Revelation: Dawn of Eternity

Chapters 12 to 22 of John's Apocalypse

Leo De Siqueira

Unless otherwise stated, scripture quotations are taken from the New American
Standard Bible® (NASB),
Copyright © 1960, 1962, 1963, 1968, 1971, 1972, 1973,
1975, 1977, 1995 by The Lockman Foundation
Used by permission. www.Lockman.org.

The Literal Standard Version (LSV) of The Holy Bible is a registered copyright of
Covenant Press and the Covenant Christian Coalition (© 2020), but has been
subsequently released under the Creative Commons Attribution-ShareAlike license
(CC BY-SA) per our desire to provide God's word freely.

Scripture quotations marked (NIV) are taken from the Holy Bible, New
International Version®, NIV®. Copyright © 1973, 1978, 1984, 2011 by Biblica,
Inc.™ Used by permission of Zondervan. All rights reserved worldwide.
www.zondervan.comThe "NIV" and "New International Version" are trademarks
registered in the United States Patent and Trademark Office by Biblica, Inc.™

Septuagint (LXX) quotations taken from C. L. Brenton, *The Septuagint with
Apocrypha in English: The Sir Lancelot C. L. Brenton 1851 Translation*, Blounstville: Fifth
Estate, 2014, online: <https://www.ellopos.net/elpenor/greek-
texts/septuagint/default.asp>.

BFBS/UBS Peshitta (Aramaic) verses are taken from the Peshitta NT published by
the British and Foreign Bible Society in 1905/1920, online:
<https://www.dukhrana.com/peshitta>.

Quotations from Flavius Josephus taken from William Whiston, M.A., *The Genuine
Works of Flavius Josephus the Jewish Historian,* London: University of Cambridge, 1737,
online: <www.penelope.uchicago.edu/josephus>.

Quotations from Tacitus taken from C. H. Moore (Histories) and J. Jackson
(Annals) *Tacitus: Histories, Annals (Loeb Classical Library)*, Latin texts and facing
English translation, Translation by C. H. Moore (Histories), and J. Jackson
(Annals), Cambridge: Harvard University Press, 1925 thru 1937, online:
<www.penelope.uchicago.edu/Thayer/E/Roman/Texts/Tacitus/home.html>.

Early Christian writings taken from Peter Kirby, *Early Christian Writings: New
Testament, Apocrypha, Gnostics, Church Fathers*, 2019, online:
<www.earlychristianwritings.com>.

Jewish religious texts taken from Sefaria, 195 Montague St, 14th Floor, Suite 1203
Brooklyn, New York 11201, 2019, online: <https://www.sefaria.org>.

Unveiled Publishing
Calgary, Canada
Revelation: Dawn of Eternity – Chapters 12 to 22 of John's Apocalypse
Leo De Siqueira
Copyright © 2024 by Leo De Siqueira
All rights reserved.
ISBN-13: 978-1-9995060-8-7

Printed in the United States of America and Canada

This book may not be reproduced, in whole or in part, in any form by any means without the express permission of the author. This includes reprints, excerpts, photocopying, recording, or any future means of reproducing text.

For permission, please contact the author through www.leodesiqueira.com.

DEDICATION

To my children Michaela, Ethan and Evelyn. May my ceiling become your floor. You were born to soar.

CONTENTS

PREFACE	IX
1 JUDAS & THE FATE OF THE WORLD	1
2 A TALE OF TWO WOMEN: CH. 12	19
3 THE EMPIRE STRIKES BACK: CH. 13 PART 1	49
4 THE EMPEROR AND HIS MARK: CH. 13 PART 2	83
5 THE SHEEP AND THE GOATS: CH. 14	111
6 THE SONG OF MOSES: CH. 15	135
7 THE PLAGUES OF WAR: CH. 16	147
8 THE UNFAITHFUL WIFE: CH. 17	179
9 JERUSALEM FALLS: CH. 18	199
10 HARLOT FALLS, WIFE ARISES: CH. 19	217
11 THE AGE OF MESSIAH BEGINS: CH. 20:1–6	231
12 AGE OF MESSIAH COMPLETED: CH. 20:7–9	245
13 THE SEA OF FIRE: CH. 20:10	273
14 THE FINAL JUDGEMENT: CH. 20:11–15	309
15 ALL THINGS NEW: CH. 21	341
16 FINAL EXORTATIONS: CH. 22	353
17 CONCLUDING THOUGHTS	363
ABOUT THE AUTHOR	366

PREFACE

What an honour and a privilege it is to be here, at the final installment in this series. First, I'm honoured to be able to have had the grace from our Heavenly Father to write. I can tell you that this journey has been one of learning when the grace is on, and when it lifts. It's been such a delight to discern the flow of His Spirit; when he calls me to work, and when he calls me to rest. Sometimes my passion would have me want to write, but He would instead have me give extra attention to family matters or work. Suddenly, things would shift and I would feel God inviting me back to this project. I've had to learn to submit to His timing and entrust the *when* to Him. When the grace is on, the pages flow without effort. Otherwise, it can be like paddling against a waterfall.

The second great honour for me is to be able to touch upon some of the greatest topics of not only our Faith, but of humanity in general. Life, death, heaven and hell, salvation, judgement, restoration, and the fate of our very existence. These are not trivial things. Yet they are themes found within John's Apocalypse, though indirectly, and help shape our understanding of God's grand love story with mankind. Such matters cannot be taken lightly. And I don't. Rather, with much humility and reverential awe of our Heavenly Father, I have done my best to yield my heart and mind so as to carefully work through both the Scriptures and the New Covenant framework as revealed by Jesus in order to best communicate what I believe to be God's heart on these topics.

Lastly, it has been a true delight to discover more about Jesus and God our Father, more than I ever thought possible. I have had so many awe and wonder moments throughout this journey, and these moments alone have made all the effort worthwhile. What could be better than to know God more intimately? This is an important distinction.

I've never felt like I was walking away with more information after writing these books. Repeatedly, after all of the translating, fact-finding, and cross-referencing, I have come away with an intimate *knowing*; like when you and your spouse, or a loved one, have a heart-to-heart conversation where you are vulnerable enough to share some of the deepest parts of your hearts. That is what it's like for me when I do this. I walk away more in love with God and knowing more of His heart. This endeavour for me has led me into a deeper relationship with Him – and for that I am forever grateful.

I want to thank you, the reader, for making it this far. I want to encourage you to prayerfully work through these pages and ask the Holy Spirit to lead you and guide you in all truth. May God highlight to you all that He has breathed on in this book, and may God shut your ears to anything in this book that is not of Him. The religious leaders of Jesus' day were masters of theology, yet they missed Emmanuel who invited them in person to follow Him. May we continue to grow in humility and hunger for Him all the more. His sheep hear His voice. May you hear the voice of our Lord Jesus the Messiah throughout this volume.

HOW WESTERN CHRISTIANITY DRIFTED FROM ITS ROOTS

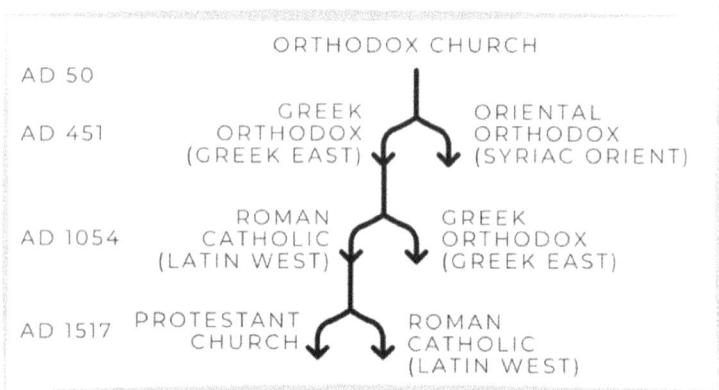

Whether we are aware of this or not, Western Protestantism and its derivatives (Baptists, Charismatics, Evangelicals, etc.) are 1,500 years into a long history of divisions. Moreover, these divisions were often because of differences of what we should and should not believe about God. It is somewhat audacious of anyone today to be convinced that our current belief system is "right", without first having understood our own history. I would like to suggest that tracing our theology back to the reformation is insufficient, for by that point we were already too far compromised. Our theological framework today is at minimum three times removed from that of the early church.

The Oriental (Semitic) Churches were mostly based in the far-eastern regions of the Roman Empire. With the Holy Land as the centre, the Oriental (meaning far-east) Orthodox communities spanned south to Egypt, north west to Asia Minor (where the seven churches of Revelation were), and east to Nineveh and beyond. Whereas the Eastern (Greek) Orthodox communities were predominately in Greece and Rome, and some of the Holy Land regions as well.

From the council of Jerusalem in AD 50 (found in Acts 15), to the Council of Chalcedon in AD 451, the church was mostly unified. Historically, we call the church from this time "the Orthodox Church". "Orthodox" can be understood as conforming to established doctrines as well as describing the beliefs and interpretations handed down by Early Church Fathers. But in AD 451 the church became divided. On what issue did they divide? The argument was rooted mainly in how one should define Jesus' nature as both divine and human. People at that time got really hung up on wording while focusing less on intent or meaning. In the end, the church split into the Semitic and Greek Churches. Sadly, it all came down to semantics.[1]

Outside of the Counsel, there were also debates surrounding eschatology (the study of end-times) and soteriology (the study of salvation). I argue that the Semitic Fathers as a whole were more grace-centric, in contrast to the Greek Fathers who were often more "eternal damnation" focused. This isn't a hard line, but rather a general observation. Then when the Latin Church (Roman Catholic) split with the Greek Orthodox, Latin Christianity really became more "fire and brimstone" focused.

So even though the Protestants broke off from the Catholics, they took with them all the faulty core beliefs about hell and eternal damnation. Therefore, I think it's time that all denominations reconsider their early Patristic roots. I'm not advocating for any specific denomination or liturgical

---

[1] Thankfully, in 1961, 1971, 1985, 1989, and 1990 reconciliation and unity discussions between Oriental and Eastern Orthodox groups have taken place.

practices, but simply suggesting that we look at what the earliest leaders and theologians believed about God and His economy of salvation. We need to return to our Semitic roots.

MY SOTERIOLOGICAL / ESCHATOLOGICAL POSITION

If I were to give my theological position a title, I think I would call myself a Reconciliationist or Restorativist (even though I don't believe either of these words exist). In short, I subscribe to the early Semitic Patristic thought about God's grand love story (His economy), and not the successively impoverished iterations of theology we've inherited in the Protestant West.

Most importantly, I embrace the mystery of how God weaves these things together, for He goes far beyond our pea-brained paradigms which we call "systematic theology". All the books in the world, all the great minds, all the opinions, all the dogmas, all the doctoral theses - these are but a speck in the infinite sky of God's vast wisdom and foresight.

We are safest when we walk in childlike wonder. Never judging. Never condemning. Hoping for the best. Believing the best. Staying in reverential awe and wonder of our loving Father, Papa, Abba. Our big Brother Jesus says there's much to receive in such a posture.

That's my position.

So how did I get here?

In concert with all of the digging I've done throughout this project, which in and of itself has radically shaped my theology, I've also gone back to early Patristic writings. As I mentioned earlier, I've sought the thoughts and conclusions of some of the earliest church thinkers and teachers because they were closer to Jesus in both time and society than we are today. These beliefs were expressed in letters, commentaries, treaties, prayers, hymns, and poems.

Here are the most common themes that have stood out to me in my studies of the first 600 years of Christianity:
Apocatastasis
Recapitulation
Reconciliation
Jesus' harrowing of Sheol
A Gehenna-Fire that purifies and heals
(You should Google these.)

Here is an elementary definition of what I call my Reconciliationist or Restorativist view, which is a rough sampling of some Patristic thought:

God's plan for the world is for a final bodily resurrection and complete restoration of His creation, most especially mankind, into total union with the Triune God. This hinges exclusively on the salvific efficacy of Jesus the Son of God, and God's grand foresight, loving-kindness, and mysterious providence.

Evil is temporal, not eternal. Death is temporal, not eternal. Evil and death will be completely abolished (1 Cor 15). Mankind, made in the image of God, will be purified by fire, either in this life or the afterlife (αἰώνιον), until all that remains is gold.

In the beginning mankind walked in fellowship with God. And God himself will not only accomplish this again, He will take it a step further: Heaven and Earth will become one, and God and mankind will become one.

God will be "all in all".

Beliefs not in my Reconciliationist or Restorativist framework are:

- There is no "hell" (Sheol, Gehenna, Lake of Fire, etc.)
- Everyone immediately "goes to heaven" when they die
- God doesn't deal with the problem of evil
- You can live in as much evil as you want without consequences

Here are a few (of many) Scriptures that help set the guideposts for a Reconciliationist view:

> *"And when I am lifted up from earth, I will drag all people to myself."*
> *(John 12:31–32)*

> *"Father . . . glorify your Son, that your Son may glorify you, because you have entrusted him with every human being, that he may give eternal life to every being that you have given him. Eternal life is that they know you."*
> *(John 17:1–2)*

> *"Jesus Christ, who was handed over for you. Heaven must keep him until the times of the restoration of all beings [ἀποκαταστάσεως πάντων], of which God has spoken by means of his holy prophets from time*

immemorial."
(Acts 3:20-21)

"He made known to us the mystery of his will, according to his purpose, which he set forth in Christ as a plan for the fullness of time, to unite [lit. recapitulate] all things in him, things in heaven and things on earth."
(Ephesians 1:9-10)

"[God is] not willing for any to perish, but for all to come to repentance."
(2 Peter 3:9)

"He was put to death in the body but made alive in the Spirit, in whom He also went and preached to the spirits in Sheol."
(1 Pet 3:18-19, Aramaic)

"For the love of Christ controls us, having concluded this, that one died for all, therefore all died; and He died for all, so that those who live would no longer live for themselves, but for Him who died and rose on their behalf… All this is from God, who reconciled us to himself through Christ and gave us the ministry of reconciliation: that God was reconciling the world to himself in Christ, not counting people's sins against them. And he has committed to us the message of reconciliation."
(2 Corinthians 5:14–15, 18–19)

"But if their [Israel's] transgression means riches for the world, and their loss means riches for the Gentiles, how much greater riches will their full inclusion bring!
…For if their [Israel's] rejection brought reconciliation to the world, what will their acceptance be but life from the dead?
… After all, if you were cut out of an olive tree that is wild by nature, and contrary to nature were grafted into a cultivated olive tree, how much more readily will these, the natural branches, be grafted into their own olive tree!
…I do not want you to be ignorant of this mystery, brothers and sisters, so that you may not be conceited: Israel has experienced a hardening in part until the full number of the Gentiles has come in, and in this way all Israel will be saved…
For God has bound everyone over to disobedience so that he may have mercy on them all."

REVELATION: DAWN OF ETERNITY

(Romans 11:12, 15, 24–26, 32)

"for even as in Adam all die, so also in the Christ all will be made alive."
(1 Corinthians 15:22

"[God] wants all people to be saved and to come to the knowledge of the truth." (1 Timothy 2:4)

"For the grace of God has appeared, bringing salvation to all people…"
(Titus 2:11)

"We have seen and testify that the Father has sent the Son to be the Savior of the world." (1 John 4:14)

"For it was the Father's good pleasure for all the fullness to dwell in Him, and through Him to reconcile all things to Himself, whether things on earth or things in [ad]?? heaven, having made peace through the blood of His cross." (Colossians 1:19–20)

There are many more Scriptures, and I'm sure there is one you like that I missed. Nevertheless, these are both powerful and thought provoking. Then there are the thoughts of the Disciples, the ones we call the Early Church Fathers. Patristic thought is something two-thirds of the global church places great value on, while for the most part Protestants and their derivatives do not. This is so sad because there is much edification and inspiration found in their words. These are people who often endured persecution, fought against various heresies, pastored churches, and some even lead monastic and celibate lives by choice, not religious duty.

As it pertains to the restoration of mankind, here is a sampling of Patristic thought:[2]

> "The Logos, when its flesh was lifted up like the brazen serpent in the desert, dragged all human beings to itself for their eternal salvation…
>
> …when the Godhead has manifested itself in human form for the novelty of absolutely eternal [ἀϊδίου] life. What has been

---

[2] All references are from Ramelli, Ilaria L. E. . A Larger Hope?, Volume 1., Cascade Books, an Imprint of Wipf and Stock Publishers. Kindle Edition.

established by God has begun: from then on, all beings have been put in motion for the providential realization of the destruction of death."

Ignatius of Antioch (c. 50-117 AD)

"The God of the universe has disposed everything for universal salvation, in general and singularly... And the necessary corrections, inflicted out of goodness by the great Judge who chairs—either through the angels who surround him, or by means of preliminary judgments, or with the complete and final judgment— force to repentance those who are too hardened.... The Lord brought the good news even to those who were in Hades.... God's punishments save and educate! They induce sinners to convert and want them to repent and not to die... It is certainly demonstrated that God is good and the Lord is able to save with impartial justice those who convert, here or elsewhere. For God's operative power does not reach only on earth, but it is everywhere, and it operates always."

Clement of Alexandria (150-215 AD)

"If God had not freely granted salvation, we would never have received it with certainty, and if the human being had not been united to God, it would never have been able to participate in incorruptibility.... The Son passes through all the stages of life, restoring for all the communion with God... For, just as because of the disobedience of one human being, molded from virgin earth, all were made sinners and had to renounce life, so also was it necessary that, thanks to the obedience of one human being, born from a virgin, all be justified and receive grace... God recapitulated in himself the original whole of humanity, so to kill sin, deprive death of its power, and vivify humanity."

Irenaeus of Smyrna and Lyons (130-202 AD)

"Every being will be restored to be one, and God will be "all in all". However, this will not happen in a moment, but slowly and gradually, through innumerable aeons of indefinite duration, because correction and purification will take place gradually, according to the needs of each individual... Once he [Jesus] has 'handed the kingdom to God the Father', that is, presented to God as an offering all, converted and reformed, and has fully performed the mystery of the reconciliation of the world, then they will be in God's presence, that God's word may be fulfilled: 'Because I live—the Lord says—every knee will bend before Me, every tongue will glorify God.'"

Origen of Alexandria (185-253 AD)

"For, what else does 'until the times of universal restoration' signify to us, if not the aeon to come, in which all beings must receive their perfect restoration? . . . On the occasion of the restoration of absolutely all beings, Paul said that creation itself will be transformed from slavery into freedom... The refining fire will come to each soul judging each according to its deeds done while alive, and cleansing and refining it by fire, like gold, and purifying the minds of all... after being instructed by punishment for a short time, they will be restored again to their previous condition... "The facts that were pre-established before the foundation of the world, and will be fulfilled at the end of the aeons; . . . once all evilness has been eliminated and the last enemy, death, has been destroyed, God will be 'all in all.'"

Eusebius of Caesarea (260-339 AD)

"Christ was made a human being, that we might be deified... Flesh was taken up by the Logos to liberate all humans and resurrect all of them from the dead, and ransom all of them from sin... to set free all beings in himself, to lead the world to the Father and to pacify all beings in himself, in heaven and on earth... Christ has banished death from us and has created us anew (bringing the knowledge of God everywhere) even in the abyss, in Hades... the totality of the peoples has entered, so that every human be saved... He has redeemed from death and liberated from hell all humanity."

Athanasius of Alexandria (296-373 AD)

"[This] fire of the corrective punishment is not active against the substance, but against [bad] habits and qualities. For this fire consumes, not creatures, but certain conditions and certain habits... The Father has given to Christ the power and dominion over all beings, that no being that has been handed to him should perish... because it was necessary that the totality of those who will have submitted to him and have arrived in the hands of the omnipotent Logos of God be saved... God not only keeps creatures in life, but also brings back to life those who have lost it, by resurrecting them from the dead. This is why we rise again... in God, who will vivify us even in case we should end up in death..."

Didymus the Blind of Alexandra (313-398 AD)

"The peace given by the Lord extends for all eternity; it knows neither boundaries nor limits. Indeed, all beings will submit to him, and all will recognize his authority. And when God will be all in all, once those who created confusion with apostasies will be restored to peace, they will sing praises to God in a symphony of peace... God's threat manifests God's beneficial action: Iniquity will be burnt away as by fire. Indeed, our good Master, as a benefit to human beings, providentially established that the matter provided by iniquity should be consigned to annihilation... deserving of being devoured by the purifying fire... He shows that earthly things are handed to the punishing fire for the sake of the soul. . . . He does not threaten destruction, but shows the purification, according to what the Apostle says: 'If one's work is burnt, one will suffer loss, but will be saved; only, as through fire' [1 Cor 3:15]."

Basil of Caesarea (330-379 AD)

"No being will remain outside the number of the saved... no creature of God will fall out of the Kingdom of God... Once, after the revolving of long ages, evil has been wiped out from nature, while now it is completely mixed and confused with it, when there will be the restoration of those who now lie in evilness into their original state, a unanimous thanksgiving will be elevated by the whole creation, both those who have been punished in purification and those who did not need even a beginning of purification. These and such things are allowed by the great Mystery of the inhumanation of God."

Gregory of Nyssa (335-395 AD)

"I know of a purifying fire, which Christ came to kindle on earth. Christ is called "fire" himself with metaphorical and mystical words. This fire consumes matter and the evil disposition, and Christ wants that it is kindled as soon as possible [Luke 12:49]. For he ardently wants the Good to be made immediately, since even the inflamed coals he gives us in order to help us. I also know a fire that is not only purifying, but also punishing: it is the fire of Sodom, which pours down like rain on all sinners... that this fire is applied for the love of human beings, and in a way that is worthy of the One who punishes... [Jesus] loosed all those who groaned under the chains of Tartarus... [Jesus] will liberate from Hades as many mortals as it has imprisoned."

Gregory of Nazianzus (329-390 AD)

"Blessed is the sinner who in Gehenna has received mercy and is deemed worthy of having access to the area of Paradise! Even if one was formerly out of the latter, one can get to graze there by grace... Between the fire of hell and Paradise, those who have found mercy can obtain punishment and then forgiveness. Glory to the Right One who reigns with His grace; He is the Good One who never puts limits to His goodness; in his compassion He bends toward the wicked; His divine cloud spreads over all that belongs to Him. He has dew rain even onto the fire of punishment... Our Lord has freely forgiven many persons for their sins... no sin will resist repentance [or] prevent a person from being justified. God, after giving retribution in Gehenna, will reward this person in the Kingdom."

Ephrem the Syrian (306-373 AD)

"Is the coming of Christ in any way commensurate with the works of the generations prior to it? Does this infinite compassion seem to you a retribution for those evil deeds? If God is one who punishes, and does so by retribution, what adequate retribution can you possibly see here? ...Even regarding the affliction and condemnation of Gehenna, there is some hidden mystery, with which the wise Creator has taken as a point of departure for his future success the evilness of our actions and will. He uses this as a means to bring his salvific plan to perfection."

Isaac of Nineveh (613-700 AD)

So what happened to the wide-spread belief that God is indeed merciful, and His aim is to restore and reconcile all humanity back to Himself? Why don't we hear about it in church today? In my estimation, it is a matter of religion and politics. The Early Church always had internal disagreements, but once Rome made Christianity a state religion, some leaders sought control over those they disagreed with. Emperor Justinian is a great example of this.

This is conjecture, but in my observations it seems that the religious and spiritual culture of the Greek churches closer to Rome (known at the time as Eastern) were very different from their Semitic brethren (known at the time as Oriental), and diversity wasn't celebrated by the religious leaders of the

Roman church. What was a priority, however, was control, so Eastern (Roman) religious leaders pressured Emperor Constantine (272-337 AD), then later Emperor Theodosius II (401-450 AD), and later still Emperor Justinian (527-565 AD) to hold major councils. The religious leaders' intentions and actions were muddy. On the one hand they did need to deal with some errant doctrines. On the other, they leveraged the might of the Empire to silence Fathers they did not agree with.

So while the Council of Nicaea (325 AD), Council of Ephesus (431 AD), and the 2nd Council of Constantinople (536 AD) brought about some good, they also caused much division between Eastern (Greek) and Oriental (Semitic) Christianity. Many church leaders were cursed and excommunicated (anathema). As a result of these councils, saints like Origen and Nestorius were demonized and their teachings distorted to make them out as heretical (much has been written about this by scholars). **Now let me be clear: I'm not advocating for or against Nestorius or Origen**. Though indeed some of their views are incorrect, many are simply misunderstood because of semantics and cultural nuances. More specifically, it is the different meanings of Greek and Aramaic words surrounding the personhood of Jesus that got lost in translation and caused men to miss each other's hearts. **What *meant* is not what was *heard*.** The tragedy is the resulting anathemas – such actions only grieve Holy Spirit. So disagreements on the nature of Christ led to the splitting of the Oriental (Semitic) and the Eastern (Greek) churches after the Council of Chalcedon in 451 AD.

Then there was the Great Schism of 1054 AD. This is where things can get a little confusing because names of places and church groups changed over time. Here is an overly simplistic explanation:

As we read earlier, Greek speaking churches of the Roman Empire (Eastern) distanced themselves from many of the churches EAST of them (Holy Land, Egypt, Assyria, etc. "Oriental" meant *really* far east of Rome). The Greek churches of the East centered themselves around Constantinople (formerly Byzantium), named after Emperor Constantine.

Later, Constantinople became a new capital city for the Roman Empire. Since Christianity had become the state religion, many church leaders there vied for position and power. Meanwhile in Rome (Western), where Latin had become the dominant language, the church communities located there began to distance themselves from their Greek (Eastern) brethren because of language and cultural differences.

Tensions grew over time as political and theological disputes went unresolved. So now the Latin (Western) churches were at odds with the Greek (Eastern) churches, and this culminated in a second divorce called the Great Schism. As a result, the churches of Rome became known as Roman Catholic, and the churches of Constantinople became known as Eastern Orthodox. The Roman Empire was (again) formally divided.

As the influence and power of institutionalized Christianity grew, so did the need (and opportunity) for control. Therefore, the Western (Catholic) church placed the pope in supreme power, while the Eastern (Greek) and Oriental (Semitic) churches carried on with their previously established groups of fathers (patriarchs), so that no one could consolidate power.

Now, more conjecture on my end: For whatever reason (maybe because of how it is structured), the Catholic Church became more powerful than the Orthodox Church, and as the power of the imperialized church continued to move to the West, the language and philosophy of those centers started overshadowing more traditional Christian doctrine. Remember, Christian thought began in the Holy Land and Semitic regions (the Levant) where the language was Hebrew, Aramaic, and Syriac (a dialect of Aramaic), and many of the early Patristic writings (and I would argue the original New Testament) were written in those languages (Coptic as well). Our faith migrated west into the Greek and Latin Roman Empire, north west into Europe, then England, and eventually to the Americas. In stages and in varying degrees, Christianity moved further and further away from its Semitic roots. The Greek and Latin church fathers, writers, and leaders, whose philosophy and world-views differed greatly from that of their Middle Eastern brethren, dominated Christian thought and doctrine, as it still does today.

Also, consider how one simple mistranslation (of many) from one language to another had a devastating impact:

> "Augustine was only seeking to be true to Scripture, but he knew little or no Greek and was unaware that "aeternus (eternal) fire" in his Latin Bible translated the Greek "αἰώνιον/aiōnion fire," which does not mean "eternal fire," but "otherworldly fire" or "long-lasting fire."
>
> Unfortunately, in Latin, both ἀΐδιος/aïdios and αἰώνιος/aiōnios were rendered with aeternus (eternal), which generated a terrible confusion that surely facilitated the birth of the idea of "eternal" punishments in hell. Because of his lack of awareness, Augustine in his To Orosius (5:5; 8:10) argued that the fire of

hell must be "eternal," otherwise the eternal beatitude of the just could not be eternal."[3]

This is just an example of how original thought and meaning was either lost or misunderstood as Christianity moved further West.[4] As the western trajectory continued, some ancient doctrines we altered, and others we lost. Instead of recapitulation atonement (c. 2nd century), the idea of penal substitution arose (c. 16th century). Instead of God working providentially within our free will (c. 1st century), John Calvin championed Predestination (originally called determinism, an errant teaching the Early Church fought against). Instead of God working within aeons and ages, the Reformation and beyond promoted an expectation of a literal 1000 year reign. (Originally called Millenariansim, another errant teaching the Early Church fought against). Then came what I'll call Rapture Theology, a novel idea that John Nelson Darby in the 1800s heavily promoted. Finally, instead of union with God by dying to the first Adam and being re-created as beloved children of God, the last 150 years or so brought about an evangelistic movement that – though not exclusively, certainly at large – focused primarily on escaping hell and getting to heaven.

What we consider normal Christian thought today is almost foreign to the Early Church. So I invite you to study Orthodox theology – not liturgy, but what the Early Church believed about God, His plan of salvation, the Incarnation, and so on. I believe it can greatly enrich your journey with Abba and add some missing puzzle pieces to your understanding of God's great love story.

THE ONGOING ISSUE OF ETERNITY / FOREVER

In my previous two books, much effort is made to explain the translational challenge we face when dealing with Hebrew, Greek, and Aramaic (Syriac) words that convey the meaning "age-enduring". In most cases, translators have defaulted to the word "eternity" or "forever" instead. Worse still, the countless volumes of Patristic writings that have been translated into English also suffered the same fate: "age-enduring" is almost always translated as "eternity" or "forever".

---

[3] Ramelli, Ilaria L. E. . A Larger Hope?, Volume 1., Cascade Books, an Imprint of Wipf and Stock Publishers. Kindle Edition.
[4] The "filioque" debacle of 6th c. Latin church is another.

I have greatly appreciated the works of Ilaria Ramelli and David Bentley Hart, and specifically their explanation of the eternity / forever dilemma. So here I will cite some of their observations, as they have articulated things so well. First, let us begin with Ramelli:

> [Ramelli] surveys the uses of two ancient Greek adjectives—aiōnios and aïdios, commonly translated as "eternal"—from their earliest occurrences in poetry and pre-Socratic philosophy down through the Septuagint (and a thorough comparison with the Hebrew Bible), the New Testament, and the Christian theologians, from the earliest to Maximus the Confessor. The monograph examines the rise of the idea of infinitely extended time (generally denoted by aïdios), and Plato's innovative introduction of a concept of a timeless eternity, which in Platonic technical vocabulary—and only there—was denoted by aiōn, with aiōnios meaning "eternal" in the sense of "transcending time." In all the rest of Greek literature, however, and—what is most relevant to us here—in the Greek Bible, aiōnios has a wide range of meanings, but does not denote absolute eternity. Since only aiōnios, and never aïdios, is applied to the punishment of humans in the afterlife, Origen could find support in the biblical usage for his doctrine of universal salvation and the finite duration of hell…
>
> Plato introduced the concept of metaphysical, timeless eternity, in reference to the model that the demiurge followed in creating the sensible universe by looking "to the eternal" (to aïdion)… Plato goes on to say that it was the nature of the living being to be aiōnios, but that this quality could not be attached to something that was begotten (gennēton). The creator therefore decided to make "a kind of moving image of eternity" (aiōnos), and so as he arranged the universe he made "an eternal image [aiōnion eikona] moving according to number of the eternity [aiōnos] which remains in one," and this he called "time."
> …However, Plato's conception of a timeless eternity remained specific to Platonism in antiquity.
>
> In Aristotle's oeuvre there are nearly three hundred instances

of aïdios, which is Aristotle's preferred word to designate things eternal. It is clear that Aristotle was not moved to adopt Plato's novel terminology… because he felt that aiōnios was an unnecessary addition to the philosophical vocabulary, given the respectability of aïdios as the appropriate technical term for eternity.

In the *Stoics*, aïdios occurs over thirty times in the sense of that which endures forever… Thus, in Stoic terminology—as generally in all of Greek literature, apart from technical Platonic language—aiōnios does not mean "absolutely eternal," a meaning that is reserved for aïdios.

The Epicureans, too, regularly employed aïdios to designate the eternity of such imperishable constituents of the universe as atoms and void. Epicurus uses aiōnios in reference to the future life that non-Epicureans expect, with its dreadful punishments: that is, to an afterlife in which Epicureans do not believe, and which does not deserve the name "eternal" (aïdios), properly reserved for truly perpetual elements.

Coming to the Bible, in the Septuagint, aïdios occurs only twice, both times in late books written originally in Greek: 4 Maccabees and Wisdom. In addition, there is one instance of the abstract noun, aïdiotēs, again in Wisdom. On the other hand, aiōnios occurs with impressive frequency, along with aiōn; behind both is the Hebrew 'olām, which has a wide range of meanings, but per se does not mean "eternal." Only when it refers to God can it acquire this meaning. For example, aiōnios can refer to a time in the remote past or future, or to something lasting over generations or centuries, or can even mean "mundane," with a negative connotation. Of particular interest is the mention in Tobit 3:6 of the place of the afterlife as a topos aiōnios, the first place in the Bible in which aiōnios unequivocally refers to the world to come. In 2 Maccabees, the doctrine of resurrection is affirmed and aiōnios is used with reference to life in the future world. This meaning will become prevalent in the New Testament.

The adjective aïdios, as mentioned, occurs in the Septuagint only in 4 Maccabees and Wisdom… [The] contrast between the parallel but antithetical expressions olethros aiōnios ("otherworldly ruin") and bios aïdios ("eternal life") is notable: whereas retribution is described with the polysemous term aiōnios, to life in the beyond is applied the more technical term aïdios, denoting a strictly endless condition. Only life is explicitly declared to be eternal; death or ruin is "otherworldly," possibly "long-lasting," but not strictly "eternal."

In the New Testament, there are only two uses of the more philosophical term aïdios. The first (Rom 1:20) refers unproblematically to the power and divinity of God, which is eternal in the absolute sense. In the second occurrence, however (Jude 6), aïdios is employed in connection with divine punishment—not of human beings, but of evil angels, who are imprisoned in darkness "with eternal chains" (desmois aïdiois). But there is a qualification: "until the judgment of the great day." The angels, then, will remain chained up until judgment day—likewise in 2 Peter 2:4, evil angels are said to have been sent by God to Tartarus, "to be held for judgment." We are not informed of what will become of them afterwards. Why is aïdios used of these chains, instead of aiōnios, which is used in the next verse of the fire of which the punishments of the Sodomites is an example? Perhaps because they continue from the moment of the angels' incarceration, at the beginning of the world, or perhaps even before the world, until the judgment that signals the entry into the new aiōn: thus, the term indicates the uninterrupted continuity throughout all time in this world—this could not apply to human beings, who do not live through the entire duration of the present universe; to them applies rather the sequence of aiōnes or generations.

In the New Testament, as in the Old, death, punishment, and fire are described as aiōnia, pertaining to the world or aiōn to come, but never as aïdia or strictly eternal. This point, which I made for the first time in the above-mentioned monograph, had escaped scholars, but it is so important that the Greek Fathers almost unanimously followed the biblical usage carefully, and therefore called death, punishment, and fire aiōnia or "otherworldly," or at most "long-lasting," but never aïdia or "everlasting, absolutely eternal." Some Latin theologians who, unlike Ambrose, Cassian, or Eriugena, did not know Greek, such as Augustine, relied on Latin translations of the Bible in which the rigorous differentiation of aiōnios and aïdios of the Greek Scriptures was completely blurred, since both adjectives were generally translated with aeternus or sempiternus. Thus, Augustine came to believe that in Scripture death, punishment, and fire in the other world are actually declared to be eternal, and his perspective proved immensely influential in the Latin West, especially among those who did not know Greek. This, of course, bears enormously on the development of Western eschatology. It is significant that the Latin theologians who did know Greek, such as Marius Victorinus, St. Ambrose, St. Jerome, Rufinus, Cassian, and Eriugena, did not think that the Bible unequivocally proclaims eternal punishment, death, or fire, and Eriugena was even one of the most radical supporters of universal salvation...

Origen followed the Bible in never calling death, punishment, or fire "eternal," but only "otherworldly" or "long-lasting," is not surprising in the light of his own eschatological convictions: fire, punishment, and death imposed by God cannot be but remedial, and therefore they cannot be eternal. But what is striking is that, as emerges from *Terms of Eternity*, a number of other patristic thinkers closely followed this biblical usage. Among them there are, of course, all the supporters of apokatastasis, such as Didymus the Blind, St. Gregory of Nyssa, St. Evagrius Ponticus, Diodore of Tarsus, Theodore of Mopsuestia, etc. But there are also others who are usually not regarded as supporters of universal restoration, such as Eusebius, St. Athanasius, St. Basil the Great, St. Gregoy Nazianzen, Pseudo-Dionysius, and St. Maximus the Confessor. It is significant that... all of these are in fact likely to have had a penchant for the theory of universal restoration.[5]

And now we will turn to David Bentley Hart's thoughts on eternity/forever:

> Then too, of course, so many serious exegetical debates coil and roil around the question of whether Christ's teachings about judgment can be said to concern the difference between time and eternity at all, at least as a governing motif, rather than the difference between this age (in Hebrew, 'olam ha-zeh) and the Age to come ('olam ha-ba). Much depends, naturally, on how content one is to see the Greek adjective αἰώνιος, aiōnios, rendered simply and flatly as "eternal" or "everlasting." It is, after all, a word whose ambiguity has been noted since the earliest centuries of the church. Certainly the noun αἰών, aiōn (or aeon), from which it is derived, did come during the classical and late antique periods to refer on occasion to a period of endless or at least indeterminate duration; but that was never its most literal acceptation. Throughout the whole of ancient and late antique Greek literature, an "aeon" was most properly an "age," which is simply to say a "substantial period of time" or an "extended interval." At first, it was typically used to indicate the lifespan of a single person, though sometimes it could be used of a considerably shorter period (even, as it happens, a single year). It came over time to mean something like a discrete epoch, or a time far in the past, or an age far off in the future...

> For Plato, chronos and aiōn were not, respectively, time and eternity, but rather two different kinds of time: the former is characterized by change, and therefore consists in that successive state of duration (measured out by the sidereal rotations of the heavens) by which things that cannot exist in their entirety all at once are allowed to unfold their essences through diachronic extension and through a process of arising and perishing; the latter is characterized by changelessness and

---

[5] Ramelli, Ilaria L. E. . A Larger Hope?, Volume 1: Universal Salvation from Christian Beginnings to Julian of Norwich (pp. 215-221). Cascade Books, an Imprint of Wipf and Stock Publishers. Kindle Edition.

repletion, the totality of every essence realized in its fullness in one immutable state. Thus, the aeon above is the entire "Age" of the world, existing all at once in a time without movement (which is to say, change), wherein nothing arises or perishes, while chronos is the "moving image of the aeon," the dim reflection of that heavenly plenum in a ghostly procession of shadowy fragments…

For educated Jewish scholars of Christ's time (or thereabouts) who wrote in Greek, such as Philo of Alexandria (c. 20 BC –c. 50 AD) and Josephus (37–c. 100), an aeon was still understood as only a limited period of time, often as brief as a single lifespan, occasionally as long as three generations.

Neither did the derivative adjective aiōnios—as ἀΐδιος (aïdios) or ἀτελεύτητος (atelevtētos) did—have the intrinsic meaning of "eternal." It could be used defectively to indicate eternity, in much the way that English words like "enduring" or "abiding" can do today. But it generally had a much vaguer connotation. And the term's plasticity was certainly fully appreciated by the Christian universalists of the Greek and Syrian East in later centuries: Clement, Origen, Gregory of Nyssa, Makrina, Diodore of Tarsus, and so on… John Chrysostom (c. 349–407) once even used the word aiōnios to describe the reign of Satan over this world precisely in order to emphasize its transience, meaning thereby that Satan's kingdom will last only till the end of the present "age." And, if one is willing to consult the witness of pagan writers—and, after all, the Platonists believed in the torments of "hell" long before the Christians fastened upon the idea—it is worth noting that, as late as the sixth century, the Neoplatonist philosopher Olympiodorus the Younger (c. 495–570) thought it obvious that the suffering of wicked souls in Tartarus is certainly not endless, atelevtos, but merely very long in duration, aiōnios. There were, moreover, regions of the Christian world where such thinking persisted well beyond antiquity. East Syrian tradition remained especially hospitable to the notion of a temporary hell and of God's eventual universal victory over evil. In the thirteenth century, for instance, the East Syrian bishop Solomon of Basra (fl. 1220s and after), in his marvelous Book of the Bee, remarked in a quite matter-of-fact manner that in the New Testament le-alam or aiōnios does not mean "eternal," and that of course hell is not an interminable condition. And the fourteenth-century East Syrian Patriarch Timotheus II (presided 1318–c. 1332) clearly saw it as uncontroversial to assert that hell's aiōnios pains will eventually come to an end for everyone, and that the souls cleansed by its fires will enter paradise for eternity…

After three centuries of Hellenization, the lingua franca of the entire region [of Galilee] was koinē Greek. Still, nevertheless, we can say with considerable confidence that, when he addressed the multitudes, who were principally the peasantry of Galilee and Judaea, Jesus would certainly have done so in the region's indigenous "vulgar" tongue, Aramaic. And so, if one assumes that the teachings recorded in the gospels are indeed faithful transpositions of the Semitic terms he used into their recognized Greek equivalents, then one must ask precisely which of the former lurk behind the latter in the texts of the New Testament. Here, happily, the Septuagint provides something of a guide. In its pages, the words aiōn and aiōnios correspond to various forms and uses of the Hebrew 'olam (or alma in Aramaic), which can mean an "age," or "epoch," or a time hidden in the far past or far future, or a "world" or "dispensation," or even occasionally perhaps "forever," but which can also mean simply any extended period with a natural term, and not necessarily a particularly long period at that. In Deuteronomy 15:17, for example, where the Hebrew text uses 'olam to indicate the lifespan of a slave, the Greek uses aiōn. And, to be honest, there really was no ancient Hebrew term that naturally carried the meaning of "eternity" in a precise sense, understood either as interminable temporal duration or as a temporal changelessness. Rather, Hebrew texts used a number of idiomatic phrases—metaphorical, hyperbolical, periphrastic—by which to convey an impression of extraordinary duration, sometimes so extraordinary as to suggest virtual endlessness. Some of these idioms are visible just below the surface of certain repeated Greek usages in both the Septuagint and the New Testament. Take, for example, the Greek phrase εἰς τὸν αἰῶνα (eis ton aiōna), which is typically rendered into English as "forever," is correct if one is pedantically precise about the etymological presence of the Latin word aevum in the English word "forever," but which might better be rendered today as something like "unto the age" or "for the age." This is the equivalent of the Hebrew le-olam or ad-olam, whose principal connotation would be something like "from now till the end of this age." Or take the phrases εἰς τοὺς αἰῶνας τῶν αἰώνων (eis tous aiōnas tōn aiōnōn)—often translated as "forever and ever," but literally meaning "unto the ages of the ages"—and ὁ αἰὼν τῶν αἰώνων (ho aiōn tōn aiōnōn)—"the age of the ages." These are standard Greek correlates of such Hebrew phrases as le-olam va-ed ("unto an age and beyond") or le olamei-olamim ("unto ages of ages"), which perhaps indicate something like eternity, but which also might be taken as meaning simply an indeterminately vast period of time.[6]

In closing, we can appreciate that there exists a translational challenge with the mistranslation of words like "eternity" or "forever", which should be translated as "age" or "age-enduring".

TRANSLATIONS FROM THE ARAMAIC

As before in my previous books, I provide my own translation directly from the Syriac (Peshitta) Bible, a dialect of Aramaic. I have used as a base the BFBS and UBS Peshitta, along with the Syriac and Hebrew Peshitta NT based on George A. Kiraz's SEDRA 3 database. I also cross reference with the Crawford Codex, Roth's Aramaic English New Testament, the works of David Bauscher, and the Hebrew New Testament (known as the Buchanan or Cochin manuscripts). Lexical citations have been through www.dukhrana.com, which has been a tremendous resource for me. And lastly, I am grateful for Accordance Bible Software, which has undergirded my translational efforts.

---

[6] Hart, David Bentley. That All Shall Be Saved: Heaven, Hell, and Universal Salvation (pp. 120-127). Yale University Press. Kindle Edition.

LEO DE SIQUEIRA

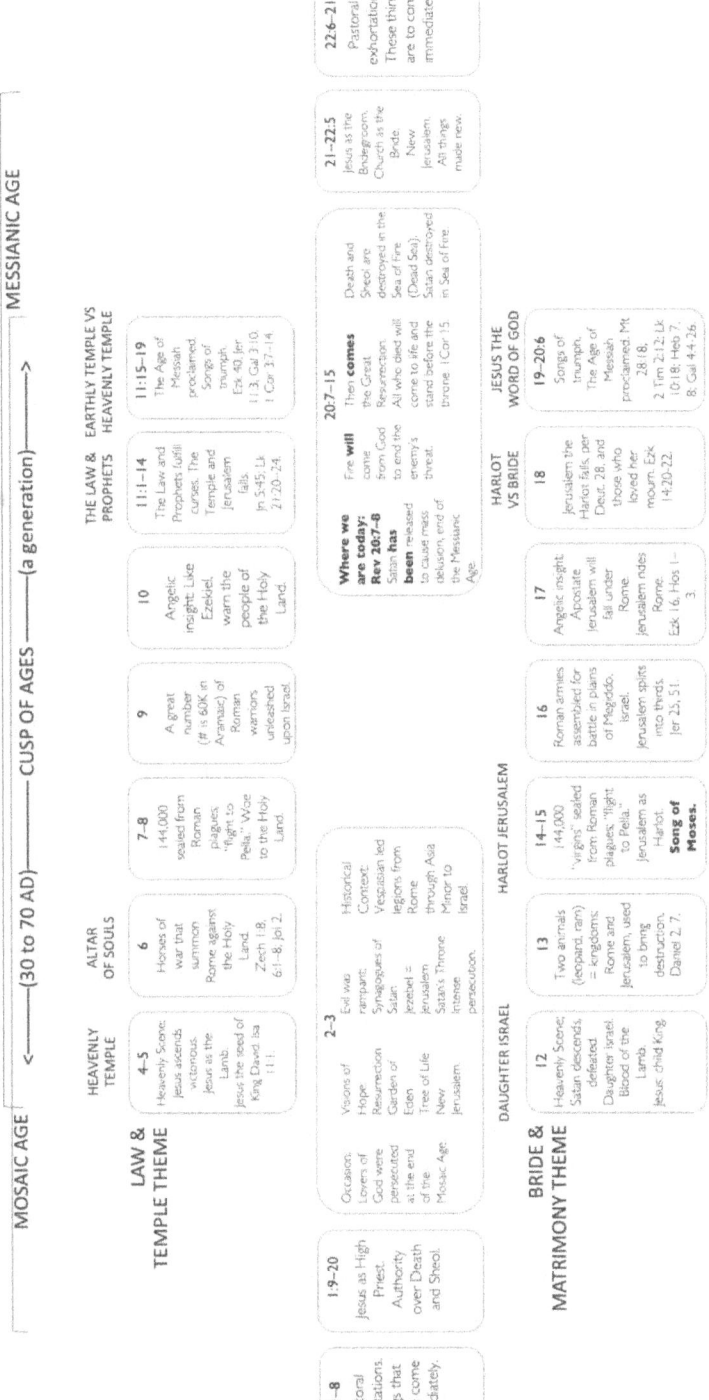

1 JUDAS & THE FATE OF THE WORLD

"'Judas, are you betraying the Son of Man with a kiss?'"
Luke 22:48 (NASB)

It would have been much easier for me to begin this book by diving immediately into Revelation 12 – believe me, that was my initial intent. But there was a growing conviction in my heart that I could not ignore, one prompting me to place what some might read as a bombshell here at the start. It is a big risk to share such thoughts on my part, and yet, I am compelled. For I am of the belief that the lens by which we perceive Judas Iscariot can either sharpen our vision of God's grand love story, or blur it.

I've been deeply immersed in John 13 to 18 for quite some time now. God our Father has been ministering to my heart from it almost daily. And of the many profound things that are found in those chapters, there is one story that I believe deeply relates to Eschatology: the fate of Judas. I believe the life of Judas is perhaps the most misunderstood one in the Gospels. And because our understanding has been skewed, so have our conclusions. So I would like to share some thoughts regarding the Judas narrative, and I will trust Holy Spirit to lead you and guide you in all truth.

First, we must begin with names. Judas is a Greek rendering of the Hebrew יהודה Judah, as in the *tribe of Judah*. And that is how I will refer to him moving forward, because his name is significant to his story. Judah is mentioned in John as Judah son of Simon יְהוּדָה בֶּן־שִׁמְעוֹן ; Judah means "God be praised", while Simon means "to listen", a derivative of שָׁמַע "shema". Some of you might have heard of the Jewish prayer known as the Shema. It is the Jewish equivalent of the Lord's Prayer for followers of Jesus. The Shema is recited as follows: "Hear O Israel: the Lord is our God, the Lord is one," quoting Deuteronomy 6:4. His other name, Iscariot אִישׁ־קְרִיּוֹת, means "man of Kerioth", which was a city in the tribe of Judah.[7] "God be praised" (Judah) was a "son of one who hears" (Simon), from a city in Judah.

Judah Iscariot seemed to be cut from the right cloth. Contrast Judah with another apostle, John, who in Mark 3:17 is introduced with his brother as בְּנֵי־רְגוֹשׁ Bnai-regesh, "sons of thunder".[8] Together, these made up part of the Twelve who were called to follow Jesus. Over time, they all experienced radical transformations. John went from being a son of thunder (tumult, rage) to becoming the apostle of love. Simon son of John ("Yochanan", meaning "Yahweh is gracious") became Peter the Rock. Early church writings also suggest that Judah (Judas) was "was son of the brother of Caiaphas the priest".[9] This seems plausible given Judah (Judas) was the only disciple not from Galilee but rather the tribe of Judah where the Temple was.

But Judah regressed. So much so that his name too had changed from son of Simon to בֶּן־הָאֲבַדּוֹן son of destruction ("Abaddon" in Hebrew. See John 17:12).

Thankfully, John and Luke provide insight on why this regression took place:

> *"the devil having already put into the heart of Judas Iscariot, the son of Simon, to betray [Jesus]... Satan then entered [Judas]." John 13:2, 27*

> *"And Satan entered Judas..." Luke 22:3*

---

[7] Karioth mean "cities". I don't subscribe to the alternate interpretation of Iscariot, that it is Syriac for Sicarii, suggesting that Judah was part of that notorious group of Jewish rebels known as "dagger men".

[8] Mark 3:17 בְּשֵׁם בְּנֵי־רְגוֹשׁ הוּא בְּנֵי־רָעַם "He gave the name of B'nai-regesh, which is, sons of thunder". Greek has "Boanerges", which is a transliteration of Aramaic. "Thunder" could also mean "rage" or "tumult".

[9] Translated by Alexander Walker. From Ante-Nicene Fathers, Vol. 8. Edited by Alexander Roberts, James Donaldson, and A. Cleveland Coxe. (Buffalo, NY: Christian Literature Publishing Co., 1886.) Revised and edited for New Advent by Kevin Knight. <http://www.newadvent.org/fathers/0813.htm>

Given that Satan had something to do with Judah's identity crisis, the name ben-abaddon (son of destruction) makes sense. In the Hebrew Bible, abaddon אבדון appears 6 times: in Job, Psalms, and Proverbs. All of them are in relationship with Sheol (the grave, or erroneously, hell). We can therefore draw a line connecting abaddon with Satan (Heb 2:14). Further, in my previous book, I discuss at length the relationship between Abaddon in Revelation 9:11 to Vespasian, and the "son of Abaddon" (בֶּן־הָאֲבַדּוֹן) in 2 Thessalonians 2:3 with his son Titus. There too a connection was made between Abaddon and Satan. Lastly, in Matthew 23:15, Jesus remarks that the religious leaders were בֶּן־גֵּיהִנֹּם sons of Gehenna ("sons of hell" in most Bibles), and that their converts were twice the sons of Gehenna that they were. Here as well, we can connect sons of Gehenna with Satan.

Where am I going with this? "Son of" can be understood as either a legal name or a prophetic foretelling of where someone's heart is. John *was* a son of thunder but later became an intimate friend of Jesus. As children, the religious leaders of Matthew 23 likely didn't begin Torah school as "sons of Gehenna" (Mt 23:15), but over time they became completely calloused (cf. Rom 11:7, 25). And Judah, son of one who hears, likely because of the fractures in his heart based on the destroyed identity he (and we) inherited from the fall of Adam, gave Satan a doorway that led to deception.

> *"And you were dead in your offenses and sins, in which you previously walked according to the course of this world, according to the prince of the power of the air, of the spirit that is now working in the sons of disobedience."* Ephesians 2:1–2 (NASB)

But what about the Scriptures that predestined Judah to betray Jesus? This is an illegitimate question because "predestined" isn't found in the Scriptures.[10] Judah did fulfill prophecies, but that is not the same thing. Judah

---

[10] In honor and sensitivity to those whose denominations trace their lineage back to John Calvin, I understand such a statement may be jarring. Therefore, I offer a few thoughts: 1. My focus throughout this series has been on returning to the Patristic-era theology and not relying on Reformation-era theology. 2. Predestination was first known as Determinism in the early church, and most church fathers were against such a notion. The only notable church father in favor of it was Augustine. 3. I argue that all of the "predestination" passages in the New Testament concerned Jews who would escape the Jewish holocaust of 66 to 70 AD and were therefore not eschatological statements. 4. Notions of Predestination or Determinism must be crossed referenced with Scriptures like: John 12:31-32; 17:1-2; Acts 3:20-2; Romans 11:12, 15, 24-26, 32; 1 Corinthians 15:22; 2 Corinthians

was part of the story, but even if he didn't betray Jesus, He still would have made it to the cross.

> *"Do you think that I cannot call upon my Father and he will not provide me at this moment with more than twelve legions of angels? But then how would the scriptures be fulfilled which say that it must come to pass in this way?"* Matt 26:53–54 (NASB)

> *"'You foolish men and slow of heart to believe in all that the prophets have spoken! Was it not necessary for the Christ to suffer these things and to come into His glory?' Then beginning with Moses and with all the Prophets, He explained to them the things written about Himself in all the Scriptures."* Luke 24:25–27 (NASB)

But what about the "woe to him" quote from Jesus?

> *"And the Son of Man goes as it is written concerning Him. Woe to him though, that person through who's hand the Son of man is delivered! Better would it have been for that man if he had not been conceived."* Matthew 26:24, Aramaic Text

Jesus' woe was not one of judgement. It was a lament delivered in hyperbole. For instance, in Mark 9, Jesus says, "Whoever causes one of these little ones who believe in Me to sin, it is better for him if a heavy millstone is hung around his neck and he is thrown into the sea. And if your hand causes you to sin, cut it off; it is better for you to enter life maimed…" (Mk 9:42–43). Is the cutting off of the hand literal? Of course not! How many followers of Jesus have you met who cut off their hand or foot in order to not sin? Then how can the millstone be literal if it is in the same sentence? Hyperbole.

Amazingly, when Judah arrives in the Garden of Gethsemane, he is still greeted with affection from Jesus:

> *"And immediately Judas went up to Jesus and said, 'Greetings, Rabbi!' and kissed Him. But Jesus said to him, 'Friend, do what you have come for.' Then they came and laid hands on Jesus and arrested Him."* Matthew 26:49–50 (NASB)

5:14-15, 18-19; Ephesians 1:9-10; Colossians 1:19-20; 1 Timothy 2:4; Titus 2:11; 1 Peter 3:18-19; 2 Peter 3:9; and 1 John 4:14.

Ivan Rogers offers a fascinating hypothesis in his book, *Judas Iscariot: Revisited and Restored,* which I feel is appropriate here:

> Judas did "deliver" Jesus into the hands of the temple priests. But that raises another question: Why? Was it a case of malice forethought? Human justice makes a distinction between crimes committed intentionally and those committed in ignorance…
>
> God's justice (from which all true human justice is derived) also makes generous provisions for those who "sin through ignorance" (Num 15:25-28 with Heb 5:1-2 KJV). From his cross, Jesus (the Great High Priest) prayed for his tormentors, saying, "Father, forgive them, for they do not know what they are doing" (Lk 23:34). In his address at the temple gate, the one called "Beautiful", Peter said to those of his countrymen who had disowned Jesus, "Now, brothers, I know that you acted in ignorance, as did your leaders" (Acts 3:17). The Apostle Paul would later write, "None of the rulers of this age understood it, for if they had, they would not have crucified the Lord of glory" (1 Cor 2:8)…
>
> And is it not significant that Paul himself, who had once persecuted Christ and his followers, would later write, "I was shown mercy. because I acted in ignorance and in unbelief" (I Tim 1:13). Shall Paul obtain God's mercy in direct proportion to his "ignorance" and "unbelief," but Judas be denied that same mercy? Someone will be quick to point out that Paul did finally repent and serve Christ. True, but he gets no credit for doing so…
>
> I am convinced that Judas' actions in delivering up Jesus were largely the result of ignorance…
>
> But God, who understands human ignorance, has always provided a way out of our collective dilemma. Thus, even under the Law of Moses, we read, "If a soul commit a trespass, and sin through ignorance, in the holy things of the LORD; then he shall bring for his trespass unto the LORD a ram without

blemish out of the flocks, with thy estimation by shekels of silver...for a trespass offering" (Lev 5:15 KJV)...

Judas, whose sin of ignorance was committed under Mosaic Law, did, in fact, bring his sacrificial Ram (Jesus) - the one "without blemish" - the one that had been properly "estimated by (thirty] shekels of silver for a trespass offering." And if the blood of old covenant animal sacrifices atoned for ignorant sinners, then surely we can believe that Judas' new covenant "Ram without blemish" would do no less for him.

Undoubtedly Judas didn't realize that by delivering Jesus to the priests, he was, in effect, bringing to the Temple his own personal trespass offering. Thus did Judas ignorantly participate in the sacrifice of God's one and only Redeemer-Ram...

In another demonstration of God's accommodation to human ignorance, he mercifully provided six "cities of refuge" for those Israelites who had unintentionally (ignorantly) killed a neighbor. In such cases, the accused had to remain in a designated city of refuge until the death of the reigning high priest, after which he was to be exonerated and allowed to return home (Num 35:28). Likewise Judas, who ignorantly delivered up Jesus to death, could only be finally exonerated upon the atoning death of the greatest High Priest of them all [Jesus] (Heb 9:11-12).[11]

JESUS AND JOSEPH

But as for the New Testament Scriptures concerning Judah, I want to focus on one specifically. All the footnotes in our Bibles (or online Bibles) thoroughly explain the prophecies concerning Judah. For instance, "He who eats My bread has lifted up his heel against Me," (John 13:18, cf. Ps 41:9). But there is one that seems to lack any supporting references:

"While I was with them, I was keeping them in Your name, which You

---

[11] Rogers, Ivan. Judas Iscariot: Revisited and Restored. Xulon Press. Location 192–241. Kindle Edition.

have given Me; and I guarded them, and not one of them perished except the son of destruction, so that the Scripture would be fulfilled."
John 17:12 (NASB)

Footnotes for John 17:12 are non-existent, save for a few, and those usually state something along the lines of, "no direct reference is known." By no means am I suggesting I have a definitive answer to which Old Testament prophecy Jesus was referring to in John 17:12, but I can offer the following: During one of the times I was meditating on John 13 (which tells of Jesus washing the disciples' feet, including the feet of Judah), I asked God to teach my heart to love this way. Something then came to mind – that the story of Joseph in Genesis in many ways foreshadows the story of Jesus, including his betrayal.

In case you've never pondered this before, the life of Joseph is a prophetic picture of the life of Jesus: Joseph goes into the pit (a Hebrew image of death), then he goes into the jailhouse (a Hebrew image of Sheol), and then he ascends to be second to Pharaoh over the largest kingdom of that day (Jesus sitting at the right hand of God). Yet there is one aspect of Joseph's story that precedes all this: his betrayal. In Genesis 37, it was Judah, brother of Joseph, who had the idea to sell Joseph for money (37:26–27). And they did so for 20 pieces of silver. **In this way, the betrayal of Joseph in Genesis 37 corresponds with the words of Jesus in John 17:12**.

Now, if the life of Joseph is a prophetic archetype of the life of Jesus, then how can we forget the most powerful moment in the Joseph narrative?

"Then Joseph said to his brothers, 'Please come closer to me.' And they came closer. And he said, 'I am your brother Joseph, whom you sold to Egypt. Now do not be grieved or angry with yourselves because you sold me here, for God sent me ahead of you to save lives. For the famine has been in the land these two years, and there are still five years in which there will be neither plowing nor harvesting. So God sent me ahead of you to ensure for you a remnant on the earth, and to keep you alive by a great deliverance. Now, therefore, it was not you who sent me here, but God; and He has made me a father to Pharaoh and lord of all his household, and ruler over all the land of Egypt.'" Genesis 45:4–8 (NASB)

Here is a man who walked in a measure of love and forgiveness we seldom see today even amongst followers of Jesus, and he did so without the regenerative power of the Holy Spirit! In light of this incredible end to the Joseph story, let's go back to John 13:

"Jesus, knowing that His hour had come that He would depart from this world to the Father, having loved His own who were in the world, He loved them to the end. And during supper, the devil having already put into the heart of Judas Iscariot, the son of Simon, to betray Him, Jesus, knowing that the Father had handed all things over to Him, and that He had come forth from God and was going back to God, got up from supper and laid His outer garments aside; and He took a towel and tied it around Himself. Then He poured water into the basin, and began washing the disciples' feet and wiping them with the towel which He had tied around Himself." John 13:1–5 (NASB)

Jesus "loved them to the end", including Judah. John wants his readers to understand that Jesus is fully aware of *His* identity in God, and that Jesus is fully aware that Satan is entering Judah in order to deliver him to the religious leaders. As such, knowing who He is and what is going on with Judah, Jesus does not kick Judah out of the room so he can break bread with the remaining eleven. He washes the feet of the Twelve, *including* Judah's. And He breaks bread and celebrates the New Covenant meal with the Twelve, *including* Judah.

There is one more important parallel I would like to draw from. In Genesis, we read that all the 12 sons (tribes) of Israel reject Joseph. It is interesting that Joseph did not have a tribe named after him. Fast forward to the time of Jesus. The land of Judah (known as Judea to the Romans) was the last of what remained of the original 12 tribes of Israel. The land of Judah is where Jerusalem and the Temple remained. And just like in Genesis, Judah Iscariot rejects Jesus his brother. Judah Iscariot in this sense was a prophetic representation of not just the land of Judah (Judea) but the rest of the Holy Land. Judah Iscariot's earthly fate (an important distinction) can also be seen as a prophetic archetype of the Holy Land's.

"Then when Judas, who had betrayed Him, saw that He had been condemned, he felt remorse and returned the thirty pieces of silver to the chief priests and elders, saying, 'I have sinned by betraying innocent blood.' But they said, 'What is that to us? You shall see to it yourself!' And he threw the pieces of silver into the temple sanctuary and left; and he went away and hanged himself." Matthew 27:3–5 (NASB)

So what was Judah Iscariot's eternal fate? The Aramaic literally says Judah was "convicted" or "self-judged". Sadly, instead of seeking absolution from the One who fulfilled the Law, and because of his interaction with the stewards of the Law in the presence of the Temple, Judah attempts to seek atonement through his own works by taking his life. This is exactly what the Law produces: death (see Hebrews 9 and 10). Likewise, the first century Jews who chose to stay bound to the requirements of the Law, striving through their own works to keep it yet continually failing to do so, saw the Law bring about their own demise. Judah Iscariot's rejection of Jesus led to the destruction of his flesh. Likewise, Judea and the Holy Land's rejection of Jesus led to the destruction of their flesh and their land.

JESUS IN SHEOL

So what does the fate of Judah (Judas) have to do with the fate of the world? Because whatever we think happened to Judah after he died either sharpens or blurs our perspective of Revelation and Eschatology in general. What I mean is if your lens is one where you see God's economy of salvation as ongoing, gracious, and shrouded in sovereign mystery, then you will see Revelation through that lens. In contrast, if your view of salvation is one where you see it as a finite formula, then such a lens will *taint* John's Vision. If you've read my first two books, you'll recall how many times I cite Romans 9 to 11—that Paul is adamant all of Israel will be saved. Let me ask you: is Judah Iscariot, as a Jew, exempt from those prophecies?

I also discuss in *Dawn of All Hope* how in 1 Peter 3 we are told **Jesus descends to Sheol and preaches to those who are there**. This event is known as *The Harrowing of Hades (Sheol)*, which was understood for so long but for many today it's new. Roughly two-thirds of the Christians in the world today hold in their doctrine an understanding of the Harrowing of Sheol (aka, *Descensus Christi ad Inferos*). Christ's descent is mentioned in the Apostle's Creed (~120–250 AD) and the Athanasius Creed (~500 AD), and the majority of the church at large hold the Saturday of Easter Weekend as a holy day. Only the Protestant denomination and its derivatives (representing the other third) have little to no knowledge of this event. For whatever reason, this teaching was dropped in Protestantism (which includes Pentecostalism and Evangelicalism), and therefore millions of well-meaning Christians today have no clue about the doctrine of Christ's descent. Nevertheless, ignorance (whether conscious or unconscious) doesn't make it any less true!

Here are some anchoring Scriptures that have helped inform the Christian understanding of what took place between Yeshua's death and resurrection for nearly 2000 years:

"Where can I go from Your Spirit?
Or where can I flee from Your presence?
If I ascend to heaven, You are there;
If I make my bed in Sheol, behold, You are there."
Psalm 139:7–8 (NASB)

"[My] soul has been filled with evils and my life has arrived at Sheol! I am counted with those who descend to the pit and I have been like a man who has no helper…
My eyes have melted from affliction and I called you, LORD JEHOVAH, every day, and have stretched forth my hands to you! Behold, **you work wonders to the dead and mighty ones will stand and confess you!** *And they will tell your kindness which is in the tombs and your faithfulness in destruction!* **Your wonders will be known in darkness and your righteousness in the land that was forgotten!** *And I have cried to you, LORD JEHOVAH, and at dawn my prayer will come before your presence! Do not forget my soul, LORD JEHOVAH, and do not turn your face from me!"*
Psalm 88:3–4, 9–14 (Aramaic, emphasis mine)[12]

"For as Jonah was three days and three nights in the belly of a huge fish [Jonah 2:2 says he was in Sheol], so the Son of Man will be three days and three nights in the heart of the earth." (Matthew 12:40)

"Because you will not abandon me to Sheol, you will not let your Holy One see decay." (Acts 2:27 Aramaic)

"I tell you, you are Peter, and on this rock I will build my Church, and the gates of Sheol shall not resist her."
(Matthew 16:18 Aramaic)

"I died, and behold I am alive forevermore, and I have the keys of Death and Sheol." (Revelation 1:18 Aramaic)

"Therefore it is said, 'He ascended to the heights and took captivity prisoner and he has given gifts to the children of men. [Ps 68:18]' But that he ascended, what is it but that also he **first descended to the lower regions** *of The Earth? He who descended is the same who*

---

[12] Bauscher, David. The Holy Peshitta Bible Translated (pp. 1189-1190). Lulu.com.

*also ascended higher than all Heavens **to restore all things**."*[13]
Ephesians 4:8–10 (Aramaic, emphasis mine)

And in 1 Peter 3 and 4 the Apostle blows our minds when he casually mentions the following:

"He [Jesus] was put to death in the body but made alive in the Spirit, in whom He also went and preached to the spirits in Sheol."
(1 Pet 3:18-19 Aramaic)

"[God] is going to judge the dead and living. For because of this, The Good News was proclaimed also to the dead that they would be judged as children of men in the flesh and they would live in God by The Spirit."
(1 Peter 4:5–6 Aramaic)

Consider also Paul's prophetic statement in Philippians 2:9–11:

*"God highly exalted Him, and bestowed on Him the name which is above every name, so that at the name of Jesus every knee will bow, of those who are in heaven and on earth **and under the earth**, and that every tongue will confess that Jesus Christ is Lord, to the glory of God the Father."*

"Under the earth" is a Hebraism that refers to Sheol. In light of Peter's (1 Peter 3, 4) and Paul's (Ephesians 4) revelation that Jesus both descends into Sheol and preaches to those held there, it makes sense why every knee in Sheol would also bow and their tongues confess that Jesus is Lord.

On a technical note, in Philippians 2:11 quoted above, the word "confess" תּוֹדָה is the exact same word used in Romans 10:9–10:

*"If you declare [lit: "confess"] with your mouth, 'Jesus is Lord,' and believe in your heart that God raised him from the dead, you will be **saved**. For it is with your heart that you believe and are justified, and it is with your mouth that you profess [lit: "confess"] your faith and are **saved**." (NIV)*

The Aramaic reads as follows: "And if you will *confess* with your mouth

---

[13] Bauscher, David. The Holy Peshitta Bible Translated (p. 2370). Lulu.com. Kindle Edition.

our Lord Jesus, and believe in your heart that God raised Him from the abode of the dead you will **live**. For the heart that believes in Him is made justified and the mouth that will *confess* Him will **live**."

While the Greek says "saved", the Aramaic goes much deeper with "live". Jesus is the resurrection and the life. In Revelation 1:18, Jesus also proclaims that He "holds the keys of Death and Sheol". So in Romans 10:9, the Aramaic reminds us that Jesus was raised from the abode (lit. "house") of the dead (i.e. Sheol) and was resurrected from death into life. Is it possible that those in Sheol, given that they too will confess that Jesus is Lord (Philippians 2:10), will be justified and given life as a result of their confession (Romans 10:9–10)? Only time will tell.

One of the most fascinating illustrations we have regarding Sheol actually comes from Jesus. Prior to his own death-descent into Sheol, he tells a story about a wealthy Jew (who in church tradition is named Dives) who dies and descends to Sheol. There, he encounters Abraham and remarks,

> *"'Father Abraham, but if someone goes to [my brothers] from the dead, they will repent!' But he said to him, 'If they do not listen to Moses and the Prophets, they will not be persuaded even if someone rises from the dead.'" Luke 16:30–31 (NASB)*

What point is Jesus trying to make in illustrating this conversation between Dives and Abraham? First, we must understand that this story is a *parable*, not a recounting of a historical event. Second, take note of who Jesus was speaking to: Religious leaders. The message is directed towards a group of "white-washed tombs" who are more concerned about their social status and outward appearance than having their hearts humbled and transformed. Most likely, the rich man (Dives) is a depiction of a Jewish religious leader, and the parable a hyperbolic illustration of the ironic turn of events such ones would experience when their time came (cf. Luke 15:1–2; Matt 23). The shock that Dives experiences is likely due to the expectation that he was in good standing with Yahweh during his life (for example, material blessing equaled God's favor in Jewish culture), only to end up on the wrong side of the chasm. Nevertheless, I will propose that Dives has a change of heart in Sheol based on the nature of his interaction with Abraham. Seeing that there is nothing he can do about his own situation, he now hopes that he can at least help his next of kin.

We now have to shift out of parable and into reality. Dives is sobered, and Jesus' message will have hopefully sobered those who are criticizing his ministry to sinners as well. Let that sink in. A bunch of people who knew the

Bible (OT) and supposedly have God all figured out can't stand that Jesus is extending grace and compassion to those who they think don't deserve it. Yet these same people ultimately end up in Sheol (cf. Matt 23). **But Jesus isn't petty**, so He goes down to Sheol. I imagine Jesus then finds the very same religious leaders who criticized him during his ministry, only to now find themselves sobered like Dives. Again, Jesus isn't petty**, so they would not have heard "I told you so," but rather, "I love you so."** To quote Peter once again,

> *"[Jesus] was put to death in the body but made alive in the Spirit, in whom He also went and preached to the spirits in Sheol… [God] is going to judge the dead and living. For because of this, The Good News was proclaimed also to the dead that they would be judged as children of men in the flesh and they would live in God by The Spirit."*
> *(1 Peter 3:18-19; 4:5–6 Aramaic)*

We need to rediscover that Sheol was seen as a place of refining by many early Church Fathers.

> The Lord brought the good news even to those who were in Hades. . . . God's punishments save and educate! They induce sinners to convert and want them to repent and not to die. . . . It is certainly demonstrated that God is good and the Lord is able to save with impartial justice those who convert, here or elsewhere. For God's operative power does not reach only on earth, but it is everywhere, and it operates always.
>
> Clement of Alexandria (c. 150-215 AD)

> Blessed is the sinner who in Gehenna has received mercy and is deemed worthy of having access to the area of Paradise! … Between the fire of hell and Paradise, those who have found mercy can obtain punishment and then forgiveness… He is the Good One who never puts limits to his goodness; in his compassion he bends toward the wicked… He has dew rain even onto the fire of punishment… Our Lord has freely forgiven many persons for their sins… no sin will resist repentance [or] prevent a person from being justified. God, after giving retribution in Gehenna, will reward this person in the Kingdom.

Ephrem the Syrian (c. 306-373 AD)

For, what else does 'until the times of universal restoration' [Acts 3:21] signify to us, if not the aeon to come, in which all beings must receive their perfect restoration? . . .

On the occasion of the restoration of absolutely all beings, Paul said that creation itself will be transformed from slavery into freedom…

The refining fire will come to each soul judging each according to its deeds done while alive, and cleansing and refining it by fire, like gold, and purifying the minds of all… after being instructed by punishment for a short time, they will be restored again to their previous condition…

The facts that were pre-established before the foundation of the world, and will be fulfilled at the end of the aeons; . . . once all evilness has been eliminated and the last enemy, death, has been destroyed, God will be 'all in all.'

Eusebius of Caesarea (c. 260-339 AD)

Christ was made a human being, that we might be deified… Flesh was taken up by the Logos to liberate all humans and resurrect all of them from the dead, and ransom all of them from sin… Christ has banished death from us and has created us anew (bringing the knowledge of God everywhere) even in the abyss, in Hades… the totality of the peoples has entered, so that every human be saved… He has redeemed from death and liberated from hell all humanity.

Athanasius of Alexandria (c. 296-373 AD)

I know of a purifying fire, which Christ came to kindle on earth. Christ is called "fire" himself with metaphorical and mystical words. This fire consumes matter and the evil disposition, and Christ wants that it is kindled as soon as possible [Luke 12:49].

> For he ardently wants the Good to be made immediately, since even the inflamed coals he gives us in order to help us. I also know a fire that is not only purifying, but also punishing... this fire is applied for the love of human beings, and in a way that is worthy of the One who punishes... [Jesus] loosed all those who groaned under the chains of the Abyss... [Jesus] will liberate from Hades as many mortals as it has imprisoned.

Gregory of Nazianzus (c. 329-390 AD)

Some of you may be thinking, "This is nonsense!" I'm not here to tell you what to think, but simply to give you some things to think about. I find it fascinating that over 1700 years ago, followers of Jesus, many of whom could trace their discipleship lineage back to one of the original Apostles of Jesus, penned these words. These people were closer to Jesus and the Apostles in terms of chronology and culture compared to us today. So at minimum, we should pause to reflect instead of judge and dismiss.

Suffice to say that if we approach Revelation and Eschatology with an impoverished Western paradigm that has its roots in Jonathan Edwards' *Sinners in the Hands of an Angry God,* then we cannot possibly begin to comprehend what God conceived to do before time began.

> *"May [Christ] dwell in your hearts through faith; and that you, being rooted and grounded in love, may be able to comprehend with all the saints what is the width and length and height and depth, and to know the love of Christ which surpasses knowledge, that you may be filled to all the fullness of God." Ephesians 3:17–19 (NASB)*

Now let's conclude this section by revisiting the topic of Judah (Judas) Iscariot with one final thought. Given that Judah dies before Jesus does (Matthew 27), Judah would be in Sheol when Jesus arrives (as per 1 Peter 3 and 4). What do you think their interaction would have been like? Is it possible Judah too was "judged in the flesh" so that he "may live in the spirit" according to the will of God? Time will tell.

> "God is everywhere. You decide whether you are close to Him or not." — St. John Chrysostom (d. 407 AD)

Instead of trying to impose a Western-Evangelical or Protestant framework into this event, we should again pause for reflection: Yeshua, the one I know and love, who has picked me up out of my mess over and over again, went into Sheol. Wow. What would that have *looked* like? Deep darkness would have been overwhelmed by the light of his glory. What would that have *felt* like? I imagine that all those people there must have felt such overwhelming hope. "But did they pray the prayer?" some of you may ask. Such a limited scope is to miss the magnitude and significance of the event. Jesus, who leaves the 99 to go after the one, descends into Sheol. Wow. **Theologically speaking, when we add together Psalms 139:7–8, Colossians 1:16–17, and Hebrews 1:3, Jesus is *constantly* in Sheol because not only is He in all realms, but by Him and through Him all realms are held together!**

> *"Where can I go from Your Spirit?*
> *Or where can I flee from Your presence?*
> *If I ascend to heaven, You are there;*
> ***If I make my bed in Sheol, behold, You are there."***
> *Psalm 139:7–8 (NASB, emphasis mine)*

> *"by Him [Jesus] all things were created, both in the heavens and on earth, visible and invisible, whether thrones, or dominions, or rulers, or authorities—all things have been created through Him and for Him. He is before all things, and **in Him all things hold together."***
> *Colossians 1:16–17 (NASB, emphasis mine)*

> *"He [Jesus] is the radiance of His [God's] glory and the exact representation of His nature, and **upholds all things** by the word of His power." Hebrews 1:3 (NASB, emphasis mine)*

WHAT IS THE POINT OF THE GOSPEL?

Everything we believe about God we must be able to see in Jesus. He is the paradigm in which we see the Father (John 14:9). If you have an angry God, then you must have an angry Jesus. The two cannot be different. The Hebrew Scriptures are not the last word on who God is. Jesus is the last word.

> *"God, after He spoke long ago to the fathers in the prophets in many portions and in many ways, in these last days has spoken to us in His Son… And He is the radiance of His glory and the exact representation of His nature…" Hebrews 1:1–3 (NASB)*

And Jesus is the one who introduced Israel and the world to Yahweh as *Father*, which forever changed the way we see both Him and ourselves. For instance, in Luke 15:11–32 we have God the Father dealing with orphan spirits. Each of the sons have a distorted view of both their father and themselves. One repents on his own, and the other has a revelation from their Father about who their Abba is and who he is as a son. Amazingly, the story ends with both sons at home in their Father's house.

Or consider Jonah who takes offense at the goodness of God. "Should I not also have compassion on Nineveh?" (Jonah 4:11) Yahweh asks. But Jonah's religious mindset could not fathom Yahweh delivering Nineveh from destruction. Nineveh was the largest city in the inhabited world and it was known to be notoriously evil. Interestingly, Nineveh in Aramaic means "abode of fish". Jonah ended up in the wrong "fish" as a result of his hardened heart! God is not only merciful towards Nineveh, but He is also merciful to Jonah who symbolically descends into Sheol (Jonah 2:2; Matthew 12:40). Yet he cries out to God, and God grants him life again.

> *"For I am convinced that neither death, nor life, nor angels, nor principalities, nor things present, nor things to come, nor powers, nor height, nor depth, nor any other created thing will be able to separate us from the love of God that is in Christ Jesus our Lord."*
> Romans 8:38–39 (NASB)

I'm not taking some flippant position that suggests we can live however we want with no eternal consequences. The ethereal experience of Sheol is real, and so is the refining fire of the Sea of Fire and Sulfur (Revelation 20). And there *will* be a final bodily resurrection, a final judgement, and a final purging of the cosmos of all evil (which we will fully dive into in this book). But the story of God is not binary - saved or damned. In addition to meaning "saved", *sozo* in the Greek also means to restore to health, to make whole, and is a reflection of the Hebrew word *shalom*. The concept has little to do with fire insurance, and much to do with restoration.

> *"heaven must receive [Jesus] until the period of restoration of all things."*
> *(Acts 3:21)*

Where the Greek reads "saved" in most of our Bibles, the Aramaic has the word "life" instead. Jesus is the way, truth, and *life*. He came that we would have *life,* and have it in abundance. This is because *death* came through Adam. Therefore, to know Jesus is to have age-enduring life (John 17:3).

> *"Therefore, just as through one man sin entered into the world, and death*

through sin, and so death spread to all mankind… For if by the offense of the one, death reigned through the one, much more will those who receive the abundance of grace and of the gift of righteousness reign in life through the One, Jesus Christ." (Romans 5:12, 17)

We cannot approach God's grand love story with His creation through a finite lens of saved or damned, heaven or hell. Jesus said that Abraham, Isaac, Jacob, and all the prophets would be in God's kingdom realm (Luke 13:28), though they never prayed the proverbial sinner's prayer. Enoch wasn't "saved", yet he ascended into heaven. Elijah was not "saved", yet he too ascended into heaven. Moses was buried in the wilderness because of his disobedience and died under the Law of sin and death (Rom 8:2). And in Jewish tradition, it is believed that Moses too ascended like Elijah. Yet both he and Elijah appeared before Jesus in glory (Mat 17:1–8). How does *that* work?

Is it possible that God's framework for life goes beyond the scope of saved vs. damned, heaven vs. hell? Is it possible there is a much greater, more complex mystery of restoration and reconciliation at work? At minimum, this question must be asked: is a ticket to heaven even the ultimate goal? If so, why is God bothering with making a new earth (Is 65:17; Rev 21:1)? Why will a new Jerusalem descend *from* heaven *to* a renewed earth (Rev 21:2)? Why will there be trees on earth whose leaves are for the healing of the nations (Ez 47:12; Rev 22:2)? What good will the great bodily resurrection do if we are to live in heaven (1 Cor 15:12–56)? What is the purpose of God making His future dwelling place amongst mankind on earth, after He has made all things new (Rev 21:3)?

"Thus you nullify the word of God by your tradition that you have handed down." Mark 7:13 (NIV)

How we answer these questions will actually shape our understanding of how Jesus could look ahead before creation began, factor in all that it would cost Him to make mankind in His image, and still decide that we were worth it. If we can get a hold of His heart in *that* context, then we have a hope of grasping what His heart is towards Judah (Judas) and all of mankind – past, present and future.

"And He has caused us to have experiential knowledge of the mystery of His will, which came before time to be established and performed in Himself for the governance of the consummation of the times: that everything from the beginning will be renewed in the Messiah, that which is in Heaven and in the earth." (Ephesian 1:9–10, Aramaic Text)

2 A TALE OF TWO WOMEN: CH. 12

"The Zodiac in the skies. That's the first Bible. Man was to look up to realize that God is from above. Follow the Zodiac; did you ever study it? It even gives every age... It gives the beginning, the birth—the birth of Christ. What is the first figure in the Zodiac? The virgin. What's the last figure? Leo the lion. The first coming and the second coming of Christ, all of it is written in there." William Branham, (1909–1965)

A major shift in the narrative takes place between Revelation 11 and 12. The final scene in chapter 11 is the Holy Land (more specifically, the Holy Temple) being ravaged by the Roman legions. Significantly, the curses of the Law and the Prophets – Moses and Elijah – have come to pass. Just one chapter prior (ch. 10), John is commissioned to warn his fellow kinsmen of their impending doom.

Judgement has come upon the Holy Land. The Age of Moses is ending. The scene closes with John seeing a vision of Yahweh's heavenly tabernacle where His copy of the contractual agreement He had with them was kept. Because *heavens* and *skies* are the same word in Hebrew, it's hard to know if the heavens in 11:19 and 12:1 are the same locale. As is often the case with dreams and visions, it isn't always supposed to make logical sense, for the message is in the symbolism.

Either way, the curtain closes on the previous scene. Now comes a new stage, new props, and a new cast of characters. We are taken from a tactile, in-the-dirt type vision to the ethereal and mystical in this new act. And the curtain opens with a very familiar (to John's culture) setting: an astrological one.

Pause. In my experience, once you mention the word "zodiac", "astrology", or even "astronomy", many people are immediately put off. If this is you right now, let me assure you that there is no hidden agenda here. Any discussion I engage in surrounding this topic does not conclude with me trying to convince you to accept some sort of "new age" belief system!

However, it is nearly impossible to have a proper Biblical understanding of constellations and the heavens without at least acknowledging that stargazing was a *normal* practice that shaped the worldview and widely-held belief systems of antiquity. Star mapping was a big deal, and not just in Israel – it was a huge component of life in almost every ancient civilization on every continent. You really need to ponder that for a bit.

God was very aware of this reality because He orchestrated it that way. To be dismissive of this fact is to rob yourself of a significant interpretive key. [14]

> *"Then God said, 'Let there be lights in the expanse of the heavens to separate the day from the night, and **they shall serve as signs and for seasons**, and for days and years...'"*
> *Genesis 1:14 (NASB, emphasis mine)*

> ***"The heavens tell*** *of the glory of God;*
> *And **their expanse declares** the work of His hands.*
> *Day to day pours forth speech,*
> *And night to night reveals knowledge.*
> *There is no speech, nor are there words;*
> *Their voice is not heard.*
> ***Their line has gone out*** *into all the earth,*
> *And their words to the end of the world."*
> *Psalm 19:1-4 (NASB, emphasis mine)*

Civilizations depended on the constellations to understand the seasons

---

[14] For those who are very uncomfortable with the subject of astronomy, rest assured, God's warnings remain intact: Deut. 18:9-13; 2 Kings 23:3-5; Isa. 8:19-20; 44:24-25; 47:8-15.

for harvesting, to navigate across vast open seas, to interpret the transition of epoch seasons and ages, and even to anticipate the coming of the Messiah. Jews referred to the prophetic significance of stars and constellations as the Mazzaroth מַזָּרוֹת, which we see in Job 38:

> *"Can you tie up the cords of the <u>Pleiades</u>*
> *or loosen the belt of <u>Orion</u>?*
> *Can you lead out the constellations of the zodiac [lit. "mazaroth" מַזָּרוֹת]*
> *in their season*
> *or guide the <u>Great Bear</u> and its cubs?*
> *Do you know the laws of the sky?*
> *Can you determine how they affect the earth?" Job 38:31–33*
> *(CJB, emphasis mine)*

God predetermined to use celestial events and signs in the heavens as a means to communicate with man. In His story, spelled out in figures in the sky, stars are the characters and constellations are the storyline. Over time it seems apparent that star-gazing became both sophisticated and well established in many civilizations. Consider the Magi. These individuals were Jewish sages from Persia. They were part of the diaspora Jews from the time of the Medo-Persian Empire (Babylon) during the time of Daniel and others who were taken as POWs to Babylon.

> *"[B]ehold, magi from the east arrived in Jerusalem, saying, 'Where is He who has been born King of the Jews? For we saw His star in the east and have come to worship Him.'…*
> *Then Herod secretly called for the magi and determined from them the exact time the star appeared." Matthew 2:2, 7 (NASB)*

They knew the prophecy of Numbers 24:17 and Isaiah 7:14, of the star of Jacob and the virgin who would conceive. But how did they know *which* star to look for, or *when* to start looking for it? That prophecy in Numbers took place almost 1300 years prior! They were star-gazers. And think of how little light pollution there would have been then; they likely would have seen thousands if not millions of stars in the sky! Thus there had to have been some sort of established guidance in place, some sort of tradition, that helped them.[15]

---

[15] "The constellation of the Virgin giving birth to the Messiah would, of course, have been viewed as quite coherent by the Magi… since the sign we know as Virgo has strong associations with other ancient 'mother goddess' figures who would produce divine kings." Heiser, Michael. *John's Use of the Old Testament in the Book of*

Here's a fun "Easter egg" in Revelation 1:20: Jesus walks amongst the seven stars. If you pull up the constellation Pleiades (aka The Seven Sisters) and overlay it on a map of the seven cities of Revelation in Asia Minor (Turkey), you'll see that they line up quite closely. Pleiades is sort of in a shape of a question mark (?), and the seven cities of Revelation are aligned in an arch with a longer right side as well! Recall that Pleiades is also mentioned in Job 38:31, quoted above.

Lastly, who can forget Joseph when he went before his family and shared the following dream:

> *"[B]ehold, the sun and the moon, and eleven stars were bowing down to me.' He also told it to his father as well as to his brothers; and his father rebuked him and said to him, 'What is this dream that you have had? Am I and your mother and your brothers actually going to come to bow down to the ground before you?'" Genesis 37:9–10 (NASB)*

How could his father have immediately interpreted this dream? It seems like Joseph's dream-interpretation gift may have run in the family! He (Israel) as the sun is the symbolic father of a future nation, and his wife Rachel (as the moon) is the symbolic matriarch of Israel. The eleven stars (Joseph's brothers) are the eleven other tribes of Israel, and the one star that appears to be situated above them all is Joseph.

Everything we have covered so far becomes our interpretive framework for what John sees in Revelation 12. It is not a like-for-like vision to that of Joseph's, but the key themes are there. Further, John is shown a great deal concerning the shift in the balance of heavenly powers, so the constellations as a prophetic canvas is fitting.

> ✶ *(1) Now a great phenomenon appeared in the heavens: a woman who was enveloped with the Sun, and the Moon under her feet, and a tiara of twelve stars upon her head.*[16]

Revelation: Notes from the Naked Bible Podcast (p. 210). Naked Bible Press. Kindle Edition.

[16] This woman was the remnant of Israel birthing both the Messiah and the Messianic Age (cf. Isa 21:3, 26:17, 37:21, 66:7; Jer 4:31, 6:24, 13:21, 14:17, 18:13; 31:4, 21; 4 Ezra 9:38–10:54; 2 Kings 19:21; Amos 5:2; Lam. 1:15; 2:13).

> א *(2) And she was pregnant, and crying out and travailing—incredibly anguished—ready to be giving birth.*

The word "enveloped" evokes a sense of being surrounded, covered, and even clothed. This is clearly an allusion to Yahweh God, the Heavenly Father. But contextually, this enveloping mostly likely represents Holy Spirit, because it is God's Spirit that overshadows Mary so that she would conceive (Luke 1:35). The woman is generally understood to be "virgin daughter Israel", which is a common Old Testament prophetic motif.[17] Church tradition has also held a long-standing view that the woman is the Virgin Mary.[18]

> "Scholars agree that verses 2–6 'reveal that this woman is a picture of the faithful community (Israel), which existed both before and after the coming of Christ.' Israel, of course, is described as the virgin of Zion in the Old Testament and produces the Messiah in fulfillment of Old Testament prophecy. More specifically, of course, Mary comes to mind as the Jewish girl who gives birth to Jesus, but 'Virgin Israel' best fits both parts of the description of the woman…
>
> [The] word 'sign' used by the author of the book of Revelation to describe this celestial display was the same one frequently used by the ancients to denote the zodiacal constellations."[19]

The tiara of the twelve stars is an obvious depiction of the Twelve Tribes of Israel, and in her womb are the prophetic promises of the Messiah – "it is those very Scriptures that testify about Me" (John 5:39).

> "[This] woman, who now takes centre stage in God's purposes for his world, is the 'priestly kingdom, holy nation' of Exodus 19.6. She represents the entire story of God's people, chosen to carry forward his plans for the nations and indeed for the whole

---

[17] See Isaiah 26:17, 66:7–10; Micah 4:10. But especially Ezekiel 16.
[18] Given that Mary did not suffer persecution (12:6), this interpretation is unlikely.
[19] Heiser, Michael. John's Use of the Old Testament in the Book of Revelation: Notes from the Naked Bible Podcast (p. 208–209). Naked Bible Press. Kindle Edition.

creation."[20]

Interestingly, some, like Dr. Martin Trench, have also made a connection between this starry vision and the constellation Virgo.[21] One thing we should keep in mind is the *interpretation* of constellations varied depending on both culture and time period. In John's time and location, Greco-Roman culture prevailed. Thus, to them, Virgo was the virgin daughter of the deity Zeus. She also had wings, much like the symbolism here (12:14). And around the time of Jesus' birth, it is estimated that the sun could be seen in the middle part of the constellation Virgo during the month of Elul (sixth month in Hebrew calendar), forming the image of the Holy Spirit coming upon her womb.[22] It was in the sixth month that the angel Gabriel visited Mary (Luke 1:26). Hence, the imagery was fitting for John's context where this type of interpretation was taught in schools and widely accepted by society. Of note, I am not suggesting John believed the Roman mythologies of the gods and goddesses!

> "The apostle John saw the scene when the Sun was 'clothing' or 'adorning' the woman. This surely indicates that the position of the Sun in the vision was located somewhere mid-bodied to the woman, between the neck and the knees. The Sun could hardly be said to clothe her if it were situated in her face or near her feet. The only time in the year that the Sun could be in a position to 'clothe' the celestial woman called Virgo (that is, to be mid-bodied to her, in the region where a pregnant woman carries a child) is when the Sun is located between about 150 and 170 degrees along the ecliptic. This 'clothing' of the woman by the Sun occurs for a 20-day period each year. This 20-degree spread could indicate the general time when Jesus was born.[23]

Finally, we have the moon. Early Church fathers like Hippolytus and Victorinus saw the moon as "heavenly glory" or "fallen saints". However these fail to resonate with the symbolism of early Jewish thought. But the 6th

---

[20] Wright, N. T. Revelation for Everyone, The New Testament for Everyone, p. 108. Presbyterian Publishing Corporation. Kindle Edition.
[21] See, Trench, Martin. Eyes Wide Open (pp. 67).
[22] Chevalier, Jacques M. A Postmodern Revelation: Signs of Astrology and the Apocalypse (Toronto: University of Toronto Press, 1997), pp 342.
[23] Martin, E. L. chapter 5, cited from the text at: http://www.askelm.com/star/star006.htm.

century author Oecumenius, who penned the earliest extant Greek commentary on Revelation, offers a reasonable assertion.

> "[The] moon, that is, the worship and citizenship according to the law, being subdued and become much less than itself, is under her feet, for it has been conquered by the brightness of the gospel. And rightly does he call the things of the law by the word *moon*, for they have been given light by the sun, that is, Christ, just as the physical moon is given its light by the physical sun."[24]

I think Oecumenius was on to something. That he connected the Law to the moon is interesting for two reasons. First, the Hebrew slaves who came up out of the sun-worshiping Egyptian culture with Moses were in Exodus 12 commanded to abandon Egypt's sun-based calendar (where the sun god Ra was central), and instead adopt a lunar-based one where Yahweh was central. New Moon observance (Rosh Chodesh) became a religious practice from that day forward.[25] Hence Paul's remarks in Colossians 2:16-17:

> *"Therefore, no one is to act as your judge in regard to food and drink, or in respect to a festival or a <u>new moon</u>, or a Sabbath day—things which are only a shadow of what is to come; but the substance belongs to Christ."*

So in the case of John's vision, we have the 12 stars in place with Yahweh assuming the role of the sun via His Spirit. But there remains room for another aspect of Israel to be represented here. We may use Joseph's dream as an interpretive framework, but also understand that it's ok to have a slight divergence in symbolism. Therefore, it is safe to suggest that the moon in John's Vision is the Torah since it is the bedrock of Jewish faith, and its words point to the Messiah. The Torah dimly reflects the glory and character of God (Heb 1:1–3). Again, to quote Paul,

> *"[God] made us adequate as servants of a new covenant, not of the letter [of the Torah] but of the Spirit; for the letter kills, but the Spirit gives life.*
>
> *But if the ministry of death, engraved in letters on stones, came with glory so that the sons of Israel could not look intently at the face of Moses because*

---

[24] Weinrich, William C., eds. Revelation. vol. 12 of Ancient Christian Commentary on Scripture. ICCS/Accordance electronic ed. (Downers Grove: InterVarsity Press, 2005), 175.

[25] Often translated in our Bibles as new month. Num. 10:10, 28:11-15; 2 Chron. 2:4, 8:13; Ezra 3:5; Neh. 10:33.

of the glory of his face, <u>fading as it was</u>, how will the ministry of the Spirit fail to be even more with glory? For if the ministry of condemnation has glory, much more does the ministry of righteousness excel in glory… For if that which fades away was with glory, much more that which remains is in glory…

[Thus] we are not like Moses, who used to put a veil over his face so that the sons of Israel would not stare at the end of what was fading away. But their minds were hardened; for until this very day at the reading of the old covenant the same veil remains unlifted, because it is removed in Christ." 2 Corinthians 3:6–14 (NASB, emphasis mine)

The imagery becomes very powerful then: the true and pure Israel (a polis, a collective bride) is being elevated above the Law. The Torah will no longer define her, nor will it bind her.[26] How is this possible? By way of the Child she was about to conceive.

Lastly, Wright offers a thought worth mentioning:

> "The second image behind the woman in this passage may well be Eve, the original mother of all human life. It is Eve, after all, who is told that her 'seed' will crush the serpent's head (Genesis 3.15). The two identities go together. If the woman is 'Israel', she is for that reason the one in whom God's purposes for humanity are to be realized."[27]

DOPPELGANGER

A contradistinction between Virgin Daughter Israel, or Virgin Daughter Zion, and Apostate Israel, or Apostate Jerusalem, will become one of the main frameworks for interpreting chapters 12 to 19 and 21 in John's Apocalypse. The tale of two women is in fact a tale of the same woman who suffers different fates as a result of her actions. Of course this is where the symbolism becomes blurry.

---

[26] See Galatians 4:1–31.
[27] Wright, N. T. Revelation for Everyone (The New Testament for Everyone) (p. 108). Presbyterian Publishing Corporation. Kindle Edition.

We must understand that we are dealing with two groups of people, and it is these two groups who collectively make up the representation of these symbols. Those who were faithful to Yahweh and discerned the promised Messiah in Jesus collectively represent the Virgin Israel, or Daughter Zion.[28] The unfaithful, which the New Testament characterizes at length, collectively represent Apostate Israel, or Jerusalem the Harlot.

The faithful bride first introduced here in chapter 12 is contrasted against a sort of doppelganger of herself in the ensuing chapters, specifically 14 to 19, with a heart-wrenching crescendo in 18 where she is further personified as fallen Babylon. The scene then shifts back in 19:7 to the true bride, Daughter Zion, who is now betrothed to her Messiah.

These themes will be explored at length as we progress through this book. But for now we must turn our attention back to the astrological fireworks which dazzled before John's eyes.

> א *(3) But another phenomenon appeared in the heavens — Behold! A great Leviathan,[29] which was fiery[30] and had seven heads and ten horns, and upon its heads seven crowns.*
>
> א *(4) And its tail was dragging a third of the stars which were in the*

---

[28] 2 Kings 19:21; Isaiah 1:8, 37:22, vs. Isaiah 1:8, 21. And again, Ezekiel 16.
[29] Literally "sea-serpent". The Aramaic is the same as Hebrew (Strong's H8577): תנין "tannin". If you have a look at a lexicon (many Bible sites have them) you will see this word has been poorly and inconsistently translated. This is due to two predominant factors: first, changes in cultural contexts over millennia. Second, changes in English vernacular over centuries. Culturally, the *tannin* of the Hebrew Bible can also be found in Ancient Mesopotamia (Ugaritic) as *tunnanu*, also known as *ushumgal*, and in Greek mythology as *hydra*, to name a few. These creatures all had several heads (eg. Ps 74:13–14), and hydra specifically had seven (like we see in Revelation). Leviathan לִוְיָתָן (Strong's H3882) is a derivative of tannin, since both share the root תַן "tan" (Strong's H8565). Both tannin and leviathan were depicted as water-based serpents in antiquity. Therefore, I will maintain the origin of the word in mind. But because the creature is airborne, *dragon* is a fitting image as well.
[30] The Aramaic, including the Crawford and Harklean, both have "of fire" or "fiery".

heavens and forced them down[31] *upon The Land,*[32] *while the Leviathan was elevating himself before the woman, who was preparing herself to give birth, so that when she had delivered, it could devour her Son.*

Several comments are required here. First, the Fiery Leviathan (aka Dragon) is clearly Satan. Much has been written on this, so there is no need for me to add.[33] As Victorinus (d. c. 304 AD) first noted, the seven heads are the seven Roman emperors up to the Fall of Jerusalem.[34] This vision is not a facial composite or witness description of Satan. It is a message being communicated in symbol and imagery.

There are also ten horns. Six heads each have a horn, representing their reign, rule, or dynasty (cf. Luke 4:5–7).[35] The seventh head has three horns, corresponding with the Flavian dynasty: Vespasian, Titus, and Domitian. These seven heads and ten horns also connect with the vision of the sea-beast in 13:1.

A SKY FULL OF STARS

I don't know about you, but as a kid I remember growing up hearing about Satan taking a third of the angels of heaven with him when he was kicked out. Revelation 12:4 is where that theory originated. However, after a quick step back and pause for reflection, one will note that that Biblical chronology makes no sense. Satan falls before Adam and Eve! So it's safe to

---

[31] The verb "to cast down, set, place" is intensified with the Aphel inflection, which implies a forceful action. It may be translated, "he threw them." There is a contrast between the Leviathan's self-elevation. Also, as we will see, the stars were likely religious leaders and priests. Therefore the imagery may suggest that they were also brought to their knees in obeisance.

[32] This is the first instance of אֶרֶץ "the land", referring to the "Land of Israel". I have discussed at length in books one and two of this series how *eretz* in Hebrew (and Aramaic) almost always was used in reference to the Holy Land. Therefore, I will not digress here. For further reading, see "The Gospel and the Land", by W. D. Davies.

[33] Of note, Heiser and others make a link to the constellations Hydra and Scorpio (see Heiser: *John's Use of the Old Testament in the Book of Revelation*). To me however, over-emphasis on the constellations takes away from the broader focus.

[34] Julius Caesar, Augustus, Tiberius, Caligula, Claudius, Nero, Vespasian.

[35] Also see The Apocalypse Commentary of Tyconius (d. c. 390).

say that the third of angels theory doesn't fit.[36]

So then what does "its tail was dragging a third of the stars which were in the heavens" mean?

The most common Biblical symbolic use of stars is to represent *people*:

- God to Abraham, his seed likened to the stars (Gen 22:17)
- Joseph's dream, where his brothers were stars (Gen 37:9)
- Deborah, 10,000 Hebrew soldiers alluded to as stars (Jud 4:6; 5:20)
- Daniel's vision, where the priests of God were stars (Dan 8:10)
- Daniel's vision, where the "wise" shine as bright stars (Dan 12:3)
- The Magi's journey, where the star represented Jesus (Matt 2:2)
- Vison of Jesus, who holds stars – messengers - in his hand (Rev 1:20)

Perhaps some of the Scriptures cited above require clarification. Early Christians knew Daniel 7 is a vision of Jesus birthing the Kingdom Age at his advent, his *first* coming. And Jewish sages have long concluded that Daniel 8 was fulfilled during the Maccabean Revolt, which is the "reason for the season" of Hanukkah.

So when you read Daniel 8:9–14, it is Antiochus IV Epiphanes (the little horn) who touches the stars of heaven by touching Yahweh's ministers – the priesthood. In short, when you messed with the Temple you were messing with Heaven itself, for the two were directly linked. It was the only place in the universe where heaven and earth were one because that was God's earthly residence (hence the alternate Old Testament name for it – the "House of God").

> Ephrem The Syrian (c. 306 – 373 AD): "He signifies here the priestly order, which he compares with the host of heaven. 'It threw down to the earth some of the host and some of the stars and trampled on them.' Here he prophesies about the sons of Semona and the allies killed by Antiochus."[37]

---

[36] Interestingly, Victorinus was the first early church source to suggest this idea, though many others followed suit.
[37] Kenneth Stevenson and Michael Glerup, eds. *Ezekiel, Daniel*. vol. 13 of Ancient Christian Commentary on Scripture. ICCS/Accordance electronic ed. (Downers Grove: InterVarsity Press, 2008), 252.

Antiochus IV Epiphanes's arrogance reaches the heavens, and the holy ones of Yahweh God are struck down. Literally. This topic is worth researching, but is beyond the scope of this book. [38]

As for Revelation 1:16 and 20, we must be thankful that the vision received self-interpretation, or else there would be no end to theories.[39] Though many in recent times have suggested that Jesus was holding angelic hosts in his hand, this interpretation lacks practicality. Angels are never in danger.[40] But those early churches about to go through hell on earth were, especially the overseers who had to keep and encourage their flocks. By the time John saw this vision, his own brother had already been killed (Acts 12:2), as had Jesus' half-brother, James (Josephus: Ant. 20:9:1), and later Paul and Peter (Eusebius: History, 2:25). They were but first-fruits.

So when we get to Revelation 12, the vision of stars has sufficient Biblical references to guide our interpretation. One should also note that Revelation 12:4 says a "third" of the stars are swept down. As we will read in subsequent chapters, *a third* becomes a prophetic number synonymous with the fall of Jerusalem. Therefore, based on all the Scriptures referenced above, it is safe to suggest that the stars John sees in chapter 12 are Jewish people in a broad sense. And more specifically, **these stars likely represent the religious leaders, especially the Temple priests**.[41]

Early on in our history as the Bride of Messiah, this association had already been made:

> Tyconius (d. c. 390 AD): "The 'tail' is the iniquitous prophets who throw down to earth the stars of heaven, namely, those simple persons who join themselves to them. When he speaks of 'a third part of the stars,' he is speaking of the Jews and their leaders who rejected Christ and with impious voices cried out that they did not want Christ to be over them but rather Caesar,

---

[38] Alter, and many others, see Daniel 8:10 as a "violation of the Temple cult by Antiochus, which is understood as an assault on God." Alter, Robert: The Hebrew Bible, Vol. 3. W. W. Norton & Company: New York, 2019, pp. 782.

[39] This is a common pattern in the Book of Daniel: Dan. 2:31-35 cf. Dan. 2:36-45; Dan. 7:1-14 cf. Dan. 7:15-28; Dan. 8:1-12 cf. Dan. 8:13-27; 9:20-27; Dan. 10:1-12:4 cf. Dan. 12:5-13.

[40] Also note that the Hebrew and Aramaic word for angel is also the same word for messenger. Discerning which English word to use is based entirely on context.

[41] Honorable mention must be made to the infants slaughtered by Herod's decree (Matt 2:16–18), as some authors have believed the stars represented these children.

and therefore they killed him."[42]

In the first two volumes of this series, I reference at length the various accounts of the apostacies of the priesthood and religious leadership recorded by Josephus. The reader must keep these in mind in order to believe that a third of them would be brought into submission under Satan. Sadly, history supports this theory.

> א *(5) Yet she delivered the male Son who was destined to shepherd[43] all the nations[44] with a rod of iron.[45] And her Son was caught up to God and to His throne.[46]*

> א *(6) And the woman fled to the wilderness region,[47] where she had there a place made ready by God where she would be sustained one thousand two hundred and sixty days.[48]*

The pastoral description of Jesus cannot be overlooked. He was destined – indeed He himself made the decision before creation took place – to be a shepherd to all nations! The Good Shephard, who leaves the 99 in search of one lost sheep, is born. And to him is given a rod of iron. Three times in Revelation the "rod" is mentioned: 2:27, 12:5, and 19:15. The word for this rod or scepter in Aramaic is the same as the Hebrew, shebet שֵׁבֶט. Shebet is used in the renown twenty-third Psalm: "thy rod (שֵׁבֶט) and thy staff, they

---

[42] William C. Weinrich, eds. *Revelation.* vol. 12 of Ancient Christian Commentary on Scripture. ICCS/Accordance electronic ed. (Downers Grove: InterVarsity Press, 2005), 179.
[43] The word here means "to feed" or "to tend", and is therefore nurturing.
[44] Or, "Gentiles". Same word.
[45] Compare with Rev 2:27 and 19:15; clearly referring to Jesus. More specifically, this is a quote from Psalm 2:7–9. The rod of iron that follows means his shepherd's rod will never fail – a staff that can never be broken – a picture of his endless fidelity and love toward mankind.
[46] Speaking of the resurrection of Jesus.
[47] This wilderness trek likely went across the Arabah (where Jesus was tempted and where Ezekiel saw water flow from the Temple) and beyond to the trans-Jordan. The Aramaic word is חורבא which corresponds to the Hebrew עֲרָבָה H6160.
[48] The 3.5 year period, along with the flight into the wilderness, clearly connects this image to the flight to Pella made by the first-century Jews prior to the fall of Jerusalem by the Romans. This event is discussed in great detail in the first two books of this series. It was chronicled by early church historian Eusebius and others.

comfort me" (23:4).

The iron scepter, or rod (same word), is one that cannot be broken. Jesus' rule cannot be challenged, nor can his reign cease. This is in contrast to kingdoms and rulers who *did* have their scepters shattered.

> *"[Israel] will take up this taunt against the king of Babylon, and say,*
> *'...The Lord has broken the staff of the wicked,*
> *The scepter of rulers...'" Isaiah 14:4–5 (NASB)*

The Son, Yeshua the Messiah, then ascends to Yahweh God after his resurrection. His descent into Sheol is not mentioned here because the focal point of this vision is not the life and ministry of Jesus, rather it is the Virgin and the Harlot Israel.

1,260 DAYS?

The theme of a 3.5 year period is hit upon again here in 12:6. As in other places of Revelation (11:2, 3; 12:14; 13:5), John is reminded over and over that the tribulation period (from 66 to mid 70 AD) is going to last three and a half years. To Yahwists, 1,260 is quite close to Daniel's 1,290 and 1,335 days (Daniel 12:11, 12). In the same way Jesus pulls on Daniel's prophecies when he speaks of the abomination that causes desolation (Mt 24:15; Mk 13:14), John is pulling on some Daniel prophecies as well through these time spans that amount to roughly 3.5 years each. Since we are on the topic of Daniel, let's take a little detour and understand how the 1,290 and 1,355 days can be likened to John's 1,260 days.

Chapters 7, 8, 9, and 12 of Daniel make reference to some date ranges that are often confusing: 1,290 days, 1335 days, 70 weeks, 2,300 evenings and mornings, and "time, times, and half a time". But these are all unique ways of describing the same approximate interval of time: 3.5 years. As we will see, this period is from 66 to mid-70 AD (the Jewish-Roman War). Let's compare John's use of these date ranges with that of Daniel's:

Daniel 7:25; 12:7	Time, times, half-time (3.5)
Revelation 12:14	Time, times, half-time (3.5)

Daniel 12:11, 12:12, 8:14   1290 days, 1335 days, 1150 days[49] (~3.5 years)
Revelation 11:3; 12:6   1260 days (3.5 years)

Daniel 9:27   Half a week (3.5 days)
Revelation 11:2; 13:5   Forty-Two Months (3.5 years)

Now for those of you who did the math, you'll have noticed that some of the dates don't quite line up with our modern-day Gregorian calendars. Daniel was likely using the simplified 360 day lunar calendar with each month consisting of 30 days. Additionally, a common Greek practice in antiquity was to employ intercalary (leap) months once every other year, in order to consistently align calendars with seasons (the Jewish calendar today still does something similar).[50] Nevertheless, the theme is consistent.

But why does Daniel have 1,290 and 1,335, while John has 1,260? Because from the time Eleazer (a Jewish priest who was sort of a catalyst to the Jewish-Roman war) stopped offering scarifies in the Temple on behalf of Caesar (6th Av, 66 AD) to when the Romans surrounded Jerusalem in preparation for their final assault (Shevat, 70 AD), it was 1,260 days. And the 1,335 are from the time when the Romans worshiped their idols on the Jewish Temple mount (9th Av, 70 AD) to when the entire Roman campaign against the Holy Land ended (16th Nisan, 74 AD), following the battle of Masada. After this period, some followers of Jesus began to return to the Holy Land. So Daniel's prophecies had to do with an approximate three and a half year period leading up to the fall of Jerusalem, to a three and a half year period following Jerusalem's fall. The entire Roman campaign was seven years long, according to history.

Now for a mini digression. When the Romans sacrifice to their pagan god on the Temple mount, this is in fulfillment of Jesus' prophecies about "the abomination of desolation". This prophecy is based upon a historical event that Daniel 8:11; 8:14; 9:25–27; 11:31; and 12:11 also speaks of: **Antiochus IV Epiphanius** desecrating the Jewish Temple.[51]

After the Persian Period of Daniel (500s to 400s BC) comes the

---

[49] 1,150 is from Daniel 8:14: "2,300 evenings and mornings". 2300/2 = 1150. An allusion to Ex 29:38–42 and the order of the morning and evening sacrifices.
[50] For the Greek intercalary months, see Herodotus: Solon and Croesus, from *The Histories*, https://sourcebooks.fordham.edu/ancient/herodotus-creususandsolon.asp
[51] Though I referenced these verses in relation to the Jewish-Roman War, they are dualistic in the sense that they also speak of a more immediate time relative to Daniel's day. This has been true of many of the OT allusions in Revelation.

Hellenistic (meaning Greek) Period (300s to mid-100s BC), which brings new troubles in the Holy Land. A madman named Antiochus IV becomes ruler of Greco-Syria. He names himself Epiphanes, meaning "god manifest". Soon after rising to the throne, he starts targeting the Jews.

In his desire to radically Hellenize (make them like Greeks) the Jews in his empire, Antiochus IV realizes he must abolish their religion. He attempts to do this by first adding Greek-styled buildings in Jerusalem. He continues by removing the High Priest, looting the Temple treasury, and stripping the Temple of all its sacred vessels – including the Menorah. He even forbids circumcision. When the Jews revolt, he has thousands of them slaughtered.

But the most horrendous thing Antiochus IV Epiphanes does is this: he places a statue of Zeus *inside* the rebuilt Temple – the Temple that was destroyed by Nebuchadnezzar and later miraculously rebuilt by Nehemiah and others. Worse, Mr. "god manifest" then sacrifices pigs upon the Holy Altar within. **This, folks, is what Jews (starting with Daniel) called the "abomination of desolation".** So when you read in the New Testament, "you shall see the abomination of desolation, spoken of by Daniel the prophet," this is the event they are referring to.

The key: Daniel speaks of a time ahead of him when Antiochus IV will come and do all that we've just reviewed. In the New Testament, this *historical* event known as the "abomination of desolation" is being used **to warn Jews of a similar type of event** that will come upon the Holy Land again! This event is the Roman siege of Jerusalem. Instead of Antiochus IV, it will be Titus (son of Vespasian) who will desecrate the Temple when his soldiers offer up sacrifices to their gods on the Temple Mount.[52]

Daniel and Revelation are linked together through these enigmatic dates because Daniel and John both prophesy about the same events: the tribulation of the end of the Mosaic Age and the dawning of the Messianic

---

[52] Some may be wondering about Daniel's 70 weeks. In Daniel 9, the angel Gabriel speaks about a 70 week period, which is really puzzling at first. But when you line up the dates with Jesus' ministry, things fit! Seventy weeks are 490 years. And at the end of the 69th week the Messiah appears. From 457 BC (the decree to rebuild the Temple) to the start of Jesus' ministry in 27 AD is 483 years. Three and a half years after that Jesus is then "cut off" (His crucifixion) half-way through the 70th week. That's how Jesus makes "an end of sin… atonement for guilt… [and brings] in everlasting righteousness" (9:24) and "[puts] a stop to sacrifice and grain offering" (9:27). Now overlay this on top of the Jewish-Roman war: half-way through the 7-year period, sacrifices ceased once and for all when the Temple was destroyed. Such is the nature of the reuse of OT prophecies in NT writings.

Age.⁵³ Now if we return to the woman in Revelation 12:6, it makes sense that she leaves the Holy Land for a 3.5 year period, which historically is the event known as the Flight to Pella. The remnant of Yahweh's faithful lovers, personified as a woman, go to "a place made ready by God where she would be sustained one thousand two hundred and sixty days". An entire company of saints leaves the Holy Land just before the hammer falls.⁵⁴

Lastly, we cannot miss the reference to Isaiah 26 and 27 here in Revelation 12:6:

"As a pregnant woman about to give birth
cries out and writhes in her labor pains,
so we have been at your presence, Adonai —
we have been pregnant and been in pain…

For see! Adonai emerges from his place
to punish those on [the land] for their sin.
Then the [land] will reveal the blood shed on it
and no longer conceal its slain.

On that day Adonai,
with his great, strong, relentless sword,
will punish [Leviathan] the fleeing serpent,
the twisting serpent [Leviathan];
he will slay the sea monster." Isaiah 26:17–27:1, abridged (CJB)

I SAW SATAN FALL LIKE LIGHTING FROM HEAVEN

א *(7) Then there was war in the heavens.*⁵⁵ *Michael and his angels*

---

⁵³ For the curious, the dates of the start and finish of Antiochus IV's desecration of the Second Temple are revealed in Maccabees. First Maccabees 1:54 says it started on Kislev (December) 15, 167 BC. And First Maccabees 4:52–53 mentions the rededication on Kislev 25, 164 BC (the date of Hanukkah), signifying the finish. This equals 1,090 days (360 x 3 + 10 days), plus two intercalary months, 60 days, totaling 1,150 days. But where do we get 1,500? From Daniel 8:14 and the 2,300 mornings and evenings 2300/2 = 1150, mentioned in the footnote above.
⁵⁴ Eusebius and other early church writers recorded this event.
⁵⁵ There is no clear indication if this is God's Heaven (3ʳᵈ), the heavens (general sense), or the skies. Both the Hebrew and Aramaic word are the same, and it is

engaging with the Leviathan, and the Leviathan and his angels engaged them.[56]

(8) But they couldn't prevail, and no domain could he gain for them in the heavens.

(9) So the Master[57] *Leviathan was brought down,*[58] *that ancient serpent, who is called the Accuser and Adversary,*[59] *who deceived everyone from the Land. So he was brought down upon the Land, and his angels were brought down with him.*

This identity of the Leviathan, or Dragon, which are depictions of Satan, is often disputed. Oddly, even Christians will dismiss the notion of Satan's existence, which I find puzzling. So a quick tour of the Scriptures is in order so we can all be on the same page.

Revelation 12:9 connects four nouns and equates them all to the same persona: leviathan (dragon), serpent, accuser/slanderer, and adversary. It is a culmination of predominately (but not exclusively) Old Testament depictions of Satan. [60] They are one and the same creature. Here are a few references from the Hebrew Scriptures:

---

always plural. So I chose the second option in order to be in the middle of both ends of the possible spectrum.

[56] "Engaging" and "engaged". Both are the same word. And is also found in Revelation 2:16: "to approach, drawn near, encounter". It can also mean "draw close for the purpose of war". Context is key. In 2:16, Jesus was not drawing near for war, as I explained in the previous book, because the sword of His mouth – His words – cleanses us (see John 15:3), they don't harm us. Here, however, the angels *are* drawing near (Aphel active participle) for the purpose of war. So I chose military verbiage, "to engage".

[57] The word rabba רבא here does not imply a physical attribute like the Hebrew "gibor" (mighty). Rather, it refers to significance, prominence, or position. It can mean "rabbi", "teacher", or "chief". Given the military context, one could suggest "commander" or "leader". I have opted for "master" for its broader meaning.

[58] The same verb used in 12:4 for the stars who were "forced down" is used here. The irony is intentional. The Leviathan, who in arrogance threw down people, is now thrown down itself, humiliated and defeated.

[59] "Accuser/slanderer" in Aramaic is akhelqartza (or akhel qartza), and "adversary" is satan (same as Hebrew).

[60] Belial בְלִיַּעַל and Beelzebub בַּעַל-זְבוּב were also common names for Satan in John's time. Later, Jewish sages wrote: "Satan, the Evil Inclination, and the Angel of Death are the same" (Talmud, Bava Bathra 16a).

"Now The Serpent (הַנָּחָשׁ) was most cunning of all the beasts of the field that YHWH God had made." Gen 3:1 (Hebrew)

"It happened one day that the sons of God came to serve Adonai, and among them came the Adversary [Satan שָׂטָן]. Adonai asked the Adversary, 'Where are you coming from?' The Adversary answered Adonai, 'From roaming through the earth, wandering here and there.'" Job 1:6–7 (CJB)

"He showed me [Joshua the High Priest] standing before the angel of Adonai, with the Accuser [Satan שָׂטָן] standing at his right to accuse him. Adonai said to the Accuser, 'May Adonai rebuke you, Accuser! Indeed, may Adonai, who has made [Jerusalem] his choice, rebuke you! Isn't this man a burning stick snatched from the fire?'" Zechariah 3:1–2 (CJB)[61]

"The Adversary [Satan שָׂטָן] now rose up against Isra'el and incited David to take a census of Isra'el." 1 Chronicles 21:1 (CJB)

"On that day Adonai,
with his great, strong, relentless sword,
will punish [Leviathan] the fleeing serpent,
the twisting serpent [Leviathan]..." Isaiah 27:1 (CJB)

It should be noted that at times in the Hebrew Bible, "satan" is not a proper name, but instead it is referring to "the adversary" (ha satan הַשָּׂטָן). Now when we get to the New Testament, references to "Satan" or "The Adversary" abound:

As a being:

The Accuser or Slanderer,[62] Matthew 4:3
Prince of Demons, Matthew 12:24; Mark 3:22; Luke 11:15

---

[61] Midrash: "On the day of Atonement Satan comes to accuse Israel, enumerating their sins" (Pesiqta Rabbati 185b).
[62] The Talumd makes reference to a tempter of immorality איצרא דעבירה (Yoma 68b).

Baal (ruler) of the Flies (Beelzebub), Matthew 12:25–28
The Enemy, Matthew 13:39
The Evil One, Matthew 13:38
The prince of the previous age (*not* world), John 12:31; 14:30
The father of lies, and a murderer, John 8:44
The god ("Elohim" in Aramaic, in the Old Testament sense of a lower spiritual being) of the previous age (*not* world), 2 Cor. 4:4
Who fashioned himself as an angel of light, 2 Cor. 11:14
Prince of the power of the air [אאר in Aramaic, emphatically not heaven, or lower heavens, which is שָׁמַיִם], and is the spirit that works in the disobedient, Ephesians 2:2
The *master of slander* (more on this below), 1 Peter 5:8

And in reference to his actions:

He placed betrayal into the heart of Judas, Jn 13:2, 27
Evil people are called his sons, Matthew 13:38; 1 John 3:8, 10
He sows tares among wheat, Matthew 13:38, 39
And snatches the Word from hearers, Matthew 13:19; Mark 4:15; Luke 8:12
He bound a woman for 18 years, Luke 13:16
And caused Ananias to lie, Acts 5:3
Gentiles are (or were) under his power, Acts 26:18
He blinds the minds of unbelievers, 2 Cor. 4:4
He caused Paul's thorn in the flesh, 2 Cor. 12:7
And hindered Paul's missionary plans, 1 Thess. 2:18
Could produce false miracles, 1 Thes. 2:9

But for those in Christ:

"He said to them, 'I watched Satan fall from heaven like lightning. Behold, I have given you authority to walk on snakes and scorpions, and authority over all the power of the enemy, and nothing will injure you.'"
Luke 10:18–19 (NASB)

He will flee if resisted, James 4:7
He is overcome by faith, 1 Peter 5:9
He is overcome by the blood of the Lamb and the word of His testimony, Revelation 12:11

One fascinating discovery I came across in this study was the curious case of 1 Peter 5:8. Most Bibles will read something like, "your enemy/adversary, Satan, is like a roaring lion." But as I inquired about this particular Aramaic word in 1 Peter 5:8, translated as "enemy", I learned that it is a compound word: ܒܥܠܕܒܒܐ ܒܥܠܕܒܒܐ, master/lord (ܒܥܠ בעל) of slander (ܕܒܒܐ דבבא). What's more interesting is the connection to Matthew 12:24–28: Jesus is accused of casting out demons by Beelzebub (which is equated to Satan in verse 26). Beelzebub/baal-zebub (ܒܥܠܙܒܘܒ בעלזבוב) is also a compound word: master/lord (ܒܥܠ בעל) of flies (ܙܒܘܒ זבוב).[63]

Both Matthew 12:24, 27 and 1 Peter 5:8 have "baal", a name that appears in the Hebrew Bible several times ("baal" בַּעַל) and also used very commonly in the ancient Levant. And Peter's use may even be an alternate spelling of Beelzebub,[64] however the word is an adjective there, while Matthew's word is a proper noun. Nevertheless, one may translate 1 Peter 5:8 as follows: "Watch and be mindful, because *he who is a master of slander towards you*,[65] Satan, like a lion roars..."

Matthew 12:25–28, the Beelzebub remark, then concludes with verse 29, the binding of the strong man. This is a fitting image for Revelation 12:

> *"How can someone enter a strong man's house and plunder his goods, unless he first binds the strong man? Then indeed he may plunder his house." Matthew 12:29 (ESV)*

The failed coup in Revelation 12 is the beginning of several staged setbacks for the celestial antagonist. While a short period of time is permitted for Satan to wreak havoc upon the Holy Land, the prophetic picture of the Strong Man in Matthew 12:29 will ultimately be fulfilled in Revelation 20:2, which we will explore in more detail later in this book.

We must also mention Daniel 12 here, as the first verses of that chapter are being referenced here in Revelation 12:

"And in that time Michael shall stand up [lit. יַעֲמֹד 'take his stand'], the great prince who stands over the sons of your

---

[63] Beelzebub comes in various forms and languages, and has a very long history of variants and interpretations beyond the scope of this book. These include: ba'al-zəbûb (lord of the flies), ba'al-zəbûl (lord of the high place), and beel-zebul/Beelzeboul (prince of demons).

[64] דבב – there could be a switch between ד and ז because of the Protosemitic letter "dh". But I lack the expertise in Aramaic/Syriac to be certain of this.

[65] ד-בעל-דבב-כון

people, and it shall be a time of distress the like of which has not been since the nation came to be until that time. And in that time your people shall escape, all who are found in the book.[66]

Like the rest of Daniel's visions, the opening verses of chapter 12 are packed full of meaning. I could spend several chapters on the first three verses alone, but I will try to keep the focus on how they related to Revelation 12.[67] First, we must understand that Daniel 11 concludes with the famous political drama between the Seleucids (Greeks), the Ptolemies (Egyptians), and a particular Caesar (obviously a Roman). The melodrama of Antony and Cleopatra (Daniel 11) then takes us right into the time of Herod and the pending birth of Jesus (Daniel 12).

How do we know this? Because in Daniel 12:1 we are told that Michael, the great angel, takes his stand. The angel is summoned for the "time of distress which has not been". This distress is depicted in Revelation 12, where Satan seeks to destroy Daughter Israel, her Son, and her people. This time of distress is also prophesied by Jesus in Matthew 24:21 and Luke 21:25. So while Daniel is only told *what* Michael would do, John actually gets to *see* the spiritual battle unfold.

> א *(10) And I heard a significant voice from Heaven which said, 'Behold! Now has come the deliverance, and the military might, the kingdom of our God, for the Prosecutor[68] of our brethren is brought*

---

[66] Alter, Robert: The Hebrew Bible, Vol. 3. W. W. Norton & Company: New York, 1923, pp. 797.

[67] If you are wondering about the resurrection mentioned in Daniel 12:2, I cover that when we get to the Age of Messiah (Rev 20) later in this book.

[68] We now have a new noun for Satan, מָסוֹר the "delator" in Aramaic, and "moser" in Hebrew. A moser or delator was one who indicated to a court another as having committed a punishable deed. In other words, a snitch. This title was based on a Roman profession that was corrupt. Because the root of the word (מסר, mesirah, "to delate", "lay accusation") is also used again in this verse, I chose "Prosecutor" and "prosecutes" to preserve the wordplay. The role of the moser was present in Jewish history as well. Even Maimonides (12th c.) wrote that a moser should be killed because it was a horrible deed. "Nothing was more severely punished by the Jews than talebearing; and no one was held in greater contempt than the informer. On account of the fact that his deeds frequently caused mischief and even entailed death and destruction, the sages of the Talmud compared the "moser" to a serpent." (Jewish Encyclopedia, "moser").

down, who was prosecuting them night and day⁶⁹ before our God.

(11) But they were victoriously acquitted⁷⁰ through the blood of the Lamb and by the agency of the word of His testimony.⁷¹ Yet they loved not their lives, even unto death.

These two verses, 10 and 11, astound me. As I've been working through the texts and pondering these words, I'm moved to tears. Jesus is speaking on my behalf. He testifies on my account. I've been acquitted of all charges of sin against me. How? Yeshua has done it all: His blood, His testimony. We know this, but do we *know* this in the innermost parts of our being?

"And as they went, they entered a village of the Samaritans, to prepare for Him. But they did not receive Him… And when His disciples James and John saw this, they said, 'Lord, do You want us to command fire to come down from heaven and consume them, just as Elijah did?'

But He turned and rebuked them, and said, 'You do not know what manner of spirit you are of. For the Son of Man did not come to destroy

---

⁶⁹ The word order here is classically Hebrew. Since Genesis 1, for the Jews, the day always begins in the evening, not the morning.

⁷⁰ The verb זכא here means several things: "to be innocent", "blameless", "righteous", "to acquit", "to justify". But it can also mean to overcome or to conquer, like in Hebrews 11:33, "through faith conquered kingdoms". Revelation 6:2 uses this word three times: "he went forth conquering, so that in conquering he might conquer." So it comes down to context. Satan is presented as a litigator, litigating the lovers of Yahweh God, especially those who had been bound under the Law of Moses. Hence, I have decided to present both meanings; it was a *legal victory*, having won a court battle. Yet there is also the broader victory for *all of us* through His Blood.

⁷¹ וּבְיַד מֶלְתָא דְסָהֲדוּתָהּ - literally, "and through *the hand* of the word of His testimony". The word "hand" in this context should be understood as "by means of" or "because", but I chose "agency" to keep with the theme. The theological implications of this verse are mind-blowing: as the court case motif continues, the saints of Yahweh are acquitted from the charges brought forth by the Litigator, on the grounds of what Jesus had to say about them, not what they had to say in their defense. What was his word? It could only have been one: "innocent". Selah.

men's lives but to save them.'" Luke 9:52–56 (NKJV)[72]

Satan accuses. Satan condemns. So if we accuse others of their sins, who are we partnering with? There is no grace from God behind such ministry. Isn't it amazing that the Apostle John was one of the ones rebuked by Jesus in Luke 9? Perhaps that is why he later became known as the Apostle of Love.

> *"Now all these things are from God, who reconciled us to Himself through Christ and gave us the ministry of reconciliation, namely, that God was in Christ reconciling the world to Himself, not counting their wrongdoings against them, and He has committed to us the word of reconciliation." 2 Corinthians 5:18–19 (NASB)*

> *"But you have come to Mount Zion and to the city of the living God, the heavenly Jerusalem… and to God, the Judge of all, and to the spirits of the righteous made perfect, and to Jesus, the mediator of a new covenant, and to the sprinkled blood, which speaks better than the blood of Abel." Hebrews 12:22–24 (NASB)*

> *"Behold, the Lamb of God who takes away the sin of the world!" John 1:29 (NASB)*

As 2 Corinthians 5:19 says, God has entrusted to *us* this word, this message of reconciliation. He is not holding the trespasses of mankind against them. This is what God has asked us to share.

> א *(12) As a result of these things:*
>   *Rejoice! O Heavens and also those who dwell within you!*
>   *Woe! O Land and Sea!*
>   *Upon which the Accuser descends towards them,*
>   *having incredible anger towards them,*
>   *once he discovered his timeframe was short.'*

I'm not entirely sure why, but I felt this verse needed to be read in a chiastic form. The structure of it breaks from the norm of conjunctive, verb, subject, repeat. When Hebrew or Aramaic feels cryptic, it is sometimes

---

[72] "For the Son of Man did not come to destroy men's lives but to save them." Though considered a later addition to the text, the early church obviously felt it was necessary to explain Jesus' heart.

because the author is trying to be poetic. And that is sort of what this verse felt like.

Whether that is the case or not doesn't really matter, for the contrast is clear. While Heaven celebrates, the Holy Land braces for impact. Satan is falling from heaven like lightening. The defeated foe now seeks to bring havoc upon those residing within the ancient boundaries of Israel. The lighting strike would be felt by all.

HIS TIME WAS SHORT

Because of what Jesus accomplished at Calvary, Satan was dethroned from lordship over the earth. We know this first and foremost through Jesus: Luke 10:18 and Matthew 28:18. Satan fell, and now all authority in Heaven and on earth has been given to Jesus. Think of the humiliation Satan felt!

> *"Then the devil, taking Him up on a high mountain, showed Him all the kingdoms of the world in a moment of time. And the devil said to Him, 'All this authority I will give You, and their glory; for this has been delivered to me, and I give it to whomever I wish.'"* Luke 4:5–6 (NKJV)

Do you understand that after the Age of Moses ended and the Age of Messiah came fully into effect, this statement of Satan's was no longer true? When he fell, for reasons we don't really know, he was given a small window of time to still manipulate and coerce the kingdom of Israel (Judea, Galilee, and Samaria) to persecute Jesus' followers. He was also granted permission to bring the kingdoms of Rome and Israel together for war – but even then his scope was limited. And since he presided over the Mosaic Age, he was able to continue to litigate against those bound to the Law. Hence, he **was** "the prince of this age" (Jn 12:31, 14:30), the "god (*elohim* in the sense of a lower spiritual being) of this age" (2 Cor 4:4), and "the prince of air" (Eph 2:2 ["air" אאר in Aramaic, not "heaven" שָׁמַיִם, because spiritual beings could be understood as floating above our heads]).

Equally important, this window of time was tied to **the cusp of ages**, the 40-year window from 30 to 70 AD ("this generation will not pass away until") which I have written about at length in the first two books of this series.[73]

---

[73] I can anticipate someone asking, "Leo, if Satan was dethroned, can you please explain all the crazy in the world today?" Yes, we will touch on this when we get to Revelation 20. Spoiler alert (to save you from waiting until then): You and I are living in Revelation 20:7–8 today, right now. This is where our chronology lines up

This reference to the "short timeframe" in verse 12 actually connects us to Daniel 7. The time between the late prophet's vision of the birth of Jesus to the destruction of the Holy Temple was being fulfilled. In chapter 7 of Daniel, there are four rulers of empires that succeed each other: the Babylonian Empire, the Medo-Persian Empire, the Greek Empire, and lastly the Roman Empire. Then all hell breaks loose until the Antient of Days intervenes:

"And behold, with the clouds of heaven
One like a son of man [Jesus] was coming,
And He came up to the Ancient of Days [God]
And was presented before Him.
And to Him was given dominion,
Honor, and a kingdom,
So that all the peoples, nations, and populations of all languages
Might serve Him…

These great beasts, which are four in number, are four kings who will arise from the earth. But the saints of the Highest One will receive the kingdom and take possession of the kingdom forever, for all ages to come…'

I kept looking, and that horn was waging war with the saints and prevailing against them, until the Ancient of Days came and judgment was passed in favor of the saints of the Highest One, and the time arrived when the saints took possession of the kingdom….

And he will speak against the Most High and wear down the saints of the Highest One, and he will intend to make alterations in times and in law [of Moses]; and they will be handed over to him for a time, times, and half a time. But the court will convene for judgment, and his dominion will be taken away, annihilated and destroyed forever. Then the sovereignty, the dominion, and the greatness of all the kingdoms under the whole heaven will be given to the people of the saints of the Highest One."
Daniel 7:13–14, 17–18, 21–22, 25–27 (NASB)

---

with John's Vision. It's the tail end of the Age of Messiah, and Satan has been granted permission to once again deceive the nations for a short period of time.

Many wonderful commentaries have been written about how Daniel 7 predicts the fall of Jerusalem and the Holy Temple in 70 AD. And while the cast of characters here do include 1. The Roman Empire, 2. The Julio-Claudian Dynasty (Nero), 3. The Flavian Dynasty (Vespasian and Titus, who warred against the Jews), and 4. The lovers of Yahweh God, *behind the scenes* we ultimately have two forces at work: The Kingdom of Heaven and the Kingdom of Darkness. Suffice to say, Satan tries to persecute and overcome the saints and is resistant to the shift in epoch seasons that was upon him. Nevertheless, God and His saints prevail.

> א *(13) Now when the Leviathan saw that it had been brought down upon the Land, it persecuted the woman who had given birth to the Male.*

> א *(14) But two wings from the Master Eagle[74] were granted to the woman to fly into the desolate region[75] to her place, to be sustained there for a time, times, and half a time, away from the presence of the face of the Leviathan.*

In verse 14 we see a reference again to Daniel 7, "a time, times and a half a time". By now we should all be very familiar with the 3.5 year period as it pertained to Jerusalem. So instead, I'd like to discuss the reference to the Master Eagle as an image of God.

First, it is a contrast to the Leviathan, as these two creatures are set in juxtaposition (see also Prov. 30:19). Second, a reference to the Exodus motif cannot be missed:

> *"In the third month after the sons of Israel had gone out of the land of*

---

[74] תְּרֵין גַּפִּין דְּנִשְׁרָא רַבָּא – two wings from the master/chief/great eagle. The word "Master" was used to match the title given to the Leviathan in verse 9, as it's the same word. Also, the "eagle" has a "determined" state, like the Hebrew definite article. Basically this means "THE Great Eagle" and not "a great eagle". Yahweh is likened to an eagle (נֶשֶׁר) in the Old Testament (Ex 19:4), and that Exodus motif is referenced here. The eagle has to be Yahweh, for who else can deliver His people? Hence, the juxtaposition between the Leviathan (Satan) and the Great Eagle (God) is maintained.

[75] The Arabah (עֲרָבָה), where Jesus was tempted (Luke 4:1). It spanned east of Jerusalem, across to the Jordan Valley Rift, down to the Dead Sea, and also across to the east Jordan region.

Egypt, on that very day they came into the wilderness of Sinai… And Moses went up to God, and the Lord called to him from the mountain, saying, 'This is what you shall say to the house of Jacob and tell the sons of Israel: "You yourselves have seen what I did to the Egyptians, and how I carried you on eagles' wings, and brought you to Myself. Now then, if you will indeed obey My voice and keep My covenant, then you shall be My own possession among all the peoples, for all the earth is Mine; and you shall be to Me a kingdom of priests and a holy nation."'
Exodus 19:1–6 (NASB)

Therefore in Revelation 12, the woman is delivered and carried away by Yahweh God on His wings (also Is 40:31) and is brought to the wilderness. There she becomes a kingdom of priests and a holy nation.

> א *(15) Then the Leviathan hurled from its mouth water like a river behind the woman, that she might be swept away by the water.*

> א *(16) But the Land helped the woman, and the Land opened its mouth and swallowed that river which the Leviathan hurled from its mouth.*

More contrasts. I love it! Satan's threat was stayed. Let's unpack the symbolism here so we know what John was talking about. Torrential waters can be considered a sign of adversity (Jonah 2:3, Matthew 7:25). The New Testament reveals in various places that Satan works in and through people. So it is safe to say the flood that proceeds from the Dragon is a wave of persecution, which also fits the rest of Revelation 12.

There is also a continuation of the Exodus motif – specifically the Rebellion of Korah.[76] In the wilderness, the land opened up and swallowed those who had rebelled against Moses. So in keeping with that theme, we see a symbol of Yahweh protecting those who love him from the ones who had hardened their hearts.[77]

---

[76] See Num 16:31–34; Ps 95:8; Heb 3:8, Jude 1:11.
[77] One incredible theological aspect of the Korah Rebellion is that Yahweh spares the sons of Korah from descending into Sheol that day (Num 26:10–11). Korah's descendants become a branch of the temple worshippers (2 Chr 20:19), and 11 Psalms are attributed to them (42, 44, 45, 46, 47, 48, 49, 84, 85, 87, and 88).

> א *(17) So the Leviathan was enraged[78] against the woman, and went away to wage war with the all the rest[79] of her seed – those who observe the commandments[80] of God – for them also exists the testimony of Yeshua."*

The closing verse of Revelation 12 focuses on the broader Jewish inhabitants of the Holy Land. "All the rest of her seed", in conjunction with "those who observe the commandments of God", clearly reference those who were bound under the Law of Moses. And what is it specifically The Leviathan sets out to do? Wage war. In the very next verse, 13:1, the instrument of war, the Roman Empire, will rise up out of the Mediterranean Sea.

This is very different than Christian persecution. Persecution is a promise made by Jesus. For example, we know that after the Great Fire in Rome (64 AD), Nero used Christians as his scapegoat for that great calamity for which many held him responsible. His persecution of Believers was horrific. We also know many of the Apostles were martyred by the time Jerusalem was destroyed. And in the decades and centuries that followed, this theme was constant.

The last remark in verse 17 is most peculiar. In essence, it says that the testimony of Jesus *is* or *exists* for them – those still trying to observe the 613 commandments. The proclamation of "not guilty" is available to those still bound under the Law should they *choose* to accept it. That is the Letter of Hebrews in a nutshell. The tension is clear: stay under the curse of the Law and be legally subject to the wrath of Satan, or come out from the bondage of the Law through the sacrifice of the Lamb of God and have Yeshua testify on your behalf instead.

Thus, the war Satan wages in Revelation 12:17 is not just a wave of Christian persecution, it is a full scale military campaign against the inhabitants of the Holy Land as well. We are talking about 1.1 million slaughtered and almost 100,000 sold into the slave trade, according to Josephus. It was the first Jewish holocaust. This is a big deal, to say the least.

---

[78] In verse 12 Satan has great anger (חֶמְתָא), but now his temper is even hotter, boiled into full blown rage (רְגַז).

[79] שַׁרְכָּא "the others", "the remainder", "all the rest." The implication here is not a select few, as in a remnant, but rather everyone else.

[80] This word is only used twice in the Gospels: Luke 1:6 and John 15:10. In Luke, it refers to the Law of Moses, and in John it refers to the Law of Jesus.

The unfolding of Satan's wrath through the agency of two man-made kingdoms will be the focus of the next chapter.

3 THE EMPIRE STRIKES BACK: CH. 13 PART 1

"Luke, you can destroy the Emperor. He has foreseen this. It is your destiny. Join me, and together we can rule the galaxy as father and son."

— Darth Vader, *Star Wars Episode V: The Empire Strikes Back* (George Lucas, 1980, Lucasfilm Ltd.)

The father-son parody in Revelation 13 cannot be missed. Historically, Vespasian and his son Titus, after their successful campaign against the Holy Land, landed themselves the ultimate earthly throne: Emperor of the Roman Empire. Symbolically, as we will see, Satan plays off the father-son imagery of Yahweh and Yeshua in a twisted depiction of Zeus and Dionysius. Everyone, it seems, wanted to rule the galaxy – or at least the Known World.

John has been on a wild ride so far. While on Patmos, he is taken up into highest Heaven (ch. 4), then placed in Jerusalem to stand upon the Temple Mount (ch. 11). His attention is then drawn upward to the skies as he sees the unfolding of a new drama through the constellations (ch. 12). The Apostle looks back down and suddenly finds himself standing on the sandy Judean beaches off the coast of the Mediterranean Sea.

Given how beautiful the beaches of modern-day Israel are today, I can only imagine how much more stunning they would have been in John's day! This new scene begins with John looking to his left where he notices something along the blue horizon to the east: a scary-looking seven-headed leopard ascending up over the Sea. Then to his right he sees another animal, a lamb (perhaps a Jacob, Awassi, or Arabi breed) with horns, rising up over the Holy Land. Nothing appears intimidating about this animal in comparison to the leopard; it probably seemed harmless at first. Yet John will soon understand that this is a wolf in sheep's clothing.

The interpretation of Daniel's visions are yet again a critical interpretive key and the framework by which we must understand John's vision here in chapter 13. In Daniel, we learn that wild animals, or "beasts", represent kingdoms, empires, and nations. There is then the more practical exercise of deciphering which beast represents which empire, one of which is as relevant to Daniel as it is to Revelation. Daniel records his visions of the beasts in chapters 7 and 8, and we get even more information about these empires in chapters 2 and 10-12. Of the fourth empire, Rome, Daniel says the following:

> *"And in the days of those kings the God of heaven will set up a kingdom which will never be destroyed, and that kingdom will not be left for another people; it will crush and put an end to all these kingdoms, but it will itself endure forever." Daniel 2:44 (NASB)*

Any sort of future-dating for Daniel's visions, especially chapters 2, 7, and 8, completely misses the occasion and audience which the prophet's book served. Jewish sages and later commentaries especially recognized the importance of Daniel's visions as they related to their history.

> The "long year" looked like the last year, the last of all years, even to the Roman historian Tacitus. Consider the way the world looked then to a Jew in the Diaspora. From the island of Patmos in 69 CE, a Jew named John looked to the east and saw the holy city of Jerusalem besieged by the armies of Rome but standing valiantly, awaiting its deliverance. Beyond Jerusalem, the ghost of Nero or a Nero who never really died -threatened to lead the armies of Parthia against his former dominions.
>
> Looking to the west, John saw the convulsions of the great beast that was Rome: war raged on Italian soil, each emperor slew his predecessor, each so-called ruler of the world was

unable to rule even his own city. It appeared that the Empire was drunk on its own corruption, lurching toward its dissolution. As he looked around the province of Asia, John saw the army of the latest pretender leaving the siege of the holy city of Jerusalem and marching on to assault the great city of Rome. Myriads of soldiers under the command of Gaius traversed the province of Asia on their way to install the fourth emperor of the year.

Closer still to home, John saw his own Jewish community living dangerously among the nations, derided and scapegoated by their neighbour over the war in Judea, tempted to abandon the commandments of God for the ways of the nations.[81]

With these things in mind, let's dive into chapter 13!

> א *(12:17a) So the Leviathan was enraged against the woman, and went away to wage war with the all the rest of her seed..."*
>
> א *(13:1) Then I was standing upon the sand of the Sea,[82] and I saw a savage animal[83] ascending from the Sea, which had ten horns and seven heads, and upon its horns, ten diadems, and upon its heads The Name, which was blasphemy.[84]*

---

[81] Marshall, John W., Parables of War: Reading of John's Jewish Apocalypse (Waterloo: Wilfrid Laurier University Press, 2001), p 1.
[82] יַמָּא here referring to a large body of water. In this case, the Mediterranean.
[83] חַיְוְתָא literally means "wild, carnivorous animal." I like Dr. John W. Etheridge's translation: "beast of prey".
[84] Lit. "the name of the blasphemy". But it could be "The Name", in conjunction with a clue in Rev. 13:6 ("to blaspheme by The Name"). The Aramaic, in contradistinction to the Greek text, "name" is singular and in the *determined* state (like having a Hebrew definite article): שְׁמָא "the name". So I will submit my hypothesis that the beast had the divine name of God יהוה YHWH (Yahweh) written on it in mockery. To misrepresent the divine name was highly blasphemous in Jewish culture and religious life (Lev 24:11; Ex 20:7; Dt 5:11, 28:58), and in reverence, when referring to Yahweh, Jews to this day say "HaShem" (which means "The Name") instead. This kingdom of the Sea is portrayed as a doppelganger to the Kingdom of God. So just as those in the kingdom of God are marked with His Name on their foreheads (Rev. 7.3; 9.4), Satan's puppet kingdom

> א (13:2) *And the savage animal that I saw resembled a leopard, and its feet as those of a bear*[85] *and its mouth as those of lions.*[86] *And to it the Leviathan gave its military might, its throne, and great authority.*

It can sometimes be disappointing to learn that the "beast of the sea" is not Godzilla. I mean, sure, if you're in the bush and come across a leopard (or in my personal experience in Alberta, a cougar/mountain lion), you'll feel a chill down your spine and understand this thing could take your life. But in the Evangelical West, the hype around this creature has been so built up that the truth can feel deflating! Nevertheless, truth is what we are all here for, and the *imagery* surrounding the leopard in this context is much deeper and more fascinating than some sort of pre-historic creature anyway!

I purposefully chose to begin the translation with chapter 12 verse 17a to remind us that Satan went off to *wage war* against the seed of Daughter Israel. Now we see how that plays out in Revelation 13. But what is this leopard? The first clue to the identity of this wild animal is to identify where it came from. From John's vantage point, the leopard arises from the Mediterranean Sea, west of where he is standing. And because we know from the prophet Daniel that beasts represent empires and kingdoms, Rome easily fits (and will continue to be substantiated in the coming verses). Because Rome was the most powerful empire of its day, it makes sense that Satan would bestow upon it "military might, its throne, and great authority".

I find it fascinating that the Greek text refers to "the name<u>s</u> of blasphemy", whereas the Aramaic reads "the name of blasphemy". Moreover, the Aramaic can be translated as either "the name of blasphemy",

---

has God's name written in vain upon it, which would have been the greatest blasphemy in Judaism.

[85] Can also be "wolf". Syr *debbā*; hence spelling confusion with *dēḇā*, "wolf." See *The Comprehensive Aramaic Lexicon*, dukhrana.com.

[86] "Leopard… bear… lions." This description is first and foremost an allusion to Jeremiah 5:6, who like Ezekiel, prophesied concerning the destruction of Jerusalem and her Temple. Secondly, Revelation 13 draws heavily from Daniel 7 and 8 where the prophet also saw wild animals (empires) emerging from the Mediterranean ("great sea", Dan 7:2). These empires were Babylon, Achaemenid (Medo–Persian), Greece, and Rome, with each taking a turn at ruling vast amounts of the Known World. Lastly, there is some semblance (perhaps intentional) to the Capitoline Wolf (*Lupa Capitolina*), the she-wolf who rescued Romulus and Remus, the founders of Rome.

or "The Name, which is blasphemy." Because of the definite article, I'm willing to risk going with the second translation option.

Moving on to the next part of verse one, what's the deal with all the heads?

First, we need to keep in mind that this is a prophetic experience. Much like dreams, the logic side of your brain isn't dominating the scene. Dreams just seem to flow, and somehow it works for things like an animal to have a bunch of heads on it. But thankfully, Scripture itself helps us a great deal:

> *"(7) And the angel said to me, 'Why do you marvel? I will tell you the mystery of the wife and of the savage animal that bears her, which has seven heads and ten horns.'*
> *(8) 'The savage animal which you saw – which was, and is not – prepares to come up from the Sea and it moves forth for destruction. But they that inhabit the Land will marvel – whose names are not written in The Book of The Living from the foundations of the Age[87] – when they see the savage animal which was, and is not, and is approaching.'*
> *(9) 'Here is the mind which has wisdom: seven heads, they are seven mountains where the wife sits upon them. (10) And these are the seven kings; five have fallen, and one that exists. The other has not yet come, but after a little while he will come, and it will be granted to him to remain.*
> *(11) But the Leviathan and the savage animal that exists and is not: there's an eighth, which is from the seventh, and it moves forth for destruction.*
> *(12) 'And ten horns which you saw, they are the ten kings who until now were not of the kingdom. However, they took on authority like the kings for one moment to be capturing alongside the savage animal.' (13) These ones have a single desire: to offer their own military might and power to the savage animal.'*
>
> *Revelation 17:7–13*
> *(my translation from the Aramaic, see Revelation 17 for footnotes)*

That was so helpful! An angel again gives John an interpretation. I will

---

[87] For other Scriptures that speak of God's redemptive foresight, see 1 Pet 1:18-21, 2 Tim 1:9, Rom 8:29, 1 Cor 2:7, Eph 1:4-7; 2:10.

cover Revelation 17 in detail when we get there, but in short, the leopard who was, was not, and then came represents how Rome, at the height of its power, was plunged into chaos when Nero committed suicide. The Known World held its breath as the Year of Four Emperors ensued.[88] Incredibly, the empire rebounded from the brink of collapse when Vespasian (who ironically was dispatched by Nero to destroy the Holy Land) finally assumed the throne as Caesar and ruler of the Known World. **Vespasian was the seventh head.**

Suetonius, a well know early Roman historian, wrote of Nero's dispatching of Vespasian into the Holy Land. Little did Nero know that he would be sending Vespasian into a future destiny of power and the very throne of the Empire. And like all ancient historians, omens and oracles were very much a part of how human history unfolded.

> "On the tour through Greece, among the companions of Nero, [Vespasian] bitterly offended the emperor by either going out often while Nero was singing, or falling asleep, if he remained. Being in consequence banished, not only from intimacy with the emperor but even with his public receptions, he withdrew to a little out-of-the-way town, until a province and an army were offered him while he was in hiding and in fear of his life.
>
> There had spread over all the Orient an old and established belief, that it was fated at that time for men coming from Judaea to rule the world. This prediction, referring to the emperor of Rome, as afterwards appeared from the event, the people of Judaea took to themselves; accordingly they revolted and after killing their governor, they routed the consular ruler of Syria as well, when he came to the rescue, and took one of his eagles. Since to put down this rebellion required a considerable army with a leader of no little enterprise, yet one to whom so great power could be entrusted without risk, Vespasian was chosen for the task, both as a man of tried energy and as one in no wise to be feared because of the obscurity of his family and name.

---

[88] This refers to the Empire's first civil war, a time spanning from Nero's death to Vespasian's succession, 68 to 69 AD. Three men vied for the throne: Galba, Otho, and Vitellius. Each one reigned but a few months before either being killed, or in Otho's case, committing suicide. Vespasian was proclaimed Caesar by his faithful legions, and he took this to heart. Thus, he left the Holy Land, stormed the capital, killed Vitellius, and seized the throne. Stability then returned to the Roman Empire.

Therefore there were added to the forces in Judaea two legions with eight divisions of cavalry and ten cohorts…

When [Vespasian] consulted the oracle of the God of Carmel in Judaea, the lots were highly encouraging, promising that whatever he planned or wished however great it might be, would come to pass; and one of his high-born prisoners, Josephus by name, as he was being put in chains, declared most confidently that he would soon be released by the same man, who would then, however, be emperor. Omens were also reported from Rome: Nero in his latter days was admonished in a dream to take the sacred chariot of Jupiter Optimus Maximus from its shrine to the house of Vespasian and from there to the Circus. Not long after this, too, when Galba was on his way to the elections which gave him his second consul-ship, a statue of the Deified Julius of its own accord turned towards the East; and on the field of Betriacum, before the battle began, two eagles fought in the sight of all, and when one was vanquished, a third came from the direction of the rising sun and drove off the victor."[89]

Now the seven hills of Rome (Palatine, Capitoline, Quirinal, Viminal, Esquiline, Caelian, and Aventine) are the seven heads. There are also seven kings: Julius Caesar, Augustus, Tiberius, Caligula, Claudius, Nero, and Vespasian. Five had fallen by the time John was experiencing this vision (mid-late 60s AD), meaning Julius Caesar, Augustus, Tiberius, Caligula, and Claudius were already dead. "The one [that] was" is Nero.

The other who would come in a little while is Vespasian, for he began the work of invading the Holy Land. Suddenly, there is mention of an eighth king in 17:11, even though there were only seven heads initially. The eighth king, an eighth head, is "from the seventh". This of course speaks of Titus, offspring of Vespasian (the seventh), who fought alongside his father in the Jewish-Roman war. In the middle of that campaign, they halted their forces so that Vespasian could assume the throne in Rome.

---

[89] Suetonius, *The Life of Vespasian*, 4–5, https://penelope.uchicago.edu/Thayer/E/Roman/Texts/Suetonius/12Caesars/Vespasian*.html

Titus oversaw four legions and auxiliary troops and completed the task of breaching Jerusalem's three massive walls. The men under his watch also destroyed the Holy Temple. The text does not say the eighth is going to be destroyed, but rather, "there's an eighth, which is from the seventh, and it moves forth for destruction." Revelation 17:10–11 tells us that while Vespasian assumes the throne in Rome, Titus will depart for Jerusalem to have it destroyed.

The ten horns and ten rulers will be discussed when we cover Revelation 17.

WHY A LEOPARD?

An important question. Of all the animals Yeshua could have used in John's vision, why this one? What we need to understand is *what* the leopard symbolized in first-century Jewish context.

The incredible early Church Father Ignaitus of Antioch, a direct disciple of the Apostle John, wrote letters to several churches during his long journey to Rome. He was under arrest and was going to be executed for his faith. Speaking of his Roman guards, these soldiers were said to be like leopards:

> "All the way from Syria to Rome I am fighting wild beasts, on land and sea, by day and night, chained as I am to ten leopards, that is, a detachment of soldiers, who prove themselves the more malevolent for kindnesses shown them."[90]

We will also see that the second animal, the lamb, was likened to Jesus as the sacrificial lamb. And we read that this beast of the Sea has written upon it the Divine Name of Yahweh (HaShem). Satan was using parody, mockery, and blasphemy against Yeshua, as he had done while our Messiah walked the earth.

> *"Then the soldiers of the governor took Jesus into the governor's headquarters, and they gathered the whole battalion before him. And they stripped him and put a scarlet robe on him, and twisting together a crown of thorns, they put it on his head and put a reed in his right hand. And*

---

[90] Ignatius of Antioch (d. 108 AD), Letter to the Romans, 5.

kneeling before him, they mocked him, saying, 'Hail, King of the Jews!' And they spit on him and took the reed and struck him on the head. And when they had mocked him, they stripped him of the robe and put his own clothes on him and led him away to crucify him." Matthew 27:27–31 (ESV)

The leopard itself was a targeted symbol of blasphemy towards the Messiah, as I will soon explain. First, we must note that Dionysus (aka Bacchus) was a key messianic figure in Greco-Roman lore. The son of the great god Zeus, Dionysus was conceived by a human mother, Semele. See the contrast to Yahweh God and Mary, mother of Jesus? But how does the leopard tie into this? Dionysus was often depicted riding a leopard.[91] He and the animal were synonymous. The son of Zeus was also said to have died and been resurrected back to life. Lastly, and most culturally relevant to John's audience, Jews had faced much slander and accusation relating to Dionysus from non-Jews in the two most prosperous and influential cities in the Known World: Rome and Alexandria. Specifically, they were accused of participating in the Cult of Dionysus because their religious rituals were misunderstood.[92]

> א *(3) Now one of its heads seemed crushed to death, but its death blow was healed! And all those of The Land were astonished in wake of the savage animal.*

Technically speaking, five of the heads should have been limp and dead given that the first five emperors of Rome had deceased a long time prior. But such is the nature of prophetic visions! Regardless, John's attention is drawn to the sixth head, Nero. The death blow is literal in the case of Nero because he committed suicide in 68 AD. But figuratively, to the Roman Empire it was the leopard itself. So the deathblow healing does not mean Nero came back to life.[93] Rather, it was that the Empire came out of near

---

[91] One of the most famous pieces of surviving artwork capturing this theme is the 4th century BC floor mosaic in the House of Dionysos at Pella, Greece.
[92] Plutarch, *Morals, Quaestiones Convivales* 4:671D–672B. Tacitus, *Histories*, 5:5
[93] This may also be a nod to the Nero Redivivus legend. Surviving accounts of the belief that Nero would return from the dead can be found in The Sibylline Oracles (4, 155-159.178-180; 5.137-141; 5.361-396), Dio Chrysostom (Discourse 21, On Beauty), and Augustine of Hippo (City of God 20.19.3). Within a 20-year period following his death, three imposters had emerged, some with their own respective armies, claiming to be Nero (known as Pseudo-Neros).

collapse when the seventh head, Vespasian, rose to power.

From a Jewish perspective, consider the sense of relief and elation when they first heard that Nero had died. He authored their destruction by dispatching Vespasian and Titus to raze the Holy Land. And hearing of his death, Vespasian and Titus paused their assaults, and the 60,000 troops were now stationary. Surely this was the end of the opresive Roman regime. Judaea would now regain it's freedom, and the Roman boot would lift off of their Land. But it was not so. The Empire did not collapse.

Rather, Vespasian took the throne, and the Roman war machine fired up again. Titus came with full force against Jerusalem. Rome would remain. Indeed, the revival of the leopard astonished those in the Holy Land.

> א *(4) And they paid obeisance[94] to the Leviathan—who gave authority to the savage animal—and they were bowed in submission to the savage animal, saying, 'What can compare to this savage animal, and who is able to wage war with it?'*

I don't believe that those in the Holy Land worshiped the Leviathan. Impossible. The text does not outright say as much. Nor were they even aware of the Leviathan's schemes. So it is much more fitting that the focus remain on the Roman Empire and the Holy Land's relationship with it. The Holy Land was under Roman subjection and under Hellenistic influence. Hence, "What can compare to this savage animal, and who is able to wage war with it?" A fitting question.

Rome seemed invincible at this point. Mind you, this sentiment was not universally shared, or else there would not have been a revolt against Rome. But those who had the most to lose – the aristocratic elites and those in positions of religious influence – definitely felt incredibly overpowered.

> א *(5) And its mouth was permitted to be saying great things and blasphemy. And there was granted to it authority to make war for forty two months.*

---

[94] Or "paid homage". סגד means "to bow down in respect" or "to cause to be venerated". The *implication* can be worship, but this is based on context (see same word in Dan 2:46 or Gen 47:31). Given the context of kingdoms and empires, "obeisance" or "homage" is more fitting than "worship".

> ℵ *(6) And it opened its mouth to blaspheme before God: to blaspheme by His Name and by the dwelling place of those who dwell in Heaven.*[95]

> ℵ *(7) And it was granted to it to be waging war with the saints and to conquer them. And it was granted to it authority over all tribes, nations, tongues, and Gentiles.*

The time period of 42 months (3.5 years) anchors us again within the timeframe of the Jewish-Roman War. Flowing from Revelation 12, the Leviathan (Satan) through the leopard (Rome) attempts to wage war upon both those bound under the Law of Moses and those in covenant with Yeshua the Messiah. This war, which was not just through sword but also persecution, will be felt throughout the Empire: "over all tribes, nations, tongues, and Gentiles" (13:7).

> ℵ *(8) And all the inhabitants of The Land will bow in submission to it – those who are not written in The Book of Living*[96] *of the Lamb slain before the foundations of the Age.*[97]

This was a key interpretative element for the Jews living within (and pilgrimaging to) the ancient boundaries of Israel and Judah. Those who did not heed the warnings of Yeshua the Messiah and his Apostles – who pleaded with them to escape the pending calamities of the curses of the Law of Moses – did not have their names written in The Book of The Living of the Lamb. As it concerns us here, did you notice how the text said Jesus was slain before the foundations of the "Age"? Yes, we could likely translate "Age" here as "world", but that isn't necessary. The plural "foundations" suggests we are going back to the genesis of the age of mankind, to before creation itself. **We are talking about the Age of Mankind.**

For Jesus to have been slain before creation ever took place means Father, Son, and Spirit looked ahead, saw the long path of what mankind would do, and counted the cost. **They knew full well a great plan of salvation and**

---

[95] Perhaps in defiance of the words of Jesus in Matthew 5:34–36.
[96] "Life" is conjugated as determined plural emphatic noun, hence, "The Living".
[97] For other Scriptures that speak of God's redemptive foresight, see 1 Pet 1:18-21, 2 Tim 1:9, Rom 8:29, 1 Cor 2:7, Eph 1:4-7; 2:10.

reconciliation involving the enfleshment of Yeshua would be required if they created mankind. Yet knowing all this, they decided it was worth it. That's when the Lamb was slain – outside of time and before creation began – a conscious decision for Yeshua to become like us so that we might become like him. It was at that point Yahweh said, "Let there be light," and "Let us make man in our image and likeness."

Selah.

THE BOOK OF THE LIVING

We have to quickly touch on this subject, though it will be covered again when we get to Revelation chapter 20. First, the "Book" is a reference to living a life unto Yahweh God, here in this lifetime. It originally had nothing to do with a final judgment or an afterlife.

> *"See, I set before you today **life** and prosperity, **death** and destruction… keep his commands, decrees and laws; then you will live and increase… But if your heart turns away and you are not obedient… you will certainly be destroyed. You will not live long in the land…*
> *This day I call the heavens and the earth as witnesses against you that **I have set before you life and death**, blessings and curses. Now **choose life**, so that you and your children **may live** and that you may love the Lord your God, listen to his voice, and hold fast to him. **For the Lord is your life**, and he will give you **many years in the land he swore** to give to your fathers, Abraham, Isaac and Jacob." Deuteronomy 30:15–20 (NIV, emphasis mine)*

In light of this God-life in the here and now, to be "blotted out" implies dying prematurely and outside of the covenant promises. We are first introduced to this notion in Exodus 32:

> *"But now, if you will forgive their sin—but if not, please blot me out of your book that you have written." But the LORD said to Moses, "Whoever has sinned against me, I will blot out of my book." Exodus 32:32–33 (ESV)*

This chapter is where the exiled Hebrews make the golden calf and worship it. Interestingly, their priest, Aaron, is their overseer while Moses is in the mountains with Yahweh. In anger, Moses smashes the tablets of the covenant and has those who do not want to be in covenant with Yahweh slaughtered (death). Ouch. Therefore, to be inscribed in the "Book" means receiving a new identity (specifically a covenant identity) that was to be contrasted against the identity of a slave. Conversely, "blotting out" means "I don't want to be in covenant with Yahweh."

> *"Beware lest there be among you a man or woman or clan or tribe whose heart is turning away today from the LORD our God to go and serve the gods of those nations…*
> *the LORD will blot out his name from under heaven. And the LORD will single him out from all the tribes of Israel for calamity, in accordance with all the curses of the covenant written in this Book of the Law…*
> *[And when] all the nations will say, 'Why has the LORD done thus to this land? What caused the heat of this great anger?' Then people will say, 'It is because they abandoned the covenant of the LORD."*
> *Deuteronomy 29:18, 20–21, 24–25 (ESV)*

Every single Hebrew slave that Moses led out of Egypt was automatically written into God's book. Yahweh was inviting them to experience a unique and blessed life in a new land. This life had everything they needed, including an opportunity to live out a life where the focal point was to get to know God, even if only through a veil. The life and the covenant which legally bound one to that life (think matrimony) was synonymous; to be in this God-life was to be in covenant, and to be in covenant was to be in God-life.

Within a Jewish context, this idea of being written into or being blotted out of a book is first and foremost an image of either being in or out of covenant with Yahweh God. Therefore, a *qualifying* nuance is inserted in Revelation 13:8: "those who are not written in The Book of The Living of the Lamb." Again, covenant language. What does this mean? It means (loosely speaking) Yahweh was transposing names from the book of the covenant of Moses to the book of the covenant of Jesus. This is why it is The Book of The Living of *the Lamb* - because he was the sacrifice of this covenant.

Then later in his life, when speaking of the future (70 AD), Moses prophesies:

> *"All these curses shall come upon you and pursue you and overtake you till you are destroyed, because you did not obey the voice of the LORD your God, to keep his commandments and his statutes that he commanded you. They shall be a sign and a wonder against you and your offspring forever." Deuteronomy 28:45–46 (ESV)*

Fast forward to the end of the Mosaic Age, to the First Century AD when the Romans were destroying the Holy Land and the Temple: those who kept their names in the book of Moses suffered under the consequences of that covenant.

> א *(9) Whosoever are those who have ears, let them be hearing:*
>
> א *(10) Whosoever forces one in to captivity,*
> *in to captivity he will go.*
> *And one who slays by the sword,*
> *by the sword will he be slain.*
> *Here is faith and the endurance of the saints.*

"Whosoever are those who have ears" is Jesus-talk. Matthew 11:15; 13:9, 43, Mark 4:9, 23; Luke 8:8, and 14:35 are all instances where Jesus says this exact phrase. In all those instances, though His words have practical application that transcends time and season, they *were first* spoken in an immediate historical context. They are words of warning to a Jewish audience still bound under the Law of Sin and Death.

The immediacy of the warning in Revelation becomes more specific in verse 10. What is the message? It is an echo of Jesus' words in the Beatitudes:

> *"You have heard that it was said, 'Eye for eye, and tooth for tooth.' But I say to you, do not show opposition against an evil person; but whoever slaps you on your right cheek, turn the other toward him also...*
>
> *You have heard that it was said, 'You shall love your neighbor and hate your enemy.' But I say to you, love your enemies and pray for those who persecute you, so that you may prove yourselves to be sons of your Father who is in heaven..." Matthew 5:38–39, 43–45 (NASB)*

And who can forget the wisdom of Yeshua on the night he was handed over to the religious leaders?

> *"Then Jesus said to him, 'Put your sword back into its place; for all those who take up the sword will perish by the sword.'" Matthew 26:52*

The message was clear: for those who chose to stay under the curse of the Law, things would be easier for them if they did not put up a fight. Indeed, even Vespasian and Titus (and Josephus) tried at various times to negotiate a peaceful surrender with the Jewish rebels, but to no avail.

And for those who abided in Yeshua, perseverance and endurance would also be required. Indeed, the call for endurance in verse 10 is a direct reference to Matthew 24 and Luke 21:

> *"Then they will hand you over to tribulation and kill you, and you will be hated by all nations because of My name… But the one who endures to the end is the one who will be saved [Aramaic = "will live"]. This gospel of the kingdom shall be preached in the whole world [Aramaic = "through the entirety of this age"] as a testimony to all the nations, and then the end will come.*
> *Therefore when you see the abomination of desolation which was spoken of through Daniel the prophet, standing in the holy place—let the reader understand—then those who are in Judea must flee to the mountains." Matthew 24:9, 13–16 (NASB)*

> *"But before all these things, they will lay their hands on you and persecute you, turning you over to the synagogues and prisons… and they will put some of you to death… By your endurance you will gain your lives.*

> *"But when you see Jerusalem surrounded by armies, then recognize that her desolation is near. Then those who are in Judea must flee to the mountains, and those who are inside the city must leave, and those who are in the country must not enter the city; because these are days of punishment, so that all things which have been written will be fulfilled… for there will be great distress upon the land, and wrath to this people; and they will fall by the edge of the sword, and will be led captive into all the nations; and Jerusalem will be trampled underfoot by the Gentiles until the times of the Gentiles are fulfilled." Luke 21:12, 16, 19–24 (NASB)*

Isn't this amazing? Look how crystal clear the Scriptures are when they align together. There is so much packed into Revelation 13:10!

א *(11) Then I saw another savage animal, this one ascending from the Land, and it had two horns, and a resemblance of the Lamb;*[98] *but it was speaking according to the Leviathan.*

THE LAMB = THE HOLY LAND

Recall Revelation 13:8 and the verbiage of "the Lamb slain". This refers to Jesus and sets us up for the phrase "resemblance of *the* Lamb" in 13:11. John is communicating that this creature looked similar to the Lamb he first saw in 5:6. Immediately we know we are dealing with Temple and sacrificial imagery. But the horns and defiled speech of this lamb reveal that this is not Jesus, the true sacrificial Lamb of God.

If the lamb of Revelation 13:11 is instead depicting a ram or goat, then I could also allude to several Old Testament images. For instance, there is the provision of a ram for Abraham in Genesis 22:13, the sacrificial ceremony of rams in Exodus 29, and it may even allude to the peculiar case of Azazel (scape-goat) in Leviticus 16. In any case, what we have here is an expanded vision unfolding before John. To his right-hand-side, while standing upon the shores of the Holy Land, a lamb (or ram) is now seen ascending upon their terra.

We have discussed the significance of the epoch seasons many times in this series. And most recently, in chapter 12, we explored how even the *constellations* reveal the transition of ages. To build on this further, some scholars have expounded on the notion and believe that constellations represent not just transition, but ages or epoch seasons in and of themselves. For example, it is believed that Aries (a ram or "horned lamb") represents the Age of Moses, and that Pisces, which followed after Aries, represents the Age of Messiah. **So it is fitting to have a ram (Aries, same word in Rev 13:11) represent the Holy Land and specifically the Age of Moses!** This is the first of many clues as to the identity of the second animal, the lamb (or ram).

How does the lamb speak like the Leviathan? Revelation 12 informs us

---

[98] Or "Aries". Aries and lamb are the same word (אמרא), sort of like Scorpio and scorpion. The allusion to Daniel continues: Daniel 7 contains a series of animals you would see in a safari, and Daniel 8 contains a ram or goat. Alternatively, because of the definite article, Aries can be translated "the lamb". Because of the proximity to 13:8 where the Lamb is mentioned, a clear contrast to Jesus as the Lamb is being made.

that "the Prosecutor of our brethren is brought down, who was prosecuting them night and day before our God." Satan brought forth slander and legal accusation against the covenant people of Yahweh. Likewise here, the lamb heaped up legal accusations and laid heavy burdens upon the people bound under the Law of Moses. This reality was foreshadowed by Jesus Himself:

> *"The scribes and the Pharisees have seated themselves in the chair of Moses... And they tie up heavy burdens and lay them on people's shoulders, but they themselves are unwilling to move them with so much as their finger... You blind guides, who strain out a gnat and swallow a camel!" Matthew 23:2, 4, 24 (NASB)*

> *"You [scribes and Pharisees] are of your father the devil, and you want to do the desires of your father. He was a murderer from the beginning, and does not stand in the truth because there is no truth in him. Whenever he tells a lie, he speaks from his own nature, because he is a liar and the father of lies." John 8:44 (NASB)*

The Lamb, or Horned Ram, represents the leadership of Jerusalem that was made up of corrupted religious and political officials in Jerusalem, much like the first beast represented Nero and the power of the Roman Empire.

"But the Pharisees and the experts in the law rejected God's purpose for themselves..." Luke 7:30 (NASB)

> א (12) *And all the authority of the first savage animal will it exercise on behalf of it, and it will force the Land and those who dwell within it to bow in submission to the first savage animal—that one which had its death-blow healed.*

In simple terms: the lamb/ram (Judea) has the authority of the leopard (Rome) and will force the inhabitants of the Holy Land to submit to Rome. On the identity of this lamb, Russell shares the following observations:

> "If our conclusions respecting the identity of the first beast are correct, it ought not to be difficult to discover who is intended

by the second beast. It will be observed that in many respects there is a strong resemblance between them: they are of the same nature, though one is supreme and the other subordinate; but there are also points of difference. It will be proper, however, in this case also, to bring into one view the various particular characteristics which assist to identify the individual intended:

1. The second beast rises up from the land.
2. He has only two horns, and they are like a lamb's.
3. He speaks like a dragon.
4. He is clothed with the delegated authority of the first beast.
5. He compels men to pay homage, or worship, to the beast.
6. He pretends to exercise miraculous powers.
7. He rules with tyrannical force and cruelty.
8. He excludes from civil rights all who refuse abject submission to the beast.

Looking at these characteristics it becomes at once perfectly clear that we must seek the antitype to this symbolic figure in a man of kindred character with the monster Nero himself. He is evidently the alter ego of the emperor, though his proportions are drawn on a smaller scale.

1. His rising out of the land, while the first beast rises out of the sea, denotes that the second beast is a domestic or home authority, ruling in Judea; while the other is a foreign power.
2. His having two horns like a lamb, while the first beast has ten, denotes that his sphere of government is small,

and his power limited, compared with the other.

3. That he speaks as a dragon, or serpent, denotes his crafty and deceitful character.

4. His being clothed with the authority of the first beast indicates that he is the official representative and delegate of Nero in Judea."[99]

In the same way the horns of the first animal, the leopard, represent people in positions of authority and influence, so must it be so for the second animal. And as Russell noted above, the two horns represent a much smaller sphere of government in comparison to the leopard's eight.

THE TWO HORNS OF THE LAMB

Much effort has been given by scholars over the years in trying to identify who the horns of the land animal represented. My caution is that anyone wishing to embrace this undertaking should first spend a considerable amount of time familiarizing themselves with the political environment of first century Judaea, especially at the time of the Jewish-Roman War.

> "[John's] interest here lies in *character determination through summation* rather *than chronology development through sequencing.* Therefore John brings the lesser beast on stage after presenting the first beast's war with the saints (Rev 13:5, 7, the Neronic persecution in A.D. 64–68) and Rome's revival under Vespasian (Rev 13:3, A.D. 69) without incongruity. Regarding the statement that 'he exercises all the authority of the first beast,' … this presents us with an *'unholy alliance' between Rome and Jerusalem* rather than an accentuation of the imperial state's authority. The 'authority' of the Land beast is expressly rooted in that of the sea beast."[100]

On this "unholy alliance", it is worth mentioning that Titus, son of

---

[99] Russell, J. Stuart: The Parousia. Baker Book House: Grand Rapids, 1983, pp. 466.
[100] Gentry Jr, Kenneth L. Navigating the Book of Revelation: Special Studies on Important Issues (p. 124). Victorious Hope Publishing. Kindle Edition.

Vespasian – the dynamic duo who were dispatched by Nero to crush the Jewish rebellion – had a sexual love affair with Berenice, daughter of Herod Agrippa I. Oh, and this happened during the war! That's messed up. It is quite likely you've never heard of her. Yet she is not only mentioned in Acts 25:13, 23; 26:30, but also by early sources.[101] She was not only the daughter of King Herod Agrippa I, but also sister of King Herod Agrippa II. The Herodians were a dynasty of Jewish puppet rulers installed by the Romans over the Holy Land in order to represent the interests of Rome.

Further, in the Jewish canonical book of 1 Maccabees, we learn of an even earlier and more official political alliance that was made between the Holy Land and Rome. Known as the **Jewish–Roman Treaty**, this covenant was established in approximately 160 BC:

> "Judas, who is also called Maccabeus, and his brothers and the people of the Jews have sent us to you to establish alliance and peace with you, so that we may be enrolled as your allies and friends." The proposal pleased them, and this is a copy of the letter that they wrote in reply, on bronze tablets, and sent to Jerusalem to remain with them there as a memorial of peace and alliance:
>
> 'May all go well with the Romans and with the nation of the Jews at sea and on land forever...'" 1 Maccabees 8:20–23 (NRSV)

In contrast to Rome, Israel had a long history of dual rulership, whereby both a monarch and a priest presided. Each of the two horns of the ram therefore were representative of this dualistic governance. This then leads to the identity of the two horns. Jesus already primed us to understand the significance of the two horns when he warned against the religious and political "leaven".[102]

*"And He [Jesus] was giving orders to them, saying, 'Watch out! Beware of the leaven of the **Pharisees**, and the leaven of **Herod**.'" Mark 8:15 (NASB, emphasis mine)*

---

[101] Josephus, Suetonius, Tacitus, Dio Cassius, Aurelius Victor, and Juvenal.
[102] Leaven or yeast in the Gospels represents worldviews, ways of thinking, and conduct. In contrast to the political and religious leaven is the leaven of the Kingdom (Matt 13:33).

For the monarchy, the infamous Herodian Dynasty was a consistent cancer in Judea, beginning with Herod the Great. For Christians, he is best known for infanticide, an edict he enforced in the hopes it would kill Jesus. As the years passed, a seventh Herodian reigned as puppet-king over Judea: Herod Agrippa II. In the same way Vespasian was the seventh horn because he was the seventh ruler over Rome, the last ruler of the Herodian line was the seventh. In fact, Agrippa II (also mentioned in Acts 25:13, 23; 26:30) supported Vespasian during the War. He was the one who sent the Apostle Paul off to Rome in chains.

Agrippa II was pro-Roman, and he did everything he could to stop the people from rebelling in order to keep them under Roman subjugation.[103] He embodied verse 11: *"And all the authority of the first savage animal will it exercise on behalf of it, and it will force the Land and those who dwell within it to bow in submission to the first savage animal."* But the Jewish people in favor of rebellion proceeded. And though Agrippa II was kicked out of Jerusalem, he didn't stop his tyranny. He aided Vespasian in several military campaigns against fellow Jews and provided the Roman warlord with 2000 soldiers for combat.

The second horn, representing the religious ruler over the Holy Land, was the High Priest Ananus ben Ananus.[104] Wait, who?

You see, the horns for both the leopard and the lamb coincide with the events leading up to and including the destruction of the Holy Land and the Temple of Jerusalem. This is an important point to keep in mind: John is seeing *who* the key players are that would *catalyze* events for the War. In regards to the leopard (Rome), you would not have had the War if it weren't for Nero, Vespasian, and Titus. Hence, they are the three horns highlighted.

As for the lamb, Herod Agrippa II was responsible for allowing the Jews to be provoked into rebellion.[105] He was a Jewish king installed by Rome. The symbolism of a wolf in sheep's clothing acting as a puppet for the beast of Rome best fits the narrative. As for the second horn, the priestly one, Ananus ben Ananus was a key figure in the Jewish Rebellion of 66 AD, ultimately contributing to the fall of Jerusalem and the Temple in 70 AD.

Why? First, before the War even began, he had ordered the execution of

---

[103] Josephus, Wars. 2:15–26.
[104] Also known as Anan Son of Anan.
[105] This included the provocations of Lucceius Albinus, Gessius Florus, and Cestius Gallus. But these men, though significant contributors to the start of the war, did not preside as kings of the Jews. They were overtly Romans.

the Apostle James (James the Just), brother of Jesus of Nazareth.[106] James was the key leader of the Jerusalem Council, which was sort of the mothership for all churches outside of the Holy Land. He was the major overseer of all fellowships under the banner of Christ.

Ananus presided over the Sanhedrin, the Jewish council which had jurisdiction over religious, civil, and criminal matters. Think of it like a Jewish Supreme Court. It was before the Sanhedrin that James was given the death sentence and subsequently stoned to death. Years earlier, Caiaphas the High Priest had condemned Jesus of Nazareth (Matt 26), and all the priests prophetically cemented their ties with Rome with their chilling statement in John 19:

> *"So they shouted, 'Away with Him, away with Him, crucify Him!' Pilate said to them, 'Shall I crucify your King?' The chief priests answered, 'We have no king except Caesar.' John 19:15 (NASB)*

Now the plot twist. After the execution of James, Ananus was kicked out of office by Herod Agrippa II, the other horn. So the two also share being displaced in common. But just as Agrippa II continued to be involved in the War, so did Ananus. He became one of the key leaders in the Jewish Revolt against the Romans and headed up the newly established Judean provisional government. His voice of deception helped fuel the delusion that the Jewish forces had Yahweh's favor in overcoming the Roman legions and liberating the Holy Land.

Then in 68 AD, the same year that Nero (the sixth horn of the leopard) died, Ananus also died. He was killed while fighting in the Zealot Temple Siege in Jerusalem. Ananus was *the last legitimate High Priest* in Judea before all hell broke loose. Four people assumed the role of High Priest, but merely in title and none of them lasted long.[107]

The lamb, a wolf in sheep's clothing, had upon its head two horns: a king and a High Priest, representing the unique dual-rulership over the Jewish people. Each horn had interactions with perhaps the two most prominent figures in the Apostolic Church: Paul and James. Each horn was the last of

---

[106] Josephus, Wars. 20:9:1.

[107] Jesus son of Damneus was kicked out in less than a year, Joshua ben Gamla was killed in the war in about a year, Mattathias ben Theophilus was also kicked out in less than a year, and Phannias ben Samuel didn't really count because he was appointed by the Zealots. Also, according to Josephus, he "was a man not only unworthy of the high priesthood, but that did not well know what the high priesthood was." Josephus, *Wars*, 4:151–158.

their respective lines in the traditional sense.

> א *(13) And it was performing great signs, like making fire fall from the skies across the Land in front of people.*

SIGNS

Commentators and well-meaning Christians have been bent out of shape over this one verse forever. To take this verse literally is to take a seven-headed leopard with a harlot saddled to its back literally as well. You can't have a vision with unrealistically-symbolic animals and then vacillate between figurative and literal interpretations.

Let's take a step back and review the basics. Scripture clearly illustrates that it was not uncommon for people to fall under the deception of signs and wonders.

> *"Now a man named Simon had previously been practicing magic in the city and astonishing the people of Samaria, claiming to be someone great and all the people, from small to great, were paying attention to him, saying, 'This man is the Power of God that is called Great.' And they were paying attention to him because for a long time he had astounded them with his magic arts." Acts 8:9–11 (NASB)*

Here in the Book of Acts we hear the story of one man (though there certainly were several others like him everywhere) who performed magic and "astonished" the people. And they called him "the Power of God". Now, what was the magic? What were the signs? How did he perform them? It seems like the questions we would ask today are not the questions of first-century Jews. We are unnecessarily obsessed with the what and how. But you will find that the Bible will not glorify darkness. It's not worth the real-estate on the scrolls.

Or how about this occasion, going all the way back to Exodus:

> *"Aaron threw his staff down before Pharaoh and his servants, and it turned into a serpent. Then Pharaoh also called for the wise men and the sorcerers, and they too, the soothsayer priests of Egypt, did the same with their secret arts. For each one threw down his staff, and they turned into*

serpents…

[Aaron] lifted up the staff and struck the water that was in the Nile in the sight of Pharaoh and in the sight of his servants; and all the water that was in the Nile was turned into blood… But the soothsayer priests of Egypt did the same with their secret arts…

[Then] Aaron extended his hand over the waters of Egypt, and the frogs came up and covered the land of Egypt. However, the soothsayer priests did the same with their secret arts, making frogs come up on the land of Egypt." Exodus 7:10–12, 20–22; 8:6–7 (NASB)

The famous faceoff between Moses and Aaron and the magicians who later became known as Jannes and Jambres was legendary, especially to the Jewish people. But again we are faced with 21st century questions: how did they do it? How did the magicians turn their staffs into snakes, turn the Nile to blood, or cause frogs to come over the land? We are given no answer from the Hebrew text. Why? It wasn't an important question. As I just said, the Bible will not glorify darkness. No credit will be given because God is greater.

The truth is, in the same way God enables saints to work miracles, the powers of darkness enable seekers of darkness to wrought supernatural works as well. And if you doubt this, go and find missionaries who have worked with indigenous tribes in Central America or Central Africa. They'll have some stories to tell you.

"Beware of the false prophets, who come to you in sheep's clothing, but inwardly are ravenous wolves." Matthew 7:15 (NASB)

"For many will come in My name, saying, 'I am the [messiah],' and they will mislead many people… And many false prophets will rise up and mislead many people… For false [messiahs] and false prophets will arise and will provide great signs and wonders, so as to mislead, if possible, even the elect. Behold, I have told you in advance."
Matthew 24:5, 11, 24 (NASB)

This is where you need to have a superior Christology. In a post-Cessationist, post-Dispensationalist Christian society, we are coming out of a "big devil, little Jesus" paradigm. We were taught to study the signs of the devil and learn the scale of his ability and power while we congruously inherited a powerless Gospel. From this paradigm, the Christian is glorified in defeat, and their only hope is escapism. It's blasphemy.

We need to ask Holy Spirit to bring us back into alignment with the truth: We have a BIG, MASSIVE God and a BIG, MASSIVE Jesus. We shouldn't give a second of our attention to what the devil does because he is miniscule in comparison to Yeshua!

> *"For He rescued us from the domain of darkness, and transferred us to the kingdom of His beloved Son, in whom we have redemption, the forgiveness of sins.*
>
> *He is the image of the invisible God, the firstborn of all creation: for by Him all things were created, both in the heavens and on earth, visible and invisible, whether thrones, or dominions, or rulers, or authorities—all things have been created through Him and for Him. He is before all things, and in Him all things hold together."*
> *Colossians 1:13–17 (NASB)*

Can I get an "Amen", please!

Moving on. We know that the lamb of Revelation 13 represents apostate Israel, the Holy Land. And the two horns on that lamb represents kings and priests who have historically shared authority over Jews.

This symbolic animal is also likened to **a false prophet**, sort of an anti-Moses or anti-Elijah (Israel's two greatest prophets). Now besides the Law and Prophets, what else did Moses and Elijah represent? They represented spiritual authority to govern and lead the people of Israel.

So what do "great signs" (Moses) and "fire fall" (Elijah) symbolize? That the lamb – which was comprised of false rulers, false priests, and apostates – had been able to falsely convince the inhabitants of the Holy Land that spiritual guidance and divine authority from God were in place to lead and govern them. And yes, as I recorded in book one of this series, there were many false messiahs and prophets. And yes, it was recorded that both Vespasian and Titus performed "signs" and "miracles" But that's just icing on the cake. The substance of the verse here is bigger than that. By seeing the great signs, **the nation itself was under the delusion that Yahweh God was blessing their cause, however varied and opposing those** causes happened to be.

Consider the words of Josephus, the Jewish historian and eye witness of the Jewish-Roman War. On the day the Holy Temple was destroyed, he recorded the following (emphasis mine):

> "A false prophet was the occasion of these people's destruction, who had made a public proclamation in the city that very day, that **God commanded** them to get upon the temple, and that there they should receive **miraculous signs** of their deliverance. Now there was then a **great number of false prophets suborned by the tyrants to impose on the people,** who denounced this to them, that they should wait for deliverance from God; and this was in order to keep them from deserting, and that they might be buoyed up above fear and care by such hopes…
>
> Thus were the miserable people persuaded by these deceivers, and **such as belied God himself**; while they did not attend nor give credit to the signs that were so evident, and did so plainly foretell their future desolation, but, like men infatuated, without either eyes to see or minds to consider, did not regard the denunciations that God made to them.
>
> [In contrast, here are the real signs that God provided:] **there was a star resembling a sword**, which stood over the city, and a comet, that continued a whole year. Thus also before the Jews' rebellion… so great **a light shone round the altar and the holy house**, that it appeared to be bright day time; which lasted for half an hour…. At the same festival also, **a heifer**, as she was led by the high priest to be sacrificed, **brought forth a lamb** in the midst of the temple…
>
> [And another] certain prodigious and incredible phenomenon appeared… before sun-setting, **chariots and troops of soldiers in their armor were seen running about among the clouds**, and surrounding of cities. Moreover, at that feast which we call Pentecost, as the priests were going by night into the inner court of the temple… they **felt a quaking**, and heard **a great noise**, and after that they heard **a sound as of a great**

multitude, saying, 'Let us remove hence'…

Now if any one consider these things, he will find that God takes care of mankind, and by all ways possible foreshows to our race what is for their preservation; but that men perish by those miseries which they madly and voluntarily bring upon themselves…

But now, what did the most elevate them in undertaking this war, was an ambiguous **oracle that was also found in their sacred writings**, how, 'about that time, one from their country should become governor of the habitable earth.' The Jews took this prediction to belong to themselves in particular, and many of the wise men were thereby deceived in their determination. Now **this oracle certainly denoted the government of Vespasian**, who was appointed emperor in Judea."[108]

One last thought on verse 13. As stated above, the mention of "signs" and "fire fall" immediately contrasts these false prophets from the great prophets of Israel, Moses and Elijah. Only two chapters prior (Revelation 11), we see the true prophetic authority of Moses and Elijah (representing the Law and Prophets) in effect. By contrast, a false spiritual authority (i.e. religious manipulation) mis-representing the Law and the Prophets is playing out here in chapter 13.

> א *(14) And it will cause those who dwell upon the Land to be lead astray by way of the signs that were being granted to it to be performing before the savage animal.*[109]

> א *(15) And it was granted to it to give spirit to the genius of the savage animal, and as a result all who do not bow in obeisance*[110] *to*

---

[108] Josephus, *Wars*, 6:5.
[109] The Peshitta lacks part B of verse 14, "to say to those who dwell upon the Land to make the genius of the savage animal which had the wound by the sword; yet lived."
[110] Or "paid homage". סגד means "to bow down in respect" or "to cause to be venerated". The *implication* can be worship, but this is based on context (see same word in Dan 2:46 or Gen 47:31). Given the context of acknowledging the divinity of Caesar, obeisance or homage is more fitting than "worship".

the genius of the savage animal will be killed.

Thanks be to Holy Spirit who leads us and guides us into all truth. When our hearts are awestruck by the supremacy of Jesus Christ, fear is displaced. We need not fear these verses, for Scripture sheds light upon itself. First, we are dealing with the image (the genius) of the savage animal, which we have already established is Rome.

THE IMAGE

We then need to understand the meaning of "image", which I have translated as "genius". The word "image", tzalmo צַלמָא in Aramaic, primarily meant a picture, a statue, an image on a coin, or an idol.[111] Within the Roman context, all of the above were used to depict the Caesars. From ensigns to marble busts, the Caesars were immortalized throughout the Empire. More specifically, this immortalization was not always of the emperor in flesh, but sometimes the emperor's essence or divine nature was used. This "essence" is what is referred to as their *genius*. This was core to the religious belief system of the Roman imperial cult.

> "This second Beast endeavors to get the earth dwellers to make a statue or image of the first Beast. There were legends about Simon Magus bringing statues to life or at least making them talk, but more to the point are the attempts to deceive worshipers into believing a god was speaking to them through the artifice of having them addressed by a statue (see Lucian's Alexander the False Prophet 12, 26). In addition Roman emperors were notorious for bringing magicians to court to practice various forms of astrology."[112]

Therefore, the implication goes beyond the face of Nero stamped into a coin (though it is inclusive of this). The significance here is the deification of the Caesars and how their deification permeated Roman religion, commerce, and even warfare.

---

[111] See J. Payne Smith's *A Compendious Syriac Dictionary,* pp 480.
[112] Witherington III, Ben: Revelation. Cambridge, United Kingdom, 2003, pp 184–184.

"Nero was particularly infatuated with Apollo; he even claimed the title 'Son of Apollos,' and appeared ostentatiously in this role. Seneca, one of young Nero's tutors and a powerful influence in the era of Nero's reign designated the *Quinquennium Neronti*, convinced Nero that he was destined to become the very revelation of Augustus and of Apollo...

Suetonius remarks of Nero that 'since he was acclaimed as the equal of Apollo in music and of the Sun in driving a chariot, he had planned to emulate the exploits of Hercules as well.' An inscription from Athens speaks of him as: 'All powerful Nero Caesar Sebastos, a new Apollo.' Nero's portrait appears on coins as Apollo playing the lyre...

The Senate erected a statue of Nero 'on divine scale in the Temple of Mars at the Forum Augusti . . . , thus introducing the cult into the city of Rome.' The statue was the same size as that of Mars in Mars's own Temple. That Nero actually was worshiped is evident from inscriptions found in Ephesus in which he is called 'Almighty God' and 'Saviour.' Reference to Nero as 'God and Savior' is found in an inscription at Salamis, Cyprus...

In A.D. 66 Tiridates, King of Armenia, approached Nero in devout and reverential worship, as recorded by Dio Cassius:

Indeed, the proceedings of the conference were not limited to mere conversations, but a lofty platform had been erected on which were set images of Nero... Tiridates approached and paid them reverence; then, after sacrificing to them and calling them by laudatory names, he took off the diadem from his head and set it upon them. . . .

Tiridates publicly fell before Nero seated upon the rostra in the Forum: 'Master, I am ...thy slave. And I have come to thee, my god, to worship thee as I do Mithras...'

Dio notes also the fate of one senator who did not appreciate Nero's 'divine' musical abilities: "Thrasaea was executed because... he never would listen to the emperor's singing and lyre-playing, nor sacrifice to Nero's Divine Voice as did the rest.'"[113]

MORE SIGNS

Just as there was much fervor in the Holy Land with respect to Messianic signs (which I discuss at length in the previous book), the Romans were looking for a sign that would point to the next Emperor. Interestingly, they looked to Judea (Israel) for that sign!

> "Few [Jews] interpreted these omens as fearful; the majority firmly believed that their ancient priestly writings [The Old Testament] contained the prophecy that this was the very time when the East should grow strong and that [Jewish] men starting from Judea should possess the world. This mysterious prophecy had in reality pointed to [the Romans] Vespasian and Titus, but the common people [of Judea], as is the way of human ambition, interpreted these great destinies in their own favour, and could not be turned to the truth even by adversity."[114]

> "When [Vespasian] consulted the oracle of the God of Carmel in Judea, the lots were highly encouraging, promising that whatever he planned or wished however great it might be, would come to pass."[115]

> "Now if any one consider these things, he will find that God takes care of mankind; and by all ways possible foreshews to our race what is for their preservation... For the Jews, by demolishing the tower of Antonia, had made their temple four

---

[113] Gentry, Kenneth L. Jr.: Before Jerusalem Fell. Institute for Christian Economics: Tyler, Texas, 1989, pp 271–273.
[114] Tacitus, *Histories,* 13:1, https://penelope.uchicago.edu/Thayer/E/Roman/Texts/Tacitus/Histories/5A*.html
[115] Suetonius, *The Life of Vespasian,* 5:6, https://penelope.uchicago.edu/Thayer/E/Roman/Texts/Suetonius/12Caesars/Vespasian*.html

square: while at the same time they had it written in their sacred oracles, that 'then should their city be taken, as well as their holy house, when once their temple should become four square.'

But now what did the most elevate them in undertaking this war, was an ambiguous oracle, that was also found in their sacred writings; how 'About that time one, from their country, should become governor of the habitable earth.' The Jews took this prediction to belong to themselves in particular: and many of the wise men were thereby deceived in their determination. Now this oracle certainly denoted the government of Vespasian: who was appointed emperor in Judea. However, it is not possible for men to avoid fate: although they see it beforehand. But these men interpreted some of these signals according to their own pleasure; and some of them they utterly despised: until their madness was demonstrated, both by the taking of their city, and their own destruction."[116] *[117]

The "signs" spoken of in Revelation 13:14 were various schemes and spiritual deceptions involving four groups of people in two opposing camps: 1) the Jewish imperial priesthood and puppet rulers and 2) false prophets and messiahs. The first group claimed it was acceptable to yield to Rome and serve them. In contrast, the second group conspired to convince the Jewish people to instead rebel against Rome. Both groups' activities led to ruin.

---

[116] Josephus, *Wars,* 6:5:4.
[117] There is much speculation on exactly which portions of the Old Testament or extra-canonical books were referenced in relation to these prophecies. It may also have been teachings or writings of the Essenes or other sects whose writings would therefore be lost to us were this the case. However, Josephus and others clearly understood that Vespasian's march to Rome for the throne of the Empire (which commenced from the east – from Judea), was in fulfilment of some Jewish prophecy.
One must also keep in mind that in Antiquity, oracles and omens were common place, and anything could be seen as a "sign". So these Roman writers simply accepted that a Jewish oracle foretold of the new emperor without much second thought. And because Josephus was so against the Revolt, he may have persuaded the Romans in their adoption of the Jewish prophecy narrative. Consider too that when Josephus was first captured, he prophesied to Vespasian that he would become Caesar.

One key issue on which these two camps clashed was emperor worship. A false spiritual authority was imposed on the people when priests started presenting sacrifices in the Temple for the Caesar. "We have no king but Caesar" (John 19:15) may be evidence of this worship.

> "The Hellenistic-Jewish author Philo of Alexandria (20 BC – 50 CE), who argued for perfect harmony between Jews and the Greek and Roman world, presented imperial sacrificial gifts to the Temple as a gesture of genuine good will of the Roman emperor toward the Jews, as well as an expression of admiration and reverence toward their god."[118]

Interestingly, the trigger event which toppled the first domino and led the Roman legions to descend upon the Holy Land was when these sacrifices on behalf of Caesar ceased.[119] According to Josephus, a priest and nationalist named Elazar convinced some lower ranking temple priests to stop sacrificing on behalf of Caesar (and all non-Jews). Hearing this, the high priests and other influential men tried to convince them to continue on with the sacrifices. However, revolt was in the air, and these radicals did not heed the high priests. War soon followed.[120] The degradation of the religious leaders and aristocratic elites of the Holy Land is well documented by Josephus.

Outside the Holy Land, followers of Yeshua were also put to the test. Approximately 40 years after the fall of Jerusalem, the historian Pliny the Younger sought counsel from Emperor Trajan while serving as his imperial magistrate:

> "I have never participated in trials of Christians. I therefore do not know what offenses it is the practice to punish or investigate, and to what extent… Meanwhile, in the case of those who were denounced to me as Christians, I have observed the following procedure: I interrogated these as to whether they were Christians; those who confessed I

---

[118] Balberg, Mira. Imperial Gifts Between Romans and Rabbis, 2015. < https://quod.lib.umich.edu/cgi/p/pod/dod-idx/imperial-gifts-between-romans-and-rabbis.pdf?c=fia;idno=11879367.2015.012;format=pdf>
[119] Sacrifices were offered twice a day for both Caesar and the Roman people. See Josephus, *Wars* 2:10:4, and, *Against Apion* 2:5.
[120] See Josephus, *Wars*, 2.17.2

interrogated a second and a third time, threatening them with punishment; those who persisted I ordered executed...

An anonymous document was published containing the names of many persons. Those who denied that they were or had been Christians, when they invoked the gods in words dictated by me, offered prayer with incense and wine to your image, which I had ordered to be brought for this purpose together with statues of the gods, and moreover cursed Christ–none of which those who are really Christians, it is said, can be forced to do– these I thought should be discharged. Others named by the informer declared that they were Christians, but then denied it... They all worshipped your image and the statues of the gods, and cursed Christ.

...For the contagion of this superstition has spread not only to the cities but also to the villages and farms. But it seems possible to check and cure it...

Trajan to Pliny

You observed proper procedure, my dear Pliny, in sifting the cases of those who had been denounced to you as Christians... if they are denounced and proved guilty, they are to be punished, with this reservation, that whoever denies that he is a Christian and really proves it–that is, by worshiping our gods– even though he was under suspicion in the past, shall obtain pardon through repentance."[121]

One final point: when dealing with the two savage animals, the beasts, we must at all times keep in mind that they are *prophetic images* that represent various personas in play. More importantly, dark spiritual forces are ultimately behind these beasts. Whether you want to call them principalities, demonic rulers, or evil spirits, the point is, *"our struggle is not against flesh and blood, but against the rulers, against the powers, against the world forces of this darkness, against the spiritual forces of wickedness in the heavenly places" (Ephesians 6:12).* We do not demonize humans, no matter how deceived they may be, for all are made in the image of God.

---

[121] Pliny, *Letters* 10.96-97.

So as we have seen, Revelation 13 is big. Actually, I'll say that our misunderstanding around it is big. Hence, there is lots to go through. So I've broken the chapter up into two parts in order to make it easier to digest. So stretch your legs, grab a coffee, and where you're ready, I'll meet you over in part 2.

4 THE EMPEROR AND HIS MARK: CH. 13 PART 2

> *"You shall therefore take these words of mine to heart and to soul; and you shall tie them as a sign on your hand, and they shall be as frontlets on your forehead…*
>
> *See, I am placing before you today a blessing and a curse …"*
> *Deuteronomy 11:18, 26 (NASB)*

Microchips. Credit cards. Injections. All things fear mongering has come up with in decades past to call "mark of the beast". Indeed, in the last 100 years alone, any new technological innovation has received this label. Not only are these predications outrageous, they would have offered zero hope or relevance to the intended audience of John's prophetic words.

The circumstances of those years were dire. Nero took his own life in June 68 AD, and Galba, a general from Spain, ascended. By the middle of January 69 AD another general, Otho, overthrew Galba and took the imperial office. Three short months later, a third general, Vitellius, supported by the northern legions, defeated Otho in a bloody battle on Italian soil. Meanwhile in Judea, Vespasian, who had been dispatched by Nero to put down the Jewish revolt, bided his time. Most of the resistance in the countryside had been squashed, and the armies of Rome surrounded Jerusalem. When Nero died, Vespasian halted the war operations as he waited to see who would succeed to the imperial office. Eventually Vespasian's troops proclaimed him emperor; he removed several legions from the siege of Jerusalem and sent them marching toward Rome. By the end of the year, Vespasian's party was victorious and he was the fourth emperor of the year…

[John] strove to make his people understand how significant and dangerous their situation was and to move them to resist the temptations of the Greco-Roman cultural complex. His vision was a parable of the war, and his message was to stand fast in the face of adversity and of the adversary…

Putting it bluntly, I argue that the Apocalypse is a Jewish and not a Christian document.[122]

> ℵ *(16) And it caused all of them—small and great, rich and poor, lords and servants—to be given unto them the brand upon their right hands or upon their foreheads,*
>
> ℵ *(17) so that no one can buy or sell afterwards, unless there is upon him the brand of the name of the savage animal or the number of its name.*

We need to come to terms with the fact that, for *many* reasons, we will never come close today to experiencing the atrocities Jews and Christians faced in the first century. Jews were slaughtered by Romans in the most brutal ways during the siege of the Holy Land. Hundreds others were crucified on a daily basis, so much so that they even ran out of trees in that region.

> "[The Jews] would be first whipped and then tortured with all sorts of torments. Then, before they died, they were crucified in front of the city wall [of Jerusalem]… the Romans caught at

---

[122] Marshall, John W., *Parables of War: Reading of John's Jewish Apocalypse* (Waterloo: Wilfrid Laurier University Press, 2001), p 2.

least five hundred Jews... Titus had those they caught nailed to the crosses, one after the other. The Romans joked that when the number of executions grew so great and no room existed for more crosses, neither would there be more crosses for Jewish bodies."[123]

A bit earlier chronologically, in Rome, Nero had also inflicted heinous tortures against the followers of Yeshua.

"Nero fastened the guilt [of the Great Fire] and inflicted the most exquisite tortures on a class hated for their abominations, called 'Chrestians' [Christians] by the populace.

Christus [Christ], from whom the name had its origin, suffered the extreme penalty during the reign of Tiberius at the hands of one of our procurators, Pontius Pilate, and a most mischievous superstition, thus checked for the moment, again broke out not only in Judaea, the first source of the evil, but even in Rome...

Accordingly, an arrest was first made of all who pleaded guilty [to believing in Christ]; then, upon their information, an immense multitude was convicted, not so much of the crime of firing the city, as of hatred against mankind [which became the charge against them]. Mockery of every sort was added to their deaths. Covered with the skins of beasts, they were torn by dogs and perished, or were nailed to crosses, or were doomed to the flames and burnt, to serve as a nightly illumination, when daylight had expired."[124]

Suetonius, a first-century AD Roman historian, also remarked,

"During [Nero's] reign many abuses were severely punished and put down, and no fewer new laws were made... Punishment was inflicted on the Christians, a class of men

---

[123] Josephus, Flavius. The Jewish Wars - A Paraphrase: Or the History of the Destruction of Jerusalem (pp. 496-497). Living Stone Books. Kindle Edition. For full excerpt, See Josephus, *Wars,* 5:11.
[124] Tacitus, *Annals,* 15.44.

given to a new and mischievous superstition."[125]

Yet perhaps worse still was the fate of those who survived the Roman invasion and conquest of the Holy Land. Escaping death by sword, torture, famine, or pestilence meant being taken alive as prisoners of war (POWs). This was a life sentence to a most brutal existence.

Josephus informs us that the approximate sum of 100,000 POWs were first hauled to Rome in order to be paraded in Titus' procession of victory. Many of the rebel leaders were tortured and mocked in that event for sport. These tens of thousands who were captured were then sold into the slave trade, but not before they were *marked*. It was a common and well documented practice in the Roman Empire to either *brand* or *tattoo* both prisoners of war and slaves with a mark – either on their hands or foreheads. This is the immediate context of the *mark of Rome*, or the *mark of Nero*.

Jesus foresaw these events ahead of time. And it broke his heart.

"When He approached Jerusalem, He saw the city and wept over it, saying, 'If you had known on this day, even you, the conditions for peace! But now they have been hidden from your eyes. For the days will come upon you when your enemies will put up a barricade against you, and surround you and hem you in on every side, and they will level you to the ground, and throw down your children within you, and they will not leave in you one stone upon another, because you did not recognize the time of your visitation." Luke 19:41–44 (NASB)

"Truly I say to you, all these things will come upon this generation. Jerusalem, Jerusalem, who kills the prophets and stones those who have been sent to her! How often I wanted to gather your children together, the way a hen gathers her chicks under her wings, and you were unwilling. Behold, your house is being left to you desolate!" Matthew 23:36–38 (NASB)

"And when [the Romans] led [Jesus] away… following Him was a large

---

[125] Suetonius, *The Life of Nero*, 16:2,
https://penelope.uchicago.edu/Thayer/e/roman/texts/suetonius/12caesars/nero*.html

> *crowd of the people, and of women who were mourning and grieving for Him. But Jesus turned to them and said, 'Daughters of Jerusalem, stop weeping for Me, but weep for yourselves and for your children. For behold, days are coming when they will say, 'Blessed are those who cannot bear, and the wombs that have not given birth, and the breasts that have not nursed.' Then they will begin to say to the mountains, 'Fall on us,' and to the hills, 'Cover us.' For if they do these things when the tree is green, what will happen when it is dry?"* Luke 23:26–31 (NASB)

> *"They will lay their hands on you and persecute you, turning you over to the synagogues and prisons, bringing you before kings and governors on account of My name… But you will be betrayed even by parents, brothers and sisters, other relatives, and friends, and they will put some of you to death, and you will be hated by all people because of My name. And yet not a hair of your head will perish. By your endurance you will gain your lives. But when you see Jerusalem surrounded by armies, then recognize that her desolation is near."* Luke 21:12–20 (NASB)

We owe it to those who have gone before us – those who died horrific deaths and endured great tortures – to not make the mark of the beast about us today. We today are the most prosperous and most privileged society in the history of mankind. Our suffering in Western Civilization pales in comparison. Yes, we suffer. Yes, we endure. But let us not try to use this passage of Scripture to contextualize our fears and woes.

Rather, we must become rooted and established in the supremacy of Christ, the efficacy of the cross, and the unfolding of His great plan.

> *"Then comes the end, when [Jesus Christ] hands over the kingdom to our God and Father, when He has abolished all rule and all authority and power. For He must reign until He has put all His enemies under His feet."* 1 Corinthians 15:24–25 (NASB)

Is he reigning, or is he a liar? Will he abolish all rule, authority, and power, or is he a liar? Where is our faith! *"Let God be true, and every human being a liar"* (Romans 3:8). We either take Him at His word, or we have no Gospel at all. What God has said is either 100% true, or it is 100% false. There is no middle ground.

Now, back to the mark. **There were three main ways this played out: branding and stigmatization, the imperial cult, and coins.**

BRANDING & STIGMATIZATION

Branding or tattooing was known as a "charagma" in the Roman Empire. In fact, the exact word is used in the Greek version of Revelation (χάραγμα G5480).

> "[The mark] was a test of loyalty to the Empire for everyone. Those willing to worship in this way received the **charagma** of the Beast on their right hand and on their foreheads. What is this **charagma**? This was a term used for the imperial stamp on commercial documents and for the impression of the Emperor's head on a coin…
>
> There is now plenty of literature and evidence showing that the imperial cult was a pervasive and growing influence in the Empire, especially in Asia. For example, all seven cities that John addresses had imperial temples, and for all but Laodicea and Philadelphia there is evidence that they had imperial altars and imperial priests. This meant various festivals in honor of the Emperor and civic responsibilities linked to the worship of Emperor…
>
> [The] implication [of the charagma] would be that individuals with this sign on them belong to the Emperor, being his slaves or devotees. Slaves and defeated soldiers were branded if they joined the Roman army. 3 Maccabees 2:28–30 says that Ptolemy IV required Jews to offer sacrifice to pagan gods. If they refused, they were killed. If they simply refrained from doing so, they were branded with the emblem of the god Dionysius… [And] when one considers 13.17, which suggests that it was a trade requirement to see the mark, a visible mark is likely. The mark is said to be the name of the Beast or rather the number of his name."[126]

The charagma would have been the ultimate sign of sacrilege and defeat for the Jewish people. It was the antithesis of Yahweh's instructions in the Pentateuch. In Exodus 13, God instructs the Hebrews to commemorate the miracle of the Exodus and their deliverance from slavery with a seven-day

---

[126] Witherington III, Ben: Revelation. Cambridge, United Kingdom, 2003, pp 184–185.

streak of eating unleavened bread. And on the seventh day, they were to feast in celebration. Oddly, this *act of commemoration* "shall serve as a sign to you on your hand, and as a reminder on your forehead, that the law of the Lord may be in your mouth" (Exodus 13:9). So the first mention of a "sign" on the hand and forehead was metaphorical.

In the same chapter, Yahweh continues, "you shall devote to the Lord every firstborn of a womb, and every firstborn offspring of an animal that you own... So it shall serve as a sign on your hand and as phylacteries on your forehead, for with a powerful hand the Lord brought us out of Egypt" (Exodus 19:12, 16).[127] Only in the later half of the chapter do we have a potential reference to something physical (albeit an object) on the forehead.

However in Deuteronomy, Yahweh goes beyond metaphor. This is the famous passages (for Jews at least) where the Shema Prayer is found. The Shema was and continues to be a daily prayer as instructed by God.

> *"Hear, Israel! The Lord is our God, the Lord is one! And you shall love the Lord your God with all your heart and with all your soul and with all your strength." Deuteronomy 6:4–5 (NASB)*

"Shema", the Hebrew word "to hear" or "to listen", is the first word of the verse. Yahweh continues,

> *"These words, which I am commanding you today, shall be on your heart... You shall also tie them as a sign to your hand, and they shall be as frontlets on your forehead.*
> *Then it shall come about when the Lord your God brings you into the land that He swore to your fathers, to Abraham, Isaac, and Jacob, to give you... be careful that you do not forget the Lord who brought you out of the land of Egypt, out of the house of slavery."*
> *Deuteronomy 6:6, 8, 10, 12 (NASB)*

So the Shema was first a daily prayer. Not only was it recited, but it was also written and bound upon their heads and hands. And like in Exodus 13, the broader context was to remined them of their Exodus miracle and deliverance from slavery. Later in Deuteronomy 11, Yahweh takes the symbolism and application of a sign on their hands and foreheads one step further.

---

[127] Robert Alter expresses doubt that the word "totafot" implied phylacteries. Instead, he is inclined to interpret it as the Egyptian styled frontlets, which rested between the eyes. See Alter: The Hebrew Bible, pp 266.

> *"You shall therefore take these words of mine to heart and to soul; and you shall tie them as a sign on your hand, and they shall be as frontlets on your forehead...*
>
> *See, I am placing before you today a blessing and a curse: the blessing, if you listen to the commandments of the Lord your God, which I am commanding you today; and the curse, if you do not listen to the commandments of the Lord your God..."*
> Deuteronomy 11:18, 26–28 (NASB)

The conditional aspect of the Mosaic Law permeates these words. The binding of Yahweh's words on their hands and heads became a matter of life and death. Deuteronomy 11 ends with a warning of curses, which in today's language meant the consequences for breach of covenant. The full list of consequences can be found in Deuteronomy 28:15 to 68. Now consider the chilling accuracy in which the prophecies of Moses found their fulfillment in the destruction of the Holy Land and Jerusalem in 70 AD:

> *"The Lord will cause you to be defeated by your enemies; you will go out one way against them, but you will flee seven ways from their presence...*
>
> *You will father sons and daughters but they will not remain yours, because they will go into captivity...*
>
> *The Lord will bring a nation against you from far away, from the end of the earth, as the eagle swoops down; a nation whose language you will not understand...*
>
> *And it will besiege you in all your towns until your high and fortified walls in which you trusted come down throughout your land, and it will besiege you in all your towns throughout your land which the Lord your God has given you. Then you will eat the offspring of your own body, the flesh of your sons and of your daughters whom the Lord your God has given you, during the siege and the hardship by which your enemy will oppress you...*
>
> *The refined and delicate woman among you... will eat [her child] secretly for lack of anything else, during the siege and the hardship with which your enemy will oppress you in your towns...*
>
> *You will offer yourselves for sale to your enemies as male and female slaves, but there will be no buyer."*

Deuteronomy 28:25, 41, 49, 52, 56, 68 (NASB)

Why did I include mention of cannibalism? Because that too took place. Josephus recorded an account that followed the prophecies verbatim.

> "A certain woman named Mary lived beyond the Jordan River… She was prominent both for her heritage and her wealth. She had fled to Jerusalem with so many others and was now besieged with no means of escape… When her hunger had swollen beyond mere hunger, and in her great need had lost any soundness of mind, she did a most unnatural thing… Mary killed her infant son and then roasted him. She ate half of the boy and then hid the other half."[128]

Why did I go through such great lengths to unravel all of these Old Covenant passages? Because it leads to the crux of the matter concerning the mark: **More than anything else, the penal stigmatization by means of charagmas on either the hand or forehead were a prophetic fulfillment of the curses of the Law of Moses. This was the significance to the first-century Jewish audience to whom these words were written.**

> "For Romans, as for the Greeks, tattooing usually signified degradation (that is, a lowering of status), because it was a treatment customarily reserved for slaves…
>
> [The marked] person is thus clearly subjected to the authority that imposed the mark, and the domination and institutional framework and hierarch relations are clearly expressed in it….
>
> [And] the name of the emperor was often tattooed on the foreheads of POWs… which is also logical given the understanding that… the crime attacks the sovereign… In this way, to mark the body of the criminal makes everyone aware of the unrestrained presence of the sovereign…
>
> "Thus there are at least three distinct variations in the mark applied to criminals in the Greco-Roman world: the most well-attested drew attention to the crime that had been committed;

---

[128] Josephus, Flavius. The Jewish Wars - A Paraphrase: Or the History of the Destruction of Jerusalem (pp. 365-366). Living Stone Books. Kindle Edition.

a second represented the ruler, the one in power, who was offended by the crime; and a third named the punishment in store."[129]

This notion continues with *stigmatization*.

"The modern word 'stigma' originates in a clutch of Ancient Greek words, derived from the root stig-, meaning to prick or to puncture… a stigma was an ink tattoo, an involuntary tattoo, pricked into human skin for 'penal and property purposes…

One of the first recorded uses of the word 'stigma' appears in a fragment of sixth-century BC poetry written by Asius of Samos, who uses the word stigmatias to describe 'a marked slave'…

Penal stigmatisation was a form of bodily inscription which, as the Roman emperor Valerius Maximus (AD 14–37) put it, turned the stigmatised into the 'image of his own penalty'.[130]

Our lack of historical knowledge and context is one of the key reasons we misunderstand and misapply John's vision of the "mark of the beast" in Revelation 13. Intuitively, we make it about ourselves and our day when we lack an original audience and original purpose.

"[Caligula had] many men of honourable rank disfigured with the marks of branding-irons and then condemned to the mines, to work at building roads, or to be thrown to the wild beasts; or else he shut them up in cages on all fours, like animals, or had them sawn asunder."[131]

For first-century Jews, stigmatization was the ultimate form of defilement.

---

[129] Gustafson, W. Mark. "Inscripta in Fronte: Penal Tattooing in Late Antiquity". Classical Antiquity, vol. 16, no. 1, University of California Press, 1997, pp. 86–97, https://doi.org/10.2307/25011055.
[130] Tyler, Imogen. Stigma (p. 34–36). Bloomsbury Publishing. Kindle Edition.
[131] Suetonius, *The Life of Caligula*, 27:3, https://penelope.uchicago.edu/Thayer/e/roman/texts/suetonius/12caesars/caligula*.html

The choice was either become a prisoner of war and be permanently branded or be put to death. Given that Josephus estimated that 1.1 million Jews were slaughtered and 97,000 were taken as POWs, we have just under a 10 to 1 ratio of those who chose death versus those who were branded. Mind you, even that assumption requires caution, because not all POWs necessarily wanted to live. Many were most likely denied the option of an honorable death and were sold into slavery as a form of humiliation.

> "[Marked] slaves are henceforth regularly and scornfully referred to with words such as literati (lettered), stigmatici (tattooed), inscripti (inscribed), and graptoi (written upon). Indeed, in the Graeco-Roman world, penal tattooing was a punishment reserved exclusively for non-citizens: slaves, indentured labourers, prisoners of war, other resident aliens, or religious minorities. As Plato wrote in The Laws, a dialogue on the ethics of government, 'if anyone is caught committing sacrilege, if he be a slave or a stranger, let his offence be written on his face and his hands'. Penal tattooing involved the inscription of words, symbols, and sometimes full sentences into the skin. These tattoos 'usually consisted of the name of a crime' inked into the face. Records of common stigmas include 'Thief' or 'Stop me, I'm a runaway', tattooed on the forehead. If you survived the torture of being tattooed (without antiseptic) you would never be free of the stigma, the 'disgrace, humiliation and exclusion' remaining 'indelibly written on one's face for all to see'...
>
> [P]enal stigmatization functioned as an injunction to a particular kind of self-knowledge: a mortifying punishment through which you were taught to 'know yourself' by 'knowing your place' in a highly stratified social order. Stigmatisation was thus an act of pedagogical violence through which a person was tutored back into a place of unfreedom..."[132]

In light of the Shema and the references we read earlier with respect to the literal and symbolic scribing of Yahweh's covenant people, you can appreciate how devastating this outcome was for the Jews who were captured

---

[132] Tyler, Imogen. Stigma (p. 34–36). Bloomsbury Publishing. Kindle Edition.

by the Romans throughout the Jewish–Roman war (which climaxed in 70 AD but ended in 73 AD at Masada). The concept of the Shema came as a result of the Exodus and is hence connected with emancipation and covenantal agreement. The Shema served as a reminder of this. Penal stigmatization is therefore the antithesis: because covenant was broken, there was a return to bondage and hence another form of "shema" was being applied. Quite tragically it served as a reminder of why this new fate came about.

> "Individuals with this sign on them belong to the Emperor, being his slaves or devotees. Slaves and defeated soldiers were branded if they joined the Roman army. 3 Mace. 2.28-30 says that Ptolemy IV required Jews to offer sacrifice to pagan gods. If they refused, they were killed. If they simply refrained from doing so, they were branded with the emblem of the god Dionysius."[133]

One really cannot underestimate the power of stigmatization in the Greco-Roman world. It was both a frightening and common phenomenon. The use of the imagery surrounding stigmatization is even found outside of Revelation 13 – though we will also see that it is alluded to again in Revelation 17.

> "Penal tattooing can in its turn be roughly divided into three kinds, again not absolute: that inflicted on delinquent slaves, on criminals, and on prisoners of war…
>
> In late antiquity there is yet another evolution in the use of tattoos: this is its extension to common soldiers and workers in military factories (fabricenses)… soldiers and military workers were marked for life with the insignia of their professions…
>
> One such metaphorical use of stigma was to have a very profound effect, St Paul's claim to have 'the marks of Jesus' on his body. It is probable that he actually refers to marks caused by ill-treatment, but regards them figuratively as the tattoos imposed on him as a slave of Christ…

---

[133] Witherington III, Ben: Revelation. Cambridge, United Kingdom, 2003, pp 184–185.

Out of St Paul grew the medieval use of the word stigma for marks received on the body by participation in Jesus' sufferings, either by self-laceration or by mystic transmission...

There may be another allusion to tattooing in the Christian New Testament, though stigma is not used. Revelation says of the Scarlet Woman, 'On her forehead was written a name of mystery, "Babylon the Great, mother of harlots and of earth's abominations [Rev 17:5]"'; the author perhaps imagines the Woman not only as a whore, but as a whore of the most degraded kind, a tattooed slave."[134]

THE IMPERIAL CULT

The second way the mark played out was in relation to emperor worship and the imperial cult. As mentioned above, a mark, or charagma, was used to brand or tattoo slaves and prisoners of war. But there was another less dramatic, day-to-day use of charagmas. This was when all people, small and great, acknowledged the divinity of the Caesar.

"No knowledge of any rescript or edict has survived from the first century which enforced emperor worship. . . . Although the emperor worship presupposed in the Apocalypse would well suit the later period of Domitian's reign, there is no conclusive evidence that it could not have occurred earlier."[135]

Worship of the Caesars or Emperors can be traced all the way back to Julius Caesar, long before Nero. We also know that temples dedicated to emperor worship were erected as far back as Augustus' reign circa 29 BC. While we know Christians were persecuted under Domitian (successions were: Nero, Vespasian, Titus, Domitian, Trajan), we have little to inform us of how emperor worship was enforced. [136] It wasn't until Trajan that the first

---

[134] Jones, C. P. "Stigma: Tattooing and Branding in Graeco-Roman Antiquity." The Journal of Roman Studies, vol. 77, 1987, pp. 139–55. JSTOR, https://doi.org/10.2307/300578.
[135] Guthrie, Donald B.: New Testament Introduction, 3rd ed. (Downer's Grove, IL: Inter-Varsity Press, 1970). Pp. 950-951.
[136] The proper translation of Irenaeus's quote concerning the dating of Revelation is: "for he (St. John the writer) was seen . . . almost in our generation toward the

official evidence for the enforcement of emperor worship has survived.

> "Surely [Nero's] character would compel him to take advantage of the emperor cult to feed his debased nature and vain pretensions. Although there are some who doubt his use of the emperor cult, there is significant evidence of not only Nero's endorsement of it, but even intimations that it may have been a factor (one of several) behind both the persecution of Christians in Rome in A.D. 64 and the overthrow of Israel in the Jewish War...
>
> Thus, whether or not the emperor Nero formally and legally demanded "worship or die," the inevitable tendency of the emperor cult, when coupled with the autocratic power of the mad emperor Nero, must necessarily result in just such an explosive confrontation."[137]

If anything, Revelation 13 (like Revelation 2 and 3) points to both the persecution of the followers of Yeshua and to the immediate and long-standing consequences for breach of covenant for those bound by the Law of Moses. Waves of Christian persecution would follow the Neronian assault against believers in the decades to come. And those under the curses of the Torah experienced the immediate consequences of the fall of the Holy Land and the Temple and suffered the long-lasting effects of defeat by the Roman super-power.

> "We do not have direct evidence of economic restrictions on Christians in the first century, although it is possible that this took place locally in one or more of the seven cities where the churches were located. For instance, it is likely that the requirement of participation in pagan rites excluded Christians from guilds, which were an important part of economic life in Pergamum and Thyatira."[138]

---

end of the reign of Domitian." For a comprehensive explanation, see Kenneth Gentry's *Before Jerusalem Fell,* pp 45–61.
[137] Gentry, Kenneth L. Jr.: Before Jerusalem Fell. Institute for Christian Economics: Tyler, Texas, 1989, pp 271, 277.
[138] Williamson, Peter S.: Revelation. Baker Publishing Group, Grand Rapids, 2015, pp 233–234.

> "It was illegal to be a Christian in 110, and it had been so for some time. Historians are not certain why the Roman imperial government regarded the sect, whose numbers at the time did not exceed eight thousand in an empire of perhaps sixty million people, as arch-enemies of the state. Clearly, however, the Christian refused to worship the Roman emperors as gods—and every emperor since Augustus, who reigned when Jesus was born, had been deified either in his lifetime or shortly after his death. Reusing to recognize the emperor's divinity was *maiestas*: treason, setting oneself up against the state, a crime punishable by death...
>
> [Under Trajan] Christians who appeared in court were to be given a chance to recant. It they repented of their faith and burnt a little incense to one of the gods or to Caesar, they were to be pardoned on the spot... Those bringing charges against [Christians] would have to prove their case in open court.
>
> This 'don't ask, don't tell' policy, which Trajan's successor, Hadrian, reaffirmed in another rescript in 124, became the official position of the Roman Empire toward Christians for nearly a century and a half."[139]

The discerning reader of Revelation must place themselves in either the Holy Land or Asia Minor (Turkey) during the first century AD. Only when we have sufficient context can we adequately resist the urge to place the prophecies of John in the future and make them about us. We can use what I call the "angry man" illustration: if you walk into work and there is a man there who looks angrily at you, many people will immediately assume the person is angry with them. But suppose you found out that man just learned he was wrongfully terminated. You would then contextualize his anger and realize he was not angry at you. In fact, *it had nothing to do with you*. This is how we must approach prophetic literature in the Bible.

> "Christians were subjected, often under duress, to one of two tests. They were required to either burn incense to the god

---

[139] Byfield, Ted. A Pinch of Incense : A.D. 70 to 250, from the Fall of Jerusalem to the Decian Persecution (Canada: Christian History Project, 2002), p 41, 46.
Author's note: This multi-volume work, broadly titled "The Christians: Their First Two Thousand Years", are phenomenal and worth purchasing. I own several and they are a wonderful resource.

Caesar... or swear by the emperor's 'genius', meaning his divine spirit. When Christians refused to do this they could be convicted of defying an imperial order and sentenced, frequently to death."[140]

Any surviving evidence that specifically points to an official start date of the requirement of a libellus has yet to be discovered. What has been discovered are dates as early as 250 AD. But it is likely that similar practices were either present or being introduced during the days of Nero.

"Certificate of sacrifice, testifying that a person during the Roman persecutions had offered sacrifice to the pagan gods. The officials were requited to superintend the sacrifices on a fixed day, receive in writing a statement from the person, and countersign the testimony in the name of the emperor. Many Christians apostatized; others bought certificates or had them procured by pagan friends. There seems to have been wholesale connivance by the officials. Those who refused to sacrifice were sentenced to prison or even death. A papyrus copy of a libellus, dating from A.D. 250, was discovered at Fayoum, Egypt. Its first part reads: 'To the Commissioners for sacrifices in the village of Alexander's island, from Aurelius Diogenes, son of Satabus, of the village of Alexander's island, aged 72; scar on right eyebrow.' The receipt of the presiding official reads: 'I certify that I witnessed his sacrifice, Aurelius Syrus. Dated this first year of the Emperor Caesar Gaius Messius Quintus Trajanus Decius, Pius, Felix, Augustus, the 2nd of Epiph. (26 Jun 250).'"[141]

COINS

As it is everywhere to this day, money was a big deal in Jewish Law and culture. The most ancient currencies were silver and gold, and their use goes all the way back to the Book of Genesis. A system of measuring the weight of these precious metals was standardized, and that is how the word "shekel",

---

[140] Ibid., p. 90.
[141] <https://www.catholicculture.org/culture/library/dictionary/index.cfm?id=34579>

meaning "weight", came into the vernacular. One ancient silver shekel weighed approximately 11 ounces.

> "By the laws of Moses, men and cattle, the possessing houses and fields, provisions, and all fines for offences, were regulated by the standard of the current value of silver. The same may be said of the contribution to the Temple, the sacrifice of animals, the redemption of the first-born, and the payment to the seer."[142]

In the fourth and second centuries BC, the Jews minted their own coins.[143] But this would not last. When the Holy Land became subject to the Roman Empire, the currencies of the Romans became status quo. By the second century BC, Rome had two royal mints in operation, one in Antioch and the other in Tyre. Here's where compromises began. Because the coins from Tyre were purer in silver than those from Antioch, the religious leaders decided to make them the official coin for the Temple Tax (aka Sacred Tribute, aka Temple Tribute).[144] But it came with a catch. The silver coins from Tyre (called "Tyrian shekels", "tetradrachma", or simply "drachma") had the god Melkhart (aka Hercules) on one side, and the inscription "Tyre the Holy and (City) of Refuge" on the other. This meant that the coffers of the Temple were filled with coins bearing the face of a pagan god.

Indeed, lots of money came into the Temple from all over the Known World, for many Jews and proselytes lived outside the Holy Land.[145] Cicero wrote,

> "As gold, under pretense of being given to the Jews, was accustomed every year to be exported out of Italy and all the provinces to Jerusalem."[146]

And Tacitus remarked,

> "[The Jews] always kept sending tribute and contributions to

---

[142] Madden, Frederic W.: Coins of the Jews. Trubner & Co., London, 1881, pp 2.
[143] Ibid., pp 65–69.
[144] Temple Tax origins: Exodus 30:13, Nehemiah 10:32–34. Also Matthew 17:24.
[145] Josephus, *Antiquities,* 18.313.
[146] M. Tullius Cicero. The Orations of Marcus Tullius Cicero, literally translated by C. D. Yonge, B. A. London. Henry G. Bohn, York Street, Covent Garden. 1856, pp 67.

Jerusalem, thereby increasing the wealth of the Jews..."[147]

One day, the Romans decided to shut down the mint in Tyre. What were the religious leaders to do if the only coin approved for the Temple Tax was going out of production? Jerusalem and Rome compromised: Rome agreed to continue to mint the coin, and Jerusalem agreed to let Rome keep the image of the pagan god on the coin so as to not stir the pot. The plot thickens.

This whole debacle of pagan coins minted for Temple use is part of the context of the time when Jesus overturns the tables of the money changers in the Gospels. Their job was to take every pagan coin and exchange it for the slightly less pagan Tyrian shekel or drachma, so that Jews and proselytes could pay their tribute to the Temple. Of course the exchange rate was pretty steep, making money-changing a profitable business.

"And Jesus entered the temple area and drove out all those who were selling and buying on the temple grounds, and He overturned the tables of the money changers..." Matthew 21:12

A fitting response. Other coins were used for the various taxes the Romans had imposed on their subjects.

"'Show Me the coin used for the poll-tax.' And they brought [Jesus] a denarius. And He said to them, 'Whose image and inscription is this?' They said to Him, 'Caesar's.' Then [Jesus] said to them, 'Then pay to Caesar the things that are Caesar's...' Matthew 22:19–21 (NASB)

About 20 years after Jesus uttered these words, the face engraved into those coins belonging to Caesar was Nero's.

> "[In the Roman Empire] standard coinage ... was discontinued in the late 50s [AD], eventually passing out of circulation. In its place, new coins were minted in Antioch with an image of Emperor Nero. This may in part explain 'buying and selling' in connection with 'the beast,' especially since the Greek term for 'mark' can refer to an image struck on a coin.[148]

Now you might be thinking, "Leo, this is a lot of information. What's the

---

[147] Tacitus, *Histories*, 5:1.
[148] Scott Hahn, Ed.: Revelation 13:17-18: Ignatius Catholic Study Bible, New Testament. Ignatius Press, San Francisco, 2010.

point?" Stay with me, we're almost there!

As I've written about in all three books of this series, in the mid 60's AD to late 70 AD, things hit a boiling point for both those under the Law of Moses and those following Yeshua the Messiah. As it relates to coins, which were the primary means of trade and daily life, things became even more difficult.

When the Jewish Revolt began in 66 AD, **Zealots captured the Temple from the Roman authorities in Judea and began minting coins.** For the next few years, they were able to mint silver shekels and bronze prutahs with inscriptions like "Jerusalem the Holy" (perhaps in jest to "Tyre the Holy") and "Freedom of Zion". This move was both a bold political and religious statement. But it would not last. Towards the end of 70 AD, Titus slaughtered most of the Zealots, burned the Temple, and killed all the priesthood.

> Hippolytus of Rome (c.170–235 AD): "Being full of guile and exalting himself against the servants of God, with the wish to afflict them and persecute them out of the world because they do not give glory to him, he will order incense pans to be set up by all everywhere, that no one among the saints may be able to buy or sell without first sacrificing. This is what is meant by the mark received upon the right hand…
>
> For in this way, too, did Antiochus Epiphanes the king of Syria, the descendant of Alexander of Macedon, devise measures against the Jews. He, too, in the exaltation of his heart, issued a decree in those times that 'all should set up shrines before their doors and sacrifice, and that they should march in procession to the honor of Dionysus, waving chaplets of ivy.'"[149]

The end of the Jewish-Roman war came with a three-fold insult to injury. First, all the wealth that accumulated for centuries in the Temple coffers from the tributes of those in and outside the Holy Land (which I mentioned earlier) went to Rome. So great were the spoils that the funding for the building of the famous Colosseum in Rome (which still stands today) came directly from the money in the Temple.

---

[149] William C. Weinrich, eds. *Revelation*. vol. 12 of Ancient Christian Commentary on Scripture. ICCS/Accordance electronic ed. (Downers Grove: InterVarsity Press, 2005), 207.

Second, the Jews' faithfulness in paying Temple Tax or Sacred Tribute gained the attention of the likes of Cicero and Tacitus and was used against them. A "Jewish Tax" (known as the "Fiscus Judaicus") was imposed on all Jews *after* the fall of Jerusalem in 70 AD. These funds were not exchanged for purer silver, and they were directed to the Temple of Jupiter in Rome.[150]

Third, when Vespasian (sent by Nero with Vespasian's son Titus to destroy the Jews) became Caesar of the Empire, he had commemorative coins minted in celebration of their victory over the Jews. The coins were stamped with the inscription "Judaea Capta" (Judea Conquered) on one side, and either a woman mourning or a male with his hands bound on the other side. These coins and other variants were minted for 25 years.[151]

> ℵ *(18) Here is wisdom: whoever has intelligence in him, let him calculate the number of the savage animal: the number of him who is indeed human: six hundred and sixty and six.*

SIX HUNDRED AND SIXTY AND SIX

In my opinion (et. al.), 13:16–18 are the most famous and most debated verses of the whole of Revelation. Entire books have been written about them. That won't be necessary here. To properly establish what these verses are about, there are only two things that must be established: one, the identity of the leopard (aka "the beast"), and two, the religious and cultural significance of the marking and branding for first-century Jews. From there, you are free to apply a Historicist or Idealist lens if you see fit. But not before one properly establishes how these two things impacted those bound under the Law of Moses in John's day. Remember: John's prophetic warning was for them first.

> "John is drawing on earlier Jewish and/or Jewish Christian traditions about Nero, for both groups had reason to despise Nero. Those who invented the numerical name 666 probably did not want outsiders to understand it, and gematria was a good way to convey the message. Like the number 888, which

---

[150] < https://www.jewishencyclopedia.com/articles/6157-fiscus-judaicus >
[151] Madden, Frederic W.: Coins of the Jews. Trubner & Co., London, 1881, pp 214–229.

is the numerical value of Jesus found in the Sibylline Oracles, this number conveyed the notion that the Emperor was in thrall to, or in league with, the forces of chaos and darkness."[152]

Some of the best commentaries on the Book of Revelation are the ones which provide the reader with an understanding of what is called the Hebrew Gematria. Gema-what? Simply put, long ago the Hebrew alphabet letters (the individual consonants or symbols) served not only as an alphabet to create words, but also as an alphanumerical system – like a cipher. It was highly efficient and similar to the more commonly known Roman numeral system: the letter I = 1; the letter V = 5; X = 10; C = 100; etc.

Gentry explains:

> "Because of the two-fold use of letters as both alphabets and numbering systems, cryptogrammic riddles were common in ancient cultures... In Rabbinic Hebrew such cryptograms were known as 'gematria' (from the Hebrew word for 'mathematical'). By the very nature of the case cryptograms almost invariably involved a riddle...
>
> Zahn provides us an example of a cryptogram discovered in excavations from Pompeii, which was buried by volcanic eruption in A.D. 79. In Greek the inscription written was: 'I love her whose number is 545'.
>
> The name of the lover is concealed; the beloved will know it when she recognizes her name in the sum of the numerical value of the 3 letters Φme i.e., 545 (Φ = 500 + m = 40 + e = 5)...
>
> In Suetonius's *Lives of the Twelve Caesars* we have recorded an interesting cryptogram from the first century. In the midst of his Latin history, Suetonius records a sample of a Greek lampoon that was circulated after the burning of Rome: 'A calculation new. Nero his mother slew.' It is interesting to note that "the numerical value of the Greek letters in Nero's name

---

[152] Witherington III, Ben: Revelation. Cambridge, United Kingdom, 2003, pp 184–185.

(1005) is the same as that of the rest of the sentence; hence we have an equation, Nero= the slayer of one's own mother. An additional example, also employing Nero's name, can be found in the Sibylline Oracles:

One who has fifty as an initial will be commander,

A terrible snake, breathing out grievous war, who one day will lay

hands on his own family and slay them, and throw everything into

confusion, athlete, charioteer, murderer, one who dares ten thousand things.

Here Nero's initial is recorded as possessing the value of 50.

Still another example is found in the Christian Sibylline Oracles (c. 150 AD):

Then indeed the son of the great God will come,

incarnate, likened to mortal men on earth,

bearing four vowels, and the consonants in him are two.

I will state explicitly the entire number for you.

For eight units, and equal number of tens in addition to these, and

eight hundreds will reveal the name.

As the translator notes: "Iesous [Jesus in Greek] has a numerical equivalence of 888.'" [153]

This leads us into the famous 666 enigma. Given that the immediate audience for whom John's prophecy was for, the Hebrew mind would have been able to make quick word of the gematria employed by John.

> "His readers would have guessed by now that he was speaking of Nero, and those who understood Hebrew probably grasped it instantly. The numerical values of the Hebrew letters in Neron Kesar (Nero Caesar) are:
>
> 50=נ

---

[153] Gentry, Kenneth L. Jr.: Before Jerusalem Fell. Institute for Christian Economics: Tyler, Texas, 1989, pp 194–195.

200=ר

6=ו

50=נ

100=ק

60=ס

200=ר

thus: 666= נרון קסר

...St. John's Biblically informed readers will have already recognized many clear indications of the Beast's identity as Rome indeed, they already knew this from reading the Book of Daniel). Now Nero has arrived on the scene as the first great persecutor of the Church..."

It is significant that all the earliest Christian writers on the Apocalypse, from Irenaeus down to Victorinus of Pettau and Commodian in the fourth, and Andreas in the fifth, and St. Beatus in the eighth century, connect Nero, or some Roman emperor, with the Apocalyptic Beast. There should be no reasonable doubt about this identification. St. John was writing to first-century Christians, warning them of things that were 'shortly' to take place." [154]

Even a non-Christian Greek Philosopher named Apollonius referred to Nero as a beast.

"[Nero's] tyranny has been established in this city so harsh and cruel, that it does not suffer men to be wise... Moreover, in traversing more of the earth than any man yet has visited, I have seen hosts of Arabian and Indian wild beasts; but as to this wild beast, which many call a tyrant, I know not either how many heads he has, nor whether he has crooked talons and jagged teeth. In any case, though this monster is said to be a social

---

[154] Chilton, David: The Days of Vengeance. Dominion Press, Ft. Worth, Texas, 1987, pp 350–351.

beast and to inhabit the heart of cities, yet he is also much wilder and fiercer in his disposition than animals of the mountain and forest, that whereas you can sometimes tame and alter the character of lions and leopards by flattering them, this one is only roused to greater cruelty than before by those who stroke him, so that he rends and devours all alike. And again there is no animal anyhow of which you can say that it ever devours its own mother, but Nero is gorged with such quarry [having killed his own mother]."[155]

It was a common practice for manuscripts and codices to have an introductory blurb in the header of a book or epistle. In the 12th century Crawford Syriac (dialect of Aramaic) manuscript of the Book of Revelation, the scribe or copyist who wrote out the text of John's vision, wrote the following in the header as an introduction:

"The Revelation which came to John The Evangelist from God
in Patmos, the island to which he was exiled by Nero Caesar."

I won't belabor this point any further. Scores of excellent commentaries and articles have been written on this subject. This single verse, verse 18 of chapter 13, is (ironically or even providentially) perhaps the *clearest* and most *unequivocal* of all the enigmatic verses in John's Apocalypse.

John's immediate audience didn't have the luxury of spending years pondering the gematria provided to them. The imminence of the tribulation against both lovers of Yeshua and those under the Law of Moses was at hand, and Nero was the catalyst. We know very well the history of the Great Fire of Rome in 66 AD, which led to the Neronian persecution of Christians. It was at that time that some were used as human torches to light up the streets of Rome.[156]

But most Christians today are ignorant to the calamities that the Jews and proselytes suffered, starting in 67 AD. Of course, I have gone to great length to bring these events to the forefront throughout this series. My point is this: readers of the Bible from the 2nd century onward have had the opportunity to make Revelation 13 whatever they wished it to mean, and with a few

---

[155] The Life of Apollonius of Tyana, by Philostratus, tr. F.C. Conybeare, [1912], at sacred-texts.com, Chapter 38, pp 438–439.
[156] Tacitus, *Annals* 15.44.

exceptions, suffered little to no consequence if (when) they got it wrong. But for John's audience it was different. It wasn't just the Christians who would suffer, it was the 1.1 million Jews who would be slaughtered and the other 97,000 that would be sold into the slave trade. That's what was at stake.

The heartbreaking reality is that, as far as we know, the warnings fell on deaf ears. This message of impending doom began with Jesus (Mt 24, 25; Lk 21, etc.) and continued on for the better part of 40 years through the mouths of his Apostles.

> *"This is now the second letter that I am writing to you, beloved. In both of them I am stirring up your sincere mind by way of reminder, that you should remember the predictions of the holy prophets and the commandment of the Lord and Savior through your apostles, knowing this first of all, that scoffers will come in the last days with scoffing, following their own sinful desires.*
>
> *They will say, 'Where is the promise of his coming? For ever since the fathers fell asleep, all things are continuing as they were from the beginning of creation.'*
>
> *But do not overlook this one fact, beloved, that with the Lord one day is as a thousand years, and a thousand years as one day. The Lord is not slow to fulfill his promise was some count slowness, but is patient toward you, not wishing that any should perish, but that all should reach repentance." 2 Peter 3:1–4, 8–9 (ESV)*

Nero, the instigator of such great suffering and turmoil for not just the people of Yahweh God, but indeed, much of the Roman Empire, would have Satan as his puppeteer. Persecution and then all-out war was coming from across the Mediterranean, through Asia Minor, then down into the Holy Land. Now, one thing that both Jews and Christians shared in common was a willingness to die for the sake of Yahweh if it came down to it. But the threat of Nero wasn't just death, it was a torturous life. *That* is the context for the verses (v.14–17) that precede the identity of Nero (v. 18).

I will quickly touch on the 616 variant. A very few but very old documents, such as the Greek Papyrus 115 (~225-275 AD) and the Codex Ephraemi Rescriptus have the number as χιϛ – 616. Because this has been so widely covered by scholars, I will summarize the consensus: Nero in Hebrew is Neron, while in Latin it is Nero. Neron in Hebrew equals 666, while Nero in Latin equals 616.[157] Most importantly, Irenaeus, a second century church leader, attested to 666 as the preferred reading (Haer. 5.30.1).

To conclude our discussion of Revelation chapter 13, I will cite Eusebius, the fourth century early church historian. Here he provides one of the best summaries of the story of Israel, the followers of Yeshua, and how Rome came into play in the first century AD. His description is fitting as it reminds us of all that took place within the lifetime of John's audience so that we may properly contextualize his prophetic book.

> "After Nero had held the power thirteen years, and Galba and Otho had ruled a year and six months, Vespasian, who had become distinguished in the campaigns against the Jews, was proclaimed sovereign in Judea and received the title of Emperor from the armies there. Setting out immediately, therefore, for Rome, he entrusted the conduct of the war against the Jews to his son Titus.

> "For the Jews after the ascension of our Saviour... had been devising as many plots as they could against his apostles. First Stephen was stoned to death by them, and after him James, the son of Zebedee and the brother of John, was beheaded, and finally James, the first that had obtained the episcopal seat in Jerusalem after the ascension of our Saviour, died in the manner already described [he was thrown off the pinnacle of the temple]. But the rest of the apostles, who had been incessantly plotted against with a view to their destruction, and had been driven out of the land of Judea, went unto all nations to preach the Gospel, relying upon the power of Christ, who had said to them, 'Go and make disciples of all the nations in my name.'

> "But the people of the church in Jerusalem had been commanded by a revelation, vouchsafed to approved men there before the war, to leave the city and to dwell in a certain town of Perea called Pella. And when those that believed in Christ had come there from Jerusalem, then, as if the royal city of the Jews and the whole land of Judea were entirely destitute of holy

---

[157] See Gentry, Before Jerusalem fell, pp 203–212, for a deeper dive.

men, the judgment of God at length overtook those who had committed such outrages against Christ and his apostles, and totally destroyed that generation of impious men.

"[Consider] the number of calamities which everywhere fell upon the nation at that time; the extreme misfortunes to which the inhabitants of Judea were especially subjected, the thousands of men, as well as women and children, that perished by the sword, by famine, and by other forms of death innumerable — all these things, as well as the many great sieges which were carried on against the cities of Judea, and the excessive sufferings endured by those that fled to Jerusalem itself... and how at last the abomination of desolation, proclaimed by the prophets, [Daniel 9:27] stood in the very temple of God, so celebrated of old, the temple which was now awaiting its total and final destruction by fire..."[158]

---

[158] Eusebius, *Church History,* Book 3, 5:1-4.

5 THE SHEEP AND THE GOATS: CH. 14

> *"And before Him shall be gathered all peoples, and He shall separate them one from another, as the shepherd separates the sheep from the goats. And He shall cause the sheep to stand upon his right hand, and the goats on his left."*
> Matthew 25:32–33 (Aramaic)

Chapter 14 of Revelation is packed with references to huge portions of Scripture. I've prayed over how to write out this chapter, and I feel like it would be a disservice to the Bible and the prophetic words John received if I were to try to just take snippets here and there of the passages being referenced. So instead, what you will find here is an invitation to take time and read through the entire portions of the Bible that will be cited.

Therefore, while this chapter will be relatively short, the additional reading from the Bible will make it whole. In the same way those under the Law were expected to be well versed in the Tanakh (Law, Prophets, and Writings), we too must have sufficient context as students of Revelation. So I trust you will take the time and do the necessary reading. Ask Holy Spirit to lead and guide you.

There are a few key themes in Revelation 14 at work. A brief overview will help us understand what is going on and what the vision seeks to explain. At the outset, we have a new Moses on a new Sinai with a new covenant given. The imagery then shifts to the Exile narrative, a time when Assyria and later Babylon were given legal right to destroy the Holy Land because the Jewish people had breached the terms of the Mosaic Covenant. Revelation draws heavily from Isaiah and Ezekiel, pulling on the imagery of adultery and harlotry which are central themes to the prophetic vision of John.

In the Exodus narrative, there was a separation of those who wanted to be in covenant with Yahweh and those who did not. So too here is a separation, and people are given a choice. Matthew 25 comes into focus as a key Scripture. Finally, Old Testament themes of restorative judgement that lead unto reconciliation abound. The wine of Yahweh's passion is painful, but through pain and fire is new life, with all things being made new!

> א *(1) And I saw and behold! The Lamb standing upon Mount Zion, and with him 144,000, who upon them there is his Name and the Name of his Father written upon their foreheads.*

The enigmatic 144,000 is covered in the previous book. Revelation 7:4–8 is where the census of the Twelve Tribes is first mentioned, and done so in greater detail.

> "The census is a specific form of list that occurs with some frequency in the OT, where it is used for purposes of taxation (Exod. 30:11–16; 2 Kgs. 15:19–20), for labor conscription (2 Chr. 2:17–18; cf. 1 Kgs. 5:13–18), for determining the cultic duties and social structure of members of the tribe of Levi (Num. 3:14–4:49), for determining Israelite descent (Ezra 2 and par. in Neh. 7 and 1 Esdr. 5), but most commonly as a means for determining military strength (Num. 1:2–46, esp. vv 2–3; 26:1– 56, esp. vv 1–2; 2 Sam. 24:1–9 [and par. 2 Chr. 21:1–6]; 2 Chr. 27:1–9)…
>
> The author's insistence on an equal number (12,000) from each of twelve tribes indicates his interest in the eschatological restoration of the twelve-tribe nation of Israel (Luke 22:30; 24:21; Acts 1:6). The eschatology of the late OT and early Jewish periods emphasized the hope of the restoration of Israel (Deut. 30:3–5; Isa. 11:11–16; 27:12–13; 49:5–6; 54:7–10; Jer.

31:7–14; Ezek. 37:15–23; Hos. 11:10–11; Pss. 106:47; 147:2; Bar. 5:5–9; 2 Macc. 2:7; Sir. 36:11; Tob. 13:13; 1 Enoch 57; 90:33; 4 Ezra 13:12–13, 39–47; 2 Apoc. Bar. 78:5–7; T. Jos. 19:4; Pss. Sol. 11:2–7; 17:26)."[159]

In short, one may consider these 144,000 as a firstfurits of a broader work of restoration for the people of Israel. As Paul wrote,

"God has not rejected His people whom He foreknew… In the same way then, there has also come to be at the present time a remnant according to God's gracious choice… But by their wrongdoing salvation has come to the Gentiles, to make them jealous. Now if their wrongdoing proves to be riches for the world, and their failure, riches for the Gentiles, how much more will their fulfillment be! …For if their rejection proves to be the reconciliation of the world, what will their acceptance be but life from the dead?

For if you [Gentiles] were cut off from what is by nature a wild olive tree, and contrary to nature were grafted into a cultivated olive tree, how much more will these [Jews] who are the natural branches be grafted into their own olive tree?

For I do not want you, brothers and sisters, to be uninformed of this mystery—so that you will not be wise in your own estimation—that a partial hardening has happened to Israel until the fullness of the Gentiles has come in; and so all Israel will be saved."
Romans 11:2, 5, 11, 12, 15, 24–26 (NASB)

Just… wow. If that doesn't challenge your soteriology then read it again! God's long plan is restoration. All of His judgements are restorative, not retributive.

I have to get into a bit of a digression here. In Romans 11, which we just read, Paul touches on the imagery of branches from an olive tree being cut off and then grafted in. I want to pick up on this as it will tie into the

---

[159] Aune, David E.: Revelation. Zondervan Academic, Grand Rapids, Michigan, 2017, 6–16, pp 436.

judgement verses here in Revelation 14. Our understanding of what it means to be cut off and grafted is *crucial* to our understanding of the purpose and nature of judgement. This learning will also serve us well when we get to Revelation 20 and the final judgement.

BRANCHES CUT OFF AND BURNED

First we need to go to the Hebrew Scriptures. This is the backbone of the two New Testament passages I will then follow with. We will be reading from Ezekiel 15.

> *"Son of man, you live in the midst of the rebellious house, who have eyes to see but do not see, ears to hear but do not hear; for they are a rebellious house. So as for you, son of man, prepare for yourself baggage for exile and go into exile by day in their sight; that is, go into exile from your place to another place in their sight. Perhaps they will understand, though they are a rebellious house… And I will bring him to Babylon in the land of the Chaldeans… So they will know that I am the Lord, when I disperse them among the nations and scatter them among the countries."*
> *Ezekiel 13:2, 3, 13, 15 (NASB)*

Within Ezekiel, we first need context. One of Ezekiel's assignments was to prophecy to the house of Israel. He was to explain to them why they were going to be taken into exile and why Yahweh would allow the Temple and Jerusalem to be destroyed. As I wrote in the previous book, John's ministry was very similar to Ezekiel's.

In light of this, we read:

> *"Son of man, how is the wood of the vine better than any wood of a branch which is among the trees of the forest? …If it has been put into the fire for fuel, and the fire has consumed both of its ends and its middle part has been charred, is it then good for anything? …Therefore, this is what the Lord God says: 'As the wood of the vine among the trees of the forest, which I have given to the fire for fuel, so have I given up the inhabitants of Jerusalem; and I set My face against them. Though they have come out of the fire, yet the fire will consume them. Then you will know that I am the Lord, when I set My face against them. So I will make the land desolate, because they have acted unfaithfully,'" declares the Lord God."*
> *Ezekiel 15:2, 4, 6–8 (NASB)*

Scary. Very scary. But there is always hope. God then shifts the imagery from burning bushes to an unfaithful wife. But the theme is the same: Israel will eat what it has sown… Until God's loving-kindness intervenes.

> *"Son of man, make known to Jerusalem her abominations, and say, 'This is what the Lord God says to Jerusalem: "Your origin and your birth are from the land of the Canaanite; your father was an Amorite and your mother a Hittite… When I passed by you and saw you squirming in your blood, I said to you while you were in your blood, 'Live!' Yes, I said to you while you were in your blood, 'Live!' …*
>
> *Then I passed by you and saw you, and behold, you were at the time for love; so I spread My garment over you and covered your nakedness. I also swore an oath to you and entered into a covenant with you so that you became Mine," declares the Lord God… Then your fame spread among the nations on account of your beauty, for it was perfect because of My splendor which I bestowed on you," declares the Lord God.*
>
> *But you trusted in your beauty and became unfaithful because of your fame, and you poured out your obscene practices on every passer-by to whom it might be tempting… Furthermore, you took your sons and daughters whom you had borne to Me and sacrificed them to idols to be devoured [in Gehenna's fire]…*
>
> *You adulteress wife, who takes strangers instead of her husband! …therefore, behold, I am going to gather all your lovers whom you pleased, all those whom you loved as well as all those whom you hated. So I will gather them against you from every direction and expose your nakedness to them so that they may see all your nakedness. So I will judge you as women who commit adultery or shed blood are judged; and I will bring on you the blood of wrath and jealousy." Ezekiel 16:2, 3, 6, 8, 14, 15, 20, 32, 37, 38 (NASB)*

Scary, again. A really cool story though. You should just read all of Ezekiel 16! It's fascinating. So we have lots of judgment going on. Israel is doomed. For sure these people were sent to burn in hell forever, right?

> *"Nevertheless, I will restore their fortunes, the fortunes of Sodom and her daughters [see Genesis 13:10], the fortunes of Samaria and her daughters,*

and along with them your own fortunes, so that you will bear your disgrace and feel ashamed for all that you have done when you become a consolation to them. Your sisters, Sodom with her daughters and Samaria with her daughters, will return to their former state, and you with your daughters will also return to your former state… I will remember My covenant with you in the days of your youth, and I will establish an everlasting covenant with you… when I have forgiven you for all that you have done,' the Lord God declares." Ezekiel 16:53–55, 60, 63 (NASB)

Ezekiel 16:53-63 is the magic key that unlocks the mystery of the fruitless branches being burned and Jerusalem the harlot being destroyed. It was all a process unto restoration. Jerusalem will be restored to her virgin youth. Sodom and Gomorrah will be restored to their former state, which was like the Garden of Eden (Gen 13:10). Does your heart not burn right now? Mine does!

Now let's go to Jesus.

*"Every branch in Me that does not bear fruit, He **props up** [Aramaic]; and every branch that bears fruit, He prunes it so that it may bear more fruit… If anyone does not remain in Me, he is thrown away like a branch and dries up; and they gather them and throw them into the fire, and they are burned." John 15:2, 6 (NASB)*

What happened in Ezekiel 15? Yahweh would allow the inhabitants of the Holy Land to be taken like wood and burned. If you only read chapter 15, you would be terrified of Yahweh God. But then you get to chapter 16 and see his heart is to restore. In the same way, we must understand that Jesus is not speaking of an eschatological burning. He is speaking of this lifetime, where we are tried and purified by fire.

Looking at the Targums (Aramaic copies of the Old Testament), consider how Ezekiel 15 was written:

> "And I will set My vengeance against them. Though they have transgressed the words of the Torah, which were given from the midst of the fire, the Gentiles, who are as mighty as fire, will destroy them, and you will know that I am the Lord, when

My wrath comes to rest upon them." (Ezekiel 15:7)[160]

These fires were Gentiles, which in this case were the Babylonians who destroyed them! It was never something in the afterlife.

Then there is Paul.

> *For if you [Gentiles] were cut off from what is by nature a wild olive tree, and contrary to nature were grafted into a cultivated olive tree, how much more will these [Jews] who are the natural branches be grafted into their own olive tree?*
>
> *For I do not want you, brothers and sisters, to be uninformed of this mystery—so that you will not be wise in your own estimation—that a partial hardening has happened to Israel until the fullness of the Gentiles has come in; and so all Israel will be saved."*
> Romans 11:2, 5, 11, 12, 15, 24–26 (NASB)

As a master of the Torah and a disciple of Yeshua, Paul brought home both Ezekiel 15 and Jesus' words in John 15. Branches may be cut off, but they are grafted back in to be restored.

This was a huge detour, but a necessary one. It's the only way we will be able to navigate verses 7 to 20 of Revelation 14.

Now to quickly finish Revelation 14:1!

THE LAMB STANDING UPON MOUNT ZION

Exodus language. Again.

> *"For you have not come to a mountain that can be touched and to a blazing fire, and to darkness and gloom and whirlwind… And so terrible was the sight, that Moses said, 'I am terrified and trembling.' But you have come*

---

[160] Ezekiel 15:7 TARG-E
<https://accordance.bible/link/read/TARG-E#Ezek._15:7>

to Mount Zion and to the city of the living God, the heavenly Jerusalem, and to myriads of angels, to the general assembly and church of the firstborn who are enrolled in heaven, and to God, the Judge of all, and to the spirits of the righteous made perfect, and to Jesus, the mediator of a new covenant, and to the sprinkled blood, which speaks better than the blood of Abel." Hebrews 12:18–24 (NASB)

Because these saints are with Jesus, who is symbolically the new Moses, and because they are now under God's new covenant, the Shema is brought to remembrance. They have the name of Jesus and Yahweh written on them, just as in Exodus 19 and Deuteronomy 6 and 11.

> א *(2) Then I heard the sound from Heaven like the sound of many waters, like the sound of a great thunder; the sound which I heard was like a lyrists strumming on his lyre.*

> א *(3) And they were praising according to a new song of worship before the throne and before the four creatures and before the elders! But no one was able to teach themselves the song of worship, except for 144,000 who were being ransomed from the Land.*

Verse 3 clearly indicates that the 144,000, the firstfruits remnant of God's future restoration, were those "being ransomed" from the Holy Land. Jews under the Law of Moses were being ransomed out of the contractual obligations of that covenant, and brought into the new covenant – Sinai to Zion – religious slavery to grace-filled freedom.

> *"For all who are of works of the Law are under a curse; for it is written: 'Cursed is everyone who does not abide by all the things written in the book of the Law, to do them.' Now, that no one is justified by the Law before God is evident; for, 'the righteous one will live by faith.' However, the Law is not of faith; on the contrary, 'The person who performs them will live by them.'" Christ redeemed us from the curse of the Law, having become a curse for us...*
> *But when the fullness of the time came, God sent His Son, born of a woman, born under the Law, so that He might redeem those who were under the Law, that we might receive the adoption as sons and daughters.*

Because you are sons, God has sent the Spirit of His Son into our hearts, crying out, 'Abba! Father!

...Tell me, you who want to be under law, do you not listen to the Law? For it is written that Abraham had two sons, one by the slave woman and one by the free woman... for these women are two covenants: one coming from Mount Sinai giving birth to children who are to be slaves; she is Hagar. **Now this Hagar is Mount Sinai in Arabia and corresponds to the present Jerusalem, for she is enslaved with her children.** *But the Jerusalem above is free; she is our mother." Galatians 3:10–13, 4:4–6, 21–22, 24–26, emphasis mine (NASB)*

Let's continue. We are going to go through verses 4 to 11 in one shot. As you read, keep these connections in mind:

Age = a fixed covenant period of time.
Babylon = Apostate Israel.
the Land = the Land of Israel.

And further down, when we hit verse 20, "City" can only mean Jerusalem.

א *(4) These are those who have not stained themselves with women, for they are chaste. These cleave to the Lamb everywhere he goes. These were redeemed from mortals, the firstfruits to God and to the Lamb.*

א *(5) From within their mouths, falsehood does not find itself, as they are without blemish.*

א *(6) Then I saw another angel flying in the midst of the heavens.[161] And there was upon him the tidings which are for an age; to proclaim unto the dwellers of the Land, and unto all people, nations,*
א *tribes and languages, (7) saying with a great voice:*

*"Be in reverence of God and be giving Him glory,
because the hour of His judgment[162] has come!
So bow down to Him who made the heavens, and the*

---

[161] The addition "who with blood", is not found in the Aramaic texts.
[162] דִּין *diyn* also means "lawsuit, court case".

              Land, and the Sea,[163] and the springs of water!"

א   *(8) Then another, a second, was connected to him and he was saying:*

            'Fallen, fallen, the great Babylon, who caused the whole of the Gentiles to drink from the fiery-passion[164] of her harlotry!'

א   *(9) Then another angel, a third, connected to them, spoke with a great voice:*

            "Whomever bows down to the savage animal and its
א   *genius and bares[165] its mark on his forehead, (10) indeed, he will drink from the wine of the fiery-passion[166] of Yahweh, which is mixed without dilution in the cup of his indignation,[167] and he will be severely chastised[168] in fire and [launder's] sulfur,[169] in the presence of the holy*
א   *angels and in the presence of the Lamb. [170] (11) And the smoke of their anguish will rise at the Age of Ages.*

---

[163] יַמֹא *yamo'* here implies the "Great Sea", i.e. The Mediterranean.

[164] חֶמְתֹא *chemto'* is literally "anger, wrath, fury". But in context here, it means to burn with passion or lust.

[165] שְׁקַל *shqal* means "to lift, take up, bear".

[166] חמר (wine) of חמת (passion) is a phonetic wordplay, loosely sounding like "hemar hemmah." Only one letter differentiates the two words.

[167] Most translations have "wrath" or "anger". My translation is not an attempt to water down the Bible. It is an attempt to best capture the context of the word, which in turn reflects the character of God. In Mark 3:17, John and James are called B'nai-Regesh, Sons of Thunder. Regesh (thunder) comes from the same root word used here in Revelation 14:10. According to Marcus Jastrow's Dictionary, the word רוגז in Revelation 14:10 can mean "excitement, anger, commotion, trouble". While William Jennings' Lexicon has "anger, indignation". Within the context of the "wine of the passion of Yahweh" in this verse, the tone of the word is one of indignation.

[168] Or "severely punished". See Payne Smith, *A Compendious Syriac Dictionary*, p. 587, and William Jennings, *Lexicon to the Syriac New Testament*, p. 227.

[169] In the Aramaic (Peshitta) Malachi 3:2, the prophet wrote, ܟܒܪܝܬܐ ܕܩܨܪܐ "launder's sulfur / fuller's brimstone". Here is the verse: ܐܝܟ ܢܘܪܐ ܗܘ ܓܝܪ ܕܨܪܦ. ܘܐܝܟ ܟܒܪܝܬܐ ܕܩܨܪܐ. Literally "(He) is like the fire which purifies and like the sulfur for washing." Revelation 14:10–11 is a fulfillment of Malachi 3. See also Payne Smith, *A Compendious Syriac Dictionary*, p. 204.

[170] Other manuscripts read, "in the presence of the throne".

REVELATION: DAWN OF ETERNITY

For there isn't breathing space, day or night, for those who bow down to the savage animal and its genius, and for him who bares the brand of its name.

To recap, Revelation 14 begins with Jesus as the Lamb standing with a symbolic number of Believers (144,000) who had been delivered from the Roman invasion of the Holy Land and Jerusalem (by fleeing to the region of Pella, East of ancient Israel). Then three angels fly over Jerusalem (likened to Babylon) and begin to speak of her destruction. Sadly, this means that many would perish by famine, plague, or the Roman sword. The ensuing verses then begin to focus in on the temporal (not eternal) fate of the individuals that would perish.

There are a total of five "day and night" (literally: "the day and the night") statements in Revelation, found in 4:8, 7:15, 12:10, here in 14:11, and 20:10. They all have one common denominator: they are employed to illustrate verbs that take place in the heavenly or spiritual realm. In other words, a literal device (day and night) is used to try to explain events taking place in a reality that is outside of the confines of time and space, or at minimum, not of the earth we walk upon. So in the same way heaven does not have a 24-hour clock, nor does its calendar depend upon the rotation of the earth around the sun, we must embrace the fact that we are dealing with a realm beyond the confines of our reality. In short, this is not flesh that is burning, but hearts (cf. Mark 7:18–23).

Central to the block we just read above is verse 10b: *"and he will be severely chastised in fire and [launder's] sulfur, in the presence of the holy angels and in the presence of the Lamb."* An unmistakable reference to Malachi 3, Revelation 14:10b places Yeshua as the key figure within Malachi's prophecy. Here are the prophet's words from the Aramaic (Peshitta) Old Testament:

> "Behold, I am sending my Messenger and he shall clear the road before me, and suddenly he whom you expect shall come to the temple of LORD JEHOVAH, and the Messenger of the covenant in whom you delight, behold, he comes, says LORD JEHOVAH of Hosts! Who endures the day in which he comes, or who can be standing when he is revealed? Because he is like the fire of a refiner and like lye that bleaches [lit. "launder's sulfur"]. For he shall return to refine and to purify as silver and he shall purify the sons of Levi and he shall purge them like gold and like silver, and they shall be bringing an offering to

LORD JEHOVAH in righteousness. And the offering of Judea and of Jerusalem will delight LORD JEHOVAH as the days of old and like the years of former time. And I shall come near to you in judgment..." Malachi 3:1–5a (Aramaic)[171]

FIRE, SULFUR AND THE FULLER

A plain reading of Revelation 14:10 has for centuries left people believing that people will be burned alive with no end in sight. Worse still, people believe that this will take place in front of Jesus and his angels in a sort of Roman-style spectacle that was put on before the Caesars and their court at the Colosseum. But this is disastrous theologically; in fact, it is dangerous. A better conclusion hinges on our understanding of the symbolism behind fire and sulfur.

The Bible tells us that fire has to do with divine presence and essence. It is a physical expression or manifestation of a spiritual reality. Here are some examples:

- *"The LORD your God is a consuming fire." Deut 4:24*
- *"The Lord your God will Himself go before you, a devouring and consuming fire." Deut 9:3*
- *"the sight of the glory of the LORD was like a consuming fire." Ex 24:17*
- *"I baptize you with water for repentance. But after me comes one who... will baptize you with the Holy Spirit and fire." Matt 3:11*
- *"[God] cleansed the bloodstains from the heart of Jerusalem by a spirit of judgment and a spirit of fire." Isa 4:4*
- *"Is not my word like fire," declares the Lord, "and like a hammer that breaks the rock in pieces?" Jer 23:29*
- *"...[And] on that which resembled a throne, high up, was a figure with the appearance of a man. Then I noticed from the appearance of His waist and upward something like gleaming metal that looked like fire all around within it, and from the appearance of His waist*

---

[171] Bauscher, David. The Holy Peshitta Bible Translated, Lulu.com. Kindle Edition. Page 1791.

and downward I saw something like fire; and there was a radiance around Him. Like the appearance of the rainbow in the clouds on a rainy day, so was the appearance of the surrounding radiance. Such was the appearance of the likeness of the glory of the Lord." Eze 1:26–28

- *"Then one of the seraphim flew to me with a burning coal in his hand, which he had taken from the altar with tongs. He touched my mouth with it and said, 'Behold, this has touched your lips; and your guilt is taken away and atonement is made for your sin.'" Isa 6:6–7*
- *"And there were seven lamps of fire burning before the throne, which are the seven spirits of God." Rev 4:5*
- *"And I saw something like a sea of glass mixed with fire, and those who were victorious over the beast and his image and the number of his name, standing on the sea of glass, holding harps of God." Rev 15:2*
- *"His head and His hair were white like white wool, like snow; and His eyes were like a flame of fire. His feet were like burnished bronze when it has been heated to a glow in a furnace." Rev 1:14–15*

Going back to Malachi 3, fire has a very specific purpose:

"And He will sit as a smelter and purifier of silver, and He will purify the sons of Levi and refine them like gold and silver, so that they may present to the Lord offerings in righteousness." Malachi 3:3 (NASB)

There is then the enigmatic paring of sulfur (aka brimstone) with fire. In antiquity, sulfur was used as a bleaching agent to whiten things such a clothes. Pliny the Elder, a Roman who wrote an encyclopedia called *Natural History* in the 1st century AD, gives us context for sulfur in the ancient world.

"There are four kinds of sulphur; the first of which is 'live' sulphur, known as 'apyron' by the Greeks… and is the only sulphur that is used for medicinal purposes. A second kind is known as the 'glebaceous' sulphur, and is solely employed in the workshops of the fullers. The third kind, also, is only used for a single purpose, that of fumigating wool, a process which contributes very greatly to making the wool white and soft; 'egula' is the name given to it. The fourth kind is used in the preparation of matches more particularly.

In addition to these several uses, sulphur is of such remarkable virtue... Applied to the loins and kidneys, with grease, when there are pains in those parts, it is marvellously effectual as a remedy. In combination with turpentine, it removes lichens on the face, and leprosy... in combination, too, with sandarach and vinegar, it is good for diseases of the eyelids... Sulphur has its place among our religious ceremonies, being used as a fumigation for purifying houses. Its virtues are also to be perceived in certain hot mineral waters; and there is no substance that ignites more readily, a proof that there is in it a great affinity to fire."[172]

What on earth was a *fuller*? If you recall, the Aramaic (Peshitta) version of Malachi 3:2 reads, *"But who can endure the day of his coming, and who can stand when he appears? For he is like a refiner's fire and like fullers' sulfur."* Understand that in ancient times, sulfur was used to whiten clothes. In this context, Malachi makes a little more sense. But what was a fuller?

Fulling has a long history. In antiquity, it was a process of washing, treating, and finishing wool clothes. In the Roman Empire, there were even fulling shops knowns as "fulleries" (fullonicae), and fullones were like laundromat workers. It was a full time job, and the work was labor-intensive. What matters most to us is *how* the fullers did their job. Fulling was a three part process that was quite symbolic:

1. Cleaning: in a wash basin or stall, the fuller would often use urine (for the alkaline chemical it contains)[173] and trample the garments with their feet. They didn't use soap.
2. Rinsing: the wool clothing was then completely immersed in clean water.
3. Finishing: the articles were then exposed to heat in order to dry. After the wool was dry, it was brushed in order to fluff it out. Lastly,

---

[172] *The Natural History. Pliny the Elder.* John Bostock, M.D., F.R.S. H.T. Riley, Esq., B.A. London. Taylor and Francis, Red Lion Court, Fleet Street. 1855. 35:50.
[173] Fun fact: Emperor Vespasian even imposed a "urine tax" on fullers. See Suetonius, *Vespasian*, 23.

"clothes were then hung on a vessel of basket-work (viminea cavea), under which sulphur was placed in order to whiten the cloth."[174]

Sulfur was part of the *finishing* process. It *restored* the garment's color back to its former glory. *"Though your sins are as scarlet, They shall become as white as snow; Though they are red like crimson, They shall be like wool"* (Isaiah 1:18). A bit later, in Revelation 14:20, we read of the trampling that took place in the great winepress. So too in the fulling process the garments are trampled upon. The winepress was unto new wine, but the fulling was part of cleansing. The garments were then baptized in water, a fitting image. Now this entire digression assumes that Revelation 14:10 is an allusion to Malachi 3:2. I'm convinced it is. Everyone, all who have ever and will ever live, will pass through the purifying fire of God, either in this life or the next.

> *"I have come to cast fire upon the earth; and how I wish it were already kindled!" Luke 12:49*

> *"For everyone will be salted with fire." Mark 9:49*

> *"each one's work will become evident; for the day will show it because it is to be revealed with fire, and the fire itself will test the quality of each one's work... If anyone's work is burned up, he will suffer loss; but he himself will be saved, yet only so as through fire." 1 Corinthians 3:13, 15*

Revelation 14:10–11 is also the fulfillment of the enigmatic words of John the Baptist and Jesus Christ himself:

> *"And the axe is already laid at the root of the trees; therefore, every tree that does not bear good fruit is being cut down and thrown into the fire. As for me, I baptize you [with water for repentance, but He who is coming after me is mightier than I, and I am not fit to remove His sandals; He will baptize you with the Holy Spirit and fire. His winnowing fork is in His hand, and He will thoroughly clear His threshing floor; and He will gather His wheat into the barn, but He will burn up the chaff with unquenchable fire." Matthew 3:10–12 (NASB)*

> *"'Explain to us the allegory of the darnel [tares] of the field.' And He*

---

[174] William Smith, D.C.L., LL.D.: *A Dictionary of Greek and Roman Antiquities*, John Murray, London, 1875. pp551-553.

answering said to them, 'He who is sowing the good seed is the Son of Man, and the field is the world, and the good seed, these are the sons of the kingdom, and the darnel [tares] are the sons of the evil one, and the enemy who sowed them is the Devil, and the harvest is [the] full end of the age, and the reapers are messengers. As, then, the darnel [tares] is gathered up, and is burned with fire, so will it be in the full end of this age; the Son of Man will send forth His messengers, and they will gather up out of His kingdom all the stumbling-blocks, and those doing the lawlessness, and will cast them into the furnace of the fire; there will be the weeping and the gnashing of the teeth. Then will the righteous shine forth as the sun in the kingdom of their Father. He who is having ears to hear—let him hear.'"
Matthew 13:36–43 (LSV)

Jesus ends in verse 43 with a cross-reference to Daniel 12 (hence, having "ears to hear"). So we need to insert Daniel 12 as well:

"And at that time stand up doth Michael, the great head, who is standing up for the sons of thy people, and there hath been a time of distress, such as hath not been since there hath been a nation till that time, and at that time do thy people escape, every one who is found written in the book.
And the multitude of those sleeping in the dust of the ground do awake, some to life age-during, and some to reproaches -- to abhorrence age-during.
And those teaching do shine as the brightness of the expanse, and those justifying the multitude as stars to the age and for ever.
And thou, O Daniel, hide the things, and seal the book till the time of the end, many do go to and fro, and knowledge is multiplied."
Daniel 12:1–4 (YLT)

I know that was quite a bit of Scripture reading. How does it all fit in? John was addressing the religious leaders, saying they would not escape the coming judgement. In Matthew 23, Jesus says the same thing to the same group. Matthew 13 talks about a judgement at the end of that age, which was the Age of Moses. And Daniel also prophesied concerning the same event. The fire burns away all the chaff, all the darnel, all the dross, all that we were never created to be. The process pains the spirit and soul, but the end is a thoroughly refined substance.

"But Daniel spoke of multitudes sleeping in the dust awakening. Isn't that the final resurrection?" you may be thinking. No, because the 1,290 days and 1,335 days at the end of Daniel 12 (as well as the weeks of Daniel 9) correspond with the fall of Jerusalem in 70 AD, starting when Eleazer ceased the daily Temple sacrifices on behalf of the Caesars in 66 AD. Further, "awakening" seems to have been a common Jewish expression for calling people to repentance:

For this reason it says,
'Awake, sleeper,
And arise from the dead,
And Christ will shine on you.'
So then, be careful how you walk, not as unwise people but as wise, making the most of your time, because the days are evil."
Ephesians 5:14–16 (NASB)

(See also Romans 13:11 and Isaiah 51:17; 52:1; and 60:1.)

This is why verses 12 and 13 below remind the followers of Yeshua to keep persevering. The stakes were high, and the 40 year window of two overlapping covenants was coming to an end. "The one who endures until the end will <u>live</u>" (Matthew 24:13, Aramaic), speaking of the end of the Age of Moses and that time of tribulation.

א *(12) Here is the perseverance of those who are holy, those who keep the commands of God and the faith of Yeshua."*

א *(13) And I heard a voice from Heaven that said,*

> *"Write, 'Blessed are the dead who have departed in Yahweh from now. Yes, says The Spirit, because they shall be at rest from their labors.'"*

א *(14) Now behold! A white cloud, and upon the cloud sat one like a man. And upon his head there was a crown of gold, and in his hand a sharp sickle.*

א *(15) Then another angel went out from the Temple. And it shouted with a loud voice to him sitting on the cloud,*

> *"Send your sickle and reap, because the hour for harvesting has come."*

א *(16) So he who sat upon the cloud thrust his sickle upon the Land,*

and the Land was harvested.

א *(17) But another angel went out from the Temple which is in*
א *Heaven, and there was with him a sharp sickle, (18) and another angel went out from the altar, who had authority over the fire, and he shouted with a loud voice to him who had the sharp sickle with him:*

> *"Send your sharp sickle and pluck the clusters from the vineyard of the Land, because its grapes are ripe."*

א *(19) So the angel thrust his sickle upon the Land and plucked the vineyard of the Land. And he cast them in the great winepress of the fiery-passion of God.*

That chapter 14 begins with Jerusalem (v. 1, Mt Zion) and ends with Jerusalem (v. 20, "outside the *City*") keeps us from wandering off into a distant, doomsday future event. To the Jewish audience John was commissioned to prophecy to, Yerushalayim (Jerusalem) was central to their religious, cultural, and theocratic existence. The historical backdrop continues to be the holocaust of AD 66 to 73, the Jewish-Roman War.

Jesus' prophetic parables provide us with interpretive clues as well. John's vision here bears a striking semblance with the word-pictures used by our Lord. Therefore, I'm providing us with a large chunk of Scripture in order for us to receive the full benefit of the intertextual interpretation available. The passages are taken from Matthew 13 and 25, and all are the words of Jesus:

> *18 "Therefore hear the parable of the sower: 19 When anyone hears the word of the kingdom, and does not understand it, then the wicked one comes and snatches away what was sown in his heart... 23 But he who received seed on the good ground is he who hears the word and understands it, who indeed bears fruit and produces: some a hundredfold, some sixty, some thirty."*

> *24 Another parable He put forth to them, saying: "The kingdom of heaven is like a man who sowed good seed in his field; 25 but while men slept, his enemy came and sowed tares among the wheat and went his way.*

26 But when the grain had sprouted and produced a crop, then the tares also appeared. 27 So the servants of the owner came and said to him, 'Sir, did you not sow good seed in your field? How then does it have tares?' 28 He said to them, 'An enemy has done this.' The servants said to him, 'Do you want us then to go and gather them up?' 29 But he said, 'No, lest while you gather up the tares you also uproot the wheat with them. 30 Let both grow together until the harvest, and at the time of harvest I will say to the reapers, 'First gather together the tares and bind them in bundles to burn them, but gather the wheat into my barn.'"

36 …Then Jesus sent the multitude away and went into the house. And His disciples came to Him, saying, "Explain to us the parable of the tares of the field."

37 He answered and said to them: "He who sows the good seed is the Son of Man. 38 The field is the world, the good seeds are the sons of the kingdom, but the tares are the sons of the wicked one. 39 The enemy who sowed them is the devil, the harvest is the end of the age, and the reapers are the angels. 40 Therefore as the tares are gathered and burned in the fire, so it will be at the end of this age. 41 The Son of Man will send out His angels, and they will gather out of His kingdom all things that offend, and those who practice lawlessness, 42 and will cast them into the furnace of fire. There will be wailing and gnashing of teeth. 43 Then the righteous will shine forth as the sun in the kingdom of their Father. He who has ears to hear, let him hear!

44 "Again, the kingdom of heaven is like treasure hidden in a field, which a man found and hid; and for joy over it he goes and sells all that he has and buys that field.

45 "Again, the kingdom of heaven is like a merchant seeking beautiful pearls, 46 who, when he had found one pearl of great price, went and sold all that he had and bought it.

47 "Again, the kingdom of heaven is like a dragnet that was cast into the sea and gathered some of every kind, 48 which, when it was full, they drew to shore; and they sat down and gathered the good into vessels, but threw the bad away. 49 So it will be at the end of the age. The angels will come forth, separate the wicked from among the just, 50 and cast them into the furnace of fire. There will be wailing and gnashing of teeth."

51 Jesus said to them, "Have you understood all these things?"

They said to Him, "Yes, Lord." Matthew 13, abridged (NKJV)

"And before Him shall be gathered all people, and He shall separate them one from another, as the shepherd separates the sheep from the goats. And He shall cause the sheep to stand upon his right hand, and the goats on his left. Then shall the King say to them on His right hand: 'come, blessed of My Father, inherit the kingdom which was to be for you from the inception of the age...'

Then shall He say also unto them on His left hand: 'remove yourselves from me, O accursed ones, to the fire which is for an age, which was intended for the accuser and for his angels...'

So these ones shall be removed for anguish which is for an age, but the righteous ones to the life which is for an age."
Matthew 25:32–34, 41, 46 (Aramaic)

Once again you've made it through one of my large Scripture reading assignments! Per usual, lots of strong images, theological bombs, and so forth. We need to narrow the focus to the topic at hand, which is Revelation 14. Here are a few themes from Jesus' teachings that I will highlight:

- In both Matthew 13 and 25, we are dealing with an age – an epoch season, a period of time with a beginning and an end. Jesus was speaking of the Mosaic Age and the judgment that came at the end of that age.
- Layered into the parables of wheat and tares are the parables of the treasure in the field and the Merchant and the pearls (Matt 13:44-46). It's important to understand that *Jesus* is the one who sold everything to buy the field because *we* were the treasure hidden in the field. And *we* are the beautiful pearls that mesmerized *Jesus,* who was the Merchant. He gave everything up so that he could ransom us from sin and death.
- In Matthew 13, Satan had a part to play with the seed that didn't bear fruit and the tares mixed in with the wheat. This is part of the Divine mystery of how things work in life.

- When men and women, all of whom were made in the image of God and have His breath of life in their lungs, are exposed to fire, it is always unto purification and restoration (this will be a key theme we shall explore in Revelation 20).

This isolated judgement was exclusive to those bound under the Law of Moses. Those judged would be the ones who refused the deliverance made available to them in the new covenant which would necessitate them bear the consequences for breach of the old covenant (see Deuteronomy 28;15-68). They are the ones who were gathered into the fire (Matt 25, goats sent to fire) to be purified and refined (as per the Refiner's Fire and Launder's Sulfur explanation above).

> ℵ *(20) And the winepress was trodden outside of the City. And the blood from the winepress went up to the horses' bridles, for twelve hundred stadia."*[175]

This graphic image was typical of ancient Near Eastern hyperbole. *"From dawn until the sun sets, they shall slay each other. The horse shall walk through the blood of sinners up to his chest; and the chariot shall sink down up to its top,"* (1 Enoch 100:2-3). Indeed, it was even typical of Jewish writers recounting their own history. After the Jewish-Roman War of AD 66-73, in the second century, Jewish rebels attempted another revolt against Rome (known as the Bar Kokhba revolt, AD 132–136). The following was written concerning this second war:

> "They [the Romans] slew the [Jewish] inhabitants until the horses waded in blood up to the nostrils, and the blood rolled

---

[175] 1200, not 1600. "Greek mss. have "a thousand, six hundred stadia"; the Greek ms. Aleph (a, 4th cent.) has "a thousand two hundred", as does the Philoxenian Syriac Version (early 6th c)… If the Aramaic is the original, how did most Greek mss. get 600 instead of 200? Ah, but the Aramaic *nytamw* is 600 and 200! How? The Aramaic language uses letters for numbers as well as words. *nytamw* can mean "and two hundred" (which it most likely does) or it can be interpreted as (hundreds) *nytam* (six) *w*, since *w* – (Waw) is also used for the number six. The Greek interpretation may have been influenced by the Hebrew form for "hundreds"- *twam*; the correct Aramaic form would be *aam*. The more accurate use of this method would actually give –"six- two hundreds" which is exactly what The Sinaiticus has! [Greek does not have a six -two hundreds. So the 4th century Greek Sinaiticus bears witness to the Aramaic text of Revelation (The only Greek ms. with 1200 stadia in this place) as does the Majority Greek Text with its subtle but sloppy use of Gematria to obtain 1600 stadia." Bauscher: The Aramaic English Interlinear Peshitta Holy Bible, pp. 196.

along stones of the size of forty se'ah and flowed into the sea a distance of four miles…

"He [Hadrian] immediately surrounded them [the Jewish rebels] with his legions and slaughtered them, so that their blood streamed as far as Cyprus."[176]

John employed imagery that was very familiar to his culture in that era to depict the brutality of the Roman assault. It must be stated that Jesus was emphatically not on a horse slaughtering people. Further, in verses 14 to 16, Jesus is the one gathering (harvesting) people to Himself. In contrast, in verses 17 to 19 it is an angel that gathers (harvests) people into the winepress. Interestingly, in verse 18 there is an angel with authority over a fire. Which fire? The same fire and sulfur from verse 10 which purifies, refines, and makes white again.

The winepress was yet another allusion to the Old Testament.

"1 Who is this who comes from Edom,
With dyed garments from Bozrah,
This One who is glorious in His apparel,
Traveling in the greatness of His strength…

2 Why is Your apparel red,
And Your garments like one who treads in the **winepress***?*

3 "I have trodden the winepress alone,
And from the peoples no one was with Me.
For I have trodden them in My anger,
And trampled them in My fury;
Their blood is sprinkled upon My garments,
And I have stained all My robes.
4 For the day of vengeance is in My heart,
And the year of My redeemed has come…

6 I have trodden down the peoples in My anger,
Made them drunk in My fury,
And brought down their strength to the earth."

---

[176] Midrash Rabbah Lamentations 2.4 and 1.45.

*7 I will mention the **loving kindnesses** of the Lord
And the praises of the Lord,
According to all that the Lord has bestowed on us,
And the great goodness toward the house of Israel,
Which He has bestowed on them according to His mercies,
According to the multitude of His loving kindnesses.
8 For He said, "Surely they are My people,
Children who will not lie."
So He became their Savior.
9 In all their affliction He was afflicted,
And the Angel of His Presence saved them;
In His love and in His pity He redeemed them;
And He bore them and carried them
All the days of old.*

*10 But they rebelled and grieved His Holy Spirit;
So He turned Himself against them as an enemy,
And He fought against them…*

*14 As a beast goes down into the valley,
And the Spirit of the Lord causes him to rest,
So You lead Your people,
To make Yourself a glorious name."
Isaiah 63:1–10, 14 (NKJV, emphasis mine)*

The incredible juxtaposition of Isaiah 63 cannot be overlooked: all the hyperbole of the winepress, the fury, and the chastisement is met with verses 7 and 14, "I will mention the loving kindnesses of the Lord… As a beast goes down into the valley, and the Spirit of the Lord causes him to rest, so You lead Your people."

All of God's judgements are unto restoration and reconciliation, whether in this Age or the one to come.

6 THE SONG OF MOSES: CH. 15

"This is what the Lord of armies says:

"Consider and call for the mourning women, that they may come...
Have them hurry and take up a wailing for us,
So that our eyes may shed tears...
For a voice of wailing is heard from Zion:
'How devastated we are!
We are put to great shame,
For we have abandoned the land
Because they have torn down our homes.'
... Teach your daughters wailing,
And have every woman teach her neighbor a song of mourning."
Jeremiah 9:17-20 (NASB)

Likely for you, the mention of the Song of Moses means little, if anything. Yet to the Hebrew mind, from the days of Sinai and the wilderness, to the first-century AD, I imagine it would be a sobering thought. This song was given by the mouth of Yahweh Himself to Moses, and with it came a command: memorize the song and pass it down from generation to generation, so that when the time of prophetic prediction came, the song would be recalled and sung.

And the purpose of the song? In short, it was to remind the Israelites that Yahweh had warned them of the dangers of breaching the vassal covenant they were under. Moreover, that Yahweh spoke out loud through Moses that they would indeed break the commandments and incur upon themselves the consequences of that contract. So generations later, when Israelites found themselves wondering, "Why has calamity come upon us?" the song was to serve as a reminder of why.

The siege of the Holy Land in 66 to 70 AD, which culminated with the fall of Jerusalem and the destruction of the Holy Temple, was the fulfillment of the Song of Moses. Hence, Revelation 15 is the prophetic reminder to those in and around the ancient boarders of Israel to help them understand what was happening during the Roman campaign.

Remember: over 1 million Jews lost their lives, and almost 100,000 were taken into slavery. Jesus wept over Jerusalem (Lk 19:41-44) as he saw what would come at the end of that generation 40 years later. The Law kills indeed (2 Cor 3:6).

> א *(1) Now I saw another great and astonishing sign in the heavens: the angels who had the seven last blows with them, for in them the fiery-passion of God fulfills itself.[177]*

> א *(2) Then I saw the likeness of a sea[178] of glass intermingled with fire, and those who were victorious over the savage animal and over its genius, and over the number of its name. And they were standing upon the sea of glass, and they had upon them the stringed instruments of God.*

A sea of fire! As I mentioned in the previous chapter, everyone – all who have ever and will ever live – will pass through the purifying fire of God, either in this life or the next. Here, the sea of fire is connected to another sea of fire in John's vision: commonly known as the Lake of Fire (19:20; 20:10, 14, 15; 21:8). The first time it is mentioned in 19:20 it literally reads, *"the sea of fire which burns with sulfur"*.

---

[177] A rare instance of the reflexive Eshtaphal verb conjugation in the perfect tense, similar to the Hebrew Hithpael.
[178] יַמָּא is the word for a large sea, like the Mediterranean. In contrast, יַמְתָא was used throughout Luke's Gospel and once in John's (6:19) for the *"sea"* of Galilee, and it was to be understood as a smaller body of water.

Every Divine fire has one, and only one, chief aim – to purify:

> *"...and he will be severely chastised in fire and [launder's] sulfur, in the presence of the holy angels and in the presence of the Lamb."* Revelation 14:10b

> *"I have come to cast fire upon the earth; and how I wish it were already kindled!"* Luke 12:49

> *"For everyone will be salted with fire."* Mark 9:49

It seems that these lovers of Yahweh in Revelation 15:2 have already passed through the ethereal and purifying fires of God through the agency of the Holy Spirit who baptizes with fire (Matt 3:11; Isa 4:4). And as we will explore in Revelation 19, 20 and 21, the sea of fire (aka Lake of Fire) is also a purifying fire.

> *"each one's work will become evident; for the day will show it because it is to be revealed with fire, and the fire itself will test the quality of each one's work... If anyone's work is burned up, he will suffer loss; but he himself will be saved, yet only so as through fire."*
> 1 Corinthians 3:13, 15 (NASB)

> *"And have mercy on some, who are doubting; save others, snatching them out of the fire; and on some have mercy with fear, hating even the garment polluted by the flesh."* Jude 1:22–23 (NASB)

However, that fire is not a pleasant experience to say the least. More on that topic later in this book.

> ܐ *(3) And they were singing the song of Moses, the servant of God, and the song of the Lamb. And they were saying:*

>> *"Great and marvelous are your works, Yahweh God, Keeper of All[79]. Reproving and steadfast are your actions, King of the Ages!*

---

[79] This combination of words, ܐܚܝܕ ܟܠ (keeper/holder/maintainer of all/everything), found uniquely in Revelation (4:8; 11:17; 16:7, 14; 19:6, 15; 21:22) is usually translated as "Almighty" or "Omnipotent". But I believe the native word choice actually has greater impact on the reader. Implied reading: God is the one

> א (4) *Who doesn't revere you, Yahweh, and glorify your Name?*
> *For you alone are holy.*
> *For all the nations will come and bow down before you.*
> *For you make right."*

> א (5) *But after these things, I looked, and the Temple of the Tabernacle of the Testimony was opened in Heaven.*

A temple… in Heaven?

"Therefore even the first covenant [of Moses] was not inaugurated without blood… And in the same way he sprinkled both the tabernacle and all the vessels of the ministry with the blood. And almost all things are cleansed with blood, according to the Law, and without the shedding of blood there is no forgiveness.

Therefore it was necessary for the copies of the things in the heavens to be cleansed with these things, but the heavenly things themselves with better sacrifices than these. For Christ did not enter a holy place made by hands, a mere copy of the true one, but into heaven itself, now to appear in the presence of God for us… but now once at the consummation of the ages He has been revealed to put away sin by the sacrifice of Himself."
Hebrews 9:18, 21–24, 26 (NASB)

It is beyond the scope of this book to get into the theological implications of Jesus entering into a heavenly temple, but suffice to say that what Moses and Solomon built was merely a shadow of a spiritual reality.

Back to the text at hand, the "Tabernacle of the Testimony" literally means *"dwelling place of the witness"* in both Numbers (Old Testament Hebrew) and here in Revelation (New Testament Aramaic). What was the witness? The Law of Moses.

"And you shall appoint the Levites over the tabernacle of the testimony, and over all its furnishings and over everything that belongs to it… the Levites shall camp around the tabernacle of the testimony, so that there will be no divine wrath against the congregation of the sons of Israel. So the Levites shall be responsible for service

---

who is continuing to take care of everything, even the reconciliation of wayward sons and daughters, even if it means passing through judgement and fire.

to the tabernacle of the testimony." Numbers 1:50, 53 (NASB)

The crucial verse here in Revelation 15 is verse 3 – they sang the Song of Moses.

*"Do not think that I [Jesus] will accuse you before the Father; **the one who accuses you is Moses**, in whom you have put your hope." John 5:45 (NASB, emphasis mine)*

WHAT WAS THE SONG OF MOSES?

When Moses instructed Israel concerning the Commandments in the wilderness, the incredibly long list of moral and civic laws began and ended with a warning:

"See, I am placing before you today a blessing and a curse: the blessing, if you listen to the commandments of the Lord your God, which I am commanding you today; and the curse, if you do not listen to the commandments of the Lord your God…" Deuteronomy 11:26–28 (NASB)

Then in Deuteronomy 28 the warnings become more specific.

"Now it shall be, if you diligently obey the Lord your God, being careful to do all His commandments which I am commanding you today, that the Lord your God will put you high above all the nations of the earth. And all these blessings will come to you and reach you if you obey the Lord your God…

But it shall come about, if you do not obey the Lord your God, to be careful to follow all His commandments and His statutes which I am commanding you today, that all these curses will come upon you and overtake you…" Deuteronomy 28:1-3, 15 (NASB)

There are roughly 10 to 12 blessings (depending on your interpretation), and up to 40 curses (same) listed in Deuteronomy 28, and you should stop and read them now (it will help here). Shockingly, when the curses are read with the devastation the Holy Land experienced during the Roman campaign against it, **we see that the curses were fulfilled *verbatim*.**

Deuteronomy 29 and 30 then follow with prophetic allusions to Israel's future disobedience and breach of covenant (breaking the Law), along with God's mercy and plan to restore them. Things then get even more serious in chapter 31. God tells Moses straight up,

> *"Behold, you are about to lie down with your fathers; and this people will arise and play the prostitute with the foreign gods of the land into the midst of which they are going, and they will abandon Me and break My covenant which I have made with them." (Deuteronomy 31:16)*

Yahweh continues,

> *"Now then, **write this song** for yourselves, and teach it to the sons of Israel; put it on their lips, so that this song may be a witness for Me against the sons of Israel… Then it will come about, when many evils and troubles find them, that this song will testify before them as a witness (**for it shall not be forgotten from the mouth of their descendants**)… So Moses wrote down this song on the same day, and taught it to the **sons of Israel**."*
> *(Deuteronomy 31:19–22, emphasis mine)*

Chapter 32 of Deuteronomy is the Song of Moses. Go ahead and read it now…

Done? Good.

I'm not sure how anyone could have memorized that! But I guess when your life is on the line you figure out a how. The song is a heavy and cryptic read – very layered and sometimes hard to understand. But what is obvious is the content is not good. Not at all.

Now come back to Revelation 15. We read in verse 4 that Jewish followers of Yeshua then began to sing the Song of Moses (per Deut 31:21), then in verse 5 God's copy of the Law of Moses was pulled out from the heavenly archives. Why? Because the consequences for breach of the contractual obligations of the Law were about to be **fulfilled**, just as Yahweh said in Deuteronomy 28 to 32.

This, my brothers and sisters, is what Revelation 15 is all about. So take a deep breath, exhale some relief, and give God praise that none of these things are coming upon us today or at a future time. More importantly, pause to reflect on the dire consequences that the Law brought about. It is sobering.

In this light, we understand the zeal and passion behind the letters of Paul in Galatians, Romans, Colossians, and Hebrews, warning his fellow Jews to not place themselves back under the yoke of slavery.

> *"For all who are of works of the Law are under a curse…*
> *Christ redeemed us from the curse of the Law, having become a curse for us…*
> *I, Paul, tell you that if you have yourselves circumcised, Christ will be of no benefit to you. And I testify again to every man who has himself circumcised, that he is obligated to keep the whole Law. You have been severed from Christ, you who are seeking to be justified by the Law; you have fallen from grace." Galatians 3: 10, 13, 5:2–4 (NASB)*

Once the Temple was destroyed in AD 70 and the requirements of the Law fully satisfied, it became (and continues to be) impossible to place oneself under the Law of Moses. That covenant and its requirements are no longer in force. Legalism stands today in the hearts and minds of millions of well-intentioned but misinformed Believers. Oh that the Apostle's prayer would come to pass in the Body of Christ today!

> *"[I pray] that the God of our Lord Jesus Christ, the Father of glory, may give you a spirit of wisdom and of revelation in the knowledge of Him. I pray that the eyes of your heart may be enlightened, so that you will know what is the hope of His calling, what are the riches of the glory of His inheritance in the saints, and what is the boundless greatness of His power toward us who believe…" Ephesians 1:17–19 (NASB)*

Lord Jesus, have mercy on us all.

> ℵ *(6) Then the seven angels went out from the Temple – they who had with them the seven blows – while wearing pure and bright linen and girded with a golden belt around their chests.*

> ℵ *(7) And one of the Four Creatures gave to the seven angels seven vessels full of the fiery-passion of the God who is the Life unto the Age of Ages. Amen!*

> "And aptly did he say "golden", for the wrath of God is worthy, bearing within itself that which is good and beneficial rather than just, even though those who are tormented might

experience distress."[180]

Oecumenius (quoted above), who wrote the first known Greek commentary on Revelation, had little to say about the angels with the *blows* ("plagues" in most Bibles) and vessels ("bowls" in most Bibles). I love his heart though, giving God the benefit of the doubt and deciding that God's wrath (fiery-passion) was good and beneficial.

What we cannot fail to miss here is yet another clear allusion to the Book of Ezekiel. Early in the prophet's work he has a very similar prophetic experience.

> *"9:1 And he [Yahweh] called in my ear with a loud voice and said: 'Come, avengers of the city [of Jerusalem], and each man with the weapons of his vengeance in his hand!' 9:2 And I saw six men coming from the way of the gate upper that looks to the north, and each man with weapons of his vengeance in his hand, and one man among them was wearing fine linen and was bound with sapphire around his loins, and they came and they stood on the side of the altar of brass 9:3 And the glory of the God of Israel went up from the Cherub who was standing at the corner of the house, and he called to the mighty man that wore fine linen and was bound about the loins with sapphire.*
>
> *9:4 And LORD JEHOVAH said to him: 'Go through within the city, within Jerusalem, and make a mark on the forehead of the men who groan and are tormented because of all the abominations and the evils that are done within her.' 9:5 And to those who were with him he said: 'Pass before my eyes within the city after me and destroy, and your eyes shall not have pity and you shall not show mercy...'*
>
> *9:7 And he said to them: 'Defile the house and fill the courts with the slain. Go out. Kill in the city!...'*
>
> *9:11 And I saw the mighty man who was wearing fine linen, who answered and said: 'I have done just as you have commanded me.' 10:1 And I saw the Tabernacle above the head of the Cherubim as the appearance of stone of sapphire, and like the appearance of the form of a*

---

[180] Oecumenius, *Commentary on the Apocalypse* (6th century AD). William C. Weinrich, eds. *Revelation*. vol. 12 of Ancient Christian Commentary on Scripture. ICCS/Accordance electronic ed. (Downers Grove: InterVarsity Press, 2005), 242.

throne above them 10:2 And he called to the mighty man who was wearing the fine linen, and he said to him: 'Enter in between the wheels under the Cherubim, and fill your hands with coals of fire from between the Cherubim, and scatter them over the city.' [Ezekiel 9:1–10:3][181]

So in Ezekiel, we have angels assigned to the destruction of Jerusalem and the First Temple. We know historically that at that time, Jerusalem fell and the Temple was destroyed by the sword of the Babylonians. Now in John's day, it would happen again by the Romans. Those "sealed" in Ezekiel can be likened to those who were singing the Song of Moses in Revelation 15.

Moreover, in the same way John saw the doors of the tabernacle in Heaven open, with angels departing from within that same tabernacle (symbolic of the Temple), **the eyewitness-historian Josephus records parallel accounts he witnessed from the Temple in Jerusalem!**

> "Thus also before the Jews rebellion, and before those commotions which preceded the war… at the ninth hour of the night, so great a light shone round the altar, and the holy house [the Temple], that it appeared to be bright day time. Which light lasted **for half an hour**… Moreover the eastern gate of the inner [court of the] Temple, which was of brass, and vastly heavy, and had been with difficulty shut by twenty men, and rested upon a basis armed with iron, and had bolts fastened very deep into the firm floor; which was there made of one entire stone: was seen to be opened of its own accord, about the sixth hour of the night…
>
> [then] a certain prodigious and incredible phenomenon appeared… at that feast which we call Pentecost; as the priests were going by night into the inner [court of the] Temple, as their custom was, to perform their sacred ministrations, they said, that in the first place they felt a quaking, and heard a great noise: and after that they heard a sound, as of a multitude, saying, 'Let us remove hence.'"[182]

To paraphrase, the supernatural multitude said, "Let's depart from here." And how about the door of the Temple opening on its own? As the

---

[181] The Aramaic Old Testament (Peshitta OT), by Bauscher, David. The Holy Peshitta Bible Translated (pp. 1564-1565). Lulu.com. Kindle Edition.
[182] Josephus, *Wars*, 6:5:3, emphasis mine.

tabernacle in heaven was opening, so was the one on earth. Crazy! Now I underscored the part where he said the light shone for "half an hour", as it connects us back to Revelation 8 and the seals. Why? **Because Revelation 6 to 11 and 13 to 19 run in parallel, highlighting the same event but from two different prophetic vantage points.**

Tacitus, the Roman historian, also recorded the same event:

> "Prodigies had indeed occurred... and suddenly the Temple was illumined with fire from the clouds. Of a sudden the doors of the shrine opened and a superhuman voice cried: 'The gods are departing': at the same moment the mighty stir of their going was heard... Such was the city [Jerusalem] and people [Jews] against which Titus Caesar now proceeded."[183]

Now check this out. Above we read Ezekiel 9 and a bit of 10. Let's continue into Ezekiel 10, in light of Josephus and Tacitus.

"And He spoke to the man clothed in linen and said, "Enter between the whirling wheels under the cherubim and fill your hands with coals of fire from between the cherubim, and scatter them over the city." And he entered in my sight.

Now the cherubim were standing on the right side of the temple when the man entered, and the cloud filled the inner courtyard. Then the glory of the Lord went up from the cherub to the threshold of the temple, and the temple was filled with the cloud, and the courtyard was filled with the brightness of the glory of the Lord...

Then the glory of the Lord departed from the threshold of the temple and stood over the cherubim..." Ezekiel 10:2, 3–4, 10 (NASB)

Therefore, taking into consideration Ezekiel and Josephus, not only do we have a Biblical connection to the *first* time such events happened in the Holy Land (Babylonian invasion), but we also have a connection from a "boots on the ground" perspective in Jerusalem the second time around (Roman invasion). Incredible!

---

[183] Tacitus, *Histories,* 5:13.

> א *(8) Then the Temple was filled with the smoke of the glory of God and of his power, so that no one was able to be going in to the Temple until the seven blows of the seven angels had brought about their fulfillment.*[184]

We read above in Ezekiel 10 that the glory of Yahweh filled the Temple during the prophet's encounter. Here too, in Revelation 15:8, the glory of God fills the tabernacle. Why?

Simply put, to remind Israel of Exodus 40. The entirety of this chapter is focused on the tabernacle and the ark of the testimony (the tablets of the Law). Moses records the painstaking procedure of getting everything set up exactly to Yahweh's precise specifications. The chapter concludes with Yahweh filling the tent with His glory, to the point that not even Moses can enter in. This is how Exodus ends. John the Revelator's vision take him back to the images and themes of Sinai, the tabernacle, and the Law of Moses, which only further hits home the single point: all that God (and Moses) said would happen to Israel when they broke the covenant was now coming to pass.

One of the key themes of Exodus is the great and powerful wonders Yahweh performed in order to deliver the Hebrews from the bondage of Egypt. By the staff of Moses, great plagues were sent over Egypt. Now, here in Revelation 15, the notion of plagues (*blows*) is being conjured up again. Verse 8 specifically take us right to the end of Exodus. But as we will see in Revelation 16, we will have a sort of regression in the Exodus narrative, where we start with the glory but end with plagues.

Exodus, Egypt, and plagues – keep these in mind as we venture into chapter 16.

---

[184] As if to bookend the chapter, again John employs the rare Eshtaphal verb conjugation, now in the imperfect tense. It took five English words to attempt to convey the full meaning of this one verb "to fulfill/complete" in a special conjugation. Perhaps this was used so as to juxtapose the Divine eternal plan of Yahweh (in verse 1) against the execution of said plan in the temporal and chronological realm. From John's perspective, writing prior to AD 70, this event was yet to take place.

LEO DE SIQUEIRA

7 THE PLAGUES OF WAR: CH. 16

"Taking Megiddo is like capturing a thousand cities."

— *Egyptian Pharaoh Thutmose III, 1468 BC*

Perhaps second only to the "Mark of the Beast", the so-called "Battle of Armageddon" is a top contender for most misunderstood themes in the Book of Revelation. But the fanciful fictions people have created over the years in their ubiquitous Doomsday predictions, or even Hollywood movies, are nowhere near the reality of the text. Mainstream interpretations of "Armageddon" not only fail to follow the narrative flow of the text, they also fail to provide any meaning to the original first-century audience. But perhaps most importantly, the popularized interpretations of a world-ending, World War III-scale event fail to capture the Father heart of God.

So, let's get at it. The fateful region is first and foremost known as Har or Tel Megiddo: "Armageddon" is from the Hebrew הַר מְגִדּוֹ Har Megiddo (har means mount), but our Bibles read it from the Latinized "Armagedon". Mount Megiddo is situated some 125 km/77 miles north of Jerusalem by car, near the Mediterranean coast. It is indeed the focal point of chapter 16 of John's Vision, but for a very different reason that most understand. The entire narrative flow of chapters 15 and 16 are a symbolic digression that takes Israel back into Egypt. It is an illustrative undoing of all the great things that became part of the Jewish story.

In Revelation 16, God invokes memories of the Kingdom of Egypt and the Exodus and contrasts these against the former united Kingdom of Israel and the fall of its royal capital, Jerusalem. The plagues are the appetizer to the Exodus theme, but Megiddo is the main course since Megiddo was historically a place of one of Egypt's greatest triumphs and one of Judah's greatest defeats (more on this below).

The personification of Israel, Judah, and Jerusalem into her various evil archetypes, such as Babylon, Egypt, and an unfaithful wife, is a central theme in Revelation. Chapters 15 and 16 then are primarily focused on symbolic-Israel becoming the very thing she despised: Egypt, the house of bondage (Ex 20:2).

> א *(1) And I heard a great voice from the Temple which said to the seven angels: 'Go and pour out seven vessels of the fiery-passion of God upon the Land.*

"Revelation 15–16 would have immediately recalled the only other biblical occurrence of plagues as judgment—Exodus 7–11. In fact, we can find some stunning direct parallels between the two lists of plagues. For example, the second and third bowls are about water turning to blood, which happened to the Nile during the plagues of Egypt (see Exod. 7:20). And the fifth bowl covers the land with darkness just like the ninth plague of Egypt (see Exod. 10:21–29). In Exodus, the Egyptian armies pursued the Hebrews, and the water swallowed them up so the Hebrews were delivered. Yet in the sixth bowl judgment, ironically, an army rises from the river and brings destruction.

In other words, the basic concept in Revelation 15–16 is a clear reversal of the Exodus story. Revelation 11:8 tells us that God saw first-century Jerusalem as being like Egypt and Sodom. Later, we see the Christians make an exodus out of Jerusalem, as represented by the 144,000 who are marked by the Lord (see Rev. 7; 14). Historically, we know that all the Christians fled Jerusalem and found safety in the nearby mountain of Pella, so that no Christians were killed in the destruction of Jerusalem…

This is the big picture of the bowls. Now Jerusalem has become like Egypt..."[185]

> א *(2) So the first went and poured his vessel upon the Land, and there came about a painful and malignant boil upon whichever man had the brand[186] of the savage animal upon them, and those who paid obeisance[187] to its genius.*

In chapter 15 of Revelation, the Song of Moses was sung to remind us of Deuteronomy, and specifically all the curses of chapter 28.

> *"The Lord will strike you with the boils of Egypt and with tumors, the festering rash, and with scabies, from which you cannot be healed... The Lord will strike you on the knees and thighs with severe boils from which you cannot be healed, and strike you from the sole of your foot to the top of your head." Deuteronomy 28:27, 35 (NASB)*

Josephus recorded the fulfillment several times over. Here is one occasion:

> "For they [the Jews] were come up from all the country to the feast of unleavened bread; and were on a sudden shut up [in Jerusalem] by an army; which at the very first occasioned so great a straitness among them, **that there came a pestilential destruction upon them**..."[188]

These plagues have *nothing* to do with you, your country, or your day and age. Nothing. Now, that should provide you with some measure of comfort and relief. However, there is also the issue of how do we see God's love and kindness in all this? *That* is the more important question.

---

[185] Welton, Jonathan. The Art of Revelation (pp. 109-110). BookBaby. Kindle Edition.
[186] As discussed in Revelation 13, branding (or stigmatization) was known as a *charagma* in the Roman Empire. It was common practice for slaves, criminals, and prisoners of war to receive the *charagma*, especially on the forehead or hand.
[187] Or "paid homage". סגד means "to bow down in respect", or "to cause to be venerated". The *implication* can be worship, but this is based on context (see same word in Dan 2:46 or Gen 47:31). Given the context of kingdoms and empires, obeisance or homage (even forced) is more fitting than worship.
[188] Josephus, *Wars,* 6:9:3.

Paul (or whoever you think wrote Hebrews), writing to Jews who had come out from under the Law of Moses, reminds his kinsmen of the big picture when it comes to chastisement.

> *"You have not yet resisted to the point of shedding blood in your striving against sin; and you have forgotten the exhortation which is addressed to you as sons,*
> *"MY SON, DO NOT REGARD LIGHTLY THE DISCIPLINE OF THE LORD,*
> *NOR FAINT WHEN YOU ARE PUNISHED BY HIM;*
> *FOR WHOM THE LORD LOVES HE DISCIPLINES,*
> *AND HE PUNISHES EVERY SON WHOM HE ACCEPTS."*
>
> *It is for discipline that you endure; God deals with you as with sons; for what son is there whom his father does not discipline? But if you are without discipline, of which all have become partakers, then you are illegitimate children and not sons. Furthermore, we had earthly fathers to discipline us, and we respected them; shall we not much more be subject to the Father of spirits, and live? For they disciplined us for a short time as seemed best to them, but He disciplines us for our good, so that we may share His holiness. For the moment, all discipline seems not to be pleasant, but painful; yet to those who have been trained by it, afterward it yields the peaceful fruit of righteousness.*
> *Therefore, strengthen the hands that are weak and the knees that are feeble, and make straight paths for your feet, so that the limb which is impaired may not be dislocated, but rather be healed."*
> Hebrews 12:4–13 (NASB)

Further, Paul wrote:

> *"each one's work will become evident; for the day will show it because it is to be revealed with fire, and the fire itself will test the quality of each one's work. If anyone's work which he has built on it remains, he will receive a reward. If anyone's work is burned up, he will suffer loss;* **but he himself will be saved**, *yet only so as through fire."*
> 1 Corinthians 3:13–15 (NASB, emphasis mine)

Also,

> *"I say then, God has not rejected His people, has He? Far from it! For I too am an Israelite...*
> *... But by their [the Jewish people] wrongdoing salvation has come to the Gentiles, to make them jealous. Now if their wrongdoing proves to be riches for the world, and their failure, riches for the Gentiles, how much more will their fulfillment be!*
> *... For if their rejection proves to be the reconciliation of the world, what will their acceptance be but life from the dead?*
> *... For I do not want you, brothers and sisters, to be uninformed of this mystery... that a partial hardening has happened to Israel until the fullness of the Gentiles has come in; and so all Israel will be saved.*
> *... For God has shut up all in disobedience, so that He may show mercy to all." Romans 11:1, 2, 11, 12, 15, 25, 26, 32 (NASB)*

Therefore, keep these truths we have just read in mind as you continue to work through Revelation. We have to elevate our perspective beyond the temporal, and see that God always has a bigger plan in play.

> א *(3) And the second angel poured his vessel into the sea[189], and it became like the sea of the dead, and every living animal in the sea died.*

> א *(4) And the third angel poured his vessel into the rivers, and into the springs of water, and they became blood.*

Of the Mediterranean Sea, Josephus recorded this account:

> "[Through] the violence of the Romans... much lamentation there was when the ships were dashed against one another... But some of them thought that to die by their own swords was lighter than by the sea, and so they killed themselves, before they were drowned; although the greatest part of them were

---

[189] Most likely the Sea of Galilee, as the same word is used for Galilee. But also for the "Great Sea", the Mediterranean. Either way, Josephus tells us in *Jewish Wars* that both seas were red with blood.

carried by the waves, and dashed to pieces against the abrupt parts of the rocks, **insomuch that the sea was bloody a long way**, and the maritime parts were full of dead bodies, for the Romans came upon those that were carried to the shore, and destroyed them; and the number of the bodies that were thus thrown out of the sea was four thousand, and two hundred."[190]

Of the Sea of Galilee, Josephus recorded this account:

"for their [the Jews] ships were small and fitted only for piracy; they were too weak to fight with Vespasian's vessels, and the mariners that were in them were so few, that they were afraid to come near the Romans, who attacked them in great numbers…

and when they ventured to come near the Romans, they became sufferers themselves, before they could do any harm to the other, and were drowned, they and their ships together. As for those that endeavoured to come to an actual fight, the Romans ran many of them through with their long poles. Sometimes the Romans leaped into their ships, with swords in their hands, and slew them; but when some of them met the vessels, the Romans caught them by the middle, and destroyed at once their ships, and themselves who were taken in them. And for such as were drowning in the sea, if they lifted their heads up above the water, they were either killed by darts, or caught by the vessels; but if, in the desperate case they were in, they attempted to swim to their enemies, the Romans cut off either their heads or their hands; and indeed they were destroyed after various manners everywhere… **one might then see the lake all bloody, and full of dead bodies, for not one of them escaped.**

And a terrible stink, and a very sad sight there was on the following days over that country; for as for the shores they were full of shipwrecks, and of dead bodies all swelled; and as the dead bodies were inflamed by the sun, and putrified, they

---

[190] Josephus, *Wars,* 3:9:3.

corrupted the air… The number of the slain, including those that were killed in the city before, was six thousand and five hundred."[191]

Of the Jordan River, which connects the Sea of Galilee to the Dead Sea (which Josephus called lake Asphaltitis because it spewed bitumen), Josephus recorded this account:

> "Now this destruction that fell upon the Jews, as it was not inferior to any of the rest in itself; so did it still appear greater than it really was. And this because, not only the whole country through which they fled was filled with slaughter, and **Jordan could not be passed over by reason of the dead bodies** that were in it; but because the lake Asphaltitis was also full of dead bodies, that were carried down into it by the river."[192]

> ℵ *(5) And I heard the angel of the waters saying, 'Righteous are You, who was and is. Holy are You who legally determines these things.*

> ℵ *(6) Because the blood of the prophets and of the saints they have shed, now this blood you have given them to drink as their due.'*

Two major themes intersect here. First, in verse 3, which we just read, we know that the Sea of Galilee was red with blood. John saw the vision, and Josephus wrote of the account. Interestingly, it was to a very large crowd that had followed him from the Dead Sea to Capernaum that Jesus said:

> *"Truly, truly, I say to you, unless you eat the flesh of the Son of Man and drink His blood, you have no life in yourselves. The one who eats My flesh and drinks My blood has eternal life, and I will raise him up on the last day. For My flesh is true food, and My blood is true drink. The one who eats My flesh and drinks My blood remains in Me, and I in him." John 6:53–56 (NASB)*

The Jews were of course enraged at this statement. They protest to Jesus, saying that their ancestors ate manna in the wilderness when Moses led them.

---

[191] Ibid., 3:10:9.
[192] Ibid., 4:7:6.

They asked what sign could Jesus perform to validate these words. Of course, this was *after* he had multiplied food to feed them!

"Your fathers ate the manna in the wilderness, and they died. This is the bread that comes down out of heaven, so that anyone may eat from it and not die," Jesus said, alluding to the fact that the Law would not bring life, only death, but that His body and blood (representing the New Covenant) would bring life.

The second major theme is that of the blood of the prophets and saints, which has already been covered at length in this series. Nevertheless, a reminder:

> *"Woe to you, scribes and Pharisees, hypocrites! For you build the tombs for the prophets and decorate the monuments of the righteous, and you say, 'If we had been living in the days of our fathers, we would not have been partners with them in* **shedding the blood** *of the prophets.' So you testify against yourselves, that you are sons of those who murdered the prophets. Fill up, then, the measure of the guilt of your fathers…*
>
> *Therefore, behold, I am sending you prophets and wise men and scribes; some of them you will kill and crucify, and some of them you will flog in your synagogues, and persecute from city to city, so that* **upon you will fall the guilt of all the righteous blood shed** *on earth, from the blood of righteous Abel to the blood of Zechariah, the son of Berechiah, whom you murdered between the temple and the altar. Truly I say to you, all these things will come upon* **this generation***. Jerusalem, Jerusalem, who kills the prophets and stones those who have been sent to her!"* Matthew 23:29–32, 34–37 (NASB, emphasis mine)
>
> *"I [Jesus] must go on My journey today and tomorrow and the next day;* **for it cannot be that a prophet would perish outside Jerusalem***. Jerusalem, Jerusalem, the city that kills the prophets and stones those who have been sent to her! How often I wanted to gather your children together, just as a hen gathers her young under her wings, and you were unwilling! Behold,* **your house is left to you desolate***."* Luke 13:33–35 (NASB, emphasis mine)

And most tragically,

> *"Now when Pilate saw that he was accomplishing nothing, but rather that a riot was starting, he took water and washed his hands in front of the crowd, saying,* **'I am innocent of this Man's blood**; *you yourselves shall see.' And all the people replied,* **"His blood shall be on us and on our children!"***"*
> Matthew 27:24–25 (NASB, emphasis mine)

Lord Jesus, humble our hearts. Break every trace of pride in us. Bring us to repentance and reverential awe of you. As Paul wrote, "[Gentiles] do not be arrogant toward the branches; but if you are arrogant, remember that it is not you who supports the root, but the root supports you," (Romans 11:18). Jesus, cover us in Your Blood, and wash us by the water of your Word! You are the Logos. We need you, Jesus.

> א *(7) And I heard the altar saying: 'Yes, Yahweh God, Keeper of All[193]! Steadfast and honest are your judgments.'*

> א *(8) And the fourth angel poured his vessel over the Sun, and it was given it to scorch the sons of man[194] with fire. (9) So the sons of man were scorched with great heat,[195] and they blasphemed the Name of Elohim who has authority over these blows, and they did not change course or give Him glory.*

The voice from under the altar connects us to Revelation 6:9-11 where the souls of those slain called out to God to ask how long until they were avenged. This of course is in fulfillment of Matthew 23:34-36 which was discussed in the previous book and again above.

As for the heat, I offer three thoughts. First, there is first the immediate

---

[193] This combination of words, ܐܚܝܕ ܟܠ (keeper/holder/maintainer of all/everything), found uniquely in Revelation (4:8, 11:17, 16:7, 14, 19:6, 15, 21:22) is usually translated as "Almighty" or "Omnipotent". But I believe the native word choice actually has greater impact on the reader. Implied reading: God is the one who is continuing to take care of everything, even the reconciliation of wayward sons and daughters, even if it means passing through judgement and fire.

[194] While it could be rendered "human" or simply "man", ܕܐܢܫܐ, or לִבְנֵי־נֹשׁ, a contraction of son and man, is peculiar. Only in two sections of Revelation (9:4, 10 and here in 16:7, 8) is it used.

[195] "Heat" is based on the Crawford manuscript, as opposed to "fire".

prophecy of Deuteronomy 28:22 which says, "The Lord will strike you with consumption, inflammation, fever, **feverish heat**, and with the sword, with blight, and with mildew, and they will pursue you until you perish."

Second, there is specific mention of heat from Josephus, which said,

> "Now it happened that the Samaritans, who were destitute of water, were inflamed with a violent heat (for it was summertime, and the multitude had not provided themselves with necessaries), insomuch that some of them died that very day with heat."[196]

But third, and most importantly, is how the *symbolism* of fire and heat manifested itself throughout the Roman campaign to obliterate the Holy Land. The Romans set fire to every city, town, village, and field they came across as they descended upon the ancient borders of Israel and Judah.[197] They set fire to each of the three great walls that protected the might city of Jerusalem. Lastly, the Romans set ablaze the very core of Jewish social, legal, and religious life: the Holy Temple.

> א *(10) And the fifth angel poured his vessel over the throne of the savage animal*[198]*, and its kingdom became darkness, and they bit their tongues in pain. (11) And they blasphemed the Name of the God of Heaven from the pains of their boils, yet they did not change the course of their actions.*

Many commentaries will suggest that the beast or wild animal afflicted here in verse 10 is Nero or Rome. Yet Rome has no contextual connection, no Scriptural connection, and no legal (under the Law of Moses) connection to these vessels being poured out. This is a thoroughly Jewish event. Rome plays a role as an agent, or means, of fulfillment, but they are not the recipient.

Therefore, as I discussed at length in Revelation 13, the second animal (beast) was the Lamb, or Horned Ram, representing the corrupted leadership of Jerusalem that was made up of religious and political officials. The

---

[196] Josephus, *Wars*, 3.7.32.
[197] See Josephus, *Jewish Wars*, 5.6.2; 4.8.3; 4.9.7; 6.1.1.
[198] Here, contrary to the established belief, this animal is the **second beast,** the Lamb representing the Jewish religious aristocracy, not Nero or Rome.

aristocratic Jewish elites wielded both religious and political power. They were the recipients of the boils, along with their fellow countrymen.

As for the darkness, we have to stop and remind ourselves that very few visions can be taken literally in Biblical prophecy. The illustrations provided are to convey *meaning and symbolism*. Amazingly, there are three major Biblical passages that mention darkness coming over a nation; one concerning Babylon, one concerning Egypt, and one concerning Israel. Here, in Revelation, both Babylon and Egypt are symbolic of Jerusalem. So for the angel to drop an allusion to darkness is to invite a blending together of prophetic Scriptures.

In Isaiah 13, a prophecy regarding **Babylon** is given:

"The Lord of armies is mustering the army for battle.
They are coming from a distant country…
To destroy the whole land.
Judgment on the Day of the Lord…

For the stars of heaven and their constellations
*Will **not flash their light**;*
*The sun will be **dark** when it rises*
*And the moon will **not shed its light**."*
Isaiah 13:4, 5, 10 (NASB, emphasis mine)

In Ezekiel 32, a prophecy regarding **Egypt** is given:

*"Son of man, take up a **song of mourning** over Pharaoh king of Egypt, and say to him,*
'Now I will spread My net over you
With a contingent of many peoples,
*I will cover the heavens and **darken** their stars;*
*I will **cover** the sun with a cloud*
*And the moon will **not give its light**.*
All the shining lights in the heavens
*I will **darken** over you*
*And will set **darkness** on your land,'*
Declares the Lord God.
'I will also trouble the hearts of many peoples when I bring your destruction among the nations, into lands which you have not known.'"
Ezekiel 32:2, 3, 7–9 (NASB, emphasis mine)

In Amos 8, a prophecy regarding **Israel** is given:

"The end has come for My people Israel. I will not spare them any longer. The songs of the palace will turn to wailing on that day,' declares the Lord God. 'The corpses will be many; in every place they will throw them out...'

'Indeed, all of it will rise up like the Nile,
And it will be tossed about
And subside like the Nile of Egypt.
And it will come about on that day,' declares the Lord God,
*"That I will make the **sun go down** at noon,*
*And make the earth **dark** in broad daylight.'"*
Amos 8:2, 3, 8, 9 (NASB, emphasis mine)

Without a doubt, the savage animal or beast here in verse 10 is Israel.

> א *(12) And the sixth angel poured his vessel over the great river Euphrates, and its waters dried up, so as to prepare the way of the kings from the rising sun.*

I love how instead of "kings from the East" it says "rising sun". The implication is obvious, but from a literary sense it ties into the theme of sun and heat from the previous verses. I think it's so cool.

Now, the bigger deal here is the river Euphrates and those that would cross it. As I covered in the previous book, Revelation 9:14 says, "Loose the four angels that are bound at the great river Euphrates." What this meant in Revelation 9 is exactly what it means here: the Euphrates was a major natural boarder. Rivers like the Danube, Rhine, or even Brazos have played key roles in military history, and the Euphrates is no exception.

But Revelation 14:8 and 16:19 give us a very important key: each reference the fall of Babylon. We know that Jerusalem is being likened to Babylon in both cases. However, the mention of the Euphrates here in chapter 16 is an additional layer which would bring to the reader's mind a well-known historical event in those days: the fall of the literal Babylon.

Remember that Babylon was actually a great and powerful kingdom, and they were responsible for the first destruction of Jerusalem and the Temple of Solomon in 586 BC, led by King Nebuchadnezzar. Not long after, in 539 BC, King Cyrus the Great, ruler of the Persian Empire, overthrew Babylon. At the time, Babylon was considered the most powerful and fortified city in the known world.

Yet Cyrus devised a plan to divert the waters of the great Euphrates river. This allowed his troops to march through the riverbed and launch his attack. He "dried up" the waters of the Euphrates. Fitting to the narrative of Revelation, Cyrus was actually seen as a liberator for both the Jews who had been deported there during the ministry of Ezekiel and the pagan priests within Babylon itself. Like Babylon, Jerusalem had become a place of oppression, and the Roman assault brought an end to tyranny.

So in the same way, Cyrus, who was on track to becoming the greatest ruler of the greatest empire of that age (Persia), came to a city (Babylon) that was considered impenetrable and overthrew it. Likewise, Vespasian, who was on track to becoming the ruler of the greatest empire of his age (Rome), came with his son Titus and they ultimately overthrew Jerusalem, a city considered impenetrable. Moreover, Jerusalem is being likened to Babylon in John's Vision!

> "For Titus, when he had gotten together part of his forces about him, and had ordered the rest to meet him at Jerusalem, marched out of Cesarea. He had with him those three legions... [and] auxiliaries that came from the Kings... that came to his assistance from **Syria**... [and] had their places filled up out of those soldiers that came out of **Egypt** with Titus. Which were two thousand men, chosen out of the armies at Alexandria. There followed him also three thousand drawn from those that guarded the river **Euphrates**..."
>
> [After Jerusalem was defeated, Titus] sent away the rest of his army to the several places where they would be every one best situate: but permitted the tenth legion to stay, as a guard, at Jerusalem: and did not send them away beyond **Euphrates, where they had been before.**"[199]

The reference to the "kings from the rising sun" then is to remind the Semitic mind of their **greatest adversaries**: In 721 BC the Assyrians took

---

[199] Josephus, *Wars,* 5:1:6, and 7:1:3. Emphasis mine.

Israel to the North, and in 586 BC the Babylonians took Judah to the south. *Both of these empires were east of the Euphrates.* And after Babylon fell to the Persians, Alexander the Great overthrew them in 333 BC, and though he was Greek, his was headquartered in Babylon, *east of the Euphrates.* Alexander then took Jerusalem in 332 BC. Then, in 167 BC, Antiochus IV Epiphanes, the Seleucid king of the Hellenistic Syrian kingdom, terrorized the Jews and was a focal point of the Jewish Books of Maccabees. He lived in modern-day Iran, *east of the Euphrates.*

Lastly, as it pertains to the Jewish-Roman War, Vespasian and Titus had with them forces from beyond the Euphrates as well, who joined in the war effort:

"All Syria had sworn the same allegiance. Vespasian's cause was now joined also by **Sohaemus** with his entire kingdom, whose strength was not to be despised, and by **Antiochus** who had enormous ancestral wealth, and was in fact the richest of the subject princes."[200]

א *(13) And I saw from the mouth of the Leviathan, and from the mouth of the savage animal, and from the mouth of the false prophet,[201] three unclean spirits like diseased frog tongues.[202]*

א *(14) These are the spirits of demons which performs signs, which have gone upon the kings of the known world,[203] to be assembling them for the war of the Great Day of God, Keeper of All.*

---

[200] Tacitus, *Histories,* 2:81. Sohaemus, a prince of the house of Emesa, had been set up by Nero in 54 AD as king of Sophene, a district on the east of the upper Euphrates. Antiochus, of the Seleucid family, was at this time king of Commagene and of a part of Cilicia; three years later Vespasian deposed him and changed his kingdom into a Roman province.

[201] The priestly aristocracy in Jerusalem.

[202] אורדעא means "a disease of the tongue" or "rana". (Marcus Jastrow's Dictionary, p. 33). The Latin, *ranula,* meaning "little frog", is an age-old illness where a mucus cyst develops into a bubble in the floor of the mouth and looks like the cheek of a frog puffed out. Hence, the "frog" in their mouths. The condition is perhaps an ancient word-picture for someone who deceives, like we would say "forked tongue" today to invoke the image of a snake as a way to describe the negative character of a person.

[203] תאביל "habitable earth" or "known world".

FALSIFICATION OF THE OFFICE OF THE PROPHET

Out of nowhere a new character gets added to the stage. Where on earth did this "false prophet" come from? This character gets added in with no introduction! So we are left with the task of employing some deductive reasoning and contextual investigation in order to understand how he fits. Now I use the term "he" loosely because like most things in Revelation, the "false prophet" is a symbol – a representation – of broader message, not a villain like Sauron in the Lord of the Rings!

Going back to Revelation 13, we know we have Satan (Leviathan), Nero/Rome (first animal, a leopard), and Israel (second animal, a lamb). We also learned that the horns on the lamb represented the puppet kings and priests of Jerusalem. Now here in chapter 16, we have Satan again (verse 13, Leviathan) and Israel (verses 10 and 13, lamb). Jerusalem and Israel are the focal point of John's vision, and certainly that theme continues here.

Revelation 19:20 also gives us a clue, because it places the beast of the land from Revelation 13:14–17 in connection with the false prophet. You will see that the descriptions of both the land beast and the false prophet are very similar. Here's what I mean:

(13:14–17, speaking of the land beast, Israel) "And it will cause those who dwell upon the Land to be lead astray by way of the signs that were being granted to it to be performing before the savage animal. And it was granted to it to give spirit to the genius of the savage animal, and as a result all who do not bow in obeisance to the genius of the savage animal will be killed. And it caused all of them—small and great, rich and poor, lords and servants—to be given unto them the brand upon their right hands or upon their foreheads, so that no one can buy or sell afterwards, unless there is upon him the brand of the name of the savage animal or the number of its name."

(19:20, speaking of the false prophet) "But the savage animal was ensnared and the false prophet with it – that which did signs before it, in which he caused those who received the brand of the savage animal to be led astray, and those who did obeisance to its genius."

When it comes to the Holy Land, if you think back to the Old Testament, there were always three influential leaders in place: kings, priests, and prophets. The lamb had two horns which represented kings and priests, because not since Malachi in the 400s BC was anyone recognized in Israel or Jerusalem as having a prophetic office.

But in the first century AD, imposters began to come about. And as I have covered at length in the previous books, we know from history that there were many who not only claimed to be a prophet but were also able to gain followers and influence over the people.

> "**A false prophet was the occasion of these peoples' destruction**: who had made a public proclamation in the city of Jerusalem, that very day, that 'God commanded them to get up upon the temple, and that there they should receive miraculous signs of their deliverance.'
>
> **Now there was then a great number of false prophets**, suborned by the tyrants, to impose on the people: who denounced this to them, that they should wait for deliverance from God; and this was in order to keep them from deserting; and that they might be buoyed up above fear and care by such hopes… Thus were the miserable people persuaded by these deceivers, **and such as belied God himself**."[204]

Josephus never gave us a name of this specific prophet, and nor does it matter. For what matters is that we understand there were *several* false prophets before and throughout the Jewish-Roman war. **What we have here is the falsification of the office of the prophet**, which was a significant role in the Jewish story. The prophet was never given a measure of political or authoritative status like the king or priest, which the horns of the lamb represented. The prescribed authority of the prophet (in the life and time of their peers) was based on the receptivity of those receiving the message. Jeremiah and Ezekiel, for instance, suffered persecution and were dismissed. So the prophet is now added here to the great thematic illustration of all the power, authority, and influence at play during the final years of the Mosaic Age and the fall of Jerusalem. The only other times we see this character in Revelation are in chapters 19 and 20 when "he" (the false prophet), the beast, and Satan are thrown down into the fiery lake of sulfur.

א *(15) – 'Behold! I come like a thief. Blessed is he who stays alert and*

---

[204] Josephus, Wars, 6:5:2, 3

keeps his garments, who does not walk naked and has his shame seen by others.'

The abrupt and disjunctive interjection here is to clearly warn hearers and readers of the immediacy of the events about to unfold in their time.

א *(16) And they will gather them to the region which in Hebrew is called, "Megiddo".*[205]

MOUNT MEGIDDO, AKA, ARMAGEDDON

Why this place, of all places? Because of the symbolic irony. Many, many great battles have been fought in this region, from the 15th century BC to the 20th century CE. But there are two that would have had the most meaning and would have spoken to the hearts of first-century Jews.

The first battle worth mentioning is in fact what is considered to be the first battle to have been recorded in human history. In 1458 BC, Egypt went to war with the Canaanites, Syrians, and surrounding client nations. A young Pharaoh known as Thutmose III led his armies to Megiddo to clash swords and chariots with the Prince of Kadesh.

The Battle of Megiddo took place in the 15th century BC under the Thutmosid Dynasty. Josephus identifies the woman who took the infant Moses from the Nile River as Thermuthis (aka Tharmuth, aka Thermutis), daughter of the Pharaoh (Antiquities, 2:9:5. See also Jubilees 47:5). She is generally dated to the 15th century BC. In other words, the Exodus could have taken place not long after this battle.

> "Here, in 1479 B., Pharaoh Thutmose III fought the first battle in recorded history. Here, too, battled Deborah, Barak and Sisera (Judges 4:1–24, 5:1–31); Gideon conducted the first

---

[205] מגדו Megiddo means "mound of the governor". It is where King Josiah was slain by the Assyrians because he "would not listen to the words of Neco that came from the mouth of God, but went out to fight in the plain of Megiddo," (2 Chronicles 35:22). But foremost, the mention of Megiddo is in fulfillment of Zechariah 12. It is known historically as a place where several wars have taken place, dating as far back as the 15th century BC.

known night campaign here (Judges 6:3–8:28); and Saul and his son Jonathan fought their last heroic battle in the valley (1 Samuel 28–31; 2 Samuel 1; 1 Chronicles 10). Pharaoh Sheshonq I (c. 945–924 B.C.; probably the biblical pharaoh Shishak), fought here, as did the Israelite kings Jehu and Joram and Queen Jezebel (2 Kings 9:14–37; 2 Chronicles 22:5–9). Later, Antiochus, Ptolemy, Vespasian, Saladin, Napoleon and Allenbyd fought here. Indeed, the turbulent history of Israel and Judah, Canaan and Palestine, is reflected in microcosm in this blood-soaked little valley.

But what is it about this region that has prompted an almost continuous state of warfare?

The location: Although the Jezreel Valley is only 20 miles long by 7 miles wide, it runs across the breadth of Israel, connecting the Mediterranean Sea near Acco (Acre) in the west with the Jordan River and the lands beyond in the east. To its south rise the Carmel Mountains and the Gilboa Ridge. The valley lies at the juncture of several major north-south trade and military routes, including the Via Maris (the Way of the Sea), which linked Egypt with Mesopotamia in the east and Anatolia in the north. Thus whoever controlled the Jezreel Valley also controlled, by default, the trade and traffic through the area, be it of merchants or warriors, nomads or kings...

King Solomon, too, must have recognized the strategic importance of Megiddo, which according to the Bible, he fortified (1 Kings 9:15). By John's time, at least 13 battles had been fought at Megiddo and in the Jezreel Valley (four at Megiddo itself, four at Mount Tabor, one at Mount Gilboa, one at the Hill of Moreh [Endor], one at the city of Jezreel and two at other locations in the valley)...

But even more important than John's knowledge of the Jezreel Valley as an ancient battlefield was his awareness that King Josiah—Judah's last effective, independent ruler from the House of David—had died in battle at Megiddo...

King Josiah ascended to the throne of Judah in 639 BC as a

smooth-cheeked eight-year-old boy. Midway through his reign, he instituted a series of far-reaching reforms when a scroll of laws (probably a copy of Deuteronomy)e was "found" in the Temple in Jerusalem. Realizing that the people of Judah had strayed from Mosaic Law, Josiah implemented sweeping religious and political reforms, which included expanding Judah's territory to the north and annexing Samaria and the Jezreel Valley. Hailed by later writers as a "second David," not least because he was a legitimate descendant of the House of David, Josiah set out to return Judah to the greatness of the days of the United Monarchy of David and Solomon three centuries earlier. But when Josiah died at Megiddo, his dreams for a Judahite renaissance were buried with him...

The grieving Judahites named Jehoahaz, Josiah's son, king, but Necho swiftly removed Jehoahaz to Egypt and set another son of Josiah, Jehoiakim, on the throne to rule as a puppet king.

[sources: 2 Kings 23:29–30 and 2 Chronicles 35:20–25, 1 Esdras 1:25–32, Josephus: Antiquities of the Jews 10.74]."[206]

Ok, so what's the big deal? It's how the details of this ancient battle overlap with the current one about to unfold within the Holy Land. Let's break it down:

- In May of 1458 BC, the Canaanite rebellion against Egypt began. And in May of 66 AD, the Jewish Rebellion against Rome began. In May of 67 AD, Rome first struck the Holy Land (Jotapata), and May 70 is when Titus broke through the first wall of Jerusalem.

- Canaanites assembled to revolt against Egypt to be freed from their yoke of oppression, just like the Jews in the Holy Land revolted against Rome.

- Led by the Prince of Kadesh, the Canaanites were sure of their victory. A new Pharaoh (Thutmose III) had taken the throne, and he was considered a god. Likewise, the Jews were sure of their victory against Rome, and the Empire too had a new ruler

---

[206] <https://library.biblicalarchaeology.org/article/why-megiddo/>

(Vespasian) at the time.

- Like Josephus (scribe) did with Vespasian (warlord), Tjaneni (world's first war correspondent) recorded the accounts of Thutmose III in the war.

- Megiddo was where Egypt engaged the Canaanites. Likewise, Vespasian came through Megiddo to destroy the Northern regions of the Holy Land.[207]

- The Canaanites had built up Megiddo into a heavily fortified city, just as Jerusalem was a heavily fortified city.

- Megiddo was a reminder to the Jews of the times they lost their independence, their kingdom, and their autonomy: Saul and his son Jonathan fought their last heroic battle in the valley (1 Samuel 28–31; 2 Samuel 1; 1 Chronicles 10). And King Josiah (who ascended to the throne of Judah in 639 BC when he was 8 years old) was fatally wounded at Megiddo, bringing an end to the Davidic Dynasty (historically, not theologically).

In short, the significance of name dropping "Megiddo" in Revelation 16:16 was to remind the first-century Semitic audience of all the calamities that had come upon Israel in that place. Moreover, in the same way the fortified city of the Canaanites fell at Megiddo by the most powerful empire of that day (Egypt), so too would fortified Jerusalem fall by the most powerful empire of their day (Rome). Lastly, Rome and Egypt were still in political alliance in the first century AD, and half of the legions that razed the Holy Land came from Egypt: Vespasian had two legions from Rome, but Titus brought with him two legions from Egypt.

"And I will pour out on the house of David and on the inhabitants of Jerusalem the Spirit of grace and of pleading, **so that they will look at Me whom they pierced**; *and they will mourn for Him, like one mourning for an only son, and they will weep bitterly over Him like the*

---

[207] Thutmose chose the Aruna Pass (aka Wadi Ara, aka Via Maris, aka Musmus Pass). We know from history that Vespasian led his armies through this same location. And even a Roman milestone bearing his name, "Imperator Caesar Vespasianus", was discovered in 1973 in the nearby town of Afula, believed to be erected between 69 and 70 AD (A Milestone of AD 69 from Judaea. See, The Journal of Roman Studies Vol. 66 (1976), pp. 15-19.)

bitter weeping over a firstborn. On that day the **mourning in Jerusalem will be great**, *like the mourning of Hadadrimmon in the plain of* **Megiddo."** *Zechariah 12:10–11 (NASB, emphasis mine)*

There is great irony and double meaning in Jerusalem being likened to Egypt in Revelation 16. Egypt is seen as the undoing of Jerusalem in an illustrative sense (Egypt is like Rome), and in a moral sense, Jerusalem ended up becoming the very thing she was delivered out of, a house of bondage.

> א *(17) Now the seventh angel poured his vessel into the air,[208] and a great voice went out from the temple, from before the throne, which said, "It is done!"*

> א *(18) And there were lightnings and thunders. And there was the great earthquake[209] – the likes of which there has not been since the sons of man were upon the Land as this. Thus the violent shaking was significant.*

"[F]or there broke out a prodigious storm in the night, with the utmost violence, and very strong winds, with the largest showers of rain, with continual lightnings, terrible thunderings, and amazing concussions and bellowings of the earth, that was in an earthquake. These things were a manifest indication that some destruction was coming upon men, when the system of the world was put into this disorder; and anyone would guess that these wonders foreshadowed some grand calamities that were coming."[210]

While Josephus accounts for all the dramatic signs that led up to this event, there is still the need to address "the great earthquake". John wasn't being shown literal events, he was shown symbolic-hyperbole. **In the Old**

---

[208] It is worth noting the word "air" אאר is only found here and in 1 Thes 4:17.
[209] נולא הוא רבא has the classic Hebraic/Aramaic/Syriac sequence of definite articles, meaning "the earthquake" or even "The Earthquake", as opposed to "an earthquake". The text itself implies a singular, isolated event, not a global catastrophe. This notion is reinforced in the very next verse.
[210] Josephus, *Wars,* 4:4:5

Testament, earthquakes had to do with warfare and devastation concerning Israel (see Ezk 38:17–23; Isaiah 29:1–7; Zech 14:1–5).

> "[In total] 2,700,200 persons [were] collected out of remote places. But the entire nation was now shut up by fate, as in prison; and the Roman army encompassed the city when it was crowded with inhabitants. Accordingly the multitude of **those that therein perished exceeded all the destructions that either men or God ever brought upon the world**. For, to speak only of what was publicly known, the Romans slew some of them; some they carried captives."[211]

The Great Earthquake was the collapse of their governmental system and the great destruction that was about to befall Jerusalem, as the next verse illustrates.

> ℵ *(19) And the Great City[212] became three parts. And the cities of the peoples fell.[213] So Babylon The Great was remembered before God – to give to her the cup of the wine of His fiery-passion and of His indignation.*

Three, three, and three. All the way back in Revelation 12 I touched on the symbolism surrounding the third of the stars that the Leviathan swept down. These stars were Jewish people caught up in the anarchy that ultimately led to the fall of Jerusalem. The number three continues to be used here in chapter 16 with the Great City being divided into thirds. Before Jerusalem was physically split apart in the war, it already had cultural divides. Jerusalem had three major walls, three major towers, and three major sections within it (Upper City, Lower City, and New City). But the most important fact as it pertains to this section of Revelation were the three rebel factions within Jerusalem that consumed each other in civil war.

Not only was Jerusalem at war with Rome, it was also at war with itself. The Great City was divided into three parts by gruesome and horrific guerilla

---

[211] Josephus, *Wars*, 6:9:3,4
[212] I've stated repeatedly in this series: only Jerusalem was known as the Great City.
[213] Cities / peoples / fell – all three words are in the plural form.

and phycological tactics devised by its own countrymen. Three men named John of Gischala, Simon Bar Gioras, and Eleazar Bar Simon[214] led the main factions that tore the people apart in violent exchanges with each other.

Now you may be thinking, "so what?" In a perfect scenario, you would drop this book right now and pick up a copy (online it is free!) of Josephus' *War of the Jews* aka *Jewish Wars* and read books 5 and 6. That will give you the full scope of how bad things got within the walls of Jerusalem *before the Romans even laid siege*. These rebel leaders were so twisted, so evil, that they caused widespread murder and famine. So severe was the famine that it even led to cannibalism. They even killed any of their own countrymen who tried to escape.

Here is an excerpt from Josephus of these events:

> "And now there were three treacherous factions in the city, the one parted from the other. **Eleazar** and his party; that kept the sacred first fruits, came against John in their cups. Those that were with **John**, plundered the populace, and went out with zeal against Simon. This **Simon** had his supply of provisions from the city, in opposition to the seditious… Accordingly it so came to pass, that all the places that were about the temple were burnt down; and were become an intermediate desert

---

[214] You can read a little bit about these men here:
"It was John, the son of a certain man whose name was Levi, that drew them into this rebellion, and encouraged them in it. He was a cunning knave, and of a temper that could put on various shapes; very rash in expecting great things, and very sagacious in bringing about what he hoped for. It was known to everybody that he was fond of war." Josephus, Wars, 4:2:1.

"For Eleazar, the son of Simon, who made the first separation of the zealots from the people, and made them retire into the temple, appeared very angry at John's insolent attempts, which he made everyday upon the people. For this man never left off murdering… So he being desirous of gaining the entire power and dominion to himself, revolted from John. Each of these were followed by a great many of the zealots. These seized upon the inner court of the temple, and laid their arms upon the holy gates, and over the holy fronts of that court." Josephus, Wars, 5:1:2.

"But now the tyrant Simon, the son of Gioras, whom the people had invited in, out of the hopes they had of his assistance in the great distresses they were in; having in his power the upper city, and a great part of the lower, did now make more vehement assaults upon John, and his party." Josephus, Wars, 5:1:3.

space, ready for fighting on both sides of it: and that almost all that corn was burnt, which would have been sufficient for a siege of many years. So they were taken by the means of the famine: which it was impossible they should have been, unless they had thus prepared the way for it by this procedure.

And now, as the city was engaged in a war on all sides, from these treacherous crowds of wicked men; the people of the city between them were, like a great body, torn in pieces. The aged men, and the women were in such distress by their internal calamities, that they wished for the Romans; and earnestly hoped for an external war, in order to their delivery from their domestical miseries. The citizens themselves were under a terrible consternation and fear… For guards were set at all places; and the heads of the robbers, although they were seditious one against another in other respects, yet did they agree in killing those that were for peace with the Romans; or were suspected of an inclination to desert to them, as their common enemies… But for the seditious themselves, they fought against each other while they trod upon the dead bodies, as they lay heaped one upon another: and taking up a mad rage from those dead bodies that were under their feet, became the fiercer thereupon."[215]

The civil war so crazy that even the Romans took note and used it to their own tactical advantage:

"And now all the rest of the commanders of the Romans deemed this sedition among their enemies to be of great advantage to them; and were very earnest to march to the city: and they urged Vespasian… to make haste; and said to him, that 'The providence of God is on our side, by setting our enemies at variance against one another'…

But Vespasian replied… [that] God acts as a general of the Romans better than he can do; and is giving the Jews up to them, without any pains of their own; and granting their army

---

[215] Josephus, *Wars,* 5:1:4, 5.

a victory, without any danger. That therefore it is their best way, **while their enemies are destroying each other with their own hands**, and falling into the greatest of misfortunes… and are mad one against another… the Jews are vexed to pieces every day by their civil wars, and dissensions; and are under greater miseries than if they were once taken, could be inflicted on them by us…

[We Romans] ought by no means to meddle with these men now they are afflicted with a distemper at home. For should we now conquer them, it would be said the conquest was not owing to our bravery, **but to their sedition.**"[216]

Josephus was so distraught, not just while he was there during the war where he tried to convince the Jews to surrender, but also in recounting the details many years later. In the middle of his historical account he interjects his own personal lament:

"[The] dead bodies of strangers were mingled together with those of their own country [Jews]; and those of profane persons with those of the [Jewish] priests: and the blood of all sorts of dead carcasses stood in lakes in the holy courts themselves. And now,

'O must wretched city, what misery so great as this didst thou suffer from the Romans, when they came to purify thee from thy intestine hatred? For thou couldest be no longer a place fit for God; nor couldest thou long continue in being, after thou hadst been a sepulchre for the bodies of thy own people; and hadst made the holy house itself a burying place in this civil war of thine. Yet mayst thou again grow better, if perchance thou wilt hereafter appease the anger of that God who is the author of thy destruction.'

But I must restrain myself from these passions by the rules of history: since this is not a proper time for domestical lamentations, but for historical narrations; I therefore return to

---

[216] Ibid., 4:6:2 (emphasis mine).

the operations that follow in this sedition."[217]

There is also a prophetic echo to Ezekiel here. During his time, while prophesying concerning the first time Jerusalem and the Temple were about to be destroyed, Yahweh said to Ezekiel:

"Now, son of man, take a sharp sword and use it as a barber's razor to shave your head and your beard. Then take a set of scales and divide up the hair. When the days of your siege come to an end, burn a third of the hair inside the city. Take a third and strike it with the sword all around the city. And scatter a third to the wind. For I will pursue them with drawn sword. But take a few hairs and tuck them away in the folds of your garment. Again, take a few of these and throw them into the fire and burn them up. A fire will spread from there to all Israel. This is what the Sovereign Lord says: This is Jerusalem, which I have set in the center of the nations, with countries all around her." Ezekiel 5:1–5 (NIV)

Jerusalem was the Great City divided in three. **The Great Earthquake first brought about a complete collapse of the governmental system that corrupted the monarchy and priesthood and then the complete destruction of Jerusalem and the Holy Temple within it.**

א *(20) And every island fled and the mountains were not found.*

This is simply hyperbolic-euphemism. Throughout the Old Testament, "islands" or "coastlands" (אי) represented the regions of the Mediterranean, from Greece to Rome and beyond, to their west. Likewise, the mountains in the Holy Land are all just beyond the Sea of Galilee and Jordan River which flows north-south to the Dead Sea, to their east.

So for the person standing in the fields near Jerusalem, the idea is that all surrounding regions east and west of him fled. In typical Hebraic-hyperbole, the fear and dread coming was so great that all the neighbouring regions near and far ran for cover. The Psalms and Prophets in the Bible are especially known for animating creation and using things like mountains or seas as location references (for some examples see Ezk 6:1–3; 26:15, 18; 36:1–8; 47:8; Ps 75:7, 72:10, 46:3–4; but also 1 Macc 6:29; Est 10:1, Is 24:14).

---

[217] Ibid., 5:1:3.

There is then the ominous warning that Jesus gave to those who mourned him as he carried his cross to Golgotha:

> *"Now following Him was a large crowd of the people, and of women who were mourning and grieving for Him. But Jesus turned to them and said, 'Daughters of Jerusalem, stop weeping for Me, but weep for yourselves and for your children. For behold, days are coming when they will say, "Blessed are those who cannot bear, and the wombs that have not given birth, and the breasts that have not nursed." Then they will begin to say to the mountains, "Fall on us," and to the hills, "Cover us." For if they do these things when the tree is green, what will happen when it is dry?"'*
> *Luke 23:27–31 (NASB)*

Wow. How incredibly layered are these words? Unless you understand the prophecies of Jesus about the fall of Jerusalem and the destruction of the Temple, and how the Romans fulfilled these prophecies, the words of Jesus here just go right over your head.

We should also note that this 'creation fleeing' theme is not unique to John's Apocalypse.[218] Whenever there is a judgement about to begin, a figurative precursor takes place:

> *Revelation 6:14, "The sky receded like a scroll being rolled up, and every mountain and island was moved from its place."*

> *Revelation 20:11, "The earth and the heavens fled from His presence, and no place was found for them."*

In the grand scheme of things, there are two major judgements that John focuses on: Jerusalem and the Holy Land being the first, and the Final Judgement when the dead are raised being the second. Revelation 6:14 and 16:20 *both* focus on the same event: the judgement of Jerusalem and the Holy Land. Meanwhile, Revelation 20:11 focuses on the Last Judgement at the resurrection of the dead. **Because revelation 6 to 11 and 12 to 19 are parallel prophetic illustrations of the exact same event**, it makes sense to have to read of the islands and mountains fleeing twice.

---

[218] Cf. Isaiah 34:4; Nahum 1:5; Jeremiah 4:23–24; Haggai 2:6.

> (21) *And great hailstones, about a talent,[219] fell from the sky on the children of men. So the children of men blasphemed God concerning the blow of hail, because of the great excess of the blow.*

What I'm about to share will blow your mind. Or at least, I can tell you about how it blew mine. In fact, when I first read this, tears streamed down my face. So many emotions: the discovery, the symbolism, the prophetic accuracy of Jesus and John... Here, let me share it with you:

> "These [siege] engines, that all the [Roman] legions had ready prepared for them [Jews], were admirably contrived: but still more extraordinary ones belonged to the Tenth Legion. Those that threw darts [arrows], and those that threw stones were more forcible, and larger than the rest...
>
> Now the stones that were cast **were of the weight of a talent**; and were carried two furlongs, and farther. The blow they gave was no way to be sustained; not only by those that stood first in the way, but by those that were beyond them, for a great space. As for the Jews, they at first watched the coming of the stone: **for it was of a white colour**; and could therefore not only be perceived by the great noise it made, but could be seen also before it came by its brightness.
>
> Accordingly the watchmen that sat upon the towers gave them notice when the engine was let go, and the stone came from it; and cried out aloud, in their own country language [Aramaic], **'the Son cometh!'**"[220]

First, the stones the Roman siege engines threw matched the hail of Revelation 16:21 verbatim. We know that it is impossible for water to recirculate up and down in the sky, becoming ice and growing bigger to the point that it weighs a hundred pounds (45 kilograms). This would defy gravity. I live in Alberta, Canada, where we have some of the greatest hail storms in North America. I've seen baseball sized hail, and those only weigh a pound (0.45 kg)! Within the context of the Roman siege of Jerusalem, the 100 lbs. stones they threw to break down the walls makes perfect sense.

---

[219] Approximately 100 lbs.
[220] Josephus, *Wars,* 5:6:3. Emphasis mine.

Now, if anyone wants to sit here and argue about how the hailstones are about some global catastrophic event, please do so. I won't join. For the rest of us, let's continue to unpack the eyewitness account of Josephus.

After the weight, we have a match in color: Josephus tells us the stones were white, which would look *symbolically* like hail from a distance. But if this wasn't enough, the final point is where we sober ourselves from whatever delusion we might have been under that tried to convince us that the words of John did not pertain to Jerusalem.

The guards who stood atop the third great outer wall of Jerusalem, along with the guards within the three great towers that connected the walls (see why three is major theme?) saw the great siege works and tried to defend against them. This was in vain. The Romans rolled their weapons of war within strike range, loaded up those 100 pound white stones, and made it rain doom over the Great City. Upon seeing these great stones hurled their way, they began to shout, "the Son cometh!" When I first saw this, I had to pause and read it again.

Why did they say this?

If you recall, I wrote in the first book of this series that one of the main accusation made against Jesus was that he proclaimed he would destroy the Holy Temple. This was considered treason.

> *"Destroy this temple, and I will raise it again in three days." John 2:19*

> *"This man said, 'I am able to destroy the temple of God and rebuild it in three days.'" Matthew 26:61*

> *"You who are going to destroy the temple and rebuild it in three days, save Yourself!" Matthew 27:40*

> *"For we have heard him say that Jesus of Nazareth will destroy this place and change the customs that Moses handed down to us." Acts 6:14*

Of course we know Jesus was misunderstood, but it wasn't just in John 2:19 and the other above verses. It was also in what we call the Olivet Discourse (Luke 21, Matt 23–25), where on the Mount of Olives Jesus prophesied the destruction of Jerusalem and the Temple (which is basically the whole point of book one of this series!). In the various accounts that record his warnings, he consistently drops the same prophetic references:

> *"Truly I say to you, all these things will come upon this generation. Jerusalem, Jerusalem, who kills the prophets and stones those who have been sent to her! …Behold, your house is being left to you desolate! For I say to you, from now on you will not see Me until you say,* **'Blessed is the One who comes in the name of the Lord!'"** *Matthew 23:36–39 (NASB, emphasis mine)*

> *"But immediately after the tribulation of those days the sun will be darkened, and the moon will not give its light, and the stars will fall from the sky, and the powers of the heavens will be shaken. And then the sign of the Son of Man will appear in the sky, and then all the tribes of the earth will mourn, and they will* **see the Son of Man coming** *on the clouds of the sky with power and great glory." Matthew 24:29–30 (NASB)*

> *"…and they will fall by the edge of the sword, and will be led captive into all the nations; and Jerusalem will be trampled underfoot by the Gentiles until the times of the Gentiles are fulfilled. There will be signs in the sun and moon and stars… for the powers of the heavens will be shaken. And then they will* **see the Son of Man coming** *in a cloud with power and great glory." Luke 21:24–27 (NASB)*

Then there was his triumphant entry into Jerusalem. Between what the people shouted and what Jesus said and did, you can see how it would have rubbed religious leaders the wrong way:

> *"And as soon as He was approaching, near the descent of the Mount of Olives, the whole crowd of the disciples began to praise God joyfully with a loud voice for all the miracles which they had seen, shouting:*

> *'Blessed is the King,* **the One who comes** *in the name of the Lord; Peace in heaven and glory in the highest!'*

> *…When He approached Jerusalem, He saw the city and wept over it, saying, "If you had known on this day, even you, the conditions for peace! But now they have been hidden from your eyes.* **For the days will come upon you when your enemies will put up a**

barricade against you, and surround you and hem you in on every side, and they will level you to the ground, and throw down your children within you, and they will not leave in you one stone upon another, because you did not recognize the time of your visitation. And ***Jesus entered the temple grounds and began to drive out those who were selling,*** saying to them, 'It is written: 'And My house will be a house of prayer,' but you have made it a den of robbers.'" Luke 19:37–38, 41–46 (NASB, emphasis mine)

I'm not going to revisit all the Old Testament prophecies Jesus was quoting in these statements because this has already been covered at length. Suffice to say that the Jews grew tired of the words of Jesus and those of his followers who would have repeated his warnings in the decades that followed his resurrection, warning that the Temple would be destroyed at the coming of the Son of Man, or Son of God. Though ominous, the warnings were seen as ludicrous… until now.

Consider that in and around these days when the siege began, the Jews also experienced the following events:

> "Thus there was a star, resembling a sword, which stood over the city: and a comet, that continued a whole year… [And] chariots and troops of soldiers in their armour were seen running about among the clouds, and surrounding of cities. Moreover, at that feast which we call Pentecost; as the priests were going by night into the inner [court of the] temple… and heard a great noise: and after that they heard a sound, as of a multitude, saying, 'Let us remove hence.' But what is still more terrible; there was one Jesus [not Christ], the son of Ananus, a plebeian, and an husbandman… began on a sudden to cry aloud, 'A voice from the east; a voice from the west; a voice from the four winds; a voice against Jerusalem, and the holy house'… This was his cry, as he went about by day and by night, in all the lanes of the city… And just as he added at the last, "Woe, woe to myself also," there came a stone out of one of the engines, and smote him, and killed him immediately."[221]

---

[221] Josephus, *Wars,* 6:5:3.

Taking all these things into consideration, you now understand why the Jewish soldiers exclaimed, "The Son cometh!" when they saw the hail stones hurled towards them. **The fables and folklore of these crazy *Nazarenes*, followers of the Nazarene named Jesus, whom they claimed was Messiah, were in fact true.** The warnings of the Temple being destroyed at the coming of the Son of Man, made some 37 years prior, was no longer the butt of their jokes; it was a dread in the pit of their stomachs.

PS – one final thought: in Deuteronomy 22:21 (cf. John 8:4–5), a woman who commits adultery was to be stoned to death under the Law of Moses. The great hail stones referenced here in Revelation allude to that. The imagery of Jerusalem as harlot becomes a focal point in the next two chapters of Revelation, as we shall cover.

8 THE UNFAITHFUL WIFE: CH. 17

"For I betrothed you to one husband, so that to Christ I might present you as a pure virgin." — 2 Corinthians 11:2

Betrothal was a big deal for the Apostle Paul. He taught Jewish followers of Jesus how crucial it was for them to divorce themselves from the Law through death in Christ, in order to then be in matrimony with Christ.

> *"Or do you not know, brothers and sisters (for I am speaking to those who know the Law), that the Law has jurisdiction over a person as long as he lives? For the married woman is bound by law to her husband as long as he is alive; but if her husband dies, she is released from the law concerning the husband. So then, if while her husband is alive she gives herself to another man, she will be called an adulteress; but if her husband dies, she is free from the law, so that she is not an adulteress if she gives herself to another man.*
>
> *Therefore, my brothers and sisters, you also were put to death in regard to the Law through the body of Christ, so that you might belong to another, to Him who was raised from the dead, in order that we might bear fruit for God."* Romans 7:1–4 (NASB)

Paul's analogy is derived from the Old Testament. There, Yahweh identifies Himself as Israel's *husband,* and He calls Israel His *wife.* Of course, as we know, this all goes sideways when Israel becomes unfaithful to Yahweh and earns herself the title of *harlot.* Let's explore this further.

There are a handful of very powerful prophetic accounts where **God is personified as a husband and Israel as a wife**. The formula is consistent in all instances: First, Yahweh calls out Israel for being an unfaithful wife (a harlot) and then declares that she will therefore reap the consequences of her actions. Second, Yahweh then promises to restore her to purity and matrimony with Him.

Now listen, we are going to have to do some Bible reading. Quite a bit actually. If we don't, you're not going to be fully convinced that the Whore of Babylon is Jerusalem. You might still entertain the notion that it could somehow be Rome, or worse, America. So let's spend some time familiarizing ourselves with the texts John and his audience would have already known.

First in Isaiah:

> *"This is what the Lord says:*
> *'Where is the* **certificate of divorce**
> *By which I have sent your mother away?'" Isaiah 50:1 (emphasis mine)*
>
> *"'For your husband is your Maker,*
> *Whose name is the Lord of armies…*
> *For the Lord has called you,*
> *Like a wife forsaken and grieved in spirit,*
> *Even like a wife of one's youth when she is rejected,'*
> *Says your God…*
> *'For a brief moment I abandoned you,*
> *But with great compassion I will gather you.*
> *In an outburst of anger*
> *I hid My face from you for a moment,*
> *But with everlasting favor I will have compassion on you,'*
> *Says the Lord your Redeemer." Isaiah 54:5–8 (NASB)*

Then in Jeremiah:

REVELATION: DAWN OF ETERNITY

"Go and proclaim in the ears of Jerusalem, saying, 'This is what the Lord says:

I remember regarding you the devotion of your youth,
Your love when you were a bride,
Your following after Me in the wilderness,
Through a land not sown.
Israel was holy to the Lord…

Have you not done this to yourself
By your abandoning the Lord your God
When He led you in the way?
But now what are you doing on the road to Egypt,
Except to drink the waters of the Nile?
Or what are you doing on the road to Assyria,
Except to drink the waters of the Euphrates River?
Your own wickedness will correct you,
And your apostasies will punish you…

For on every high hill
And under every leafy tree
You have lain down as a prostitute…

So the house of Israel is shamed;
They, their kings, their leaders,
Their priests, and their prophets…'"
Jeremiah 2:2–3, 17–20, 26 (NASB)

"God says, 'If a husband divorces his wife
And she leaves him
And becomes another man's wife,
Will he return to her again?
Would that land not be completely defiled?
But you are a prostitute with many lovers;
Yet you turn to Me,' declares the Lord…

<u>Yet you had a prostitute's forehead;</u>
You refused to be ashamed…

Then the Lord said to me in the days of King Josiah, "Have you seen what faithless Israel did? She went up on every high hill and under every leafy tree, and she prostituted herself there…
And I saw that for all the adulteries of faithless Israel, I had sent her away and given her a certificate of divorce*…*
Yet in spite of all this her treacherous sister Judah did not return to Me with all her heart, but rather in deception,' declares the Lord."

'Return, faithless Israel,' declares the Lord;
'I will not look at you in anger.
For I am gracious,' declares the Lord;
'I will not be angry forever."
Jeremiah 3:1, 3, 6, 8, 10, 12 NASB, emphasis mine)

"'Behold, days are coming,' declares the Lord, 'when I will make a new covenant with the house of Israel and the house of Judah, not like the covenant which I made with their fathers on the day I took them by the hand to bring them out of the land of Egypt, My covenant which they broke, although I was a husband to them,' declares the Lord. 'For this is the covenant which I will make with the house of Israel after those days,' declares the Lord: 'I will put My law within them and write it on their heart; and I will be their God, and they shall be My people.'"
Jeremiah 31:31–33 (NASB)

Then there is Hosea. This guy is a legend. God asks him to live his life as a living testimony of Yahweh's marriage situation with Israel, meaning he is asked to marry a harlot! But God asks this of Hosea in order to tell mankind throughout all the ages that even when we are unfaithful over and over, God will continue to pursue us.

"'Go, take for yourself a wife inclined to infidelity, and children of infidelity; for the land commits flagrant infidelity, abandoning the Lord.' So he went and took Gomer the daughter of Diblaim, and she conceived and bore him a son." Hosea 1:2–3 (NASB)

Gomer of course is unfaithful. But Hosea goes after her again, just as God did and does!

> *"Go again, love a woman who is loved by her husband, yet is committing adultery, as the Lord loves the sons of Israel… So I purchased her for myself for fifteen shekels of silver, and a homer and a lethech of barley. Then I said to her, 'You shall live with me for many days. You shall not play the prostitute, nor shall you have another man; so I will also be toward you.' For the sons of Israel will live for many days without a king or leader, without sacrifice or memorial stone, and without ephod or household idols.* **Afterward the sons of Israel will return and seek the Lord their God and David their king; and they will come trembling to the Lord and to His goodness in the last days.**" Hosea 3:1–5 *(NASB, emphasis mine)*

The book of Hosea is only 14 chapters long, but it contains some beautiful love notes from Yahweh God to His unfaithful bride. It is worth leafing through the pages of the prophet's words, for there are too many to list here. Suffice to say that the formula continues in Hosea, where God promises to restore his unfaithful wife.

I saved Ezekiel for last because of how much his prophetic book overlaps with John's Vision. Though we only find the allegory in chapter 16, it is packed full of grace and hope-filled eschatological themes. I can only provide snippets, but you should read the chapter in full.

> *"Son of man, make known to Jerusalem her abominations, and say, 'This is what the Lord God says to Jerusalem: Your origin and your birth are from the land of the Canaanite; your father was an Amorite and your mother a Hittite. As for your birth, on the day you were born your navel cord was not cut, nor were you washed with water for cleansing; you were not rubbed with salt or even wrapped in cloths. No eye looked with pity on you to do any of these things for you, to have compassion on you. Rather you were thrown out into the open field, for you were abhorred on the day you were born.*
>
> *When I passed by you and saw you squirming in your blood, I said to you while you were in your blood, 'Live!' Yes, I said to you while you were in your blood, 'Live!' I made you very numerous, like plants of the field. Then you grew up, became tall and reached the age for fine jewelry; your*

breasts were formed and your hair had grown. Yet you were naked and bare.

'Then I passed by you and saw you, and behold, you were at the time for love; so I spread My garment over you and covered your nakedness. I also swore an oath to you and entered into a covenant with you so that you became Mine,' declares the Lord God. 'Then I bathed you with water, washed off your blood from you, and anointed you with oil.'"
Ezekiel 16:2–9 (NASB)

Up to this point we have a truly beautiful illustration of how Yahweh God takes care of Israel, brings her up from nothing, and nourishes her into health. Note that she is covered, cleansed, and anointed with oil. She becomes a radiant woman. God then enters into a covenant with her, and she becomes His bride.

"'I also clothed you with colorfully woven cloth and put sandals of fine leather on your feet; and I wrapped you with fine linen and covered you with silk. I adorned you with jewelry, put bracelets on your wrists, and a necklace around your neck. I also put a ring in your nose, earrings in your ears, and a beautiful crown on your head. So you were adorned with gold and silver, and your dress was of fine linen, silk, and colorfully woven cloth. You ate fine flour, honey, and oil; so you were exceedingly beautiful and advanced to royalty. Then your fame spread among the nations on account of your beauty, for it was perfect because of My splendor which I bestowed on you,' declares the Lord God." Ezekiel 16:10–14 (NASB)

Here, in verses 10 to 14, we begin to see where all the imagery of the Harlot's adornment in John's Revelation comes from!

"'But you trusted in your beauty and became unfaithful because of your fame, and you poured out your obscene practices on every passer-by to whom it might be tempting. You took some of your clothes, made for yourself high places of various colors, and committed prostitution on them, which should not come about nor happen. You also took your beautiful jewels made of My gold and of My silver, which I had given you, and made for yourself male images so that you might commit prostitution with them.'"
Ezekiel 16:15–17 (NASB)

At this point we see God's heart break as Israel continually prostitues herself to other gods. But heartbreak turns into indignation in the following verses.

> *"Furthermore, you took your sons and daughters whom you had borne to Me and sacrificed them to idols to be devoured. Were your obscene practices a trivial matter? You slaughtered My children and offered them to idols by making them pass through the fire. And besides all your abominations and obscene practices, you did not remember the days of your youth, when you were naked and bare and squirming in your blood."*
> Ezekiel 16:20–22 (NASB)

These abominations are in reference to child sacrifice at the Hinnom Valley (Gehenna!), which is also mentioned in Jeremiah 7:31–32. It is an absolute horror and abomination when you think of such things being performed. Can you even imagine this day and age how people would react if they saw children being thrown into sacrificial fires? God then goes on to list the Egyptians, Philistines, Assyrians, and Chaldeans amongst her suitors, leading to the pinnacle verse:

"You adulteress wife, who takes strangers instead of her husband!" Ezekiel 16:32

Then come the consequences:

> *"'therefore, behold, I am going to gather all your lovers whom you pleased, all those whom you loved as well as all those whom you hated…*
> *I will also hand you over to your lovers, and they will tear down your shrines, demolish your high places, strip you of your clothing,* **take away your jewels**, *and will leave you naked and bare. They will incite a crowd against you,* **and they will stone you** *and cut you to pieces with their swords. And they will* **burn your houses with fire** *and execute judgments against you in the sight of many women. Then I will put an end to your prostitution, and you will also no longer pay your lovers."* Ezekiel 16:37, 39–41 (NASB, emphasis mine)

These things all came about historically when Babylon sacked Jerusalem and destroyed Solomon's Temple. The Jews were then led into captivity, which is where we get the story of Daniel in Babylon. But the overlap with the second time Jerusalem and the Temple are destroyed (this time by Rome) cannot be missed. As you will see, the parallels are heavily drawn upon in Revelation. Now, on to redemption.

> *"Now your older sister is Samaria, who lives north of you with her daughters; and your younger sister, who lives south of you, is Sodom with her daughters. Yet you have not merely walked in their ways and [aa]committed their abominations; but, as if that were too little, you also acted more corruptly in all your conduct than they…*
> **'Nevertheless, I will restore their fortunes, the fortunes of Sodom and her daughters, the fortunes of Samaria and her daughters, and along with them your own fortunes**…
> *Your sisters, Sodom with her daughters and Samaria with her daughters, will return to their former state, and you with your daughters will also return to your former state…*
> *'Nevertheless, I will remember My covenant with you in the days of your youth, and I will establish an everlasting covenant with you…*
> *So I will establish My covenant with you, and you shall know that I am the Lord, so that you may remember and be ashamed, and not open your mouth again because of your disgrace,* **when I have forgiven you for all that you have done**,*' the Lord God declares."*
> Ezekiel 16:46–47, 53, 55, 60, 62–63 (NASB, emphasis mine)

That gave me goosebumps. Do you know that the "former state" of Sodom is that it was like the Garden of Eden (see Gen 13:10)? I mean, this is the place that is considered to have been submerged beneath the Dead Sea after the rain of fire and sulfur. So if this is the extent to which God plans to restore Sodom, can you imagine the extent to which He will restore Israel?

As Paul wrote,

> *"[For] a partial hardening has happened to Israel until the fullness of the Gentiles has come in; and so all Israel will be saved… For God has shut up all in disobedience, so that He may show mercy to all… For from Him, and through Him, and to Him are all things."*
> Romans 11:25–26, 32, 36

I love how Scripture will so often speak for itself. Taking into consideration *all* of the passages we have read through, my hope is you now have an appreciation for how significant the imagery of a harlot is to the

Jewish narrative. I also hope you can see that God only had *one* bride in the Old Covenant, and she was not Rome (or America)! We now have sufficient Biblical context to begin our journey into Revelation 17.

> ℵ *(1) Now there came one of the seven angels, who had with them the seven vessels, and spoke with me saying, 'Follow me; I shall show you the lawsuit of the Harlot²²² situating²²³ over many waters,'*

> ℵ *(2) 'For the kings of the earth committed fornication with her, and all the inhabitants of earth²²⁴ are drunk with the wine of her prostitution.'*

One of the most practical illustrations of this (Josephus provides many more) is the affair between Queen Bernice (Jewish nobility, daughter of Agrippa I, see also Acts 25:13, 23) and Titus (the Roman noble who destroyed Jerusalem, son of Vespasian!). The worst part? They were lovers *during the Jewish-Roman War* while the Holy Land was being devastated. Ironically, after the siege of Jerusalem ended, Titus dumped her.²²⁵

> ℵ *(3) Then he brought me to the wilderness in the Spirit, and I saw the wife²²⁶ who was sitting²²⁷ on the blood-red savage animal²²⁸, which was full of blasphemous names, which had seven heads but ten horns.*

---

²²² ܙܢܝܬܐ = "fornicator", "prostitute", or "harlot".

²²³ Though ܝܬܒ can mean "to sit", it can also mean "to inhabit" or "to dwell". The latter translations would make sense in the context of the Diaspora Jews who lived all over the far reaches of the Empire in those days. Keep this in mind when reading verse 15, where the interpretation of the waters is "peoples and multitudes, and nations and languages".

²²⁴ One of the few instances where לָאָרֶץ "the land" takes on a broader meaning, i.e. "the earth", given the context of the verse: "For the kings of the earth... and all earth dwellers..."

²²⁵ For the full story, read Tacitus, *Histories,* 2:2:1, 2:81:2; Suetonius, *Titus,* 7:1; Cassius Dio, *Roman History,* 66:15:3–4.

²²⁶ ܐܢܬܬܐ is most often translated as "wife".

²²⁷ Same word as in verse 1, ܝܬܒ, but here the context suggests "sitting" instead of "dwelling".

²²⁸ This is the same animal from Revelation 13:1, only this time John mentions its color to us.

> א (4) *Now the wife was arrayed in purple and scarlet, and overlaid with gold and precious stones and pearls, and had a cup of gold in her hand, and it was full of the defilement and pollution of her prostitution.*

The word for "woman" here is most often translated as "wife", or at least it is implied, such as in Matthew 5:28. This, in conjunction with the definite article "the", means we are not dealing with "a" woman but rather "the" woman, or "the wife". Now think back to all the Scriptures we read above. John's vision is first and foremost about Jerusalem and the Holy Land. So "the wife" referenced here is none other than the wife of Yahweh. Verse 18 of this chapter emphasises the point further: the "Great City" (Jerusalem) is "the wife".

Because we are dealing with Jerusalem, the description of her garments carries even greater significance. As Beale has pointed out, the combination of words here is almost identical to the Septuagint's (Greek Old Testament) description of the high priest's garments.[229]

> א (5) *And upon her forehead was written: 'Mystery – Babylon the Great, the mother of harlots[230] and of the pollution of the Land.[231]*

Jerusalem's forehead is a clear allusion to Jeremiah's prophecy:

> *"And you [Jerusalem] have defiled a land*
> *With your prostitution and your wickedness.*
> *Therefore the showers have been withheld,*
> *And there has been no spring rain.*
> *Yet **you had a prostitute's forehead**;*
> *You refused to be ashamed."*

---

[229] Beale, *Revelation*, 886, citing Exod. 25:3–7; 28:5–9, 28:15–20, 35:6; 36:9–12; 36:15–21 LXX (the Septuagint). See also Chilton, *Days of Vengeance*, 429; and Gentry, *A Preterist View of Revelation*, 76.

[230] Israel as harlot is a prevalent OT theme: Ezek 16:15, 17, 28, 35, 41; 23:1–21, 44; Isa 1:21; 57:3; Jer 2:20; 3:1; 13:27; Hos 2:2–5; 4:12, 15, 18; 5:4; 9:1; Mic 1:7.

[231] לָאָרֶץ "the land" is used here because of the next verse (6) and beyond, which takes us back to the immediate context of the Holy Land and not the broad reaches of the Roman Empire.

Jeremiah 3:2–3 (NASB, emphasis mine)

And it is to be contrasted against the high priest's head-plate, since Jerusalem is being depicted as one wearing priestly garments:

> *"'You shall also make a plate of pure gold and engrave on it, like the engravings of a signet, 'Holy to the Lord. You shall fasten it on a violet cord, and it shall be on the turban... It shall be* **on Aaron's forehead**.*'" Exodus:28:36–38 (NASB, emphasis mine)*

א *(6) And I saw that the wife was drunk with the blood of the Saints and with the blood of the witnesses of Yeshua. And I was marveled with great astonishment when I saw her.*

The prophecies of Jesus now come to light:

"[For] surely no prophet can die outside Jerusalem!
Jerusalem, Jerusalem, you who kill the prophets and stone those sent to you..." Luke 13:33–34 (NIV)

"Therefore I am sending you prophets and sages and teachers. Some of them you will kill and crucify; others you will flog in your synagogues and pursue from town to town. And so upon you will come all the righteous blood that has been shed on earth, from the blood of righteous Abel to the blood of Zechariah son of Berekiah, whom you murdered between the temple and the altar. Truly I tell you, all this will come on this generation." Matthew 23:34–36 (NIV)

"God in his wisdom said, 'I will send them prophets and apostles, some of whom they will kill and others they will persecute.' Therefore this generation will be held responsible for the blood of all the prophets that has been shed since the beginning of the world [or "age"], from the blood of Abel to the blood of Zechariah, who was killed between the altar and the sanctuary. Yes, I tell you, this generation will be held responsible for it all. Woe to you experts in the law..." Luke 11:49–52 (NIV)

And who can forget the tragic and fateful words of the religious mob at the sentencing of Jesus?

"His blood shall be on us and on our children!" (Matthew 27:25)

Let us continue:

- ܐ *(7) And the angel said to me, 'Why do you marvel? I will tell you the mystery of the wife and of the savage animal that bears her, which has seven heads and ten horns.'*

- ܐ *(8) The savage animal which you saw – which was, and is not – prepares to come up from the Sea and it moves forth for destruction[232]. But they that inhabit the Land will marvel[233] – whose names are not written in The Book of The Living[234] from the foundations of the Age – when they see the savage animal which was, and is not, and is approaching.'*

Those who are written in the book of Yeshua (those who are in matrimony with him) won't marvel - because they've already been warned! They have the words of Jesus in Matthew 24 and Luke 21, and now also the visions of John. As discussed in Revelation 13, "The Book of The Living" is a reference to a God-life and covenant identity.

- ܐ *(9) 'Here is the mind which has wisdom: seven heads, they are seven hills[235] where the wife sits upon them.*

Israel's relationship with Rome deepened in the 150 years (approx.) leading up to the incarnation of Jesus. The Hasmoneans (the guys who led

---

[232] ܐܒܕܢܐ is the noun "destruction". With both a direct object marker and a definite article, this word seems to imply a specific event. It also connects us to Revelation 9:11, ܡܚܒܠ, "destroyer" or "Abaddon". The key here is to understand that the beast is not going to its own destruction, but rather it is bringing about destruction.
[233] A play on verses 6 and 7 where John is lightly rebuked for marveling. John has no need to marvel, as he is getting an early warning.
[234] "Life" is conjugated as a determined plural emphatic noun; hence, "The Living".
[235] These are the seven hills or mounts of Rome. See Caird, Revelation, 216; Richard Bauckham, The Climax of Prophecy: Studies on the Book of Revelation (Edinburgh: T. & T. Clark, 1993), 395. See also Virgil *Georgics* 2.535, Horace *Carmen Saecularae* 7, and Cicero *ad Atticum* 6.5.

the Maccabean revolt) took over the monarchy and priesthood of Jerusalem. They were able to do this because they had the political backing of Rome.

"Now when Cesar was come to Rome [and] Hyrcanus [the Hasmonean ruler over Jerusalem] sent ambassadors to him: and by them **desired that he would ratify that league of friendship and mutual alliance which was between them**. And it seems to me to be necessary here to give an account of **all the honours that the Romans and their emperors have paid to our nation**; and of the leagues of mutual assistance they have made with it: that all the rest of mankind may know **what regard the Kings of Asia and Europe have had to us**; and that they have been abundantly satisfied of our courage and fidelity... Nay, besides this, Julius Cesar made a pillar of brass for the Jews at Alexandria; and declared publicly that they were citizens of Alexandria [of Egypt]."[236]

> א *(10) And these are the seven kings; five have fallen, and one that exists. The other has not yet come, but after a little while*[237] *he will come, and it will be granted to him to remain.*[238]

The first five kings are: Julius Caesar, Augustus, Tiberius, Caligula, and Claudius. Nero was the sixth Caesar of Rome, the "one that exists". **Vespasian was the one that "after a little while he will come"**, but between Nero's death and Vespasian's rule there were three generals who fought for the throne. In what is known as the Year of Four Emperors, Galba, Otho, and Vitellius rose and fell (by assassination) in rapid succession. They were never established as Caesars, and their short stints were part of Rome's great civil war.

It was only Vespasian who saved the Empire by firmly securing the throne. It was he who was "granted to remain", in contrast with the three failed Caesars – Galba, Otho, and Vitellius – who were not granted permanence. Vespasian not only reigned for 10 years, he also established the Flavian Dynasty: Vespasian (69–79), succeeded by his two sons Titus (79–

---

[236] Josephus, *Antiquities*, 14:10:1.

[237] ܩܲܠܝܼܠ most often means "little, short, brief". It is often used in the New Testament with relation to *time*. This is also the case with John in his Gospel and Vision, using this word primarily to indicate a short time or a little while (see John 7:33; 12:35; 13:33; 14:19; especially 16:16–19; Rev 20:3).

[238] ܠܲܡܟܲܬܪܘ "to stay, remain, persist". Here in the infinitive construct, *permanence* is further emphasized.

81) and Domitian (81–96).

> א (11) *But the Leviathan and the savage animal that exists and is not: there's an eighth, which is from the seventh, and it moves forth for destruction.*[239]

As discussed above, Vespasian is the seventh king since Galba, Otho, and Vitellius didn't actually reign. Therefore, the eighth, being "from the seventh", is his son, Titus. The final confirmation of Titus' identity is his association with "Abaddon" (destruction) here in verses 8 and 11, which takes us back to Revelation 9 and the revealing of Titus. **Both the seventh and eighth head, Vespasian and Titus, "move forth for destruction".** Not their own destruction, but the Holy Land's. Though grammatically awkward, verse 11 communicates a combined effort between Satan, Rome, Vespasian, and Titus to destroy Israel and Jerusalem.

> א (12) *'And ten horns which you saw, they are the ten kings who until now were not of the kingdom.*[240] *However, they took on authority like the kings*[241] *for one moment to be capturing alongside the savage animal.' (13) 'These ones have a single desire: to offer their own military might and power to the savage animal.' (14.) 'These ones alongside the Lamb will engage them,*[242] *and the Lamb will overcome them.'*
>
> *'Therefore, He is the Lord of Power and the King of Kings and his companions are the called, the chosen, and the faithful.'*

---

[239] "Moves forth for destruction" is identical to verse 8.

[240] "Not of the kingdom". Because we have been dealing with Rome exclusively, it is the only kingdom within context. See also v. 17 below. Taking it a step further, "Empire" is implied. We know historically that Vespasian and Titus were accompanied by other kings from surrounding nations who joined forces out of hatred for the Jews.

[241] Referring to the sixth, seventh, and eighth heads, the "kings" or Caesars.

[242] ܢܩܦܘܢ "engaging them" and "engaged them". Both are the same word. And is also found in Rev 2:16: "to approach, draw near, encounter". It can also mean to draw close for the purpose of war. Aphel active participle = for the purpose of war. Hence military verbiage, "to engage".

Aren't the armies waging war against the Lamb? I argue no for two reasons. First, the sentence structure. Second, the war is against the Holy Land. Now for the first point, let us compare a similar sentence structure found in Revelation 12:7 with the one found here in Revelation 17:14. (Bear with me as we get into the technicalities of the Aramaic language.)

Comparing Revelation 12:7 and 17:14:

(12:7)
"Michael and his angels (subject)
engaged (verb) with (particle)
the Leviathan (object)
and the Leviathan and his angels (subject)
engaged them (verb that contains an object)."

(17:14)
"These ones (subject, representing Rome and allies) with/alongside (particle)
the Lamb (object of particle but technically still part of the subject)
will engage them (verb that contains an object, the inhabitants of the Holy Land),
and the Lamb (subject)
will overcome them (verb that contains an object, the inhabitants of the Holy Land)."

In 12:7 there are two groups coming together for war: Michael's group and the Leviathan's group. Therefore we can properly interpret the scene as Michael and his angels engaging **with/against** the Leviathan. But in Revelation 17:14, there are three groups coming together for war: Rome and their allies, the Lamb, and the inhabitants of the Holy Land. Therefore this text reads as Rome and their allies ("these ones") **together with** the Lamb engage in war against the inhabitants of the Holy Land ("them").

What's my point? Whoever is engaging/making war (the subject) is announced *before* the verb, and then the one who is on the receiving end of the verb (the object) comes after the verb (or the verb itself is properly conjugated [in this instance the plural, "them"]). So the traditional reading, "They made war with the Lamb" doesn't make grammatical sense in the Aramaic text.

The second reason I argue that these armies are not making war against the Lamb is the immediate context. We have been reading how Rome and the nations surrounding the Holy Land have all come together with one purpose: to wage war against the Holy Land. Jesus in Matthew 23 and 24 and Luke 19 and 21 prophesied at length concerning this war. And now it has come. **The implication of Revelation 17:14 is the armies are not fighting *against* the Lamb, they are fighting *on his behalf.*** Revelation 17:17 drives this point home:

"Indeed, God set it in their hearts to accomplish His will, and to accomplish their collective will, and to be offering up their kingdom to this savage animal until the words of God fulfill themselves."

Moving on, what do we make of the ten kings? They were people who held military rank during the Jewish-Roman War, a common career path for aspiring politicians. Vespasian himself rose to the highest office, not through the senate, but as a general.

> "On the whole, we conclude that this symbol signifies the auxiliary princes and chiefs who were allies of Rome and received commands in the Roman army during the Jewish war. We know from Tacitus and Josephus that several kings of neighbouring nations followed Vespasian and Titus to the war. Allusion has already been made to some of these auxiliaries: Antiochus, Sohemus, Agrippa, and Malchus. There were no doubt others, but it is not incumbent to produce the exact number of ten."[243]

Indeed, there were more military leaders:

> "So Vespasian sent his son Titus from Achaia, where he had been with Nero, to Alexandria, to bring back with him from thence the fifth and the tenth legions… with a considerable number of auxiliaries from the kings in that neighbourhood…
>
> Now the auxiliaries which were sent to assist the people of Sepphoris, being a thousand horsemen, and six thousand footmen, under Placidus the tribune…
>
> But as to Titus… he came suddenly to Ptolemais, and there finding his father, together with the two legions, the fifth and the tenth, which were the most eminent legions of all, he joined them to that fifteenth legion which was with his father: eighteen cohorts followed these legions: there came also five cohorts

---

[243] Russell, J. Stuart: The Parousia. Baker Book House: Grand Rapids, 1983, pp. 503.

from Cesarea, with one troop of horsemen, and five other troops of horsemen from Syria. Now these ten cohorts had severally a thousand footmen, but the other thirteen cohorts had no more than six hundred footmen a piece, with a hundred and twenty horsemen. There were also a considerable number of auxiliaries got together, that came from the Kings Antiochus and Agrippa, and Sohemus, each of them contributing one thousand footmen that were archers, and a thousand horsemen. Malchus also, the king of Arabia, sent a thousand horsemen, besides five thousand footmen, the greatest part of which were archers: so that the whole army, including the auxiliaries sent by the kings, as well horsemen as footmen, when all were united together, amounted to sixty thousand."[244]

א *(15) Then he said to me, 'The waters that you saw, which the Harlot was situating upon, are the nations, multitudes, ethnicities and languages.'*

א *(16) 'And the ten horns that you saw on the savage animal will hate the Harlot, and they will make her desolate and naked, and they will devour her flesh, and they will set her ablaze in fire.'*

Another reference to Ezekiel:[245]

"Because you poured out your lust and exposed your naked body in your promiscuity with your lovers... therefore I am going to gather all your lovers, with whom you found pleasure... I will gather them against you from all around and will strip you in front of them, and they will see you stark naked. I will sentence you to the punishment of women who commit adultery and who shed blood; I will bring on you the blood vengeance of my wrath and jealous anger. Then I will deliver you into the hands of your lovers, and they will tear down your mounds and destroy your lofty shrines. They will strip you of your clothes and take your fine jewelry and leave you stark naked. They will bring a mob against you, who will stone you and

---

[244] Josephus, *Wars.* 3:1, 4.
[245] And others: Hosea 2:3; Jeremiah 10:25; 14:2–22; Micah 3:3.

hack you to pieces with their swords. They will burn down your houses and inflict punishment on you in the sight of many women. I will put a stop to your prostitution…" Ezekiel 16:36–41 (NIV)

"They will take away your sons and daughters, and those of you who are left will be consumed by fire. They will also strip you of your clothes and take your fine jewelry. So I will put a stop to the lewdness and prostitution…" Ezekiel 23:25–27 (NIV)

As heavy as these Scriptures are, we must never lose sight of the long-path of God. All His judgements are unto restoration! Let us continue with Revelation chapter 17.

- *(17) 'Indeed, God set it in their hearts to accomplish His will, and to accomplish their own collective will, and to be offering up their kingdom to this savage animal until the words of God fulfill themselves.'*

- *(18) 'And the wife which you saw is the Great City,[246] who has for herself dominion over the kings of the Land.[247]*

Josephus provided a statement that I find fitting here:

> "[The] royal city Jerusalem was supreme, and presided over all the neighboring country, as the head does over the body.[248]

And Jerusalem, the Great City, was not only central to Jewish life, it was at the time still the headquarters of the early church.

> "Foremost and clearest stands the fact of the centrality of Jerusalem. The Church there is the unchallenged centre of the

---

[246] The "Great City", which is Jerusalem.
[247] ܐܪܥܐ "the Land" is the only option. Jerusalem's autonomy doesn't extend beyond her own boarders, so the traditional use of "the land", i.e. The Holy Land, makes the most sense. It also highlights the fragility of Jerusalem in contrast to her many enemies.
[248] Josephus, *Wars*, 3:3:5.

movement, and even Paul thinks of his mission as beginning from there. This unique status of Jerusalem would appear to be the natural consequence of the fact that Christian tradition agrees in locating there practically all the most crucial events of the Passion of Jesus, and probably also of the fact that the metropolis was the divinely appointed religious centre for all devout Jews...

Lastly, there is the evidence of the collection of alms throughout the Gentile churches for the community at Jerusalem. This duty Paul admits was enjoined on him by the three Jerusalem leaders, and he accepted it without demur, and his writings eloquently witness to the zeal with which he laboured for its fulfilment.

The picture which the Pauline documents, therefore, present of the constitution and organization of the Church is sufficiently clear in the major outlines. The various communities, whether Jewish or Gentile in racial origin, are regarded as forming a unity, which has its centre at Jerusalem with the original community of believers. In practical effect this unity expresses itself through the decisive control exercised by the Jerusalem community in matters of faith and practice."[249]

---

[249] S. G. F. Brandon, M.A., D.D., *The Fall of Jerusalem and the Christian Church, A Study of the Effects of the Jewish Overthrow of A.D. 70 on Christianity* (London: S.P.C.K, 1951)

9 JERUSALEM FALLS: CH. 18

> *"As [Jesus] approached Jerusalem and saw the city, he wept over it and said, 'If you, even you, had only known on this day what would bring you peace—but now it is hidden from your eyes.*
> *The days will come upon you when your enemies will build an embankment against you and encircle you and hem you in on every side. They will dash you to the ground, you and the children within your walls. They will not leave one stone on another, because you did not recognize the time of God's coming to you.'"*
> — *Luke 19:41–44 (NIV)*

Who was Babylon in the Book of Revelation? Those of you reading this series will (hopefully!) already know the answer to this question. Jerusalem has been the focal point of Revelation all along. Now, in these next two chapters (18 and 19), Apostate Jerusalem continues to take the main stage. In a flurry of Old Testament imagery, Jerusalem is likened to many of the wicked cities and empires of old; but most specifically, Babylon.

> ✣ *(1) Following these things I saw another angel who had descended from Heaven, who had great authority, and the Land was illuminated by his glory.*

It is very likely that this heavenly event would have had some physical correspondence with an earthly experience:

"[Then] there was a star resembling a sword, which stood over the city [of Jerusalem], and a comet, that continued a whole year. Thus also before the Jews' rebellion... so great a light shone round the altar and the holy house [the Temple], that it appeared to be bright day time; which lasted for half an hour."[250]

> *(2) And he cried out in a loud voice: "Fallen, fallen, Babylon the Great! It has become the abode for demons and the prison of all unclean and detestable spirits.*

"O blessed Isaiah; arise, **tell us clearly what thou didst prophesy with respect to the mighty Babylon. For thou didst speak also of Jerusalem, and thy word is accomplished**. For thou didst speak boldly and openly: 'Your country is desolate, your cities are burned with fire; your land, strangers devour it in your presence...'

What then? Are not these things come to pass? Are not the things announced by thee fulfilled? Is not their country, Judea, desolate? Is not the holy place burned with fire? Are not their walls cast down? Are not their cities destroyed? Their land, do not strangers devour it? Do not the Romans rule the country? And indeed these impious people hated thee, and did saw thee asunder, and they crucified Christ. Thou art dead in the world, but thou livest in Christ."[251]

> *(3) Because she mixed from the wine of her prostitution for all their*

---

[250] Josephus, *Wars,* 6:5.
[251] Hippolytus of Rome (d. 236 AD), *Fragments of Dogmatic and Historical Works*, 30.

nations,[252] *and the kings of the earth fornicated with her, and the merchants of the earth became rich through her military insanity."*[253]

Josephus is not shy in noting what the spoils of war were, as far as Rome was concerned. This of course benefited the whole of the Empire. Writing of the post-war victory procession into Rome, where Vespasian and Titus showed off the spoils of war, Josephus recounts:

> "For there was here to be seen a **mighty quantity of silver, and gold, and ivory**, contrived into all sorts of things: and did not appear as carried along [through Rome] in pompous shew only, but, as a man may say, **running along like a river**. Some parts were composed of the rarest purple hangings, and so carried along: and others accurately represented to the life what was embroidered by the art of the **Babylonians**. There were also precious stones that were transparent, some set in crowns of gold...
>
> **The images of the gods were also carried, being as well wonderful for their largeness, as made very artificially, and with great skill of the workmen. Nor were any of these images of any other than very costly materials...**
>
> The magnificence also of their structure afforded one both pleasure, and surprize. For upon many of them were laid carpets of gold. There was also wrought gold, and ivory, fastened about them all...
>
> On the top of every one of these pageants was placed the commander of the city that was taken; and the manner wherein he was taken. Moreover there followed those pageants a great number of ships. And for the other spoils they were carried in great plenty. **But for those that were taken in the temple of Jerusalem, they made the greatest figure of them all.** That is the golden table, of the weight of many talents. The

---

[252] Literally "the nations theirs", suggesting a belonging to an entity. In this case, the nations under the Roman Empire.
[253] "Military insanity", lit. "army/force" "madness/wildness". Clearly, a reference to the madness behind the Jewish revolt, where it was crazy of them to think that they could take on the might of Rome.

candlestick also, that was made of gold… **And the last of all the spoils was carried the Law of the Jews**…

After these triumphs were over, and after the affairs of the Romans were settled on the surest foundations, Vespasian resolved to build a temple to Peace. Which was finished in so short a time, and so glorious a manner, as was beyond all human expectation and opinion. **For he having now by providence a vast quantity of wealth**… he also laid up therein those golden vessels and instruments that were taken out of the **Jewish temple**, as ensigns of his glory. **But still he gave order that they should lay up their Law, and the purple veils of the holy place, in the royal palace itself; and keep them there.**"[254]

Cassius Dio, a Roman historian, also wrote about the vast sums of wealth that were brought into Rome and what Vespasian did with it:

"On reaching Rome [Vespasian] bestowed gifts upon both the soldiers and the populace. He also repaired the sacred precincts and the public works which had suffered injury and rebuilt such as had already fallen into ruin; and upon completing them he inscribed upon them, not his own name, but the names of those who had originally built them. He immediately began to construct the temple on the Capitoline."[255]

In addition to material goods, the Romans also took Jewish prisoners of war and sold them as slaves into the nations within the Empire:

"[Titus sold] the multitude, with their wives and children; and every one of them [as slaves] for a very low price: and that because such as were sold were very many, and the buyers very few…

And as for the rest of the multitude, that were above seventeen years old, he put them into bonds, and sent them to the

---

[254] Josephus, *Wars,* 7:5:5–7, emphasis mine.
[255] Cassius Dio, *Roman History,* 66:10.

Egyptian mines. Titus also sent a great number into the provinces; as a present to them: that they might be destroyed upon their theatres, by the sword, and by the wild beasts. But those that were under seventeen years of age, were sold for slaves…

Now the number of those that were carried captive, during this whole war, was collected to be ninety-seven thousand."[256]

Lastly, perhaps the greatest testament to the vast riches that came to the Roman Empire from the defeat of the Holy Land is the Colosseum. This famous wonder, which still stands today in Rome, was known in antiquity as the Flavian Amphitheatre, named after Vespasian (his full name: Titus Flavius Vespasianus). We now know today that funding for the construction of the Colosseum came directly from the spoils of the Jewish war:

"[There is a] recently deciphered inscription … a large, altar-like stone with a chiselled Latin inscription, which tells how a senator, Lampaudius, had the Colosseum restored in AD 443.

But holes still visible in the surface clearly corresponded to different lettering, this time in bronze, which had been previously fitted into the stone. After a long study, Prof Geza Alfoldy of Heidelberg University, working with Italian archaeologists, deciphered the puzzle. He concluding that the original inscription read… 'The Emperor Caesar Vespasian Augustus had this new amphitheatre erected with the spoils of war.' There is no doubt what war this was, the sack of Jerusalem."[257]

> ܐ *(4) And I heard another voice from Heaven that said, "Come out from within her my people, do not be married*[258] *to her sins, lest you*

---

[256] Josephus, *Wars,* 6:8:2, 6:9:2, 3.
[257] Johnston, Bruce. (2001, June 15). Colosseum 'built with loot from sack of Jerusalem temple'. The Telegraph.
<https://www.telegraph.co.uk/news/worldnews/1311985/Colosseum-built-with-loot-from-sack-of-Jerusalem-temple.html>
[258] ܬܶܫܬܰܘܬܦܽܘܢ lit. "be married/have intercourse with her".

receive from her blows."

To the well trained Jewish ear, these words would have immediately taken them back to the Old Testament prophets:

> *"Flee out of Babylon;*
> *leave the land of the Babylonians…" Jeremiah 50:8 (NIV)*

> *"Flee from Babylon!*
> *Run for your lives!*
> *Do not be destroyed because of her sins…*
> *Come out of her, my people!*
> *Run for your lives!" Jeremiah 51:6, 45 (NIV)*

And what does Paul say?

> *"These things are being taken figuratively: The women represent two covenants. One covenant is from Mount Sinai and bears children who are to be slaves: This is Hagar. Now Hagar stands for Mount Sinai in Arabia and corresponds to the present city of Jerusalem, because she is in slavery with her children. But the Jerusalem that is above is free, and she is our mother…*
> *But what does Scripture say? 'Get rid of the slave woman and her son, for the slave woman's son will never share in the inheritance with the free woman's son.' [Gen 21:10] Therefore, brothers and sisters, we are not children of the slave woman, but of the free woman."*
> *Galatians 4:24–26, 30–31 (NIV)*

Further, as I cover in the first two books of this series, we know from early church historical sources that prior to the siege of Jerusalem the saints of Christ had an angelic visitation in which they were warned that it was time to flee to Pella. So they headed east, beyond the Jordan, and remained there in safety until after the war.

> "So he [Aquila] passed through the city of Antioch and passed through Coele-Syria and Phoenicia and came to Palestine – which is also called Judea – **forty-seven years after the**

destruction of Jerusalem. And he went up to Jerusalem, the famous and illustrious city which Titus, the son of Vespasian, overthrew in the second year of his reign.

And he found the temple of God trodden down and the whole city devastated **save for a few houses and the church of God**, which was small, where the disciples, when they had returned after the Savior had ascended from the Mount of Olives, went to the upper room. For there it had been built, that is, in that portion of Zion which escaped destruction, together with blocks of houses in the neighborhood of Zion and the seven synagogues which alone remained standing in Zion, like solitary huts, one of which remained until the time of Maximona the bishop and Constantine the king, 'like a booth in a vineyard,' [Isa. 1:8] as it is written…

So Aquila, while he was in Jerusalem, **also saw the disciples of the disciples of the apostles** flourishing in the faith and working great signs, healings, and other miracles. For they were such as had come back from the **city of Pella to Jerusalem** and were living there and teaching. For when the city was about to be taken and destroyed by the Romans, it was revealed in advance to all the disciples **by an angel of God that they should remove from the city**, as it was going to be completely destroyed. They sojourned as emigrants in Pella, the city above mentioned, in Transjordania. And this city is said to be of the Decapolis. But after the destruction of Jerusalem, when they had returned to Jerusalem, as I have said, they wrought great signs, as I have already said." [259]

All of this was in fulfillment of what Jesus had already prophesied:

"When you see Jerusalem being surrounded by armies, you will know that its desolation is near. Then let **those who are in Judea flee to the mountains**, *let* **those in the city get out**, *and let those in the*

---

[259] Epiphanius of Salamis (b. 310 AD), *Weights and Measures* (1935), 14–15.
<https://www.tertullian.org/fathers/epiphanius_weights_03_text.htm>

country not enter the city." Luke 21:20-21 (NIV, emphasis mine)

And as N.T. Wright remarks,

> "Luke's reading of Mark is quite clear: all this language refers to the fall of Jerusalem, which is to be understood against the background of the predicted destruction of Babylon…
>
> [This] is the all-important change of roles. Jerusalem has become Babylon; Jesus and His disciples have become Jerusalem…
>
> The new Babylon was to be destroyed in an instant, and flight was the only appropriate action, the only way of salvation for Jesus' renewed Israel."[260]

א *(5) 'Because the sins in her have adhered*[261] *as high as Heaven, and God was reminded of her crimes.'*

א *(6) 'Pay her just as she also has paid you, and duplicate for her double on account of her deeds. In the cup which she has mixed, mix for her double.*[262]

א *(7) 'On account of how often she glorified herself and exalted herself,*[263] *then dole out torment and sorrow, because she said in her heart,*
  "I sit as the Queen,
    and I am not a widow,
      nor shall I see sorrow."'

א *(8) 'For this reason, in one day there will come upon her blows,*

---

[260] Wright, N.T., *Jesus and the Victory of God*, (London: SPCK Publishing, 2015) p. 356, 360.
[261] הֻדְבַּק lit. "stuck to", or figuratively "glued to".
[262] Only Israel has ever had to pay double for sins: Isa 40:2; 61:7 Jer 16:18; 17:18.
[263] וְאִשְׁתַּעֲלַיָת from the Hebrew Peshitta NT, which matches the Crawford Codex.

death, sorrow, and famine, and she will burn in fire, because only Yahweh is capable of being her judge.'

א *(9) And the kings of the earth, who fornicated with her and exalted themselves,²⁶⁴ will weep and wail concerning her, when they see the smoke of her burning.'*

א *(10) When they are standing at a distance out of fear of her affliction, they will say, "Woe! Woe! Woe! The great city Babylon! The Mighty City! Because in one hour your judgment has come!"'*

א *(11) And the merchants of the earth will weep and mourn over her, and their cargo won't have trading anymore: (12) cargo of gold and silver and of precious stones, of pearls, of fine linen, of purple, of silk, of scarlet, of every fragrant wood, and every ivory vessel, every expensive wooden vessel, and brass, iron and marble, (13) cinnamon, spices, ointments, frankincense, wine, oil, fine white flour, sheep, horses, chariots and the bodies and souls of the children of men.²⁶⁵*

In his classic work, "The Life and Times of Jesus the Messiah", Alfred Edersheim writes:

> "Altogether, Jerusalem covered, at its greatest, about 300 acres. As of old there were still the same narrow streets in the business quarters; but in close contiguity to bazaars and shops rose stately **mansions of wealthy merchants**, and palaces of princes... Outside their shops in the streets, or at least in sight of the passers, and within reach of their talk, was the shoemaker hammering his sandals, the tailor lying his needle... the butcher, the wool-comber, or the flax- spinner were carried on. In these large, shady halls, artistic trades were pursued: the elegant workmanship of the goldsmith and jeweller; the various articles de luxe, that adorned the houses of the rich; the artwork

---

²⁶⁴ וְאִשְׁתָּעֲלִיו like verse 7; Hebrew Peshitta NT, which matches the Crawford Codex.
²⁶⁵ "The bodies and souls of the children of men", meaning slaves.

of the designer, the moulder, or the artificer in iron or brass.

In these streets and lanes **everything might be purchased**: the production of Palestine, or imported from foreign lands—nay, the rarest articles from the remotest parts. Exquisitely shaped, curiously designed and jewelled cups, rings and other workmanship of **precious metals; glass, silks, tine linen, woollen stuffs, purple, and costly hangings; essences, ointments, and perfumes, as precious as gold; articles of food and drink from foreign lands**—in short, what India, Persia, Arabia, Media, Egypt, Italy, Greece, and even the far-off lands of the Gentiles yielded, might be had in these bazaars.

Ancient Jewish writings enable us to identify **no fewer than 118 different articles of import** from foreign lands… In the bazaars you might get a complete suit for your slave for eighteen or nineteen shillings, and a tolerable outfit for yourself. For the same sum you might purchase an ass, an ox, or a cow, and, for little more, a horse."[266]

But the focus here is not simply a literal approach, where we try to identify each and every item that was traded in the Holy Land. Rather, as Provan suggests,

"[It] is not simply Old Testament language and imagery which has shaped Revelation 18, but also the very form and structure of Old Testament texts—the very manner in which they have been composed… [Does] this list signify economic critique of Rome as such, or is it there simply because it is the sort of thing that one finds in biblical laments and dirges?

…How can one say that the presence of wheat on John's list [of cargoes] shows how the general population of Rome survived only at the expense of the rest of the empire, when wheat appears on the very list in Ezek 27 that provides the basis

---

[266] Edersheim, Alfred. The Life and Times of Jesus the Messiah (New York: Herrick & Co., 1886), p 115, 116. Emphasis mine.

for John's list?"²⁶⁷

> א (14) *'And the fruit of the lust of your soul²⁶⁸ has departed from you, and everything luxurious and beautiful has departed from you, and you will not see them again, (15) nor will the merchants of these things find them. These who became wealthy through her will stand at a distance for fear of her punishment, weeping and lamenting.'*

> א (16) *And they will say, "Woe! Woe! The Great City that wore fine linen and purple, and scarlet gilded with gold, and precious stones and pearls! (17) Therefore in one hour the wealth is plundered!"²⁶⁹ In this way also, every ship captain, everyone traveling on ships to places, and the sailors, and every crewman at sea, stood from afar. (18) And they wept as they watched the smoke of burning, and they were saying, 'what can compare to the Great City?'"*

As Josephus remarked,

> "Nor indeed is Judea destitute of such delights as come from the sea, since its maritime places extend as far as Ptolemais: it was parted into eleven portions, of which the royal city Jerusalem was supreme, and presided over all the neighboring country, as the head does over the body."²⁷⁰

Now we may understand James 5:1–7 in its proper context:

> *"Now listen, you rich people, weep and wail because of the misery that is coming on you. Your wealth has rotted, and moths have eaten your clothes. Your gold and silver are corroded. Their corrosion will testify against you*

---

²⁶⁷ Provan, Iain. (1997). Foul Spirits, Fornication, and Finance: Revelation 18 From an Old Testament Perspective. Journal for The Study of The New Testament. 19. 84, 86, 88.
²⁶⁸ Most likely a euphemism for her virginity, a motif found in Song of Songs.
²⁶⁹ ܐܣܬܦܩ "to be emptied" or "despoiled". In the Ethpael conjugation, "plundered" is fitting.
²⁷⁰ Josephus, *Wars*, 3:3:5.

and eat your flesh like fire. You have hoarded wealth in the last days. Look! The wages you failed to pay the workers who mowed your fields are crying out against you. The cries of the harvesters have reached the ears of the Lord Almighty. You have lived on earth in luxury and self-indulgence. You have fattened yourselves in the day of slaughter. You have condemned and murdered the innocent one, who was not opposing you. Be patient, then, brothers and sisters, until the Lord's coming." James 5:1–7 (NIV)

> א *(19) 'So they threw dust upon their heads and wailed as they were weeping, and lamenting, and saying, "Woe! Woe! The Great City, by which those who had ships in the sea became wealthy from her magnificence, which is in one hour is destroyed!"'*

It is in the context of Revelation 18 that we may properly understand the words of James, **head of the church in Jerusalem**, when he wrote:

"Come now, you rich people, weep and howl for your miseries which are coming upon you. Your riches have rotted and your garments have become moth-eaten. Your gold and your silver have corroded, and their corrosion will serve as a testimony against you and will consume your flesh like fire. It is in the last days that you have stored up your treasure! Behold, the pay of the laborers who mowed your fields, and which has been withheld by you, cries out against you; and the outcry of those who did the harvesting has reached the ears of the Lord of armies." James 5:1–4 (NASB)

> א *(20) 'Rejoice over her oh Heaven, oh saints, oh apostles and prophets! Because Yahweh has judged your court case with her!'*

A direct connection to Revelation 6:10 and Matthew 23:

"And they cried in a great voice, and they were saying, 'Until when, Yahweh, holy and true, will you not be judging and avenging our blood upon the inhabitants of The Land?'" (Aramaic)

"upon you will fall the guilt of all the righteous blood shed on earth, from

> *the blood of righteous Abel to the blood of Zechariah, the son of Berechiah, whom you murdered between the temple and the altar. Truly I say to you, all these things will come upon this generation."*
> *Matthew 23:35–36 (NASB)*

> א *(21) Then one of the angels took a mighty stone, great as a millstone, and hurled it into the sea and said, "In this way with violence, Babylon the Great City will be thrown down, and she will not be found again. (22) And the sound of the lyre, and the shofar, and music, and musicians will not be heard in you again!"*

The prophetic significance of Jesus' enigmatic words are now realized here.

> *"whoever causes one of these little ones who believe in Me to sin, it is better for him that a heavy millstone be hung around his neck, and that he be drowned in the depths of the sea."*
> *(Matthew 18:6, NASB, cf. Mk 9:42; Lk 17:2)*

Indeed, Josephus did note that after the destruction "there was nothing to make those that came thither believe it [Jerusalem] had ever been inhabited."[271] But we also know that around 130 AD, Roman Emperor Hadrian decided to re-establish Jerusalem as a Roman colony. He called it Aelia Capitolina, and upon the ruins of the Temple Mount he placed a temple dedicated to Capitoline Jupiter. And in case you didn't notice, Jerusalem is a bustling place today (as is Rome)!

The redemptive aspect of Revelation 18:21 is that the apostate persona of Jerusalem (Babylon) will not be found again. In the same way that we all must die to Adam, so too does Jerusalem die to all she was never created to be. Remember, at the end of the day, we are dealing with images and symbols that represent the nature of how human beings relate to Yahweh God. And His long-path plans are always unto restoration.

As Daniel Morais notes,

---

[271] Ibid., 7:1:1.

"Babylon was 'never found again' because old-covenant Jerusalem was destroyed in A.D. 70 and rebuilt both physically and spiritually under a new covenant. After A.D. 70 Jerusalem was rebuilt and repopulated by Christians under Christianity, the new covenant. Babylon was 'never found again' because after the Law was fulfilled and wicked old-covenant Jerusalem was destroyed in A.D. 70, new-covenant Jerusalem was then rebuilt from the ashes of the old city both literally and spiritually and given a new name in Revelation 21 and 22, the New Jerusalem."[272]

> *(23) "And the light of the lamp will not be seen by you again, and the voice of the bridegroom and the voice of the bride will not be heard in you again; because your merchants had become the great ones of the Land, because through your enchantments you caused the peoples to be led astray!"*

Verse 23 presents us with a few prophetic allusions, two of which are most clearly seen in Matthew 25 and Luke 12.

First, let's read Matthew's account:

> *"Then the kingdom of heaven will be comparable to ten virgins, who took their lamps and went out to meet the groom. Five of them were foolish, and five were prudent. For when the foolish took their lamps, they did not take extra oil with them; but the prudent ones took oil in flasks with their lamps. Now while* **the groom was delaying***, they all became drowsy and began to sleep. But at midnight there finally was a shout: 'Behold, the groom! Come out to meet him.' Then all those virgins got up and trimmed their lamps. But the foolish virgins said to the prudent ones, 'Give us some of your oil, because our lamps are going out.' However, the prudent ones answered, 'No, there most certainly would not be enough for us and you too;* **go instead to the merchants** *and buy some for yourselves.' But while they were on their way to buy the oil, the groom came, and those who*

---

[272] Morais, Daniel <https://www.revelationrevolution.org/revelation-18-a-preterist-commentary>

were ready went in with him to the wedding feast; and the door was shut. Yet later, the other virgins also came, saying, 'Lord, lord, open up for us.' But he answered, 'Truly I say to you, I do not know you.' Be on the alert then, because you do not know the day nor the hour."
Matthew 25:1–13 (NASB, emphasis mine)

Now, Luke's:

"Let your loins be wrapped and lamps be burning. And you, be like men awaiting their lord, whenever he returns from the **wedding feast***, so that when he comes and knocks they may immediately open up for him… But know this, if the master of the house knew in what hour the thief comes, he would not have allowed his house to be breached. And you, be prepared, because* **the Son of Man comes in an hour you do not expect***.'*
And Peter said, 'Lord, do you address this parable to us, or also to everyone?' And the Lord said, 'Who is the faithful, the prudent steward, whom the lord will appoint over the household attendants, to give them their rations at the proper time? How happy that slave whom his lord, on coming, will find doing so. I tell you truly that he will place him in charge over all his possessions. But if that slave says in his heart, 'My lord takes a long time in coming,' and begins to beat the slave boys and slave girls, and both to eat and to drink, and to become drunk, that slave's lord **will come on a day he does not expect and in an hour he does not know***, and* **will cut him to pieces and assign him a portion with the faithless***. And that slave who has known his lord's will, and has not made preparations or acted according to his will, will be beaten with many* **blows***. But the one who has not known, but has done things worthy of a thrashing, will be beaten with few* **blows***. And to everyone to whom much was given, from him much will be demanded, and from the one to whom much has been entrusted they will request far more. I came to* **fling fire** *upon the earth, and how I wish it were already kindled. And I have a baptism in which to be baptized, and how hard-pressed I am till it is accomplished. Do you think that I came to give peace on earth? No, I tell you, but rather* **division***. For from now on there will be five in one house divided three against two and two against three…'*
And he also said to the crowds, 'When you see a cloud rising **over the west***, you immediately say a storm is coming, and so it happens, And*

*when **a south wind blows**, you say it will be hot, and so it happens. Charlatans, you know how to discern the face of earth and sky, but how do you not discern this season?"*²⁷³
(Luke 12:35–56, abridged, emphasis mine)

We also see a redemptive allusion to Jeremiah 33. Though the entire chapter is worth reading on your own, I will quote a snippet here:

*"This is what the Lord says: 'Yet again there will be heard in this place, of which you say, "It is a waste, without man and without animal," that is, in the cities of Judah and in the streets of Jerusalem that are deserted, without man and without inhabitant and without animal, the voice of joy and the voice of gladness, **the voice of the groom and the voice of the bride**, the voice of those who say,*

"Give thanks to the Lord of armies,
For the Lord is good,
For His mercy is everlasting,"

*as they bring a thanksgiving offering into the house of the Lord. **For I will restore the fortunes of the land as they were at first**,' says the Lord.*

"This is what the Lord of armies says: 'There will again be in this place which is waste, without man or animal, and in all its cities, a pasture for shepherds who rest their flocks."
Jeremiah 33:10–12 (NASB, emphasis mine)

In addition to the prophetic allusions, there is also the symbolic significance of the voice of the groom (Yeshua) and the voice of the bride (the church) not being heard in Babylon (Jerusalem) again. Jesus and his followers had warned the inhabitants for almost 40 years – a generation – of the impending Roman invasion. But now their voice would no longer be heard. And yet we know that there is still hope because God restores all things in His appointed times.

---

[273] Hart, David Bentley. The New Testament: A Translation (pp. 137-138). Yale University Press. Kindle Edition.

א *(24) And in her was found the blood of the prophets and the saints who were murdered upon the Land.*

There are no quotation marks in the original text, so we can only do our best to try to understand where the angel's monologue ends. I believe it was in verse 23. Now, in verse 24, it seems as though John interjects an observation or word of discernment. Regardless, verse 24 closes out this chapter by again emphatically reminding us that we are dealing with Jerusalem and her alone.

It is in the context of the Jewish-Roman war that we can correctly understand Paul's words to the lovers of Yeshua in Thessalonica:

"For you, brothers and sisters, became imitators of the churches of God in Christ Jesus that are in Judea [Jerusalem], for you also endured the same sufferings at the hands of your own countrymen, even as they did from the Jews, who both killed the Lord Jesus and the prophets, and drove us out. They are not pleasing to God, but hostile to all people, hindering us from speaking to the Gentiles so that they may be saved; with the result that they always reach the limit of their sins. But wrath has come upon them fully."
1 Thessalonians 2:14–16 (NASB)

I've cited Matthew 23 and Luke 19 enough times recently for it to (hopefully) still be ringing fresh in your mind, so I won't cite it again. But suffice to say that ONLY in Jerusalem were the prophets of Yahweh slain, and ONLY Jerusalem was found guilty of all the shed blood of the saints and prophets. Additionally, Jesus very clearly says in Matthew 23:36 that judgement would "come upon this generation" (a 40 year period). He would have said this in and around 30 AD, and 40 years later was 70 AD when Jerusalem, the Temple, and the Holy Land, were razed to the ground.

But let us close with words of hope:

"For the sons of Israel will live for many days without a king or leader, without sacrifice or memorial stone, and without ephod or household idols. Afterward the sons of Israel will return and seek the Lord their God and David their king; and they will come trembling to the Lord and to His goodness in the last days." Hosea 3:4–5 (NASB)

10 HARLOT FALLS, WIFE ARISES: CH. 19

> *"'As I live!' declares the Lord God, 'I take no pleasure at all in the death of the wicked, but rather that the wicked turn from his way and live. Turn back, turn back from your evil ways! Why then should you die, house of Israel?'"*
> *— Ezekiel 33:11*

Three is a symbolic number that pertains to Jerusalem and the Holy Land's destruction. Numerology is not a focal point of this book, but suffice to say, the prominence warrants further study (8:13; 9:18; 16:13, 19 – three different scenes!). Interestingly, John dedicates three entire chapters (or sections) to the fall of the Harlot, Jerusalem.

It can seem somewhat tedious to work through so much detail and drama, especially when going over the same event, but we cannot lose sight of what was at stake and what was lost. The death toll was unfathomable, and the effects have lasted even to this day, almost 2000 years later. That's a big deal.

Even more significant is the broader framework of God's grand love story. No matter how devastating the event, it is temporary. No matter how harsh the chastisement, it is unto restoration. If God looked ahead and counted the cost of creating mankind in Their image and likeness, and if the Lamb was slain before the foundations of the Age of mankind, then His end goal was not creating humans for failure, death, and destruction. As a Father,

His goal was reconciliation and restoration.

Chapter 12 of Revelation introduces a pregnant wife (representing faithful Israel) who is faithful to Yahweh God, while chapter 19 concludes with the Harlot Jerusalem (representing apostate Israel). To bookend this seven chapter section (12 to 19) that is all about matrimony and covenant relationships, the faithful woman of chapter 12 is elevated towards Yahweh, while the Harlot here in chapter 19 falls into chastisement. Moreover, in chapter 12 we read that Satan is thrown down after the crucifixion and is granted a short season of 40 years (from ~30 to ~70 AD) to wreak havoc. And just ahead in chapter 20, Satan is again thrown down, and at a future time will be granted a short season (of which I believe we are living at the tail end of, more on that to come) to deceive the nations.

> ℵ *(1) Now after these things I heard the great voice of many multitudes in Heaven, who were saying, "Hallelujah! Redemption and glory and power to our God! (2) For His judgments are certain and honest, because he has judged the Great Harlot, who corrupted the Land with her fornication. So He has sought the blood of His servants from her hand."*

> ℵ *(3) Again they said, "Hallelujah!"*
>
> *And her smoke went up unto the Age of Ages.*

> ℵ *(4) Then the twenty four elders and the four creatures fell down and did obeisance to our God, who sits upon the throne. And they were saying, "Amen! Hallelujah!"*

> ℵ *(5) And the voice from the throne was saying, "Praise our God, all his servants, and be awestruck of His Name, everyone from least to great!"*

> ℵ *(6) And I heard the sound like that of many multitudes, and like the sound of many waters, and like the sound of mighty thunders saying,*

"HALLELUJAH!

BECAUSE YAHWEH GOD, KEEPER OF ALL, REIGNS!"[274]

> א (7) *"We celebrate and we rejoice! We give Him glory, because the wedding-feast of the Lamb has come, and His Wife[275] has prepared herself!"*

There is an intentional distinction being made between these two women (or wives) - the Harlot and the Wife. Remember too that in ancient Jewish culture, what we would call the engagement phase of a relationship would already be considered marriage. The distinction here is that those who were truly faithful to Yahweh God would have betrothed themselves to Yeshua.

> *"Husbands, love your wives, just as Christ also loved the church and gave Himself up for her, so that He might sanctify her, having cleansed her by the washing of water with the word, that He might present to Himself the church in all her glory, having no spot or wrinkle or any such thing; but that she would be holy and blameless... This mystery is great; but I am speaking with reference to Christ and the church."*
> *Ephesians 5:25–27, 32 (NASB)*

> *"... I [Paul] betrothed you to one husband, to present you as a pure virgin to Christ."*
> *2 Corinthians 11:2 (NASB)*

Meanwhile, those who rejected Yeshua as Messiah, but were once faithful to Yahweh God, became part of a collective majority personified as a harlot.

> א (8) *Now it was granted to her to be adorned with fine linen – pure and radiant – for the fine linen is the uprightness of the Saints.*

---

[274] Of course there are no upper or lower case letters in the ancient languages. However, because of John's hyperbole in describing the loudness and intensity of the many hosts who with one voice gave glory to God, I felt I needed to represent the emphasis somehow. So I used all-caps as sort of an equivalent to our vernacular.

[275] The word here ܐܢܬܬܗ "his wife" is not ܟܠܬܐ "bride" like we find in Revelation 21:2 (cf. John 3:29). There is a distinction being made between the two women, or wives; the Harlot and the Virgin (cf. Eph 5:25–27, 2 Cor 11:2).

א *(9) And they said to me, "Write: 'Blessed are they who are summoned to the supper of the wedding-feast of the Lamb!'" And one said to me, "These are the true words of God."*

א *(10) Then I fell before his feet, and I paid obeisance to him, but he said to me, "No! I am a fellow-servant of yours and your brothers; those who have the testimony of Yeshua. Worship God extravagantly!* [276] *For the testimony of Yeshua is the spirit of prophecy."*

א *(11) Then I saw Heaven opened and behold! The white horse, and He who was riding upon it is called Faithful and Steadfast, and in righteousness He is judging and advancing. (12) Then His eyes were like the flame of fire, and upon His head were many crowns, and on Him the Name was written, which no one knew except Himself.*

א *(13) And He was adorned with the garment soaked with blood, and His name is called The Word of God.*

א *(14) And the armies of Heaven were joined to Him upon white horses, and were wearing fine linen, white and pure.*

א *(15) And from their mouths* [277] *proceeded the sharp sword which by itself will smite the peoples.* [278] *But He will shepherd them with the iron staff as he treads the winepress of the indignation of Yahweh, Keeper of All.*

In what is perhaps a jarring departure from Western Tradition, the Aramaic text (including the Crawford Codex) first places the sword coming out of the mouths of the heavenly hosts, not Yeshua's (though we will see Jesus' too in v. 21). Furthermore, the sword is being personified here. It is a

---

[276] "Worship" here is the exact same verb as "did obeisance" earlier in this verse. However, within context, the angel is clearly not just suggesting John bow down in respect, which is what the verb means. With an added superlative, the intention is clear: worship!
[277] ܦܘܡܗܘܢ "from their mouths".
[278] "The sharp sword which by itself will smite the peoples" is the literal reading.

feminine noun. The verb that follows, "to smite", is also conjugated in the 3rd feminine singular. Since there are no other feminine nouns thus far in the verse, we can conclude that the sword itself is doing the smiting. The sword is the prophetic word of Yahweh God, and the angels (angel literally means messenger) are those who deliver the prophetic word.

> *"For the word of God is living and active, and sharper than any two-edged sword, even penetrating as far as the division of soul and spirit, of both joints and marrow, and able to judge the thoughts and intentions of the heart. And there is no creature hidden from His sight, but all things are open and laid bare to the eyes of Him to whom we must answer."*
> *Hebrews 4:12–13 (NASB)*

So what is Jesus doing here? Shepherding. As He oversees the fulfillment of all that God spoke through the Law and Prophets, He is also actively shepherding those on the receiving end of those calamities. This is a powerful image. How can he be shepherding if he is treading the winepress? He was making new wine. Even in death, there is grace.

> *"For Christ also suffered for sins once for all time, the just for the unjust, so that He might bring us to God, having been put to death in the flesh, but made alive in the spirit; in which He also went and made proclamation to the spirits in prison [lit. Sheol]…" 1 Peter 3:18–19 (NASB)*

> *"[They] will give an account to Him who is ready to judge the living and the dead. For the gospel has for this purpose been preached even to those who are dead, that though they are judged in the flesh as people, they may live in the spirit according to the will of God. 1 Peter 4:5–6 (NASB)*

> *"Therefore insofar as I am an apostle of Gentiles, I magnify my ministry if somehow I may move my own people to jealousy and save some of them. For if their [the Jews] rejection proves to be the reconciliation of the world, what will their acceptance be but life from the dead?"*
> *Romans 11:13–15 (NASB)*

Why does he have an iron staff? It is a symbol of Covenant, and it is a prophetic allusion to Zechariah 11.

> "'This is what the Lord my God says: 'Pasture the flock doomed to slaughter. Those who buy them slaughter them and go unpunished, and each of those who sell them says, 'Blessed be the Lord, for I have become rich!' And their own shepherds have no compassion for them. For I will no longer have compassion for the inhabitants of the land,' declares the Lord; 'but behold, I will let the people fall, each into another's power and into the power of his king; and they will crush the land, and I will not rescue them from their power.'
>
> So I pastured the flock doomed to slaughter, therefore also the afflicted of the flock. **And I took for myself two staffs: the one I called Favor, and the other I called Union; so I pastured the flock…**
>
> **And I took my staff Favor and cut it in pieces, to break my covenant which I had made with all the peoples…**
>
> Then I cut in pieces my second staff Union, to break the brotherhood between Judah and Israel.
>
> And the Lord said to me, "Take again for yourself the equipment of a foolish shepherd. For behold, I am going to raise up a shepherd in the land who will not care for the perishing, seek the scattered, heal the broken, or provide for the one who is exhausted, but will devour the flesh of the fat sheep and tear off their hoofs."
> Zechariah 11:4–7, 10, 14–16 (NASB, emphasis mine)

Just like an iron staff cannot be cut up, the Covenant of Yeshua will never be broken:

> "'For this is the covenant which I will make with the house of Israel after those days,' declares the Lord: 'I will put My law within them and write it on their heart; and I will be their God, and they shall be My people. They will not teach again, each one his neighbor and each one his brother, saying, 'Know the Lord,' for they will all know Me, from the least of them to the greatest of them,' declares the Lord, 'for I will forgive their wrongdoing, and their sin I will no longer remember.'"
> Jeremiah 31:33–34 (NASB)

This is the covenant that Yahweh desired all along for all mankind.

> א (16) *And He has on His garment – over His thigh – the name written: "The King of Kings and Yahweh of Dominions."*

> א (17) *And I saw another angel standing in the sun, and proclaiming with a loud voice, and he said to the birds flying in the midst of the skies, "Come! Be gathered together for the great supper of God. (18) Eat the flesh of kings, and the flesh of legates[279] of thousands, and the flesh of warriors, and the flesh of horses and those riding upon them, and the flesh of the nobles and the servants, and of the small and of the great."*

Clearly this is a literal, future event, right?

"Now as for you, son of man, this is what the Lord God says: 'Say to every kind of bird and to every animal of the field: "Assemble and come, gather from every direction to My sacrifice, which I am going to sacrifice for you as a great sacrifice on the mountains of Israel; and you will eat flesh and drink blood. You will eat the flesh of warriors and drink the blood of the leaders of the earth… You will eat your fill at My table with horses and charioteers, with warriors and all the men of war," declares the Lord God.

"And I will place My glory among the nations; and all the nations will see My judgment which I have executed, and My hand which I have laid on them. And the house of Israel will know that I am the Lord their God, from that day onward. The nations will know that the house of Israel went into exile for their wrongdoing, because they were disloyal to Me, and I hid My face from them; so I handed them over to their adversaries, and all of them fell by the sword. In accordance with their uncleanness and their offenses I dealt with them, and I hid My face from them."

Therefore this is what the Lord God says: "Now I will restore the fortunes of Jacob and have mercy on all the house of Israel; and I will be jealous for

---

[279] In Latin, "legatus legionis" (legion legate), was the commander of legions.

My holy name...
When I bring them back from the peoples and gather them from the lands of their enemies, then I shall show Myself holy through them in the sight of the many nations.""
Ezekiel 39:17–25, 27 (NASB)

I know, you saw that coming. The incredible thing is how chapter 39 of Ezekiel ends with an eschatological hope for the Jewish people. Because, as I have repeatedly said, God's judgements are restorative. John's prophetic experience was very clear: the gruesome scene the prophet Ezekiel saw was coming to pass in the Holy Land.

> ℵ *(19) Then I saw the savage animal and its soldiers,[280] and the kings of the Land[281] and their soldiers who were gathering to make war[282] with Him who rode upon the horse and with His soldiers.*

> ℵ *(20) But the savage animal was ensnared[283] and the false prophet with it – that which did signs before it, in which he caused those who received the brand of the savage animal to be led astray, and those who did obeisance to its genius. And both of them were cast down and they descended into the Sea[284] of the Burning Fire and the Sulfur.[285]*

> ℵ *(21) Then the remainder were slain with the sword of Him who was riding upon the horse, by that which was proceeding from His mouth, and all the birds of prey were satiated with their flesh.*

---

[280] ܢܚܫܘܠܬܗ "soldiers" are not mentioned in verse 18, but are they here. This is intentional in order to distinguish from Roman "warriors" who come to devour (v 18) and mere "soldiers" of the horned lamb (Holy Land) who fight in vain (v 19).
[281] The focus in this chapter has been exclusively on Israel, "the (Holy) Land".
[282] So far in Revelation, armies have been "drawing near" or "engaging" for war. But now this army is literally "making war".
[283] ܘܐܬܬܨܝܕ ܚܝܘܬܐ is a unique verb, meaning "to be hunted, to capture an animal, to be ensnared, to be netted". Conjugated in the Ethpeal Perfect tense.
[284] ܝܡܬܐ "small sea", i.e. The Sea of Galilee.
[285] ܝܡܬܐ ܕܢܘܪܐ ܝܩܕܬܐ ܘܟܒܪܝܬܐ sea, fire, burning, and sulfur all have definite articles. This is representative of the Dead Sea, or Salt Sea as it was known.

WHICH BEAST: LEOPARD OR HORNED LAMB?

The major key to understanding what's going on in verses 17 to 21 is to first determine **which** beast John is referring to. I'd like to propose that the beast in these verses is not the Leopard (Rome), but rather it is the **Horned Lamb** (apostate Israel). I base this on four main factors.

Before we review said factors, let's look at the ways in which the beasts are mentioned throughout John's Vision:

11:7	Beast from the Sea (Rome)
13:1–4	Beast from the Sea (Leopard, Rome)
13:11–17	Beast from the Land (Horned Lamb, Israel)
14:9, 11	Beast and his image (Rome)
15:2	Beast and his image and number (Rome)
16:2	Beast and his mark (Rome)
16:10	Angel poured bowl over throne of the beast (Israel)
16:13	Leviathan, beast, false prophet (Israel)
17:3–17	Blood-red beast with woman on it, huge army (Rome)
19:19	Beast and the kings of the Land (Israel)
19:20	Deceitful beast and false prophet seized (Israel)
20:10	Devil, beast, false prophet in Lake of Fire (Israel)

This list gives us a few clues to help us confirm the identity of the beast in 19:19–20 and 20:10. First, the last time we see the beast of Rome in 17:3-7, it is distinguished as being red in colour.

Second, as I discussed when we covered Revelation 16, the description given to the false prophet here is similar to the description given to the land beast (Israel) back in Revelation 13:

> *(13:15–17, speaking of the land beast, Israel) "And it will cause those who dwell upon the Land to be lead astray by way of the signs that were being granted to it to be performing before the savage animal. And it was granted to it to give spirit to the genius of the savage animal, and as a result all who do not bow in obeisance to the genius of the savage animal will be killed. And it caused all of them—small and great, rich and poor, lords and servants—to be given unto them the brand upon their right hands or upon their foreheads, so that no one can buy or sell afterwards, unless there is upon him the brand of the name of the savage animal or the number of its name."*

> *(19:20, speaking of the false prophet) "But the savage animal was ensnared and the false prophet with it – that which did signs before it, in which he caused those who received the brand of the savage animal to be led astray, and those who did obeisance to its genius."*

The spirits of the false prophet and the land beast are connected. We must note that **it's not people that first went into the Sea of Fire, but demonic spirits.** Also, recall that in Revelation 16:13–14, John sees unclean spirits coming out of the mouth of the Leviathan, the horned lamb, and the false prophet. Demonic spirits and the horned lamb are interwoven.

Third, here in Revelation 19:3 we read of Jerusalem's smoke rising "unto the Age of Ages". The only other mention in Revelation of smoke rising like this is in 14:11, "and the smoke of their anguish rises unto the Age of Ages", speaking of Jews who had suffered the consequences of the curses of the Law of Moses. But we should also include 18:9 which mentions the smoke of Jerusalem's burning. So now shift ahead to Revelation 20:10. There, it mentions the smoke of the devil, **the beast,** and the false prophet having their smoke rise "unto the Age of Ages". The beast beside the false prophet can only be the beast of the Land, the Horned Lamb, since all other instances of smoke rising unto the Age of Ages has to do with Jerusalem.

Fourth, do you recall the noun-verb quick analysis I did earlier? We now have one more verse to add to the list. The point I made earlier was that, up until now, no one was waging war *against* the Lamb, but rather, *on His behalf*. We compared the sentence flow to another instance in Revelation where the same verb, "to draw near or to engage", was used.

(12:7)
"*Michael and his angels (subject)*
engaged (verb) with (particle)
the Leviathan (object)
and the Leviathan and his angels (subject)
engaged them (verb that contains an object)."

(17:14)
"*These ones (subject, representing Rome and allies)* with/alongside (particle)
the Lamb (object of particle but technically still part of the subject)
will engage them (verb that contains an object, the inhabitants of the Holy Land),
 and the Lamb (subject)
will overcome them (verb that contains an object, the inhabitants of the

Holy Land)."

In 12:7a, Michael is advancing <u>against</u> the devil:
"Michael and his angels engaged with the Leviathan."

In 12:7b, the devil and his demons advanced <u>against</u> Michael:
"and the Leviathan and his angels engaged them."

Later in 17:14a, the kings are advancing <u>with</u> the Lamb:
"These ones alongside the Lamb will engage them."

Now here in 19:19, speaking of the beast, its soldiers <u>make war against</u> Him who rides (Jesus):
"and their soldiers (subject) **were gathering (verb) to make war (verb)** <u>with (particle)</u> *Him (object) who rode upon the horse (object)."*

Rome did not wage war against the Lamb or the Rider of the white horse. It was only apostate Israel and the Harlot Jerusalem – who have been the main focal point of all of Revelation thus far – that resisted Jesus. In figurative terms, they (apostate Israel and Harlot Jerusalem) waged war against Him because they waged war against Rome and all the nations that gave Rome their allegiance.

More specifically, apostate Israel and the Harlot Jerusalem waged war against the sword that proceeded from the mouths of the angels (19:15) and the mouth of Jesus (19:21). **The sword represents the prophetic words of Yahweh God**. The entire calamity that befell the Holy Land was the fulfilment of the word written in the Law and the Prophets, and the words of Jesus during his earthly ministry.

This distinction is significant. **We cannot possibly have Jesus riding around with a literal sword slaughtering people**. Such a depiction is utterly irreconcilable with the Jesus who stooped down to lift up the woman caught in adultery. Or the Jesus who upon the cross publicly proclaimed, *"Forgive them Father."* **Revelation 19 is not Jesus' passive-aggressive vendetta against humanity**, as so many ill-informed teachers and preachers proclaim.

> *"...When He approached Jerusalem, He saw the city* **and wept over it**, *saying, 'If you had known on this day, even you, the conditions for peace! But now they have been hidden from your eyes.* **For the days will come upon you when your enemies will put up a**

barricade against you, and surround you and hem you in on every side, and they will level you to the ground, and throw down your children within you, and they will not leave in you one stone upon another, because you did not recognize the time of your visitation.'" Luke 19:37–38 (NASB, emphasis mine)

The time of His visitation was to save them from the consequences of the Law coming upon them! But looking ahead, much like Yahweh looked ahead in the closing chapters of Deuteronomy, Jesus already knew their choices. **This is why Jesus wept over them.**

"Jerusalem, Jerusalem… How often I wanted to gather your children together, just as a hen gathers her young under her wings, and you were unwilling! Behold, **your house is left to you desolate.*"* *Luke 13:34–35 (NASB, emphasis mine)*

Yet, even in what seems to be the worst case scenario, in Romans 11 Paul reminds us that it is never too late for salvation. God's mercy is as far reaching as is His foresight.

"[For] a partial hardening has happened to Israel until the fullness of the Gentiles has come in; **and so all Israel will be saved…** *For God has shut up all in disobedience, so that He may* **show mercy to all…** *For from Him, and through Him, and to Him are* **all things**.*"* *Romans 11:25–26, 32, 36 (NASB, emphasis mine)*

In light of the aforementioned points, we can better understand the immediate context of both the suffering and anticipation of first century followers of Yeshua. Take for example 2 Thessalonians 1:4–10:

> "Such that we ourselves boast about you in God's assemblies, on account of your patience and your faithfulness in all your persecutions, and in the afflictions you endure: A clear indication of the justice of God's judgment in finding you worthy of God's Kingdom (on behalf of which you also suffer), Since it is just on God's part to repay those afflicting you with affliction, But you who suffer the affliction with repose in our company at the revelation of the Lord Jesus from heaven, along

with the angels under his power, In a flaming fire, exacting justice upon those who do not know God and do not heed the good tidings of our Lord Jesus—Who will pay the just reparation of ruin in the Age, coming from the face of the Lord and the glory of his might. On that day when he comes to be glorified by his holy ones and to be worshipped with wonder by all those who have been faithful (because our witness to you was trusted).[286]

Paul is in full prophetic mode here, and the similarities between his foretelling of the 70 AD event in comparison to Revelation 19 are remarkable. But we must keep in mind that though Paul's tone is harsh toward his deceived countrymen, he is also the one who penned the words of Romans 11, quoted above. Nevertheless, the monumental and catastrophic events during the three and a half years of warfare between Rome and the Holy Land left everyone shaken.

After Jesus' resurrection, the disciples naively asked, "Lord, are you at this time going to restore the kingdom to Israel?" (Acts 1:8). They of course were referring to political autonomy from Rome. Clearly, without the illumination of the Holy Spirit (which was coming), they didn't understand. "It is not for you to know the times or dates the Father has set by his own authority," was Jesus' reply. Perhaps they thought the whole "no stone will be left upon another" discussion in Matthew 24 could be avoided, given the descendant of king David was now clearly invincible – I mean, He rose from the dead on His own! But in time, they *would* understand.

> "The destruction of their Holy City and the consequent cessation of the Temple worship had a paralysing effect on the life of the Jewish people, and from it they only slowly recovered and settled to an essentially maimed existence, with their cherished religion bereft of much of its *raison d'etre*… To those Jewish Christians who survived the carnage of AD 70 the same heart-rending questions must have presented themselves, but of their reactions thereto no certain record remains."[287]

---

[286] Hart, David Bentley. The New Testament: A Translation (pp. 411-412). Yale University Press. Kindle Edition.
[287] S. G. F. Brandon, M.A., D.D., *The Fall of Jerusalem and the Christian Church*,

I made this point earlier in Revelation 13, but I will emphasize it again. When dealing with the savage animals, the beast, and the false prophet, we must at all times keep in mind that they are *prophetic images* that represent various personas in play. More importantly, there are dark spiritual forces that are ultimately behind the illustrations of the beasts and the false prophet. There is no literal horned lamb or literal person who is a false prophet in a physical sea of fire and sulfur because these are prophetic *pictures*. Whether you want to call them principalities or demonic rulers, the point is *"our struggle is not against flesh and blood, but against the rulers, against the powers, against the world forces of this darkness, against the spiritual forces of wickedness in the heavenly places"* *(Ephesians 6:12)*. We do not demonize humans, no matter how deceived they may be, for all are made in the image of God.

Let us close with these remarkable and fitting words of hope:

> *"The nations will see your righteousness,*
> *And all kings your glory;*
> *And you will be called by a new name*
> *Which the mouth of the Lord will designate.*
> *You will also be a crown of beauty in the hand of the Lord,*
> *And a royal headband in the hand of your God.*
> *It will no longer be said to you, "Forsaken,"*
> *Nor to your land will it any longer be said, "Desolate";*
> *But you will be called, "My delight is in her,"*
> *And your land, "Married";*
> *For the Lord delights in you,*
> *And to Him your land will be married.*
> *For as a young man marries a virgin,*
> *So your sons will marry you;*
> *And as the groom rejoices over the bride,*
> *So your God will rejoice over you."* Isaiah 62:2–5 (NASB)

A Study of the Effects of the Jewish Overthrow of A.D. 70 on Christianity (London: S.P.C.K, 1951), at 167.

11 THE AGE OF MESSIAH BEGINS: CH. 20:1–6

> *"Six thousand years is the duration of the world. Two thousand of the six thousand years are characterized by chaos; two thousand years are characterized by Torah, from the era of the Patriarchs until the end of the Rabbinic period; and two thousand years are the period of the coming of the Messiah."*
> — Sanhedrin 97a:14

In my previous book I cover Revelation 20:1–7 in great detail, and I strongly encourage you to go back to it and re-read that section. There is a lot there that you will want to review so it's fresh in your mind. I will continue to build upon the groundwork I laid in the previous book, as the magnitude of Revelation 20 requires many pages!

In chapters 4 to 11 (seven chapters) and 12 to 19 (seven chapters) of Revelation - some of the most powerful prophetic visions and experiences in the Scriptures – John recounts the same story from two different vantage points: the climactic end to the Mosaic Age and curses of the Law, and the fall of Jerusalem and the Holy Land. Much like his predecessor Ezekiel, the bulk of what John saw was for the immediate hearers and readers of his present day. Therefore, the descriptions are vivid and sometimes even longwinded. He gives us the smallest details, like the armour of Roman soldiers (ch. 9) and a full three entire chapters dedicated to the fall of Jerusalem (17–19).

But suddenly, the vision and the focus shifts. The imagery goes from short-range to long-range. We are no longer looking under a microscope, we are looking through binoculars. Before, we had exhaustive descriptions of events spanning multiple verses, but now we have monumental events compressed into single verses. Instead of hyper-details of garments, horns and heads, and plagues, John now drops huge, successive events with little explanation. **Revelation 20 is the gradual shift from immediate present to distant future – from John's chronological point in time**. Chapter 20 is where John departs from present exhortation and admonition to future hope. This nuance is vital to understanding Revelation as a whole.

Verses 6 and 7 of chapter 20 fast-forward us into a future that was distant from John's day. For all of Revelation, up until 20:5, the apostle John and those he wrote to were closer to the events of Revelation *chronologically* than we are today. Now, from 20:6 onward, the opposite is true: we today are closer *chronologically* to the events John saw in the rest of chapter 20 and beyond. What an exciting time to be alive!

Finally, here are two overarching Scriptures we must take to heart when pondering the figurative 1000 year reign. These are not prophecies or visions, these are concrete statements made by the Apostles of Jesus. First, to his fellow Jews at the end of the Mosaic Age, Peter offers this message:

> *"Therefore repent and return, so that your sins may be wiped away, in order that **times of refreshing may come** from the presence of the Lord; and that He may send Jesus, the Christ appointed for you, whom heaven must receive **until the period of restoration of all things**, about which God spoke by the mouths of His holy prophets from ancient times." Acts 3:19–21 (NASB, emphasis mine)*

Jesus will remain in the realm of Heaven **until** the time for all things to be restored. That word "restoration" in Aramaic translates to *consummation,* and it paints a picture of all things coming together in intimate union. In Greek, the word is *apokatastasis,* which means a returning to a perfect state. Peter says this restoration will take place **before** Jesus' return! Oh, and did you catch the part where Peter says God has spoken of restoring all things through His prophets since ancient times? Restoration, not destruction, has always been God's intent! Second, I will quote once more one of my favourite passages in the New Testament:

> *"For as in Adam **all** die, so also in Christ **all will be made alive**. But each in his own order: Christ the first fruits, after that those who are*

*Christ's at His coming, **then comes the end**, when He hands over the kingdom to our God and Father, **when He has abolished** all rule and all authority and power. For **He must reign until** He has put all His enemies under His feet. The last enemy that will be abolished is death." 1 Corinthians 15:22–26 (NASB, emphasis mine)*

Paul informs his readers that even though Adam had an effect on every human being in all history, Christ will have an even greater effect on every human being in all history. Moreover, Jesus is *actively reigning* at this present time, and He will continue to *until* He has abolished all rule and placed all enemies beneath his feet. Physical death itself will also be defeated. Only after all these things have taken place will the end come. **Peter and Paul have made it clear that our present time is one where Christ is reigning, will defeat all His enemies, and all things will be restored.** Sounds like the Messianic Age to me!

> א *(1) And I saw another angel who had descended from Heaven, who had with him the key of the Abyss[288] and a great chain in his hand.*

> א *(2) So he grabbed hold of the Leviathan, that Ancient Serpent, which is the Accuser and Adversary,[289] and bound him for a thousand years.*

> א *(3) And he hurled him down into the Abyss,[290] and shut and sealed it over, that he would no longer cause all the nations to wander in deception. After these things, it is granted to unbind him for a short season.*

In the previous chapter, I mention the first time Satan is thrown down and granted a short season to wreak havoc (recorded in Revelation 12). In fact, the lines in 12:9 and 12 are almost identical to 20:2–3:

---

[288] תְהוֹם same as the Hebrew "tehom" (as in Gen 1:2; Strong's H8415) "the deep".
[289] Or "the Devil and Satan".
[290] The same word is used in Revelation 20:10: "the accuser will throw/hurl some of you into prison". The connection is not a coincidence, and it signifies how God keeps the books on all that His Saints suffer for His name's sake.

(12:9) So the Master²⁹¹ Leviathan was brought down,²⁹² that ancient serpent, who is called the Accuser and Adversary,²⁹³ who deceived everyone from the Land. So he was brought down upon the Land, and his angels were brought down with him… (12) the Accuser descends towards them, having incredible anger towards them, once he discovered his timeframe was short.

In the same way Satan was loosed for a short season at the end of the Mosaic Age, he will be loosed for a short season at the end of the Messianic Age. Of course the great question is why? This is part of the Divine mystery, and our theology has to make room for mystery. Not all riddles of God are to be solved; many are in place to keep us humble and grow our trust in Him.

א *(4) And I saw the thrones and they were sat upon,²⁹⁴ and the judgment was granted on their behalf.²⁹⁵*

For these were the souls cut off because of the testimony of Yeshua, and because of the word of God,
and were those who didn't pay obeisance to the savage animal, nor its genius,
nor received the brand between their eyes or on their hands.

They lived, and they reigned alongside the Messiah for a thousand years.

א *(5) And this is the first resurrection.*

---

²⁹¹ The word rabba רבא here does not imply a physical attribute like the Hebrew gibor (mighty). Rather, it refers to significance, prominence, or position. It can mean rabbi, teacher, or chief. Given the military context, one could suggest "commander" or "leader". I have opted for "master" for its broader meaning.
²⁹² The same verb used for the stars in 12:4 who were "forced down" is used here. The irony is intentional. The Leviathan, who in arrogance threw down people, is now thrown down itself, humiliated and defeated.
²⁹³ "Accuser/slanderer" in Aramaic is akhelqartza (or akhel qartza), and "adversary" is satan (same as Hebrew).
²⁹⁴ It is not specified who sat upon the thrones, but implied is that it is God, perhaps Jesus, and perhaps even Saints. Cf. 1 Cor 4:8, 6:9; Dan 7:9–27.
²⁹⁵ The ethpeal/ithpeel conjugation means the verb was done to or for them.

This description of those who lay down their lives for Yeshua and Yahweh brought me to tears. What the earliest church endured is heart-wrenching. Yet they counted it an honor to give up their earthly tents, knowing that these bodies would one day rise again. And their spirits did not taste Death or Sheol; they were immediately caught up into the presence of Abba Father. This is the first resurrection.

As for the 1000 year reign, in my previous book, *Revelation: Dawn of All Hope*, I wrote extensively about the Age of Messiah. But there are two new thoughts I would like to add here, which are both new and exciting to me!

First, **the 1000 years is symbolic of Christ's undoing of Adam**. Jewish sages believed that Adam was supposed to live for 1000 years. Interestingly, they also believed that God came to Adam and showed him the future life of David and that he (David) would die as an infant. So Adam chose to take 70 years off of his own life and give them to David. This tradition is used to explain why Adam lived 930 years and David 70.

> What our sages said about Adam giving 70 years of his life to David is also true. The whole point of granting life to David was to repair the damage done to G–d's universe by Adam, without which a Messianic age and all its benefits to mankind would not be needed. Adam's צלם אלוקים, divine image, needed to be restored first and foremost through the constructive lives of the patriarchs… Once the Messiah will arrive on earth, Adam will be rehabilitated completely, will be אד"ם, the first letters respectively of the incarnations in אדם דוד משיח [Adam David Messiah].[296]

> [It was] seventy years that Adam took away from his life and gave to David ben Yishai [son of Jesse]. It was fit that he live for a thousand years, as it says "…for on the day that you eat thereof, you shall surely die." (Genesis 2:17) And a day to the Holy One is a thousand years, as it says "For a thousand years are in Your eyes like yesterday, which passed, and a watch in the night." (Psalms 90:4)[297]

---

[296] Shenei Luchot HaBerit, Torah Shebikhtav, Toldot, Torah Ohr 58, Shney Luchot Habrit by Rabbi Eliyahu Munk. <sefaria.org>
[297] Bamidbar Rabbah 14:12, Rabbi Mike Feuer, Jerusalem Anthology. <sefaria.org>

Now, I'm not asking you to believe in this tradition. I'm asking you to understand that Adam living for 1000 years was part of Jewish thought. Now transpose that to Jesus, whom Paul calls the "Last Adam" (1 Cor 15:45). We see that the 1000 years in Revelation is a throw-back to the 1000 years of Adam, and this is not by coincidence!

The second point I want to make has to do with the Tree of Knowledge and the Cross. The *issue of sin* began with a tree at the start of Adam's epoch, which I will call the Age of Adam for illustration's sake. Similarly, the *solution to sin* came from a tree (aka the Cross; cf. Gal 3:13) at the start of the Last Adam's epoch, the Age of Messiah. Moreover, at the end of the Age of Adam came death – meaning Adam died. However, through the death of Christ, this Messianic Age will bring about the end of death – death itself will die (1 Cor 15:25–26; Rev 20:14).

This notion of Jesus as the Last Adam is known as "Recapitulation", a theological term that is so old it's new to most! The early Church Fathers placed great significance on the fact that Jesus did what Adam could not, all while redeeming humanity in the process.

> [A major] emphasis in patristic teaching is that the incarnate one is the last Adam, who recapitulated in himself the human story and thus accomplished all the divine purpose. The contrast between Adam and Christ was foundational to St. Paul's teaching on sin and salvation. In the early patristic period, Irenaeus laid heavy emphasis on this theme, writing,
>
> 'When he became incarnate and was made human, he began anew the long line of human beings and, to state it briefly, furnished us with salvation. Consequently, what we had lost in Adam – namely, the image and likeness of God – we recovered in Christ Jesus. [*Against Heresies 3:18,1*]'...
>
> The last Adam saved humankind through his death and his resurrection: Cyril of Alexandria pointed out, 'He [the incarnate Son] came from Adam according to the flesh, as a second beginning for those on earth, to transform human nature in himself into a newness of life in holiness and incorruptibility through the resurrection from the dead. [*Catechetical Lectures 13:2*]' Further, Maximus the Confessor rhapsodized, 'After securing complete victory over the devil, Jesus Christ crowned

Himself with the Resurrection for our sake. Thus the new Adam renewed the old. [*The Ascetic Life 12*]'[298]

So an additional aspect to the 1000 year period in Revelation 20 has to do with Recapitulation: Christ's undoing of Adam and the restoration of all that was lost through sin and death. Sin came first, and it ultimately led to death. Likewise, the cross came first to free us from sin, and at the end of the figurative 1000 years will come the abolition of death. Paul captures this thought best in 1 Corinthians:

"For since death came through a man, the resurrection of the dead comes also through a man. For as in Adam all die, so in Christ all will be made alive." 1 Corinthians 15:21–22

THE TWO RESURRECTIONS

"And at that time stand up doth Michael, the great head, who is standing up for the sons of thy people, and there hath been a time of distress, such as hath not been since there hath been a nation till that time, and at that time do thy people escape, every one who is found written in the book. And the multitude of those sleeping in the dust of the ground do awake, some to life age-during, and some to reproaches -- to abhorrence age-during." Daniel 12:1–2 (YLT)

In the first book of this series, I explain that the resurrection, like God's Kingdom, is both now and yet to come. John (uniquely) simplified this by referring to a "first resurrection" and a "second death" (Rev 20:5-6, 14), whereby a second resurrection and a first death are so obvious that they are implied but not necessary to mention. In short, if you drop dead right now, that is the first death. In fact, Jesus (and later Paul) says that we are already dead in this life apart from Christ (Lk 9:60, Eph 2:1, Col 2:13, etc.). Everlasting life – which is the first resurrection – is knowing Jesus intimately (Lk 15:24, Jn 1:4; 5:21 26; 11:25; 14:6; 17:3, Rom 5:12, 17; 6:4, Eph 2:5, 6, Col 2:12, etc.).

---

[298] Payton, James R. Jr., *The Victory of the Cross: Salvation in Eastern Orthodoxy* (Westmont: InterVarsity Press, 2019), p. 84, 87.

"You gave Him authority over all mankind, so that to all whom You have given Him, He may give eternal life. And this is eternal life, that they may know You, the only true God, and Jesus Christ whom You have sent." John 17:2–3 (NASB)

"And you were dead in your offenses and sins… even when we were dead in our wrongdoings, made us alive together with Christ (by grace you have been saved), and raised us up with Him, and seated us with Him in the heavenly places in Christ Jesus." Ephesians 2:1, 5, 6 (NASB)

"Having been buried with Him in baptism, in which you were also raised with Him through faith in the working of God, who raised Him from the dead. And when you were dead… He made you alive together with Him." Colossians 2:12–13 (NASB)

See the pattern here? Death (1st death) and Life (1st resurrection) are *here and now*. That then leaves the second death and second resurrection for the future, and we will explore the second death when we cover Revelation 20:11–14. John saw the second resurrection, aka the Great Resurrection, in which all who *ever* died since the earth was created will come back to life in physical flesh. 1 Corinthians 15 is Paul's entire discourse on how this all plays out. Read these words carefully. Let the anointing come upon you as you ponder the weight of what is to come:

"For if the dead are not raised, then not even Christ has been raised; and if Christ has not been raised, your faith is worthless; you are still in your sins. Then also those who have fallen asleep in Christ have perished. If we have hoped in Christ only in this life, we are of all people most to be pitied.

But the fact is, Christ has been raised from the dead, the first fruits of those who are asleep. For since by a man death came, by a man also came the resurrection of the dead. For as in Adam all die, so also in Christ all will be made alive. But each in his own order: Christ the first fruits, after that those who are Christ's at His [final] coming, then comes the end, when He hands over the kingdom to our God and Father, when He has abolished all rule and all authority and power. For He must reign until He has put all His enemies under His feet. The last enemy that will be abolished is death…

But someone will say, "How are the dead raised? And with what kind of body do they come?" You fool!

...Behold, I am telling you a mystery; we will not all sleep, but we will all be changed, in a moment, in the twinkling of an eye, at the last trumpet; for the trumpet will sound, and the dead will be raised imperishable, and we will be changed. For this perishable must put on the imperishable, and this mortal must put on immortality."
1 Corinthians 15:16–26, 35–36, 51–53 (NASB)

Back to Daniel 12: "And the multitude of those sleeping in the dust of the ground do awake, some to life age-during, and some to reproaches -- to abhorrence age-during." Daniel was speaking of his Jewish brethren who would be alive at the cusp of ages, where the Mosaic Age ceased and the Messianic Age began, who would see the Light of Life (Jn 8:12). Those who walked into that light entered into the first resurrection, the Life. Those who walked away from that light were awakened into an age of death. [299]

"Truly, truly, I say to you, the one who hears My word, and believes Him who sent Me, has eternal life, and does not come into judgment, but has passed out of death into life...

Truly, truly, I say to you, a time is coming and even now has arrived, when the dead will hear the voice of the Son of God, and those who hear will live...

Do not be amazed at this; for a time is coming when all who are in the tombs will hear His voice, and will come out: those who did the good deeds to a resurrection of life, those who committed the bad deeds to a resurrection of judgment." John 5:24–25, 28–29 (NASB)

Chapter 20 verses 4 to 6 tell us that the first resurrection is synonymous

---

[299] One more passage to chew on: "And Jesus cried out again with a loud voice, and gave up His spirit. And behold, the veil of the temple was torn in two from top to bottom; and the earth shook and the rocks were split. Also the tombs were opened, and many bodies of the saints who had fallen asleep were raised; and coming out of the tombs after His resurrection, they entered the holy city and appeared to many." Matt 27:50–53 (NASB)

with the figurative 1000 years. Therefore, we who are presently living in the 1000 years are participants of the first resurrection (the born-again experience).[300] Interestingly in John's Gospel, both the first and second resurrections are cryptically alluded to in an exchange Jesus has with Martha:

> *"Martha then said to Jesus, 'Lord, if You had been here, my brother would not have died. Even now I know that whatever You ask of God, God will give You.' Jesus said to her, 'Your brother will rise from the dead.' Martha said to Him, 'I know that he will rise in the resurrection on the last day.' Jesus said to her, 'I am the resurrection and the life; the one who believes in Me will live, even if he dies, and everyone who lives and believes in Me will never die. Do you believe this?'"*
> *John 11:21–26 (NASB)*

Martha was referencing the Great Resurrection (the second resurrection), an event in which we will receive new bodies that will not suffer death or decay and will take place "on the last day". But Jesus said that knowing Him now is already a form of resurrection (the state of being born-again), and "even if [one] dies" the first death (death of the soul and body), that one will live (in spirit in God's heavenly realm). We are all born into the first death (as ones born in Adam, a fallen state); our bodies expiring are simply the final expression of that death (Jesus said, "Let the dead bury their own dead" [Lk 9:60], and Paul said, "You were dead in your sins" [Eph 2:1, also Col 2:13]). The Prodigal Son of Luke 15 was considered "dead" when he wandered off and "alive" when he returned to his Father (Lk 15:24). To know Christ is to enter into the first resurrection (the state of being born-again). So even when our bodies expire in physical death, we continue to abide in His heavenly presence in spirit. But there is more to come! The purpose of salvation – the very meaning of life! - is not to die and simply go to heaven, but for God to renew all creation (including you and me) and for heaven and earth to become one. This is what John meant by the "second resurrection". We will be given new flesh that has no fallen state, no sin, no decay, and no possibility of death (which we will discuss in more detail a little further on; see also 1 Cor 15:42-54).

> א *(6) Blessed and holy is he who has his portion in the first resurrection, and over these ones the second death has no authority. Rather, they shall be the priests of God and of the*

---

[300] Cf. John 11:25; Col 2:12, 3:1; Rom 6:4–5; Eph 2:6.

REVELATION: DAWN OF ETERNITY

Messiah, and they shall reign alongside Him a thousand years.

As I mentioned in the previous book when I covered Revelation 20:1–7, **we are presently in the figurative 1000 year reign of the Messiah.** This is where the delineation between current events (from John's historical perspective) and future events (again, future to John) takes place. Now, today, in the 21st century, **we are at the tail end of the Messianic Age.** And I believe verse 7 has already taken place, where Satan has been loosed from his restraints and has been actively deceiving the nations.

This is where I depart from full Preterism, or the notion that the Messianic Age will go on indefinitely until Believers turn the world around. My separation is from the theological position, not those who hold it! For unity in the Body of Christ is paramount, not agreement. So what I write here pertains to theology, not humans made in the image of God.

To me, full Preterism (meaning all of Revelation has already been fulfilled) is very convenient for those living in First World countries. Indeed, life is good and "heaven is here", as the saying goes. Yet full Preterism is entirely ignorant of those who currently suffer in this world. Take for instance the persecuted Christians of Iran, India, China, North Korea, and countries in Northern and Central Africa. Is their bloody reality heaven? What about the millions of children who are being trafficked in the sex trade? Is this heaven for them? Then we go back in time to the world wars, the slave trades, and all the suffering that mankind has experienced: this is heaven?

On the flipside, the view that suggests that the Age of Messiah will keep going on indefinitely until we fulfill the Great Commission or we figure out how to renew creation according to Romans 8 is to me sincere but misguided. Please don't misunderstand me: we need to pursue the Great Commission and we need to grow in our Romans 8 revelation as sons and daughters of Abba Father. But to grow in something is quite different than being solely responsible for an expected outcome. No matter how much we grow and do, there are things that only God can perform.

For instance, the Great Resurrection – which is physical not metaphorical – is something only God can do. The final and ultimate defeat of physical death (the last enemy) so that humans no longer experience it is something only God can do. Nowhere in Scripture will you find a hint that would suggest otherwise. And likewise, only God can renew all of creation, both heaven and earth, and merge them together as one. So no matter how great out intentions, we need to realize that the big stuff still rests on His shoulders.

Lastly, if you will recall in the first book of this series, *Dawn of This Age,* I use up a great many pages explaining how God works within epoch seasons. Yahweh works within beginning and end dates; He doesn't operate randomly or indefinitely. The same is true for the Age of Messiah, where the figurative 1000 year period has both a predetermined start and end date that Yahweh has already appointed.

> *"Then they gathered around him and asked him, 'Lord, are you at this time going to restore the kingdom to Israel?'*
>
> *He said to them: 'It is not for you to know the times or dates the Father has set by his own authority. But you will receive power when the Holy Spirit comes on you; and you will be my witnesses in Jerusalem, and in all Judea and Samaria, and to the ends of the earth.'*
>
> *After he said this, he was taken up before their very eyes, and a cloud hid him from their sight.*
>
> *They were looking intently up into the sky as he was going, when suddenly two men dressed in white stood beside them. 'Men of Galilee,' they said, 'why do you stand here looking into the sky? This same Jesus, who has been taken from you into heaven, will come back in the same way you have seen him go into heaven.'" Acts 1:6–10 (NIV)*

Abba Father has set the times and dates by His own authority. And Jesus will return at a set time, in the same manner He ascended.

> *"Repent, then, and turn to God, so that your sins may be wiped out, that times of refreshing may come from the Lord, and that he may send the Messiah, who has been appointed for you—even Jesus. Heaven must receive him until the time comes for God to restore everything, as he promised long ago through his holy prophets." Acts 3:19–21 (NIV)*

God has already established the kairos time for everything to be restored. And all that is needed to set the plan in motion to accomplish this is already at play. All effects of the Fall of Mankind – including sickness and disease, violence and rape, and of course death – *will* all be removed from life and creation as we know it. This is the great hope of our Faith. Dying and going to heaven is not God's ultimate end goal for mankind. It's so much more than that! In the once-again merged heaven and earth God recreates, there will no longer be any physical death. It will be a return to a Renewed Eden.

So if the really big picture stuff is still to come, what is God doing in the meantime? Reconciling sons and daughters back to Himself.

> *"For the love of Christ controls us, having concluded this, that one died for all, therefore all died; and He died for all, so that those who live would no longer live for themselves, but for Him who died and rose on their behalf…*
>
> *Now all these things are from God, who reconciled us to Himself through Christ and gave us the ministry of reconciliation, namely, that God was in Christ reconciling the world to Himself, not counting their wrongdoings against them, and He has committed to us the word of reconciliation."*
> *2 Cor 5: 14–15, 18–19 (NASB)*
>
> *"The Lord is not slow about His promise, as some count slowness, but is patient toward you, not willing for any to perish, but for all to come to repentance." 2 Peter 3:9 (NASB)*
>
> *"God our Savior… wants all people to be saved and to come to the knowledge of the truth. For there is one God, and one mediator also between God and mankind, the man Christ Jesus, who gave Himself as a ransom for all, the testimony given at the proper time."*
> *1 Timothy 2:3–6 (NASB)*
>
> *"He is before all things, and in Him all things hold together. He is also the head of the body, the church; and He is the beginning, the firstborn from the dead, so that He Himself will come to have first place in everything. For it was the Father's good pleasure for all the fullness to dwell in Him, and through Him to reconcile all things to Himself, whether things on earth or things in heaven, having made peace through the blood of His cross." Colossians 1:17–20 (NASB)*

Hence our present mission:

> *"**All authority** in heaven and on earth **has been given to me**. Therefore go and make disciples of all nations, baptizing them in the name*

*of the Father and of the Son and of the Holy Spirit, and teaching them to obey everything I have commanded you. And surely I am with you always, to the **very end of the age**."*
Matthew 28:18–20 (NIV, emphasis mine)

And how do we fulfill the Great Commission?

*"My prayer is not for them alone. I pray also for those who will believe in me through their message, **that all of them may be one**, Father, just as you are in me and I am in you. May they also be in us **so that the world may believe** that you have sent me. I have given them the glory that you gave me, **that they may be one as we are one**—I in them and you in me—so that they may be brought to complete unity. **Then the world will know** that you sent me and have loved them even as you have loved me."*
John 17:20–23 (NIV, emphasis mine)

Lastly, we must not forget that Jesus, as King of all Kings and Lord over all Lords, is actively reigning.

"Then the end will come, when he hands over the kingdom to God the Father after he has destroyed all dominion, authority and power. For he must reign until he has put all his enemies under his feet. The last enemy to be destroyed is death. For he 'has put everything under his feet.' …When he has done this, then the Son himself will be made subject to him who put everything under him, so that God may be all in all."
1 Corinthians 15:24–28 (NIV)

Does Jesus have all authority in both heaven and earth? Yes.
Is he actively reigning? Yes.
Do we have a shared responsibility in this Age? Yes.

Stop waiting for the world to end! Start partnering with Him in what He seeks to do through you in order to bring about the intended purpose of this Messianic Age!

12 AGE OF MESSIAH COMPLETED: CH. 20:7–9

> *"And 6,000 years must needs be accomplished, in order that the Sabbath may come, the rest, the holy day 'on which God rested from all His works.' For the Sabbath is the type and emblem of the future kingdom of the saints, when they 'shall reign with Christ,' when He comes from heaven, as John says in his Apocalypse: for 'a day with the Lord is as a thousand years.' Since, then, in six days God made all things, it follows that 6,000 years must be fulfilled."*
> Hippolytus of Rome, 3rd century AD

We've finally made it to the only point in the Book of Revelation that coincides with where we in the 21st century find ourselves (chronologically speaking). Not only does a practical reading of John's words lead us to such a conclusion, but so does the way in which John's writing shifts. In contrast to previous chapters, where each event or plague is followed by a long list of descriptions, the Beloved Apostle is now short on details throughout this chapter. Since we are no longer looking at the immediate present (in his time), but instead into the distant future, we will find the details to be sparse. There is much to cover, so let's dive in.

א *(7) Now whenever the thousand years are fulfilled, Satan[301] will*

---

[301] "the adversary"

> *be loosened from his restraint.*
>
> א *(8) And he will go forth to deceive all the nations in the four corners of the Earth,[302] to Gog and Magog, and to gather them for war. Their number is like the sand of the Sea.*

The great deception is already taking place. This of course is where many Christians find themselves fixated, and it's easy to get distracted by the darkness. I don't want to give unnecessary attention to what our enemy is up to, but it is important to acknowledge that the fulfillment of Revelation 20:7 is at hand. We are indeed at the tail end of the Messianic Age, and Satan has been deceiving the nations for approximately 200 years. Here are some bullet points, each of which are their own digression and far beyond the scope of this book:

1800s – Religious Deception:
- John Nelson Darby and the start of Dispensationalism, the precursor to "Left Behind" end-times theology
- Joseph Smith and the start of the Mormon Church
- Charles Taze Russell and the start of the Jehovah's Witnesses movement
- Mary Baker Eddy and the start of the Christian Science movement

1900s – Religious Persecution and World Wars:
- World War I
- Genocide of Armenian, Assyrian, Bulgarian, and Greek Christians
- USSR Soviet persecution of Christians
- World War II
- Jewish Genocide (The Holocaust)
- Rise of Christian Persecution in Muslim and communist countries

2000s – Social-Political Deception:
- Founding of the Church of Satan by Anton Levey in the 1960s
- Leftist ideologies infiltrating all aspects of society
- Legalizing the genocide of infants
- Threats against certain religious freedoms
- Targeted destruction of the family unit and the human self

---

[302] Because of the preceding noun ("nations/peoples") the focus shifts to a broader context. Hence, "the earth" instead of "the Land".

As stated above, each of these points are worth pondering and studying. For instance, it is no coincidence that Armenia, the very first nation to adopt Christianity as state-religion (not Rome) in 300 AD, was persecuted in the early 1900s in an event known as the Ottoman Genocide. A total of 2,000,000 Oriental Orthodox Christians – the ones who trace their origins as far back as the original Apostles – were targeted and killed by the Ottoman Empire between 1915 and 1923. Think about this: an *empire* rises up and specifically targets the oldest group of Christian communities and kills them *because* they are Christians. This is Satan deceiving the nations.

In the 1920s, the former Soviet Union (USSR) began to persecute their own Christians. From 1922 to 1980, it is estimated that over 20,000,000 (yes, twenty million) Christians were killed, either in concentration camps (such as the Solovki Camp of Special Purpose) or by various targeted executions. This is Satan deceiving the nations.

Then we have another empire, The Third Reich, known as Nazi Germany, which rose between 1933 to 1945. They targeted and killed Jews in the most inhumane ways. A minimum of 6,000,000 Jews were murdered specifically because of their ethnicity. This is Satan deceiving the nations.

Christian persecution has been on the rise in the 20th and 21st centuries. It is estimated that over 45 million Christians have suffered martyrdom just in the 20th century alone.[303] An even more astonishing figure is that from the 1st century AD until our time today, an estimated 70 million Christians in total have died as martyrs. This means that almost half of all the Christians who have ever died in history died in the last two centuries. This is Satan deceiving the nations.

And who can forget all the wars between nations in the 20th century? We've had two World Wars, wars in Eastern Asia, wars in the Middle East, and wars in South America. "But Leo, we've had wars, pogroms, and other horrific things in times past." Indeed. But the *grandiose, rapid, and consecutive* natures of these events in the past 200 years have no equal in human history. And now in the 21st century, the deception has moved from the battlefield to the home and to the mind. What's right is wrong, and what's wrong is right. This is Satan deceiving the nations.

---

[303] Johnson, Todd, CHRISTIAN MARTYRDOM: A GLOBAL DEMOGRAPHIC ASSESSMENT, Notre Dame, November 2012 < https://mcgrath.nd.edu/assets/84231/the_demographics_of_christian_martyrdom_todd_johnson.pdf>

GOG AND MAGOG

I'm incredibly grateful for the work of Sverre Bøe, who in my estimation wrote the most comprehensive analysis of the Gog Magog enigma, spanning nearly 400 pages. To my surprise, references to Gog Magog outside of Ezekiel are found in the LXX (Septuagint, Greek OT),[304] Samaritan Pentateuch (Torah in Samaritan Hebrew), and several variant manuscripts.[305]

What's really cool is how many times Gog Magog is found in early Jewish, Christian, and Islamic literature:

- various Sibylline Oracles
- a few times in Jubilees
- several Qumran scrolls
- many Targums
- once in 3 Enoch
- a few Early Church Fathers
- Josephus (Antiquities)
- The Koran
- an awesome reference in the Syrian Legend of Alexander (7th c. AD)

That said, the views and interpretations of who or what Gog Magog was are about as varied as their mentions. Though there is no uniform consensus, the reference to Gog Magog falls into one of two broad categories: historical or eschatological.[306] However, even the historical accounts vary from each other, and those that employ eschatological usage each do so with differing intentions and subsequent conclusions. But things are not completely scattered. There are some generalizations that can be made based on a broad sampling of the various bodies of writings available from antiquity and by relying predominately on Genesis 10:2, Numbers 24:7, and Ezekiel 38–39.

---

[304] For instance, Numbers 24:7 has Gog instead of "Agag", and Gog instead of "mowing" in Amos 7:1 – "and lo, He is forming locusts at the beginning of the ascending of the latter growth, and lo, the latter growth [is] after the mowings of the king." (see Young's Literal Translation).

[305] Gog for Og in Cod. Vat. in Deuteronomy 3:1–13; 4:47. "Haman, the Gogite" in ms. 93 to Esther 3:1 and 9:24. Gog in Cod. Vat. to Sirach 48:17.

[306] This broad brushstroke immediate presents conflicts; for instance, LXX Numbers 24:7 could fall between historical and eschatological, or it could be its own category. However, my goal here is simplification.

Key texts:

"This is the account of Shem, Ham and Japheth, Noah's sons, who themselves had sons after the flood.
The sons of Japheth:
Gomer, Magog, Madai, Javan, Tubal, Meshek and Tiras."
(Genesis 10:1–2)

"There shall come a man out of his [Israel's] seed, and he shall rule over many nations; and his kingdom shall be more exalted than Gog, and his kingdom shall be increased." (Numbers 24:7, LXX)[307]

"The word of the Lord came to me: 'Son of man, set your face against Gog, of the land of Magog, the chief prince of Meshek and Tubal; prophesy against him… Persia, Cush and Put will be with them, all with shields and helmets, also Gomer with all its troops, and Beth Togarmah from the far north with all its troops—the many nations with you.'"
(Ezekiel 38:1–2, 5–6)

When looking at the text of Ezekiel, Bøe notes:

1. All the lands listed are remote nations, geographically as well as culturally.

2. Many of the nations listed were bygone powers only heard of in historical accounts.

3. None of the peoples with whom Israel and Judah had actually been engaged in war are listed here, e.g. Babylon, Assyria, Egypt, Syria, Edom, Moab, Ammon, the Philistines, etc.

4. The only nation with whom Israel ever came to be politically involved is Persia, and that took place after the days of Ezekiel.

5. All the names, except for Gog, are also found in the tables of the nations in Genesis 10 and 1 Chronicles 1.

---

[307] Or "and the kingdom of Gog shall be exalted, and his kingdom shall be increased." The reading depends on whether you use the η as a conjunction or definite article.

6. Since these names are also found in the table of nations as ordinary nations, there is little reason to suppose that they were meant as anything but exactly ordinary nations. Theories of seeing the peoples comprising Gog's army as demons or mythological figures seem to be contrary to the way the text itself presents these peoples.

7. The directions from which Gog's army has been recruited give an impression of a universal plot against Israel; cf. the following list of the nations according to their place on a (modern) map:

38.2	Meshech	N
38.2	Tubal	N
38.5	Persia	E
38.5	Cush	SW
38.5	Put	W
38.6	Gomer	N
38.6	Bet Togarmah	N
38.13	Sheba	S
38.13	Tarshish	W
39.6	"The coastlands"	NW [308]

How does this help us understand Revelation 20:8? Ezekiel's vision places Jerusalem at the center of the circle of invaders from nations all around them. Therefore, when we read in Revelation *"all the nations in the four corners of the Earth, to Gog and Magog, and to gather them for war"*, we have Ezekiel's prophecy as a frame of reference for what that may look like. This doesn't answer the question of *where* historical Gog and Magog were located, geographically speaking.

> The geographical notes of Genesis 10 are not sufficient to allow us to place all the names in particular areas. In this respect the genealogies of the Book of Jubilees are a lot more elaborated... It is clear, however, that Magog in this text refers to a real land or people, not to a mythical region...
>
> Josephus states without hesitation that Magog is the same as

---

[308] Bøe, Sverre: Gog and Magog : Ezekiel 38 - 39 as pre- text for Revelation 19,17-21 and 20,7-10 (Tübingen: Mohr Siebeck, 2001), p 106, 107.

the people called Scythians by the Greeks... The Targumim both to Genesis as well as to 1 Chronicles, listed *Germania* as the province of Magog. It is not, however, clear what region they understood by "Germania" (sometimes *Germamia*); possibly it referred to the Cimmerians, or to *Germanicia* in Commagene in eastern Turkey, or to Germany in its modern sense or parts of it, or to the land of Beth Togarmah, like in the Targum to Ezek 27:14...

Given our ignorance, it is prudent to suggest the Magog may be located somewhere in Anatolia [Asia Minor, modern-day Turkey].[309]

For the student of Revelation, one must consider how John understood and interpreted the imagery of Gog Magog in light of his mission and audience. We have learned throughout this series how closely John's Apocalypse mirrors Ezekiel's prophetic book. However, John may not have employed Ezekiel's exact use of Gog, nor its same purpose. This nuance does not diminish John's allusion to Ezekiel: enemies who hate followers of Yahweh without cause may come, but it is Yahweh Himself who will defeat them. Sverre Bøe writes extensively and cites various Scriptures and ancient sources illustrating that Gog Magog has been used as either a name, a place, or both (ie. Gog of Magog). The identity of Gog as a person has also seen a wide range of scholarly opinions. I won't go through all the ideas proposed by academics over the years, but rather I will provide Bøe's conclusion after examining all the evidence:

[For the book of Ezekiel] a variety of proposed explanations has been suggested both of "Gog" and "Magog". There is no scholarly consensus. Among the historical identifications King Gyges of Lydia clearly stands out as the best candidate to have formed Ezekiel's Gog-figure. We have no indications, however, that John or his contemporaries sought for identifications for Gog in the remote past.[310]

So did John use Gog Magog as a person or a place? For context, Numbers 24:7 clearly considers Gog a person, and Amos 7:1 in the LXX (Septuagint)

---

[309] Ibid., p 47, 48.
[310] Ibid., p. 99.

has Gog as a person. But then in Jubilees 7:19, Magog is an individual, like in Genesis 10:2 and 1 Chronicles 1:5. Then in Qumran 1QM 11:16 Gog is also an individual. But in contrast, Sibylline Oracles 3:319-320 refers to Gog as a land. Here's what Boe has to say about Gog Magog as person or place:

> Another interesting question is whether John has thought of Gog and Magog as individual persons, as nations or as names of countries. One may also consider the possibility that John took these names as symbols or sobriquets, not intended to be identified with specific persons or nations, but rather as referring to well-known eschatological adversaries. Grammatically it is most probable that it should conform to the words to which it forms an apposition, i.e. "the nations"…
>
> In Ezekiel 38-39 Gog obviously is the name of an individual, a person, a prince. Ezek 38:2 seems to be the name of Gog's home-country, whereas Magog in Rev 20:8 seems to be a parallel name to Gog. This is traditionally seen as a shift away from Ezekiel's original intent, over to what is often said to be the more common use in the apocalyptic tradition, where the names simply come as a pair.[311]
>
> Thus the conclusion has been that "the nations at the four corners of the earth, Gog and Magog" must simply be peoples in the sense of ordinary human beings…
>
> Another major observation concerns how John reserves for God himself the task of defeating Gog and Magog. This is directly in line with Ezekiel, who similarly leaves all the fighting to God himself. This is quite different in many of the other texts which relate to the Gog and Magog traditions. Most of these texts place Israel, Messiah or some other human agent in the center…
>
> It is also important to note the very different ways Ezekiel and John continue their narratives or writings after the Gog-battle: Ezekiel speaks extensively of the cleansing of Israel, and goes on to describe the New Temple (Ezekiel 40-48). John, however, inserts the account of the general judgement (Rev 20,11-15)

---

[311] Ibid., p. 312, 313.

before he describes the New Jerusalem.

The lack of direct references to Israel, Jerusalem, the Jewish nation, etc. in Revelation 20 sets this text apart from all the other texts we have studied dealing with Gog and Magog. This is the only text presenting Gog and Magog which does not refer to their attack on Israel. At this point Revelation departs from both Ezekiel 38-39 and all the other texts referring to Gog and Magog. This lack of reference to Israel may also be the reason why John shows no interest in the burial of Gog's soldiers and the cleansing of the land after the battle.[312]

Based on all his research, Bøe deduced John did not employ Gog Magog as a person but as place-names.

A VARIANT ON ORDER OF EVENTS

Most Bibles in print today have the Masoretic Text dating back to the 9th to 11th centuries AD as their source for the Old Testament. So in your Bible, you will likely see the following order in Ezekiel:

Ch 37 Dry bones come to life
Ch 38 Gog and Magog attack and are destroyed
Ch 39 Evil is defeated by God
Ch 40 New Temple vision

However, one of the earliest surviving manuscripts of Ezekiel, known as P967 (P for papyrus), dating back to the late second or early third century AD provides us with a unique detail: the chapter orders are different.[313]

In P967, the chapter order is as follows:

---

[312] Ibid., p. 344, 345.
[313] Lilly, Ingrid E., *Two books of Ezekiel: Papyrus 967 and the Masoretic text as variant literary editions* (Leiden, Boston: Brill, 2012), at 1, e-book. On page 2, Lily writes, "the most notable features of p967 are its omission of ch. 36:23c–38 and its transposition of MT [Masoritic Text] chs. 37 and 38–39, placing the vision of the valley of dried bones after the Gog-Magog battle. Several other unique minuses of significant length (i.e., over 10 letters) are also attested (e.g., Ezek 12:26–28 and 32:24–26)."

Ch 37 (38) Gog and Magog attack and are destroyed
Ch 38 (39) Evil is defeated by God
Ch 39 (37) Dry bones come to life
Ch 40 (40) New Temple vision

In the older manuscript, Gog invades *first*, is defeated, and *then* there is a great resurrection. Now look at the sequence of events in Revelation:

20:8–9 Gog and Magog attack and are destroyed
20:10 Evil is defeated by God
20:12–13 Everyone comes to life
21 New Jerusalem vision

If this manuscript is in fact the correct order of events, then Ezekiel (and later John) saw the same events and in the same order.

WHO WAS GOG?

I want to make it clear that there is no textual or contextual evidence strong enough to conclude that John was referencing Gog as a person. I do believe, based on the evidence, John is referring to Gog as an enemy force, an antagonist. That said, for those of you curious enough to know more about the use of Gog in the Old Testament, this section is for you.

With just one glance at the book of Numbers or Matthew's Gospel, you can appreciate how much names meant to the Hebrew people. It's not just Ansestry.com type stuff. It's that a name bore a story, an image, a moral equation. Names like Korah and Balaam are generally not a big deal to Christians today, but they carried great meaning to 1st century Yahwists.[314] The same is true of the names Ham and Japheth.

Noah begat three sons, Shem, Ham, and Japheth. Ham sinned against Noah and was written off. Well-wishes were spoken over Japheth, but only Shem was blessed. From that point on, the Semitic people (Shemitic, i.e. Hebrews) were antagonized by the descendants of Ham (Northern Africa and Arabia) and the descendants of Japheth (Greece, Anatolia [Turkey], and Eastern Levant [Iran]).

Ham antagonized the Hebrews from the south through empires like Egypt (Mizraim in Hebrew) and Babylon (think Nebuchadnezzar), and from

---

[314] See Jude (Judas) 1:11; 2 Peter 2:15; and Revelation 2:14.

the north, Japheth antagonized the Hebrews through empires like the Assyrians, Persians, and Macedonians (Alexander the Great). Suffice to say the names Ham and Japheth carried a lot of weight in the days of John the Apostle. But how does this apply to Revelation?

Because Japheth had some kids, and one of them was named Magog. And while only small tidbits of history have endured the test of time, it seems he was a big deal.

> "Gog and Magog" links the name of Japheth's second son to Gyges king of Lydia, that land of Asia Minor that once belonged to the Persian Empire...
>
> Gaels of Christian times asserted firmly that they descended from Magog... Their "invasions" of Britain invariably refer to maritime routes from Asia Minor to Britain. The Phoenician "ships of Tarshish" became an immediate dimension of this Japhethite dispersion.[315]

Gog, or Gyges, reigned in modern-day Turkey, known as Asia Minor in John's day, right where all his seven churches were located. This guy was somewhat legendary, infamous even, like William Wallace ("Braveheart" for the uncultured) or Lancelot. But in a bad way because he was evil.

> "Magog could easily be identified as a war god but only after the Uruk-Aratta war, not in the pre-colonization period. In the Uruk-Aratta war Magog undoubtedly led one of the griffin armies including ancestors of the Egyptians as well as Semites. Anhur was conceived as spiritual leader of the Egyptian army. We have now seen Magog in the role of three different Egyptian gods--- Anubis, Shu and Anhur."[316]

From Noah we have a similar tale: Abraham begets Ishmael and Isaac and a rivalry ensues. Isaac begets Jacob and Esau, and there too the siblings were at odds. Esau marries a relative of Ishmael and has a grandson named Amalek

---

[315] Pilkey, John, *Noah's Family Speaks: Postdiluvian History from Noah to Abraham, Genesis 10-11 Studies Book 2* (Anacortes: R. S. Marshall, 1984). Kindle Edition.
[316] Ibid.

whose clan later became known as the Amalekites. They were more than a thorn in Israel's side. According to the Jewish sage Rashi (1040–1105), "[Amalek] came before all of them to make war with Israel." Amalek and the Amalekites became synonymous with evil in Jewish folklore. The Amalekites appear several times in the Bible, including Numbers 24, 1 Samuel 15, and throughout Esther.

Now back to Gog. As I've already mentioned, he was a historical figure also known as Gyges or Gugu, and he reigned in Lydia, the western part of Asia Minor, where John's churches were.

> "[Magog's brother] Gomer (Ezekiel 38:6 - Cimmerians) was an enemy of the Assyrians that invaded ancient Asia Minor by coming down from the north around the 8th century BC. The Assyrians called the barbarous invading Cimmerians (Gomer) "creatures of hell."
>
> These nations all coexisted in Asia Minor (modern Turkey) at a time when Magog (also known as Ludu or Lydia in both the Bible and the Assyrian texts) was led by a militant leader called Gog (685-652 BC), about 100 years before the Book of Ezekiel was written. Gog is the Hebrew spelling for the name of this militant leader from western Asia Minor, who was known as Gyges of Lydia to the Greeks. This same leader was known as "Gugu, king of Ludu" and "Gugu, King of Lydia" to the Assyrians...
>
> In the Assyrian language "the land of Gugu" is rendered as Ma-gugu, just as "the land of Zamua" is rendered as Ma-zamua. The Hebrew spelling of Magugu is "Magog," and thus, "Magog" simply means "the land of Gog." When Ezekiel 38:2 refers to Gog from the land of Magog, as the chief prince of Meshech and Tubal, scripture refers to a specific geographic area – Asia Minor; to a specific time period- when Magog (Lydia), Meshech, and Tubal were coexistent; and to a specific ruler – Gog (Gyges to the Greeks) – who led the defensive efforts of Magog, Meshech and Tubal against invading Gomer (the Cimmerians)."[317]

---

[317] Goodman, Jeffrey, *The Comets of God - New Scientific Evidence for God: Recent*

If you check out this cool document called "The Ancient Records of Assyria" or the "Assyrian Royal Court Records" dating back to 700 BC, it also mentions Gyges of Lydia/Gog of Magog:

> "Gugu (Gyges), king of Lydia, a district of the other side of the sea, a distant place, whose name, the kings, my fathers, had not heard, Assur, the god, my creator, caused to see my name in a dream. 'Lay hold of the feet of Assurbanipal, king of Assyria and conquer thy foes by calling upon his name,'
>
> On the day that he beheld this vision, he dispatched his messenger to bring greetings to me [King Assurbanipal]...
>
> He sent his forces to the aid of Tushamilki, king of Egypt, who had thrown off the yoke of my sovereignty. I heard of it and prayed to Assur and Ishtar, saying: 'May his body be cast before his enemy, may (his foes) carry off his limbs.' The Cimmerians, whom he had trodden underfoot, by calling upon my name, invaded and overpowered the whole of his land. His son seated himself upon his throne, after him (i.e., his death)"[318]

Greek historians and philosophers like Herodotus, Plutarch, and Plato also wrote of Gog/Gyges/Gugu, but I won't digress. In short, Japheth bore a son who, from the little history we can gather, was known as a military leader and was, according to Greek legend, a usurper who assassinated his king to seize the throne. Also worth noting is that the capital city of the Gog/Gyges/Gugu kingdom in Lydia was *Sardis* (Rev 3:1).

A couple pages back I make mention of the Amalekites. They were a real threat to Israel and a plague that King Saul failed to deal with (1 Samuel 15). One such Amalekite was named Agag/Gog. He's special. In Numbers 24:7–8, it reads in the Septuagint,

> *"There shall come a man out of his seed, and he shall rule over many nations; and over the kingdom of Gog [Agag in your Bible] shall be*

---

archeological, geological and astronomical discoveries that shine new light on the Bible and its prophecies (Tucson: Archeological Research Books, LLC., 2011), at 338-339, Kindle Edition.
[318] Luckenbill, Daniel David, *Ancient Records of Assyria and Babylnia Volume II* (Chicago: The University of Chicago Press, 1927) at 297–298, e-book.

exalted, and his kingdom shall be increased… he shall consume the nations of his enemies, and he shall drain their marrow, and with his darts he shall shoot through the enemy."

In Amos 7:1, it reads in the Septuagint,

"This is what my Lord God showed me: He was creating [a plague of] locusts at the time when the late-sown crops were beginning to sprout—the late-sown crops after the king Gog."

King Agag (Gog) of the Amalekites was a modern-day (in the days of King Saul and King David) manifestation of Gog (Japheth's son). Saul disobeyed Yahweh and failed to fully subdue them. As a result, hundreds of years later, the Amalekites continued to be a thorn in the side of the Hebrew people.

Then we have Haman the Agagite (Gogite) in the book of Esther. As previously mentioned, when Papyrus 967 (P967) was discovered in the early 1900s, it contained three books as one unit: Ezekiel, Daniel, and Esther. Whoever bound these books together saw meaning in their collective interpretation. The book of Esther is significant here because the antagonist of the Esther story is Haman. This anti-Semitic (anti-Shem) character is a personification of the Amalekite/Esau/Ishmael and Magog/Japheth/Ham motifs. Haman is not simply a guy with a grudge against Mordecai. He represents the constant threat against Jews.

However, the climax of the Esther story is that God himself does what King Saul failed to do: defeat Israel's enemy. Haman's execution symbolically represents the defeat of the Amalekites, and it carries an eschatological message here for all creation: what happened to Haman will happen to the figure of Gog.

In the Septuagint, Haman is introduced as "Haman, son of Hammedatha the Bugaean" (Esther 3:1), but in the Hebrew it reads, "Haman, son of Hammedatha the Agagite". As Lilly remarks,

> "The Hebrew version takes on an eschatological perspective as a cosmic struggle between Jews and gentile nations, Haman appropriately becoming the apocalyptic 'Gogite'. (cf. Ezek 38–

9)."³¹⁹

Her point is that since Agag in Numbers 24 is synonymous with Gog, the writer of Esther is telling us that not only is Haman an Amalekite (See Agag the Amalekite, 1 Sam 15), but he is also personifying Gog in this narrative.³²⁰

> "The Septuagint shows that the story of Esther was right away understood or reinterpreted as conveying a religious message. The allusions to the historic confrontation of Israel and Amalek in the book were readily picked up and amplified. But with a twist. In the Greek of 9:24, as well as in the Addition to 8:12, Haman is called a Makedon. He was "a Macedonian, an alien in fact" who, says v. 14, plotted "to transfer to the Macedonians the sovereignty now held by the Persians." On the other hand, the Jews are called by the king, "our loyal Persians" {v. 23}…
>
> In 3:I, 8:3 and 5, and 9:10 and 24, he is an Agagite (i.e., Amalekite) or, by a possible play of words with Agag, he is a Gogite (i.e., coming from the cursed city of Gog)."³²¹

CONCLUSIONS ABOUT GOG MAGOG

I know some of you are disappointed I didn't call out specific nations and place them on a watch list for upcoming doomsday events. Perhaps worse for some there is no super villain code-named Gog to lead these enemy forces. What a bummer! In all seriousness though, what can our takeaway be in light of all this information about Gog and Magog when reading John's Revelation?

---

³¹⁹ Lilly, Ingrid E., *Two books of Ezekiel : Papyrus 967 and the Masoretic text as variant literary editions* (Leiden, Boston: Brill, 2012), at 281, e-book.

³²⁰ The Septuagint surname for Haman, "Bugaean", is the source of much debate. However, the best hypothesis I've come across is by Adam J. Silverstein in his book, *Veiling Esther, Unveiling Her Story: The Reception of a Biblical Book in Islamic Lands*. Silverstein states in chapter 6 of his premise that Bougaean was the Persian equivalent to Gyges, having the same lore in that he was a schemer who assassinated his way into power. Thus, the Greek translation was still alluding to the same person using another cultural context.

³²¹ Lacocque, Andre, *Haman In The Book of Esther*, Center for Jewish-Christian Studies, Chicago Theological Seminary, p 212.

The key is to understand that the folklore surrounding the Gog figure was enough to remind Jewish readers of the constant threat against them as a people group. The nuance of grouping Gog and Magog together to represent distant nations doesn't diminish the intended effect for John's readers: Satan's legal right to cause nations to walk in deception will result in a threat against the Saints of Yahweh and Yeshua. Satan will use people to become an antagonistic force against the lovers of God. As the Psalmist wrote,

"Those who hate me without reason
outnumber the hairs of my head;
many are my enemies without cause,
those who seek to destroy me." Psalm 69:4 (NIV)

Magog has a long history going back to the table of nations, and many Jewish writings have made use of the name in various ways. However, the one constant theme is that the names Gog and Magog invoke a notion of antagonism and persecution that is as old as the Hebrew people themselves.

Thus, one may conclude that if the *last* enemy to be defeated is death (1 Corinthians 15:26), then in a figurative sense, a *second last* enemy to be defeated is the age-old thorn in Israel's side, the Gogites/Amalekites. From the perspective of John's immediate Jewish audience, they may have seen Israel's deliverance from Gog Magog as symbolic of what God aims to do cosmologically.

"Then the end will come, when he hands over the kingdom to God the Father after he has destroyed all dominion, authority and power. For he must reign until he has put all his enemies under his feet. The last enemy to be destroyed is death." 1 Corinthians 15:24–26 (NIV)

These references to Gog Magog should therefore be understood as illustrations of God's grand plan to bring down every last enemy before the renewal of the Cosmos. This concludes our Gog Magog discussion.

Revelation 20:9 is the hinge verse that catapults all of creation into the most epic, powerful, awe-inspiring sequence of events the world has ever seen. Let us turn our attention now to its reading.

א (9) *And they went up*[322] *upon the expanse of the Land.*[323] *And they surrounded the city encampment*[324] *of the Saints, and the Beloved City.*[325] *But fire descended from Heaven from God and consumed them.*

The fire descending can only be understood in light of verse 11: "But fire descended from Heaven from God and consumed them....And I saw the Great White Throne...". This fire is not an isolated object or event like the pillar of cloud that followed the Hebrews in the wilderness or the fire that Elijah the Prophet called down. **The fire in Revelation 20:9 is the beginning of the manifest presence of Yahweh God Himself descending** (cf. Daniel 7:9–10). The consequences of the intensity and magnitude of Yahweh God's figurative descent upon the earth is that all evil is consumed and Satan is cast down once and for all. More on these things later.

Let's turn our attention now to the peculiar description of the encampment outside of Jerusalem. First, it reminds us of Deuteronomy 23:9–14 where we learn how the Hebrews were to prepare themselves for an impending enemy invasion. Purity and consecration were the focal points. As it relates to what John saw, the implied context suggests the lovers of Yeshua are preparing themselves for the arrival of nations coming for war.

"Since the Lord your God walks in the midst of your camp to save you and to defeat your enemies before you, your camp must be holy; so He must not see anything indecent among you or He will turn away from you." Deuteronomy 23:14 (NASB)

Interestingly, the Saints are not *within* the confines of Jerusalem, and there

---

[322] ܣܠܩܘ The first tell-tale sign we are dealing with the Holy Land. Like the Hebrew "aliyah" (עֲלִיָּה), the Aramaic is used to describe "going up" to Jerusalem. See John 11:55.

[323] With the combination of "going up" and the forthcoming mention of "the Beloved City", we are once again dealing with the Holy Land.

[324] Or "the tent city of the Saints". Camp ܡܫܪܝܬܐ a difficult word to decipher. Mashrito' can mean camp, habitation, lodging, or it can mean military camp, garrison, fortress. It is difficult to imagine Saints in a military context, as there is no New Testament basis for Saints to take up arms. Therefore, I will stick with the conservative translation.

[325] ܚܒܝܒܬܐ "beloved" is the same word used for Jesus, "my Beloved Son". More importantly, it is an allusion to Isaiah 62:4.

is no mentions of walls, artillery, or any sort of defenses. These Saints have Yahweh God as their shield, their fortress, their deliverer. Violence and taking up arms has never been an option for the followers of Yeshua (the early church certainly demonstrated this time and time again). Clearly, the church of the future has taken this to heart as well. Therefore, it is God who will move on their behalf. These Saints may also be a prophetic fulfillment of the watchmen of Isaiah 62 who carry Jerusalem in their hearts. How so? The mention of "the Beloved City" is our clue.

JERUSALEM AS BELOVED

In chapters 17 and 19, Jerusalem is described as a harlot. Now she is called "Beloved". This is another major indicator informing us that John is now looking into a future that was distant from him chronologically. So what took place in order for Jerusalem to go from Harlot to Beloved?

"For Zion's sake I will not keep silent,
  for Jerusalem's sake I will not remain quiet,
till her vindication shines out like the dawn,
  her salvation like a blazing torch.
The nations will see your vindication,
  and all kings your glory;
you will be called by a new name
  that the mouth of the Lord will bestow.
You will be a crown of splendor in the Lord's hand,
  a royal diadem in the hand of your God.
No longer will they call you Deserted,
  or name your land Desolate.
But you will be called Hephzibah, [my delight is in her.]
  and your land Beulah; [married]
for the Lord will take delight in you,
  and your land will be married.
As a young man marries a young woman,
  so will your Builder marry you;
as a bridegroom rejoices over his bride,
  so will your God rejoice over you.
I have posted watchmen on your walls, Jerusalem;
  they will never be silent day or night.
You who call on the Lord,

give yourselves no rest,
and give him no rest till he establishes Jerusalem
and makes her the praise of the earth." Isaiah 62:1–7 (NIV)

The word "beloved" here in Revelation 20 is the same one used for Yeshua when Yahweh God declares, "this is my beloved Son in whom I take great delight (Mt 3:17)". In the Old Testament, the word דוד [326] is most commonly used in Song of Songs. **Jerusalem as Beloved has nothing to do with a rebuilt 3rd Temple or the reinstituting of the sacrificial system of the Law. What John saw was a prophetic image of the fulfillment of Romans 11!**

> *"Again I ask: Did they [Israel] stumble so as to fall beyond recovery? Not at all! Rather, because of their transgression, salvation has come to the Gentiles to make Israel envious. But if their transgression means riches for the world, and their loss means riches for the Gentiles, how much greater riches will their full inclusion bring!*
> *...For if their rejection brought reconciliation to the world, what will their acceptance be but life from the dead?*
> *... Israel has experienced a hardening in part until the full number of the Gentiles has come in, and in this way all Israel will be saved.*
> *...For God has bound everyone over to disobedience so that he may have mercy on them all." Romans 11:11, 12, 15, 25, 26, 32 (NIV)*

The most exciting part of this vision is that it takes place *in this age*, the one you and I are living in right now! Though the Messianic Age began with the fall of Jerusalem and the Holy Land, it *ends* with their restoration and reconciliation. Not in the sense of works and sacrifices, but rather in intimate union with Yahweh God and His Son, Yeshua, by way of Holy Spirit.

THE SAINTS VS THE NATIONS?

These nations all gather for war, so in a literal sense this could mean a geo-political war. But given the nature of Satan's current deceptive employments, it could also include a social-political aspect as well.. Certainly, in the 21st century, it feels like both are true. Middle Eastern tensions against

---

[326] Strong's H1730.

Israel continue to escalate over time, as do the evil political agendas. This makes the doom and gloom conspiracies very easy to buy into. But we cannot abandon all of the prophecies of hope and restoration because we are in a time of tension.

Go back to the first letters of Revelation. Consider those who have gone before us; they too were in a time of tension as one epoch season was fading and another was coming into fruition. The Age of Messiah started with great trial and difficulties for the lovers of Yeshua. They suffered greatly. So the pastoral exhortations which we read in Revelation 2 and 3 serve to bring us comfort today.

Nevertheless, the Saints do not need to do anything to defend themselves. **When John was looking ahead, he was in fact looking at us today, at least some of us.** How incredible! And what did he see us doing?

Gathering weapons? Nope.
Marching out to fight? Nope.
Hiding in bunkers? Nope.

No verbs are ascribed to the Saints, which suggests they were at peace. How is this possible?

> *"We have a strong city;*
> *God makes salvation*
> *its walls and ramparts.*
> *Open the gates*
> *that the righteous nation may enter,*
> *the nation that keeps faith.*
> **You will keep in perfect peace**
> **those whose minds are steadfast,**
> **because they trust in you."**
> *Isaiah 26:1–2 (NIV, emphasis mine)*

Instead of "perfect peace", the Hebrew literally says "shalom shalom". That is an extraordinary measure of peace! How can we enter into this measure of peace? Sadly, many Christians are addicted to fear and conspiracies because it satisfies a hunger for context and meaning when they look at the world. This is a by-product of an impoverished Christology and Eschatology, and it feeds the lies that:

We have a little God and a big devil.
We have a little Jesus and a big fantasy antagonist.

We have a weak Gospel and an enemy with a much more effective plan.
Our good news isn't good.
Escape is our hope.
Self-preservation is our empowerment.

We seek control because deep down we don't truly believe God is looking after things. So we think it's up to us. This is not our fault. We are coming up on 200 years of a false eschatology: fear-mongering, rapture, left-behind, weak, defeated, hell-in-a-handbasket type of belief systems. We've had five generations of fear and impoverished doctrine, and this is the result.

All of this is part of Satan's plan of deception: If I am spending more time reading about what the devil is up to than what God is up to, I'm heading into deception. If I am spending more time discussing what the devil is doing than what God is doing, I'm heading into deception. If my idea of the Christian fight is keeping tabs on the devil and unraveling all the secret things he is up to, I'm heading into deception. I *cannot* be in God's perfect shalom, faith, and rest while having my focus be upon the devil or his schemes. If God has less than 100% of our focus, then Satan has all of it. That's the snare. But resist the devil and he flees (James 4:7).

If I may suggest, it is much more fruitful to focus our time on developing a better Christology: the efficacy of the finished work, the power of his rule, and the increase of his dominion. Do we truly have reverential awe of Him?

> *"When I saw Him, I fell at His feet like a dead man. And He placed His right hand on me, saying, 'Do not be afraid; I am the First and the Last.'" Revelation 1:17 (NASB)*

It is much more fruitful to immerse ourselves in the hope-filled prophetic promises of what God is doing and will continue to do. **Jesus must become so big, so awe inspiring in our hearts and minds, that we laugh in the face of everything we see in the world.** The by-product of a superior Christology is a superior Eschatology.

> *"See to it that there is no one who takes you captive through philosophy and empty deception... rather than in accordance with Christ. For in Him all the fullness of Deity dwells in bodily form, and in Him you have been made complete, and He is the head over every ruler and authority." Colossians 2:8–10 (NASB)*

The Gospel – the prophecies of Jesus, the Scriptures of hope – are either entirely true or entirely false. There is no partiality. Don't look for the devil and his schemes. Seek to better understand who the real Christ is. Allow what you find to so impregnate you with faith that you give birth to hope for the world around you. You become what you behold! The devil wants your worship. He craves awe and fear of him. So why give him your attention? Don't take the bait!

One last thought with respect to the Gog Magog armies and the ingathering of nations from the four corners. In John 12:32, Jesus enigmatically states that when He is lifted up, He will draw all mankind to Himself. This is a multi-layered statement, one of which we see fulfilled in John's prophetic vision. Looking far ahead with minimal details, John sees the Saints in the middle of a number of people as great as the sand of the sea. Suddenly, the Shekinah glory of Yahweh appears. From John's perspective, you have all of humanity in one place (again, this is a prophetic *vision,* not a documentary film), and then God shows up. The following verses then have *everyone* who has ever lived standing before the Great White Throne, gathered to God, as a fulfillment of Jesus' words in John 12:32!

FIRE FALLS DOWN

"And it came to pass, in the completing of the days of His being taken up, that He fixed His face to go on to Jerusalem, and He sent messengers before His face, and having gone on, they went into a village of Samaritans, to make ready for Him, and they did not receive Him, because His face was going on to Jerusalem. And His disciples James and John having seen, said,
'Lord, will You [that] we may command fire to come down from Heaven, and to consume them, as Elijah also did?'
And having turned, He rebuked them and said,
'You have not known of what spirit you are, for the Son of Man did not come to destroy men's lives, but to save';
and they went on to another village." Luke 9:51–56 (LSV)

We have established in this series a few anchoring points relating to the nature of God, which I will recall here: a) God is not bi-polar, b) God was and is in Christ reconciling the world to Himself, c) The God of the Old

Testament can only be understood through the lens of Jesus, and d) Old Testament theophanies do not override Jesus as God in flesh because He is the express image and nature of God. With this in mind, let's examine the peculiar future event of the fire of Yahweh that descends upon these nations.

Clearly, placing our hope in Yahweh instead of trying to defend ourselves will pay off! In the end, God comes through for us, the enemy threat is neutralized, and John does not report any harm done to the Saints or the Beloved City. But what do we make of this fire?

A literal reading is highly implausible as it violates the nature of God (as revealed through the Incarnation of Yeshua) and the broader symbolism of John's vision. If the people gathered are as numerous as the sand of the sea, then it means God kills thousands or even millions of people in one shot. If we keep the literal reading going, a few verses later these same people are raised from the dead only to be burned again in the Sea of Fire and Sulfur. Now many of you are thinking, "Yes, that's what I've been taught." Friend, allow me to humbly suggest that there is *more*!

First, this is a prophetic allusion to Zechariah 2:

> *"Jerusalem is inhabited [as] open places,*
> *From the abundance of man and beast in her midst.*
> *And I am to her—a declaration of YHWH—**A wall of fire all around**, And I am for glory in her midst.*
> *Behold, and flee from the land of the north,*
> *A declaration of YHWH,*
> *For as the four winds of the heavens,*
> *I have spread you abroad,*
> *A declaration of YHWH.*
> *Behold, Zion, be delivered who are dwelling [with] the daughter of Babylon.*
> *For thus said YHWH of Hosts: He has sent Me after glory to the nations who are spoiling you,*
> *For he who is coming against you,*
> *Is coming against the pupil of His eye."*
> *Zechariah 2:4–8 (LSV, emphasis mine)*

Second, as mentioned above, **the fire of 20:9 is the beginning of the manifest presence of Yahweh God Himself. It can be likened to His Shekinah glory or the train of His robe (cf. Isa 6:1)**. Verse 11 is the key to understanding this, as the verses that follow verse 9 that speak about the

Great Resurrection and the Final Judgement all take place here on earth! Moreover, Father, Son, and Spirit are all associated with fire, and fire is a constant image employed in the Old Testament to describe Yahweh's presence.

> *"I was seeing until thrones have been thrown down, and the Ancient of Days is seated, His garment [is] white as snow, and the hair of His head [is] as pure wool,* **His throne flames of fire***, its wheels* **burning fire***. A* **flood of fire** *is proceeding and coming forth from before Him, one million serve Him and one hundred million rise up before Him, judgment has been set, and the scrolls have been opened."*
> Daniel 7:9–10 (LSV, emphasis mine)

In a scene very similar to the one John saw, Daniel describes God's throne of fire that has a *flood* of fire flowing, almost like lava before Him. Then a judgement begins. Let's take a look at some more Scriptures.

- *"for our God is also a consuming fire."* Hebrews 12:29 (Cf. Deut 4:24)

- *"[Jesus'] head and His hair were white like white wool, like snow; and His eyes were like a flame of fire. His feet were like burnished bronze when it has been heated to a glow in a furnace."* Revelation 1:14–15

- *"And there were seven lamps of fire burning before the throne, which are the seven spirits of God."* Revelation 4:5

- *"And tongues that looked like fire appeared to them, distributing themselves, and a tongue rested on each one of them. And they were all filled with the Holy Spirit."* Acts 2:3–4

- *"the sight of the glory of the LORD was like a consuming fire."* Ex 24:17

- *"I baptize you with water for repentance. But after me comes one who… will baptize you with the Holy Spirit and fire."* Matt 3:11

- *"[God] cleansed the bloodstains from the heart of Jerusalem by a spirit of judgment and a spirit of fire." Isa 4:4*

- *"Is not my word like fire," declares the Lord, "and like a hammer that breaks the rock in pieces?" Jer 23:29*

- *"...[And] on that which resembled a throne, high up, was a figure with the appearance of a man. Then I noticed from the appearance of His waist and upward something like gleaming metal that looked like fire all around within it, and from the appearance of His waist and downward I saw something like fire; and there was a radiance around Him. Like the appearance of the rainbow in the clouds on a rainy day, so was the appearance of the surrounding radiance. Such was the appearance of the likeness of the glory of the Lord." Eze 1:26–28*

If God is love and God is good, and if He is revealed to us by Yeshua as Father, **then fire must be good.** It is interesting to note that in Revelation 20:9, when God comes, the fire "consumed" (literally: ate) those who had surrounded the Saints. We are given no further details, but we understand enough from Scripture to know that God's fire consumes that which we were never created to be, in order that all that He created us for remains.

*"and the Messenger of YHWH appears to him **in a flame of fire**, out of the midst of the bush, and he sees, and behold, **the bush is burning with fire, and the bush is not consumed**. And Moses says, 'Now I turn aside and see this great appearance. Why is the bush not burned?" And YHWH sees that he has turned aside to see, and God calls to him out of the midst of the bush and says, "Moses! Moses!" And he says, "Here I [am]." And He says, "Do not come near here. Cast your shoes from off your feet, for the place on which you are standing is holy ground." Exodus 3:2–5 (LSV, emphasis mine)*

Notice how the bush was not consumed?
But isn't God a consuming fire?
So what's the deal here?

The bush was being exactly how God created it to be. Therefore there was nothing to consume. That's why the area was *holy*. Zechariah 3 reminds us of this:

"Who endures the day in which he comes, or who can be standing when he is revealed? Because he is like the fire of a refiner and like lye that bleaches [lit. "launder's sulfur"]. For he shall return to refine and to purify as silver and he shall purify the sons of Levi and he shall purge them like gold and like silver, and they shall be bringing an offering to LORD JEHOVAH in righteousness. And the offering of Judea and of Jerusalem will delight LORD JEHOVAH as the days of old and like the years of former time. And I shall come near to you in judgment…" Malachi 3:2–5a (Aramaic)[327]

Middleton remarks,

> Zechariah 13 makes clear that the fire of God is not simply destructive; or, to be precise, we might say that it is destructive of sin and not creation. The oracle begins with reference to "a fountain" by which God will cleanse his people from sin and impurity (v. 1). But the metaphor soon changes to fire, by which God will "refine them the remnant that survives judgment as one refines silver, and test them as gold is tested" (v. 9a).
>
> The result is that they will once more call on YHWH, who will acknowledge them as his people, while they acknowledge him as their God (v. 9b). God's fiery judgment is thus ultimately for salvation. The metaphor of fire as refining is even more prominent in Isaiah 1. Describing the injustice of Jerusalem as the tarnishing of silver ("Your silver has become dross" [v. 22]), the text goes on to describe the process of judgment by which repentant Zion will be restored:
>
>> "I will smelt away your dross as with lye and remove all your alloy.
>>
>> And I will restore your judges as at the first, and your counselors as at the beginning.

---

[327] Bauscher, David. The Holy Peshitta Bible Translated, Lulu.com. Kindle Edition. Page 1791.

> Afterward you shall be called the city of righteousness,
>
> the faithful city.
>
> Zion shall be redeemed by justice,
>
> and those in her who repent, by righteousness."
>
> Isaiah 1:25-27

Interestingly, the metaphor of fire continues in Isaiah 1, but this time to describe the destruction of unrepentant evildoers and their deeds:

> "The strong shall become like tinder, and their work like a spark;
>
> they and their work shall burn together, with no one to quench them." Isaiah 1:31

The image of the refining fire is perhaps most prominent in the book of Malachi. Chapter 3 begins by introducing the covenant messenger whom YHWH is sending to Israel especially to purify the Levitical priesthood.[328]

The Apostles Paul and Jude both paint a perfect illustration of the effect of God's consuming fire:

> *"if anyone builds on this foundation gold, silver, precious stones, wood, hay, straw—the work will become visible of each, for the day will declare [it], because it is revealed in fire, and the work of each, what kind it is, the fire will prove; if the work of anyone remains that he built on [it], he will receive a wage; if the work of any is burned up, he will suffer loss, but himself will be saved, but so as through fire."*
> *1 Corinthians 3:12–15 (LSV)*

> *"show mercy to those who are doubting, and rescue others by snatching [them] out of fire; but show mercy to others in fear, hating even the coat having been stained from the flesh." Jude 1:22–23 (LSV)*

---

[328] Middleton, Richard J., *A New Heaven and a New Earth: Reclaiming Biblical Eschatology* (Grand Rapids: Baker Academic, 2014) p 123–124.

In both cases, it is what defiles that is burned. What does "defiled" mean? In simplest terms, it encompasses all that we were never created to be. It is a metaphorical fire, for all that defiles comes from within: that is, the heart.

> *"[Jesus] says to them, 'So also you are without understanding! Do you not perceive that nothing from outside entering into the man is able to defile him? Because it does not enter into his heart, but into the belly, and into the drain it goes out, purifying all the meats." And He said, 'That which is coming out from the man, that defiles the man; for from within, out of the heart of men, the evil reasonings come forth, adulteries, whoredoms, murders, thefts, covetous desires, wickedness, deceit, arrogance, an evil eye, slander, pride, foolishness; all these evils come forth from within, and they defile the man." Mark 7:18–23 (LSV)*

Now let's go back to the fire that consumes the numberless multitude of nations that swarm the Saints of Yahweh. Does His fire instantaneously consume the literal flesh of millions of humans made in His image, or is there a greater work at play?

13 THE SEA OF FIRE: CH. 20:10

*"Get your facts first,
and then you can distort them as much as you please."*

— *Mark Twain*

The quote above is perhaps crude; however the severity of these next five verses cannot be understated. The Final Judgement. The eternal fate of living souls. All of life's most monumental questions are often hinged on these few verses. Getting our facts straight is perhaps one of the greatest responsibilities of anyone wishing to teach and lead others in these matters, so we cannot tread lightly.

I am now six years into this project, and I thank God for His kindness in slowing down my progress. At times I wanted to power through and keep studying and writing, but His grace would lift and I would struggle to put even a sentence together. So the proverbial pen would go back in the drawer, and I would be drawn towards the more important things like my family, my community, and the life-long process of learning to abide in Him. Over the years as I've continued to learn, ponder, and dig deeper, I realize how much my understanding has evolved. I'm thankful I didn't write about these last verses of Revelation 20 six years ago; I would have had to re-write this chapter all over again!

You may not like what you read, and you may disagree. I understand, for I too would have felt the same way six years ago. All I ask is this: place whatever offends you before our Heavenly Father, and with all sincerity ask Him to lead you, guide you, and speak to you. He will often answer in the most unexpected ways, and in His divine mystery also honor the integrity of your will to let go of what is familiar. If after some time you still feel the same way, then with all sincerity, should it come to mind, please pray for me. Ask that the eyes of my heart be enlightened, so that I will know what is the hope of His calling, what are the riches of the glory of His inheritance in the saints, and what is the boundless greatness of His power toward us who believe.

> ℵ *(10) Now the Accuser, their Deceiver,[329] was cast down into the Sea of Fire and Sulfur, where the savage animal and the false prophet are. And they shall be severely chastised[330] day and night unto the Age of Ages.*

There are a total of five "day and night" (literally: "the day and the night") statements in Revelation, and they are found in 4:8, 7:15, 12:10, 14:11, and here in 20:10. They all have one common denominator: they are employed to illustrate actions that take place in the heavenly or spiritual realm. In other words, a literal device (day and night) is implemented to try to explain events taking place in a reality that is outside of the confines of time and space, or at minimum, not of the earth we walk upon. Heaven does not have a 24-hour clock (since only earthly calendars depend upon the rotation of the earth around the sun), so we must embrace that we are dealing with a realm beyond the confines of our reality. This is important because, if you recall, there were also people in Revelation 14:11 experiencing the cleansing fire of Yahweh in the presence of Yeshua and his angels in that heavenly/spiritual realm.[331]

This is the third and final time Satan is thrown down (12:9 – the end of the Mosaic Age; 20:3 – the end of the Messianic Age; 20:10 – he will be thrown down into the Sea of Fire). He is joined by the spirits or demons known as the horned lamb and the false prophet. Again, **it's not people that first go into the Sea of Fire and Sulfur in this verse,** but evil spirits and demons. The so-called *unholy trinity* now finds itself in the Sea of Fire and

---

[329] Or "their deceiver, the Devil". I'm following the literal word order.
[330] Or "severely punished". See Payne Smith, *A Compendious Syriac Dictionary*, p. 587, and William Jennings, *Lexicon to the Syriac New Testament*, p. 227.
[331] Is it possible that Revelation 14:11 is a link to Revelation 20:15 and the Sea of Fire and Sulfur? I believe it is.

Sulfur.

WHAT IS THE SEA OF FIRE AND SULFUR?

The Lake of Fire has been a concept that I've mulled over for many years now. Here are a few of the many things I pondered. First, given how many Old Testament allusions we find in Revelation, one would expect to find the "Lake" of Fire elsewhere in Scripture. But at first glance it seems new. Second, the "Lake" of Fire has no correlation with Gehenna (the Hinnom Valley), which was (and is) the southern valley surrounding Jerusalem. Because we know very little about the Lake (lit. "sea") of Fire, it is short-sighted to simply lump the two together. As I will discuss below, the Sea of Fire is actually a prophetic allusion to the *Dead Sea within Israel*. The third thought I had was to questions if there is any sort of redemptive aspect to the Sea/Lake of Fire. If all of God's judgments are restorative, then does that include this place as well? Finally, the inclusion of the word "sulfur" (aka brimstone) was curious to me. If you fell into a volcanic mountain, with its crater filled with a large pool of lava, would it matter to you if it contained sulfur as well? In all my studies, I have come across not one person who seems to acknowledge the significance of the sulfur in the "Lake" of Fire.

When I started digging into the text, the first thing that stood out to me was that the word most Bibles use for "lake" is actually the word "sea", *yamma* in Aramaic (Syriac). This is the same word used for *Sea* of Galilee, and it specifies a smaller body of water. *(Yam* is reserved for larger bodies such as the Mediterranean.) So Revelation 20:10 doesn't read "Lake" of fire in the Aramaic (Syriac) text, it reads "sea" of fire. This changed everything. For if we are now dealing with "The **_Sea_** *of the Burning Fire and the Sulfur" (Rev 19:20)*, then we actually have yet another Old Testament allusion: the Dead Sea. The "Lake" of Fire, or more accurately the "Sea" of Fire, is the Dead Sea.

THE DEAD SEA

So let's turn our attention to the Dead Sea for a moment. Because of both the length of its existence and its renown, the Dead Sea went by many names – Sea of Salt (Gen 14:3, Deut 3:17), Sea of Arabah (Josh 3:16), and Eastern Sea (Ezk 47:18). It was Greek writers who gave it the name "lake", such as Lake Asphaltites ("lake of asphalt", Josephus), Lake Sirbonis (Strabo, though in error), and then of course the Greek New Testament calls it "Lake of Fire".

There are three significant things we must take note of in our understanding of the Dead Sea: What it was, what it is, and what it will be. For what it *was*, we can look to Genesis 13 and 14. There we learn the Dead Sea used to be dry land that was part of the Jordan Circle (13:10) located in the Valley of Siddim ("valley of the plain", location of five cities – Sodom, Gomorrah, Admah, Zeboiim, and Bela.) More importantly, Genesis specifically connects this area to the Garden of Eden by saying the area was "well-watered like the Garden of the Lord" (13:10).

For what it *is,* we look to Genesis 19 - the account of Sodom and Gomorrah's destruction. Because of the wickedness found there, fire and sulfur rained down from Heaven destroying these two cities (Gen 19) and eventually creating the Dead Sea. Much like in Revelation 14:11, the smoke of Sodom and Gomorrah ascended and Lot's wife was turned into a pillar of salt (more on this later).

Let's dive a little deeper into what people had to say about this land after it became a sea of fire and sulfur (I'll talk about what it *will be* in a moment).

> "In this ridge of mountains there is one called the Iron mountain [today called the Jordan Valley Rift], that runs in length as far as Moab. Now the region that lies in the middle between these ridges of mountains, is called the great plain [Siddim]. It reaches from the village Ginnabris, as far as the lake Asphaltitis [the Dead Sea]…
>
> It hath two lakes in it; that of Asphaltitis [Dead Sea], and that of Tiberias [aka Sea of Galilee]: whose natures are opposite to each other. For the former is salt, and unfruitful: but that of Tiberias [Galilee] is sweet, and fruitful…
>
> The nature of the lake Asphaltitis [Dead Sea] is also worth describing. It is, as I have said already, bitter and unfruitful. It is so light [or thick] that it bears up the heaviest things that are thrown into it. Nor is it easy for anyone to make things sink therein to the bottom, if he had a mind so to do. Accordingly, when Vespasian went to see it, he commanded that some who could not swim, should have their hands tied behind them, and be thrown into the deep. When it so happened, that they all swam; as if a wind had forced them upwards [not understanding the buoyancy of the salt]. Moreover the change of the colour of this lake is wonderful. For it changes its appearance thrice every day. And as the rays of the sun fall differently upon it, the light is variously reflected. However, **it casts up black clods of bitumen**, in many parts of it. **These swim at the top of the**

water, and resemble both in shape and bigness headless bulls... This bitumen** is not only useful for the caulking of ships, **but for the cure of men's bodies. Accordingly it is mixed in a great many medicines**... The country of Sodom borders upon it. It was of old a most happy land, both for the fruits it bore and the riches of its cities: although it be now all burnt up. It is related how, for the impiety of its inhabitants, it was burnt by lightning. In consequence of which **there are still the remainders of that divine fire, and the traces [or shadows] of the five cities are still to be seen**: as well as the ashes growing in their fruits."[332] (emphasis mine)

That was Josephus' account. I find it interesting that he writes that you could still see the traces of the cities that became submerged under it (Sodom, Gomorrah, Zeboiim, and Admah). Also, even though the sea was considered foul, it was still recognized for its medicinal benefits. This is important, and we will touch on it later.[333] The Sea of Fire was so renown throughout the known world that there are even historical accounts of it from outside the Holy Land. Strabo (c. 63 BC – 24 AD), the Greek philosopher and historian, wrote the following:

> The Lake Sirbonis [the Dead Sea] is of great extent... It is deep, and the water is exceedingly heavy, so that no person can dive into it; if any one wades into it up to the waist, and attempts to move forward, he is immediately lifted out of the water. It abounds with **asphaltus**, which rises, not however at any regular seasons, in bubbles, like **boiling water**, from the middle of the deepest part. The surface is convex, and presents the appearance of a hillock. Together with the asphaltus, there ascends a great quantity of **sooty vapour**, not perceptible to the eye, which tarnishes copper, silver, and everything bright—even gold...

---

[332] Josephus, *Wars*, 4:8:2–4.
[333] Diodorus wrote, "In a certain valley in this [Dead Sea] region there grows what is called balsam, from which there is a great income since nowhere else in the inhabited world is this plant found, and its use as a drug is very important to physicians." Library 8–40, 19.98.1.

> It is natural for these phenomena to take place in the middle of the lake, **because the source of the fire is in the centre**, and the greater part of the asphaltus comes from thence. The bubbling up, however, of the asphaltus is irregular, because the **motion of fire**, like that of many other vapours, has no order perceptible to observers…
>
> Many other proofs are produced to show that **this country is full of fire**. Near Moasada [Masada] are to be seen rugged rocks, bearing the marks of fire; fissures in many places; a soil like ashes; pitch falling in drops from the rocks; rivers boiling up, and emitting a fetid odour to a great distance; dwellings in every direction overthrown; whence we are inclined to believe the common tradition of the natives, that thirteen cities once existed there, the capital of which was Sodom, but that a circuit of about 60 stadia around it escaped uninjured; shocks of earthquakes, however, **eruptions of flames and hot springs, containing asphaltus and sulphur, caused the lake to burst its bounds, and the rocks took fire**; some of the cities were swallowed up, others were abandoned by such of the inhabitants as were able to make their escape.[334] (emphasis mine)

Another well-known historian was Tacitus (c. 56 AD – 120 AD). He too wrote much when he was describing the Sea of Fire in the Holy Land:

> Their [the Jews] land is bounded by Arabia on the east, Egypt lies on the south, on the west are Phoenicia and the sea, and toward the north the people enjoy a wide prospect over Syria… Of the mountains, Lebanon rises to the greatest height, and is in fact a marvel, for in the midst of the excessive heat its summit is shaded by trees and covered with snow; it likewise is the source and supply of the river Jordan. This river does not empty into the sea, but after flowing with volume undiminished through two lakes is lost in the third. **The last is a lake of great size: it is like the sea, but its water has a nauseous taste, and its offensive odour is injurious to those who live near it**. Its

---

[334] Strabo, *Geography*, H.C. Hamilton, Esq., W. Falconer, M.A., Ed., 16:2. <http://data.perseus.org/citations/urn:cts:greekLit:tlg0099.tlg001.perseus-eng2:16.2>

waters are not moved by the wind, and neither fish nor water-fowl can live there. Its lifeless waves bear up whatever is thrown upon them as on a solid surface; all swimmers, whether skilled or not, are buoyed up by them. At a certain season of the year the sea **throws up bitumen**, and experience has taught the natives how to collect this, as she teaches all arts. Bitumen is by nature a dark fluid which coagulates when sprinkled with vinegar, and swims on the surface…Not far from this lake is a plain which, according to report, was once fertile and the site of great cities, but which was later devastated by lightning; and it is said that traces of this disaster still exist there, and that the very ground looks burnt and has lost its fertility.[335]

If you take a trip to Israel today, you will notice that there is no bitumen bubbling up to the surface. But according to Diodorus (1st C BC), an actual bitumen industry formed and was run by a people named Nabateans.[336] So the Dead Sea of today is not what it was thousands of years ago. What matters to us is what first century Jews thought about the Dead Sea - what it meant to them. These stories from antiquity certainly help.

There is one more source I'd like to quote, this one from the 1600s. When I came across this book I was elated. In a *massive* work titled, *A Pisgah-Sight of Palestine and the Confines Thereof* (1650), Thomas Fuller goes through painstaking efforts to describe the entire region of the Holy Land, tribe by tribe, region by region. Fuller notes,

> "This bitumen… is a clammy, glutinous substance, useful in physic to astringe, in surgery to consolidate… [and the rich] used it for embalming their dead, being a great drier, and so preserver from corruption."[337]

So this asphalt, the aftermath of Sodom and Gomorrah's rain of fire and sulfur, was used by physicians to help their patients heal and by embalmers to preserve the bodies of the deceased. Interesting.

Now here's my favorite thing in Fuller's book – the illustrations. You can Google them by searching for his book. He carefully drew out each section of the Holy Land and added the most incredible details to them. I was so amazed that I actually had some of them blown up to hang on the wall of my

---

[335] Tacitus, *Histories,* 5:4–5.
[336] Diodorus, II, 48 and XIX, 98–99, 100.
[337] Fuller, Thomas, *A Pisgah-sight of Palestine and the confines thereof; with the history of the Old and New Testaments acted thereon* (London: William Tegg, 1869), p. 246–247.

office. For the purposes of our discussion, here is one illustration that is most fitting:

(Tribe of Judah in the Promise Land, A Pisgah-sight of Palestine and the confines thereof; with the history of the Old and New Testaments acted thereon. With facsimiles of all the quaint maps and illustrations of the original edition. 750 pp., London, William Tegg 1869)

Notice he placed the cities mentioned in Genesis at the bottom of the Dead Sea, the Sea of Fire, just like Josephus mentions! So connecting the "Lake of Fire" to the Dead Sea was a huge piece of the puzzle for me in my endeavors. But, as is often the case with the mysteries of God, there is more. The Dead Sea is only part of the enigma of the "Lake" of Fire, and I would soon discover others.

Because I have a bunch of Fuller's maps up on my wall at home, I often find myself pondering the topographical features of the Holy Land, and the only conclusion I can come to is that Jerusalem is divinely situated. For example, Mount Moriah (Zion) and the Mount of Olives sit across from each other, the Kidron Valley (the Valley of the Shadow of Death) lies between them, and then the Hinnom Valley rounds off Jerusalem's southern border. These geographical details play into the various prophecies throughout the

Bible that mention any one of these places. **As we will see next, this is true for the two seas and the two symbolic rivers of Israel as well.**

(Terra Canaan, A Pisgah-Sight of Palestine and the confines thereof; with the history of the Old and New Testaments acted thereon. With facsimiles of all the quaint maps and illustrations of the original edition. 750 pp., London, William Tegg 1869)

THE SEA OF GALILEE AND THE JORDAN RIVER

The region of Galilee is where Jesus in His foreknowledge (before time) decided He would be raised (specifically in a town called Nazareth, situated slightly southwest of the Sea of Galilee) and headquarter His ministry. The Jordan River flows out of the Sea of Galilee and travels 63 miles down to the Dead Sea. I find the flow of this water curious. Sure, one could simply say there is no symbolism and that any intent to find meaning would be purely speculative. If God were indeed distant, stoic, and lacking in creativity, then I would agree. But Abba is a face-to-face, engaged, creative genius.

"It is the glory of God to conceal a matter; to search out a matter is the glory of kings." Proverbs 25:2

So I started to search for potential symbolic meanings of the Sea of Galilee. What were the hidden gems God has invited us to find?

"Leaving Nazareth, he went and lived in Capernaum, which was by the lake in the area of Zebulun and Naphtali— to fulfill what was said through the prophet Isaiah:

'Land of Zebulun and land of Naphtali,
 the Way of the Sea, beyond the Jordan,
  Galilee of the Gentiles—
the people living in darkness
 have seen a great light;
on those living in the land of the shadow of death
 a light has dawned." [Isaiah 9:1, 2, emphasis mine]

From that time on Jesus began to preach, "Repent, for the kingdom of heaven has come near." Matthew 4:13–17 (NIV)

When I started looking for meaning in the area where Jesus lived, I realized the actual word "Galilee" was a clue. The Jews never referred to it as that. In Hebrew the area is called Kinneret כִּנֶּרֶת, and in Aramaic Ginosar גְּנֵיסָר. Named after a city bearing the same name, Kinneret[338] is named for the kinnar trees which grow extensively in the region.[339] Ok, so what's the

---

[338] Numbers 34:11, Joshua 13:27.
[339] Jerusalem Talmud, Megillah 1:1, Babylonian Talmud, Megillah, 6a.

big deal? Galilee is named after a tree? What does that have to do with Jesus? What made that tree so special?

> In Christian tradition the [kinnar] tree was identified with the thorn bush with which Jesus was crowned before his crucifixion (Matthew 27:28–29; John 19:5; Mark 15:17). This is also the source for the scientific name (*spina-christi*). This tradition was supported by the parable of the tree recorded in Old Testament Book of Judges where the bramble has been identified as the Christ thorn. In Judges 9, *Zizphus Spina-Christi* (bramble) vote to be the forest king! "All the trees said to the bramble, you come and reign over us! And the bramble said to the trees, 'If in truth you anoint me as king over you, Then come and take shelter in my shade; But if not, let fire come out of the bramble and devour the Cedars of Lebanon!'" (Judges 9: 14-15).
>
> The bramble, being the Christ-thorn, obviously represents Christ himself, who was rejected by his own people, as a result of which Jerusalem and its temple were set on fire in 70 AD when Roman forces took the city by force. Muslim as well as Christian pilgrims and travelers have described *z. spina-christi* as a large tree that grew in the Land of Israel. The tree was usually recorded for its uses and as a symbol of holiness. The pilgrims took branches of the tree back to their homeland as souvenirs in the belief that the Jesus's crown of thorns was made from such branches. In Israel *Ziziphus spina christi* is especially respected because of its red sap, which looks like blood; it appears when the tree is hurt. [340]
>
> In rabbinical literature, the plant is called "rimin" (Mishna, Demai, 1:1; Kilayim, 1:4), and in the Talmud it is called "kanari" (Bab. Talmud, Baba Bathra, 48b). It may be that it was so named because it is widespread around Lake Kinneret – the Sea of Galilee (Bab. Talmud, Mgillah, 6a)...

---

[340] Shuaibu RB, Salami KD, Boni PG. Evaluation of the Benefits Of "Christ-Thorn Jujube" Zizphus Spina-Christi (l.) Desf Tree in Nigeria. Ecol Conserv Sci. 2023; 3(1): 555601 DOI:10.19080/ECOA.2023.03.555601.

The tree is thought to groan when it's cut and its sap, red as blood, gushes out of the slashed trunk, justifying the idea that the tree has a life similar to a human's.[341]

Wow! So Kinneret (Galilee – where Jesus spent His earthly life) was named after a thorny tree called Christ's Thorn (Zizphus Spina-Christi) that fills the area. The tree was so famous, so sacred,[342] that even Jews and Muslims considered the tree holy. And according to tradition, a branch from this tree was used as the crown of thorns for Christ! Additionally, if the trunk of this tree is cut, the sap that comes out is blood red. Now consider Galatians 3:13: "Christ redeemed us from the curse of the Law, having become a curse for us—for it is written: "cursed is everyone who hangs on a tree." Another fun fact is the oldest known Christ's Thorn tree is located in Ir Ovot which is in the south of Israel. It is estimated to be between 1500 and 2000 years old![343] The Sea of Kinneret is also the second lowest body of water on earth, second only to the Dead Sea. "You made them a little lower than the angels; you crowned them with glory and honor" (Hebrews 2:7). So the Sea of Kinneret (Sea of Galilee) was filled with symbolic trees that represented Jesus. I think that's really cool.

Then you have the Jordan River which flows out of the Sea of Galilee. I won't spend as much paper on the Jordan as I did Kinneret because the Jordan is well known, but the symbolism is just as amazing. Joshua, an Old Testament representation of Jesus, led the people of Israel across the Jordan and into the Promised Land. Jesus followed the same physical path and was baptized in the Jordan as well.

> *"Or don't you know that all of us who were baptized into Christ Jesus were baptized into his death? We were therefore buried with him through baptism into death in order that, just as Christ was raised from the dead through the glory of the Father, we too may live a new life."*
> Romans 6:3–4 (NIV)

The Jordan is where our old selves die and we are born-anew of water and Spirit (John 3:4–5). Baptism is done in anticipation of new life (1 Cor 15:29) and gives us the assurance that we have put on the New Adam, the

---

[341] Dafni, Amots, Levy, Shay, Lev Efraim, Journal of Ethnobiology and Ethnomedicine: The Ethnobotany of Christ's Thorn Jujube (Ziziphus spina-christi) in Israel, 28 September 2005, p. 1, 2, 6.
[342] Marcus Jastrow, Dictionary of the Targumim, the Talmud Babli and Yerushalmi, and the Midrashic Literature, Peabody, Mass. 2006, p. 651.
[343] Grossman, Michelle Malka (24 January 2016). "Israeli trees get IDs with interactive heritage project". The Jerusalem Post. Retrieved 27 October 2019.

Son of Man, Jesus (Gal 3:27). This River Jordan then can be seen as the River of Christ that flows out from the Sea of Christ. To pass through this river is to step into a place of God's promise. And where does this River of Christ end up? The Sea of Fire and Sulfur.

All that you die to in Christ figuratively flows into the Dead Sea. Suppose you were baptized in the Jordan (for illustration sake), and your old self died and you came to life in Christ. Then you could say that the old self flowed down into the Dead Sea. Now pair this notion with what Revelation 20:14 tells us: the Sea of Fire and Sulfur is "the second death". So whatever goes into the Sea of Fire is going there to *die*. But as we will soon discover, Death then makes way for *new life*.

I mentioned a while back that there is a figurative sea and a figurative river that also flow into the Sea of Fire. We will discuss that now.

THE MOLTEN SEA AND THE RIVER OF YAHWEH

> *"[Huran] made the Sea of cast metal, circular in shape, measuring ten cubits from rim to rim and five cubits high. It took a line of thirty cubits to measure around it. Below the rim, figures of bulls encircled it—ten to a cubit. The bulls were cast in two rows in one piece with the Sea.*
> *The Sea stood on twelve bulls, three facing north, three facing west, three facing south and three facing east. The Sea rested on top of them, and their hindquarters were toward the center. It was a handbreadth in thickness, and its rim was like the rim of a cup, like a lily blossom. It held three thousand baths." 2 Chronicles 4:2–5 (NIV)*

Much speculation and debate exists over the purpose and symbolism of this gigantic water basin known as the Molten Sea or the Brazen Sea. Situated on the backs of twelve bulls, the laver stood in the south east section of the Temple grounds (2 Chr 4:10) and provided the priests with a source of water for ritual cleansing. They would wash themselves before they performed their duties, including entering the Temple.

THE BRAZEN SEA OF SOLOMON'S TEMPLE.—WITH VIEW OF SECTION.
(Restored according to Calmet.)

Jewish Encyclopedia, Volume 3, Morris Jastrow, Jr., Ira Maurice Price, Marcus Jastrow, Louis Ginzberg, p. 358.
<https://www.jewishencyclopedia.com/articles/13361-sea-the-molten>

Here's the crazy thing: this giant basin was made of either brass or bronze. And if you've ever seen a bowl made of brass or bronze filled with water, you'll know that with the sun's reflection it looks like water is on fire! Now cross reference this copy and shadow (Hebrews 8:5) of what things are like in God's realm:

> *"And there were seven lamps of fire burning before the throne, which are [the seven spirits of God; and before the throne there was something like a sea of glass, like crystal."*
> *Revelation 4:5–6*

> *"And I saw something like a sea of glass mixed with fire, and those who were victorious [a]over the beast and his image and the number of his name, standing on the sea of glass, holding harps of God."*
> *Revelation 15:2*

Sadly, the Molten Sea was destroyed by the Babylonians along with Solomon's Temple. But then came Ezekiel who, like John, was present for the destruction of Jerusalem and the Temple (Ezekiel the first time it happened, John the second time it happened). After the Temple was destroyed, Yahweh gives Ezekiel one of the most incredible prophetic experiences in the Old Testament.

> *The man [an angel] brought me back to the entrance to the temple, and I saw **water** coming out from under the threshold of the temple toward the **east** (for the temple faced east). The water was coming down from under the south side of the temple, **south of the altar**. He then brought me out through the north gate and led me around the outside to the outer gate facing east, and the water was trickling from the **south side**.*
>
> *As the man went eastward with a measuring line in his hand, he measured off a thousand cubits and then led me through water that was **ankle-deep**. He measured off another thousand cubits and led me through water that was **knee-deep**. He measured off another thousand and led me through water that was up to the **waist**. He measured off another thousand, but now it was a river that **I could not cross**, because the water had risen and was deep enough to swim in—**a river that no one could cross**. He asked me, 'Son of man, do you see this?'*
>
> *Then he led me back to the bank of the river. When I arrived there, I saw a **great number of trees on each side of the river**. He said to me, 'This water flows toward the eastern region and goes down into the **Arabah**, where it enters the **Dead Sea**. When it empties into the sea, the salty water there becomes **fresh**. Swarms of living creatures will **live wherever the river flows**. There will be large numbers of fish, because this water flows there and makes the salt water fresh; so where the river flows everything will live. Fishermen will stand along the shore; from En Gedi to En Eglaim there will be places for spreading nets. The fish will be of many kinds—like the fish of the Mediterranean Sea. But the swamps and marshes will not become fresh; they will be left for salt. Fruit trees of all kinds will grow on both banks of the river. Their leaves will not wither, nor will their fruit fail. Every month they will bear fruit, because the water from the sanctuary flows to them. **Their fruit will serve for food and their leaves for healing.**"*
> *Ezekiel 47:1–12 (NIV, emphasis mine)*

Ezekiel saw a symbolic Temple with crazy measurements and specifications (Ezekiel 40–47). The very presence of Yahweh God was there, and Holy Spirit flowed out of this figurative Temple as living waters. This Spirit-Water flowed east, south, and east again, meaning it would have flooded the Kidron Valley (valley of the Shadow of Death) on the eastern side of Jerusalem's hill, and then flooded the Hinnom Valley (Gehenna) that met the Kidron at Jerusalem's south. You've got to let that sink in. **Death and Gehenna are flooded by the living waters of Holy Spirit, which flows out from God's presence**. That gives me goosebumps, in a good way. The Spirit-Water, now a torrent (47:5), then flows a long way east across the Arabah (the wilderness where Jesus was tempted), down the escarpment known as the Jordan Valley Rift, and then into the Sea of Fire and Sulfur (47:8).

This Spirit-Water began on the Temple Mount, Mount Zion, where there used to be a Molten Sea that represented waters of cleansing. The late Henry Sulley even proposed that the dimensions of Ezekiel's Temple vision had an interior circumference that was for an *even larger* Molten Sea, based on his interpretation of Ezekiel 42:15–20 and other key passages.

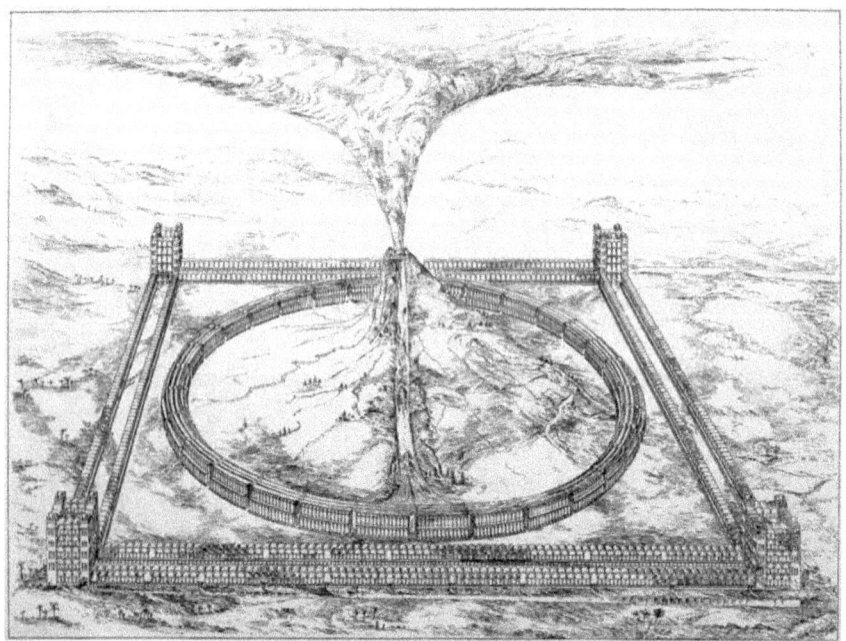

(Sulley, Henry, The Temple of Ezekiel's Prophecy (Nottingham: H. Sulley; Birmingham; Robert Roberts, 1892) Plate 1)

Whether this was the case or not, the manifest presence of Yahweh in

Ezekiel's vision, in conjunction with the two instances we see a sea of fire before Yahweh in Revelation, means we are safe to apply some type of sea of fire to the overall symbolism of Ezekiel's Temple. Equally important is the image of God's Spirit-River flowing *out of the Temple,* making its way into the Dead Sea, *and then healing the waters therein.*

> *"There is a river whose streams make glad the city of God,*
> *the holy place where the Most High dwells." Psalm 46:4*

> *"And on that day... all the brooks of Judah will flow with water;*
> *And a spring will go out from the house of the Lord*
> *And water the Valley of Shittim [aka Valley of Siddim, which is the Dead Sea region of Genesis 14]." Joel 3:18*

> *"And on that day living waters will flow out of Jerusalem, half of them toward the eastern sea [Dead Sea] and the other half toward the western sea [Mediterranean]; it will be in summer as well as in winter."*
> *Zechariah 14:8*

What does this all mean?

Go back a few pages and look at Fuller's map of Israel. You have Kinneret (Galilee) to the north which contains the Sea of Jesus, with the Jordan, which is the Spirit-River, flowing into the Dead Sea. Then apply your imagination and look to the left of the Dead Sea. Jerusalem is the location of Yahweh's Sea, the Molten Sea, and from there flows the Spirit-River towards the Dead Sea as well (per Ezekiel 47). **We have Jesus and God represented figuratively, both of whom flood the Dead Sea by way of Holy Spirit.** Give this some thought. The implications are astounding.

But it gets deeper.
Again, there is more.

John the Beloved not only sees the Dead Sea in Revelation 20, he also sees the Spirit-River of Ezekiel 47 at the end of his vision!

> *"And he showed me a river of the Waters of Life, clear as crystal, coming from the throne of God and of the Lamb, in the middle of its street. On either side of the river was the tree of life, bearing twelve kinds of fruit, yielding its fruit every month; and the leaves of the tree were for the healing*

of the nations." Revelation 22:1–2

Now only one question remains: what does the flowing of the Spirit-River, the "river of the Waters of Life", mean for the cities of Sodom and Gomorrah at the bottom of it? And a logical follow-up question would be: if John did in fact see the Dead Sea in Revelation 20, then what does the Spirit-River mean for those who are cast into the Sea of Fire and Sulfur (the Dead Sea)? These are big questions. Thankfully, God already provided an answer.

Looking at the typical *error-judgement-restoration* formula found throughout the Old Testament, in Ezekiel 16 (which I have referenced before) we find that God makes sure Jerusalem is aware of how deeply she has grieved His heart. She did all the worst things you could imagine from a covenant perspective (even burning children alive to pagan gods in Gehenna/Hinnom Valley). Yet, **in one of the most powerful and dramatic monologues in the Old Testament**, God says the following:

> *Then the word of the Lord came to me, saying, 'Son of man, make known to Jerusalem her abominations [v 3 to 34 lists them]…*

> *Therefore, you prostitute, hear the word of the Lord. This is what the Lord God says: 'Because your lewdness was poured out and your nakedness uncovered through your obscene practices with your lovers and with all your detestable idols, and because of the blood of your sons that you gave to idols, therefore, behold, I am going to gather all your lovers whom you pleased, all those whom you loved as well as all those whom you hated. So I will gather them against you from every direction and expose your nakedness to them so that they may see all your nakedness. So I will judge you as women who commit adultery or shed blood are judged; and I will bring on you the blood of wrath and jealousy'…*

> *'As I live,' declares the Lord God,* ***'Sodom, your sister and her daughters*** *have not done as you and your daughters have done! Behold, this was the guilt of your sister Sodom: she and her daughters had arrogance, plenty of food, and carefree ease, but she did not help the poor and needy. So they were haughty and committed abominations before Me.* ***Therefore I removed them when I saw it…'***

> *'Nevertheless,* ***I will restore their fortunes, the fortunes of Sodom and her daughters, the fortunes of Samaria and her daughters, and along with them your own fortunes*** *so*

that you will bear your disgrace and feel ashamed for all that you have done when you become a consolation to them. Your sisters, Sodom with her daughters and Samaria with her daughters, **will return to their former state***, and you with your daughters will also return to your former state'…*

"Nevertheless, I will remember My covenant with you in the days of your youth, and **I will establish an everlasting covenant with you***. Then you will remember your ways and be ashamed* **when you receive your sisters***, both your older and your younger; and* **I will give them to you as daughters***, but not because of your covenant. So I will establish My covenant with you, and you shall know that I am the Lord, so that you may remember and be ashamed, and not open your mouth again because of your disgrace, when I have forgiven you for all that you have done,' the Lord God declares.'"*
Ezekiel 16, abridged (NASB, emphasis mine)

I mean… wow. Where do I even begin? Maybe just go through Ezekiel 16 again because it pretty much speaks for itself. Sodom will be restored to her former state? Do you recall what that was?

"Lot raised his eyes and saw all the vicinity of the Jordan, that it was well watered everywhere—this was before the Lord destroyed Sodom and Gomorrah—like the garden of the Lord…" Genesis 13:10 (NASB)

Moreover, Jerusalem will receive Sodom as a daughter. Hello? Have you *ever* heard this taught before? I haven't. Yet it's right here. Now make no mistake, the pain of the chastisement is real. Luke 16 – Dives and Lazarus – is a great illustration of the torment of the soul. But unto what? Ezekiel 16 and Ezekiel 47 seem to suggest that it is unto **restoration**. So when we get to Revelation 20:15 ("whosoever is not found engraved in the scroll of life, he is cast down into the Sea of Fire"), we must keep this in mind. We must also keep in mind that the Sea of Fire is for this Age, it is *temporal* (20:10, "unto the Age of Ages"), not eternal.

> There have been Christians… who believe that in the end all persons will be saved and joined to God in Christ—since the earliest centuries of the faith. In fact, all the historical evidence suggests [this belief] was at its most numerous, at least as a relative ratio of believers, in the church's first half millennium

[meaning up to 500 AD]. Augustine of Hippo (354–430) referred to such persons as *misericordes*, "the merciful-hearted"… In the early centuries they were not, for the most part, an especially eccentric company. They cherished the same scriptures as other Christians, worshipped in the same basilicas, lived the same sacramental lives. They even believed in hell, though not in its eternity; to them, hell was the fire of purification described by the Apostle Paul in the third chapter of 1 Corinthians, the healing assault of unyielding divine love upon obdurate souls, one that will save even those who in this life prove unworthy of heaven by burning away every last vestige of their wicked deeds. The ["merciful-hearted"] were not even necessarily at first a minority among the faithful, at least not everywhere. The great fourth-century church father Basil of Caesarea (c. 329–379) once observed that, in his time, a large majority of his fellow Christians (at least, in the Greek-speaking Eastern Christian world that he knew) believed that hell was not everlasting, and that all in the end would attain salvation.[344]

Additionally, we can factor in the writings of Peter and Judas (Jude):

"[God] condemned the cities of Sodom and Gomorrah by burning them to ashes, and made them an example of what is going to happen to the ungodly… if this is so, then the Lord knows how to rescue the godly from trials and to hold the unrighteous for punishment on the day of judgment. This is especially true of those who follow the corrupt desire of the flesh and despise authority." 2 Peter 2:6, 9, 10 (NIV)

"So also Sodom and Gomorrah–and the neighboring towns in the same manner–having been guilty of gross fornication and having gone astray in pursuit of unnatural vice, are now before us as a specimen of the fire of the Ages in the punishment which they are undergoing." Jude 1:7 (Weymouth)

They serve to illustrate what takes place with those who experience the Refiner's Fire. Now think back to Ezekiel. Those flames are then flooded

---

[344] Hart, David Bentley. That All Shall Be Saved: Heaven, Hell, and Universal Salvation (pp. 1-2). Yale University Press. Kindle Edition.

with Spirit-water and healing takes place.

Now you may be thinking, "Ok Leo, I understand the idea of a temporal Sea of Fire with all of God's judgements being restorative not retributive. But what about Satan and the others in the Sea of Fire? Does God restore him back to the angel he was (assuming that's what he was), as well as the demons?" Big question. I don't have an answer. But I will offer this: there was a peculiar early church father named Origen of Alexandria (c. 185 AD – 253 AD) who was a genius when it came to theology. Few others championed the love and grace of God like he did, and Origen thoroughly pushed the theological limits of what that grace can look like. He was and still is often misunderstood because he was a *thinker, a muse,* and simply enjoyed pondering the vast possibilities and mysteries of God's economy. He is one who thought that, in theory, even Satan could be restored to his former state. But in the body of his works he does not provide a definitive conclusion on the matter.

> As it relates to the salvation of the devil, Origen created two problems in *PArch* [Peri Archon]: firstly by stating that the devil could choose goodness, but did not desire it, and secondly, by suggesting that the *Apocatastasis* [the doctrine that one day all free creatures will share in the grace of salvation] could be universal. Indeed, though the devil retained the ability, his consistent choosing of evil became habitual to the point where evil was the only viable choice. And, if the devil could not desire and therefore admit goodness, salvation was impossible. However, Origen's view of the *Apocatastasis* presents a different problem because he is unclear as to whether it is universal or not. If the *Apocatastasis* is not universal, the devil will not be saved. On the other hand, if it is, there is the possibility that Origen's description of the *Apocatastasis* could be different, that death could be defeated because the devil was restored to God. Ultimately, by his own speculations, Origen forces himself into a corner, and the views he presents on the salvation of Satan are contradictory.[345]

---

[345] Holliday, Lisa R. "Will Satan Be Saved? Reconsidering Origen's Theory of Volition in 'Peri Archon." Vigiliae Christianae 63, no. 1 (2009): 23. http://www.jstor.org/stable/20474897.

So my answer is I don't know and I don't want to know. The last thing I want to do is try to sit in the Seat of Judgement. Last time I checked there is only one Name written on it, and it isn't mine! Yahweh alone sees all ends and interacts with His creation from the perspective of both beginning and end at the same time. We have but a fraction of a sliver when it comes to knowing the full picture of all He created and purposed. We only see in part. Meanwhile, our Father God is at the beginning, at the end, and in the now constantly. He isn't subject to our impoverished theologies. He doesn't know what limiting thoughts or beliefs are. He has always had a plan in place before creation ever began.

Therefore, as for me, here is my heart posture:

> *"Love is long-suffering, it is kind, love does not envy, love does not vaunt itself, is not puffed up, does not act unseemly, does not seek its own things, is not provoked, does not impute evil, [does] not rejoice over unrighteousness, and rejoices with the truth; it bears all things, it believes all, it hopes all, it endures all. Love never fails; and whether [there be] prophecies, they will become useless; whether tongues, they will cease; whether knowledge, it will become useless; for we know in part, and we prophesy in part; and when that which is perfect may come, then that which [is] in part will become useless… for we now see obscurely through a mirror, and then face to face; now I know in part, and then I will fully know, as I was also known; and now there remains faith, hope, love—these three; and the greatest of these [is] love."*
> 1 Corinthians 13:4–13 (LSV)

SULFUR AKA BRIMSTONE REVISITED

Back in Revelation 14, we explored the concept of sulfur and how the fuller (a laundry person) used it to bleach clothes. Because we are now dealing with a sea of fire *and* sulfur, I want us to remind ourselves of why sulfur is included in the symbolism. Going back to my original illustration, if you fell into a pool of lava in real life, would you care that sulfur was part of the mix? I doubt it would make a difference since you'd likely be preoccupied with your flesh burning alive. But the Sea of Fire is ethereal, not physical. As such, these subtle details do matter.

> *"And He will sit as a smelter and purifier of silver, and He will purify*

the sons of Levi and refine them like gold and silver, so that they may present to the Lord offerings in righteousness." Malachi 3:3 (NASB)

Sulfur was used as a bleaching agent to whiten things such a clothes. Pliny the Elder, a Roman who wrote an encyclopedia called *Natural History* in the 1st century AD, recorded all the different ways sulfur was used in medicine for healing and in fulling (laundry) for whitening.[346] Fullers used sulfur to make garments white. The Aramaic (Peshitta) version of Malachi 3 says, *"But who can endure the day of his coming, and who can stand when he appears? For he is like a refiner's fire and like fullers' sulfur"* (3:2). **Jesus was the one coming in Malachi's vision, and Jesus was the fuller – meaning He was the one who would use sulfur to make things white and clean.** Sulfur was part of the finishing process, restoring garments back to a clean state.[347] *"Though your sins are as scarlet, They shall become as white as snow; Though they are red like crimson, They shall be like wool"* (Isaiah 1:18).

So now you have an entire sea filled with *fire* and *sulfur,* a prophetic image shared at a time in history where the only uses people had for sulfur was either medicinal or as a whitening agent. John mentions three times that sulfur is in this sea, and he was writing to an audience who knew the vision of Malachi. Again, Jesus is the Fuller (aka Laundry Guy) who would come as a *fire that refines and a sulfur that makes clean.* You can insert a "mind-blown" emoji here.

We must also be cautious of a literal reading of "fire and sulfur" and understand that it is once again Old Testament hyperbole layered in with Jewish history.

> *"The whole land [of Israel] will be* **a burning waste of salt and sulfur**—*nothing planted, nothing sprouting, no vegetation growing on it. It will be like the destruction of* **Sodom and Gomorrah, Admah and Zeboyim***, which the Lord overthrew in fierce anger. All the nations will ask: 'Why has the Lord done this to this land? Why this fierce, burning anger?'*
> *And the answer will be: 'It is because this people abandoned the covenant of the Lord, the God of their ancestors, the covenant he made with them when he brought them out of Egypt. They went off and worshiped other*

---

[346] *The Natural History.* Pliny the Elder. John Bostock, M.D., F.R.S. H.T. Riley, Esq., B.A. London. Taylor and Francis, Red Lion Court, Fleet Street. 1855. 35:50.
[347] William Smith, D.C.L., LL.D.: A Dictionary of Greek and Roman Antiquities, John Murray, London, 1875. pp551-553.

gods and bowed down to them, gods they did not know, gods he had not given them. Therefore the Lord's anger burned against this land, so that he brought on it all the curses written in this book."
Deuteronomy 29:23–27 (NIV, emphasis mine)

This multifaceted prophecy was fulfilled twice - once when the Babylonians destroyed the Holy Land and the first Temple, and then again when the Romans destroyed the Holy Land and the second Temple. There is no record of fire and sulfur raining down from heaven, yet there was much purification and refinement that took place in the hearts of people.

THE SEA OF GLASS

In Revelation 4:6 and 15:2, we are told that a sea of glass mixed with fire is situated before Yahweh's throne. Moreover, John saw the Saints standing *in* that sea holding instruments of worship. I'd like to propose that in some sort of divine mystery, this sea of glass mixed with fire is somehow connected to the Sea of Fire and Sulfur. But how?

Glassmaking is an ancient process that can be traced as far back as the empires of Mesopotamia and ancient Egypt, but the formula is more or less the same as it is today: you need sodium (salt) and heat (fire) to make glass.[348] Now this may be a stretch for some, but consider also that people (especially Israel) have often been referred to as the sand of the sea in the Bible.[349] Therefore, we may hypothetically have a sea made of glass and fire, where within it the Saints of Yeshua stand. It is possible that this sea represents the multitudes of humanity that have passed through the purifying fires of Yahweh God? Could this be part of what Jesus meant when he said, *"For everyone will be salted with fire"* (Mark 9:49)? Time will tell.

DEATH DIES?

If you recall, Revelation 20:14 reads:

"And Death and Sheol were cast down in the Sea of Fire, which is the second death."

---

[348] Sodium carbonate was used as a flux for silica (SiO^2).
[349] Gen 22:17, 32:12; Josh 11:4; Jud 7:12; 1 Sam 13:5; 2 Sam17:11; 1 Kings 4:29; Is 10:22, 48:19; Jer 15:8, 33:22; Hos 1:10; Hab 1:9; Rom 9:27; Heb 11:12; Rev 20:8.

This portion of Scripture actually connects to Paul's thoughts in 1 Corinthians 15. There, Paul discusses the great and final victory of Christ which is the final defeat of Death itself. Yes, there is a victory over death today. But Paul is talking about the culmination of that defeat, which means that no one will ever die a physical death again.

Well folks, now in Revelation 20, that time has come. The "last enemy to be defeated" is destroyed in the Sea of Fire. Paul doesn't mention that part, nor does John mention that Jesus is the one who throws Death into said Sea. This is because we all see in part. Nevertheless, Death will come to an end.

The significance of this event isn't just that people will no longer die. It's that death's destruction is the last stage of Christ's undoing of Adam, the final measure of the recapitulation of mankind.

> *"And the Lord God commanded the man, 'You are free to eat from any tree in the garden; but you must not eat from the tree of the knowledge of good and evil, for when you eat from it you will certainly die.'"*
> *Genesis 2:16–17 (NIV)*

As I have mentioned earlier in this series, Adam didn't drop dead on the day he ate of the tree. In fact, he went on to raise a family and live until he was 930 years old! So did God lie or get it wrong? Of course not! From that day on, Adam's true identity – all that he was created to become – died. And that death, this *cancer of the soul*, is what is passed down to every human afterwards. **This is the death that dies in the Sea of Fire.**

> *"On this mountain he will destroy*
>   *the shroud that enfolds all peoples,*
> *the sheet that covers all nations;*
> **he will swallow up death forever.**
> *The Sovereign Lord will wipe away the tears*
>   *from all faces;*
> *he will remove his people's disgrace*
>   *from all the earth.*
> *The Lord has spoken." Isaiah 25:7–8 (NIV, emphasis mine)*

God Himself will swallow up death. How about that for a word picture? And how does that happen? In the Sea of Fire. Here is the same Scripture again, this time from the Aramaic. Watch for the subtle nuances:

> *"And in this mountain, the face of the Ruler that was authorized over all the nations shall be wounded, and the sacrifice that was slain for the sake*

of all the nations. **And death shall be swallowed by victory** *for eternities, and LORD JEHOVAH God of Hosts shall remove the tears from every face, and the reproach of his people he shall remove from all the Earth, for LORD JEHOVAH has spoken."*
Isaiah 25:7–8 *(Aramaic, emphasis mine)*[350]

Now how can I resist sharing 1 Corinthians 15 yet again? Notice that Paul quotes the Aramaic version of Isaiah!

For since death came through a man, the resurrection of the dead comes also through a man. For as in Adam all die, so in Christ all will be made alive. But each in turn: Christ, the firstfruits; then, when he comes, those who belong to him. Then the end will come, when he hands over the kingdom to God the Father after he has destroyed all dominion, authority and power. For he must reign until he has put all his enemies under his feet. The last enemy to be destroyed is death…

Listen, I tell you a mystery: We will not all sleep, but we will all be changed— in a flash, in the twinkling of an eye, at the last trumpet. For the trumpet will sound, the dead will be raised imperishable, and we will be changed. For the perishable must clothe itself with the imperishable, and the mortal with immortality. When the perishable has been clothed with the imperishable, and the mortal with immortality, then the saying that is written will come true: 'Death has been swallowed up in victory. [Is 25:8]'"
1 *Corinthians 15:21–26, 51–54 (NIV)*

So this Sea of Fire and Sulfur is where the death that Adam died (even though he continued to live a long life) is destroyed. Whoa. This is not what I was taught in Sunday school! So does this give us a clue concerning John's "whosoever" statement regarding those who may be cast into this Sea? Is it those who still have this death cancer within them?

THE SECOND DEATH

Revelation 20:14 tells us the Sea of Fire and Sulfur is the second death. John uniquely introduces the concept of a first and second resurrection and a first and second death. In simplest terms, everyone apart from Christ is

---

[350] Bauscher, David. The Holy Peshitta Bible Translated (p. 1344). Lulu.com.

currently in the **first death**, even if they are alive and well (like Adam after he ate the fruit). As Jesus famously said, "Let the dead bury their own dead." [351] Now track with me. Borrowing from Pauline language, you therefore need to **die again, a second death, in order to be freed from Adam's death**:

*"We are those who have **died** to sin; how can we live in it any longer? Or don't you know that all of us who were baptized into Christ Jesus were baptized into his **death**? We were therefore **buried** with him through baptism into **death** in order that, just as Christ was raised from the **dead** through the glory of the Father, we too may live a new life.*

*For if we have been united with him in a **death** like his, we will certainly also be united with him in a resurrection like his. For we know that our old self was **crucified** with him so that the body ruled by sin might be **done away with**, that we should no longer be slaves to sin— because anyone who has **died** has been set free from sin.*

*Now if we **died** with Christ, we believe that we will also live with him. For we know that since Christ was raised from the **dead**, he cannot **die again**; **death** no longer has mastery over him. The **death** he **died**, he **died** to sin once for all; but the life he lives, he lives to God.*

*In the same way, count yourselves **dead** to sin but alive to God in Christ Jesus." Romans 6:2–11 (NIV, emphasis mine)*

So it would seem that the **second death** is supernatural, spiritual, and ethereal. It is not a physical (bodily) death. More importantly, **the second death is a choice.** There is a dying to all that you were never created to be - a dying to self, a dying to Adam. This death is intangible and has nothing to do with the body, though it impacts the body if we experience it.

"For whoever wants to save their life will lose it, but whoever loses their life for me will find it." (Matthew 16:25)

"In most solemn truth I tell you that unless the grain of wheat falls into the ground and dies, it remains what it was—a single grain; but that if it dies, it yields a rich harvest. He who holds his life dear, is destroying it; and he who makes his life of no account in this world shall keep it to the Life of the

---

[351] See Luke 9:60; and also 15:24; Ephesians 2:1, 5; 5:14; Colossians 2:13; John 5:25.

Ages." (John 12:24–25)[352]

In this context, this **second death** then leads to **resurrection life**: "For you died, and your life is now hidden with Christ in God." (Col 3:3). While Paul doesn't call this a second death, it nevertheless is a **voluntary and necessary death** that all must experience first before they walk in newness of life.[353] Read this again: according to Paul, **you cannot experience supernatural life until you have died a supernatural death**. This newness of life is the **first resurrection**. As Revelation 20:5 told us, the Messianic Age is the first resurrection. To know Him is to be brought into resurrection life.

"Jesus said to her, 'I am the resurrection and the life. The one who believes in me will live, even though they die.'" (John 11:25) **This "even though they die" is the caveat to the first resurrection: your physical body will still die.** That's how we know Jesus is talking about the first one. The first resurrection is to have an intimate relationship with Yahweh: "Now this is eternal life: that they know you, the only true God, and Jesus Christ, whom you have sent" (John 17:3). Physical death is still an enemy, and Paul said it is the last one to be defeated (1 Cor 15:26). And as we will see in Revelation 20:14, Death and Sheol will be defeated when they are cast down into the Sea of Fire and Sulfur. Enigmatically, **the first death is thrown into the second death.**

Then comes the **second resurrection,** which is the great and final one. In addition to John mentioning it in Revelation 20:12, Paul gives a tremendous discourse on it in 1 Corinthians 15. After this event, our *new bodies* will not experience decay, corruption, or death, which will allow us to enjoy the renewed earth with Abba, Son, and Spirit. Hopefully, the first and second deaths and the first and second resurrections now make sense.

But how does the Sea of Fire fit into this? Does a person who is not etched in The Book of The Living (and thus gets thrown into the Sea of Fire upon physical death) automatically experience the second death and then get born again into resurrection life? Not necessarily. The challenge with John is he offers us little in the way of details, but that's ok because he gave us enough to help fill in the gaps. So let's do a recap as well as set up a quick framework to help us navigate through this discussion:

---

[352] Weymouth New testament, Baker & Taylor Company (New York) and James Clarke & Co (London), 1903.
[353] See also Galatians 2:19; Colossians 2:20.

- Living in sin apart from Christ is the first death (what you are born into).
- Salvation (being "born again") is the first resurrection and begins with a "spiritual death".
- The Sea of Fire is the second death (and is only for those who don't accept Christ's work on the cross either in this life or in Sheol).
- Death and Sheol are thrown into the second death (the Sea of Fire).
- The Sea of Fire is a supernatural, ethereal place or experience.
- The Great Resurrection is the second resurrection (per 1 Cor 15).
- Revelation 21:8 (Aramaic) reads: "But to the timid, the unbelievers, the evil, the defiled, murderers, sorcerers, fornicators, idol worshipers and all liars: their part is in the burning Sea of Fire and Brimstone, which is the second death."

This is now where, like the earliest church fathers, we ponder and ask Holy Spirit to guide our thoughts and minds. The bullet points above are what we have been told about the Sea of Fire. We then have to overlay on top of the Sea of Fire what we have learned so far about the Dead Sea, the rivers of Christ and God, the restoration in Ezekiel 16 and 47, and the uses of sulfur to cleanse and fire to refine.

Now some of you may be thinking, "What about Luke 12:5?" In your Bible, it reads something like this:

> *"I will show you whom you should fear: Fear him who, after your body has been killed, has authority to throw you into hell."*

Yikes. Thankfully, digging into the text reveals a more Christ-like God.

> Aramaic (Syriac): "But I will announce to you who you should be in awe of: The One who after He has put to death, has authority to cast down into Gehenna."

The context of Jesus' admonishment is the pending Roman invasion. He is saying to his Jewish audience: don't fear the Roman soldiers (who come to fulfill the curses of the Law of Moses), but in contrast, fear (in awe and reverence that leads to repentance) Yahweh who has the authority to cast you into the judgment fire of Gehenna. This threat (the Roman invasion) is immediate, local, and by no means eschatological. Let's move on.

The most important point I want to stress in all this is we must grasp the character of God as expressed in the person of Jesus Christ. Jesus is the express image of the invisible Father. He is perfect theology:

"And when I am lifted up from earth, I will drag all people to myself."
(John 12:31–32)

"Father . . . glorify your Son, that your Son may glorify you, because you have entrusted him with every human being, that he may give eternal life to every being that you have given him. Eternal life is that they know you."
(John 17:1–2)

"Jesus Christ, who was appointed for you. Heaven must keep him until the times of the restoration of all beings, of which God has spoken by means of his holy prophets from time immemorial."
(Acts 3:20-21)

"He made known to us the mystery of his will, according to his purpose, which he set forth in Christ as a plan for the fullness of time, to unite all things in him, things in heaven and things on earth."
(Ephesians 1:9-10)

"[God is] not willing for any to perish, but for all to come to repentance."
(2 Peter 3:9)

"He was put to death in the body but made alive in the Spirit, in whom He also went and preached to the spirits in Sheol."
(1 Pet 3:18-19, Aramaic)

"For the love of Christ controls us, having concluded this, that one died for all, therefore all died; and He died for all, so that those who live would no longer live for themselves, but for Him who died and rose on their behalf… All this is from God, who reconciled us to himself through Christ and gave us the ministry of reconciliation: that God was reconciling the world to himself in Christ, not counting people's sins against them. And he has committed to us the message of reconciliation."
(2 Corinthians 5:14–14, 18–19)

"for even as in Adam all die, so also in the Christ all will be made alive."
(1 Corinthians 15:22

"[God] wants all people to be saved and to come to the knowledge of the truth." (1 Timothy 2:4)

"For the grace of God has appeared, bringing salvation to all people…" (Titus 2:11)

"We have seen and testify that the Father has sent the Son to be the Savior of the world." (1 John 4:14)

"For it was the Father's good pleasure for all the fullness to dwell in Him, and through Him to reconcile all things to Himself, whether things on earth or things in [ad]heaven, having made peace through the blood of His cross." (Colossians 1:19–20)

"But if [Israel's] their transgression means riches for the world, and their loss means riches for the Gentiles, how much greater riches will their full inclusion bring!
…For if their [Israel's] rejection brought reconciliation to the world, what will their acceptance be but life from the dead?
… After all, if you were cut out of an olive tree that is wild by nature, and contrary to nature were grafted into a cultivated olive tree, how much more readily will these, the natural branches, be grafted into their own olive tree!
…I do not want you to be ignorant of this mystery, brothers and sisters, so that you may not be conceited: Israel has experienced a hardening in part until the full number of the Gentiles has come in, and in this way all Israel will be saved…
For God has bound everyone over to disobedience so that he may have mercy on them all."
(Romans 11:12, 15, 24–26, 32)

Jesus revealed Yahweh God as a Father. So from a Father's perspective, we must carefully navigate all things "fire and brimstone". If we piece together the events John gives us and pair them with the other Scriptures we have explored, the outcome of the Sea of Fire and Sulfur may be something like this:

- We are all dead in the first death, even if you are alive.

- If you physically die apart from Christ, you descend into Sheol. Yet Jesus is there.
- If while alive you die the second death during this Age, you come into the first resurrection in Christ. To know Him and God is be born again into resurrection life in Christ.
- The physical bodies of Believers who partake of the first resurrection still die, but their souls continue in fellowship with God, face to face in His presence (aka Heaven, Paradise).
- At the end of this Age, the second resurrection (the Great Resurrection) takes place. All who ever died in all of history rise to life in mortal bodies and stand at the Great Judgement.
- Sheol is destroyed. Death is destroyed. Evil is destroyed.
- All who are judged according to Jesus get new super flesh bodies (like Jesus' when He rose from death) as a result of the Great Judgement (per 1 Cor 15:42–54).
- Those who for whatever reason said no to Jesus in life as well as in Sheol go to the Sea of Fire and Sulfur. These are the ones who still carry Adam's death within their souls.

From what we have learned from Jesus in Luke 16, Sheol is a place of contemplation and repentance. We know from Peter, the Psalms, and the early Church Fathers that Yeshua was and is present in Sheol.[354] Like God, Jesus is omnipresent. Meanwhile, the Sea of Fire and Sulfur (an experience which seems like it is 1000 times more intense that Sheol) is where Sheol and even Death are ultimately cast into. The Sea of Fire must also be a place where Jesus is present as well, since he fills the universe and literally holds all things together.

Like Sheol, the Sea of Fire must have some sort of redemptive purpose. Perhaps one can liken it to an Emergency Room for the soul; where all the Divine fiery-passion, the refining fire and sulfur, is employed at once upon those who could not help themselves – on earth or in Sheol. Perhaps it is a 911-operation of the soul to try to salvage what can be salvaged. Again, this is applying all of the layers of understanding we have obtained regarding the Sea of Fire/Dead Sea: the rivers of Christ and God, the restoration in Ezekiel 16 and 47, and the use of sulfur to cleanse and fire

---

[354] eg. Psalm 139:8 "If I go up to the heavens, you are there; if I make my bed in Sheol, you are there." 1 Peter 3:18 (Aramaic), "in which also to the spirits in Sheol having gone he [Jesus] did preach." And consider Colossians 1:17, "He is before all things, and in him all things hold together." See also Psalm 88:3–4, 9–14; Matthew 12:40; Revelation 1:18; Ephesians 4:8–10; 1 Peter 4:5–6; Philippians 2:9–11; Colossians 1:16–17; Hebrews 1:3.

to refine, and the character of God as expressed in Jesus.

> [A] number of Old Testament texts express a genuine fear that a "face to face" encounter with God could in fact kill us. And insofar as such an encounter would remove us from the ambiguous circumstances of an earthly life, perhaps it would indeed signal the end of an earthly life. But even deeper than the fear of physical death is the fear that in our present condition we simply could not endure standing "nakedly" before our Creator with no ambiguities and no comforting illusions to protect us; that is, we simply could not endure to see ourselves as we really are in our present unperfected state. It seems quite possible, then, that under the right conditions contact with the divine nature could itself be a source of unbearable torment—as the image of the lake of fire illustrates so nicely…
>
> For the lake of fire clearly represents God's holy presence rather than, as sometimes suggested, separation from him; that is, even as God's holy presence brings "refreshing times" upon the repentant (see Acts 3:19), so it also brings misery, torment, and destruction upon the unrepentant (see 2 Thess 1:9). The misery associated with the lake of fire, therefore, is simply the way in which the rebellious and the unrepentant experience God's holy presence; in that respect, being cast into the lake of fire can be likened to a forcibly imposed punishment…
>
> But there is nonetheless a hard metaphysical reality here, and those cast into the lake of fire no more choose or even anticipate their purgatorial suffering than a heroin addict typically chooses or even anticipates the suffering associated with his or her addiction. It is simply not possible for those who cling to their selfish attitudes, to their lust for power over others, or to their delusions of personal grandeur to experience God's holy presence as anything but unbearable torment.[355]

---

[355] Talbott, Thomas. The Inescapable Love of God (p. 185–186). Cascade Books, an Imprint of Wipf and Stock Publishers. Kindle Edition.

The Sea of Fire and Sulfur must by all accounts be a horrific experience. Indeed, "weeping and gnashing of teeth" (Matthew 13:42) is a fitting description. Perhaps it can be seen as the place for those who are in ultimate ignorance or in the most delusional cases of self-preservation. Regardless, everyone there is still a product of Adam and therefore not the full expression of who God created them to be. This is a great mystery, and it serves one well to remain humble about it.

> *"I will also turn My hand against you,*
> *And smelt away your impurities as with lye [a cleaning agent];*
> *And I will remove all your slag [waste produced from smelting in heat].*
> *Then I will restore your judges as at first,*
> *And your counselors as at the beginning;*
> *After that you will be called the city of righteousness,*
> *A faithful city." Isaiah 1:25–26 (NASB)*

At the same time, God honors our choice and the dignity of our will. Perhaps this is why John in Revelation 20:15 wrote, "whosoever" doesn't find their name written is cast into the Sea of Fire. The **whosoever** is key, because it means people have a choice. So if after this life and after Sheol people *still* decide to cling to the delusion of Adam, choose to remain faithless, evil, and defiled, and continue to be cowards, murderers, sorcerers, fornicators, idol worshipers, and liars to themselves, then their portion is the burning Sea of Fire and Sulfur which is the second death (21:8). They will indeed die to all that they were not created to be and take the risk that nothing salvageable will remain, for the soul might become pure dross in the refining fire, and the linen stained beyond repair by the fuller's sulfur. Though I personally believe this to be extremely unlikely (dare I say, impossible?), I do need to keep margin for the possibility since we are dabbling with hypotheticals.

Time will tell.

It's hard to believe that I dedicated an entire chapter to one verse. But let's be honest, this is one of the most challenging topics in the New Testament! Remember what I said at the beginning? You may not like what you read. You may disagree. If you do, all I ask is that you pray for the eyes of my heart be enlightened so that I will know the hope of His calling, the riches of the glory of His inheritance in the saints, and the boundless greatness of His power toward us who believe. Thank you for sticking with me this far.

"LORD JEHOVAH, God of my salvation, in the daytime I

have cried and before you in the nighttime. My prayer will enter before you and bend your ear to my prayer! Because my soul has been filled with evils **and my life has arrived at Sheol!** I am counted with those who descend to the pit and I have been like a man who has no helper! A free man among the dead, like the slain sleeping in the graves, those whom you remember no more and they were destroyed by your hands! You have laid me into the deepest pit, into darkness and the shadows of death! And your wrath rests upon me and you have brought against me all your storms! You have removed my acquaintances from me and you have made me unclean to them; I am prohibited that I may not come out. My eyes have melted from affliction and I called you, LORD JEHOVAH, every day, and have stretched forth my hands to you! **Behold, you work wonders to the dead and mighty ones will stand and confess you! And they will tell your kindness which is in the tombs and your faithfulness in destruction! Your wonders will be known in darkness and your righteousness in the land that was forgotten!**" Psalm 88:1–12 (Aramaic, emphasis mine)[356]

---

[356] Bauscher, David. *The Holy Peshitta Bible Translated* (pp. 1189-1190). Lulu.com. Kindle Edition.

14 THE FINAL JUDGEMENT: CH. 20:11–15

*"Don't judge a man by where he is,
because you don't know how far he has come."*
— C. S. Lewis

The fire that falls down in Revelation 20:9 can be likened to the train of God's robe, the beginning of the royal procession, because soon we will see the Royal Throne and the courts of Heaven descending upon the *earth*. Revelation 20:9–15 is filled with so much fire language because the earth gets filled with so much manifest presence. We see the full, uninhibited expression of the Shekinah Glory of Yahweh. Therefore all dross is melted away like slag, and only what is pure remains. Daniel too had a similar prophetic experience. In his vision, it's as if fire flowed from Yahweh Himself:

*"As I looked,
thrones were set in place,
   and the Ancient of Days took his seat.
His clothing was as white as snow;
   the hair of his head was white like wool.*
**His throne was flaming with fire,
   and its wheels were all ablaze.
A river of fire was flowing,**

coming out from before him.
Thousands upon thousands attended him;
ten thousand times ten thousand stood before him.
The court was seated,
and the books were opened." Daniel 7:9–10 *(NIV, emphasis mine)*

As stated previously, because John is looking so far ahead from where he was in time, the details of these monumental events are few. Looking through figurative binoculars instead of a microscope, John can only make general observations about the events he sees, and so these verses lack the clarity and granularity we have been privy too in subsequent chapters. In these closing verses, there is a general harmony that brings closure to some of life's greatest problems – Death and Satan – but some things are left unanswered. Nevertheless, John gives us more than enough detail to help us string together the next series of events and cross reference them with other Scriptures.

> *(11) And I saw the Great White Throne, and He was enthroned upon it, from whose face Earth and Heaven fled away, but no place was found for them.*[357]

Andrew of Caesarea (AD 563–614) shares some wonderful thoughts about this passage:

> The image of the "white throne" signifies the divine rest that God will establish among the saints, who are resplendent with virtues and among whom God will be enthroned. The flight of the earth and sky signifies their transformation from what they were into something better. And there will be found no longer any place for change. For if the creation was subjected to corruption because of us, as the apostle says, it will also be transformed with us into the freedom of the glory of the children of God,[10] being made new into that which is more brilliant.[11] [The creation] will not be subjected to complete

---

[357] Typical Jewish hyperbole that must be understood figuratively, not literally (cf. Rev 6:14; 16:20; 21:1; Jer 4:23–26; Dan 2:35; Judges 5:4–5; Isaiah 29:6; Psalm 97:2–5).

annihilation, as we learn from Irenaeus, Antipater[12] and other saints. For the blessed Irenaeus writes, "For neither is the substance nor the essence of the creation annihilated (for faithful and true is he who has established it), but the fashion of the world passes away, that is, those things among which transgression has occurred, since humankind has grown old in them. And therefore this fashion has been formed temporary, God foreknowing all things."[358]

> א *(12) And I saw the dead – great and small – who rose before the throne. And scrolls[359] were opened, but another scroll[360] was opened, which is of the Judgment,[361] and the dead were judged from those things that were written in the scroll[362] as their deeds.[363]*

THE GREAT RESURRECTION

This is the second resurrection – the Great Resurrection. John offers no commentary, just a few details, but we do have other Scriptures to guide us along. Let's look at those passages first, and then we will investigate the few details John gives us here in Revelation 20.

> *"But your dead will live, Lord;*
> *their bodies will rise—*

---

[358] William C. Weinrich, eds. Revelation. vol. 12 of Ancient Christian Commentary on Scripture. ICCS/Accordance electronic ed. (Downers Grove: InterVarsity Press, 2005), 345.

[359] ܣܦܪܐ / סָפְרָא means "scroll, document, letter, written record". Like the Hebrew *sefer* (Strong's H5612). This is different than in Rev 20:15, כְּתָבָא / ܟܬܒܐ which means "inscription, scripture". Like the Hebrew *ktav* (Strong's H3790).

[360] ܣܦܪܐ / סָפְרָא "scroll, document, letter, written record." Cf. Ex 24:7, סֵפֶר הַבְּרִית "Scroll of the Covenant".

[361] The Greek Manuscripts read "the Life". Perhaps ܕܕܝܢܐ "of Judgment" was misread as "of Life" by a Greek translator when reading an Aramaic manuscript, misreading ܕ as a ܗ , and ܢ as a ܝ .

[362] ܣܦܪܐ / סָפְרָא "scroll, document, letter, written record". Cf. Ex 24:7, סֵפֶר הַבְּרִית "Scroll of the Covenant".

[363] Cf. Psalm 62:12; Proverbs 24:12.

let those who dwell in the dust
 wake up and shout for joy—
your dew is like the dew of the morning;
 the earth will give birth to her dead." Isaiah 26:19 (NASB)

17 And if Christ has not been raised, your faith is futile; you are still in your sins. 18 Then those also who have fallen asleep in Christ are lost. 19 If only for this life we have hope in Christ, we are of all people most to be pitied.

20 But Christ has indeed been raised from the dead, the firstfruits of those who have fallen asleep. 21 For since death came through a man, the resurrection of the dead comes also through a man. 22 For as in Adam all die, so in Christ all will be made alive. 23 But each in turn: Christ, the firstfruits; then, when he comes, those who belong to him. 24 Then the end will come…
26 The last enemy to be destroyed is death…
28 When he has done this, then the Son himself will be made subject to him who put everything under him, so that God may be all in all…

35 But someone will ask, "How are the dead raised? With what kind of body will they come?" 36 How foolish! What you sow does not come to life unless it dies…

42 So will it be with the resurrection of the dead. The body that is sown is perishable, it is raised imperishable…
49 And just as we have borne the image of the earthly man, so shall we bear the image of the heavenly man…

51 Listen, I tell you a mystery: We will not all sleep, but we will all be changed— 52 in a flash, in the twinkling of an eye, at the last trumpet. For the trumpet will sound, the dead will be raised imperishable, and we will be changed…
54 then the saying that is written will come true: "Death has been swallowed up in victory." 1 Corinthians 15, abridged (NIV)

Paul's remarks provide us with incredible insight to John's prophetic experience. Of note, we see that resurrection life can only come after death. In Paul's language, we sow into death in order to reap unto life. Reconciling this with Johannine language, the second death (dying to self, submitting to Christ) is a necessary path that ultimately leads to the second resurrection. (Reminder, the first resurrection is salvation, the second resurrection is the Great Resurrection at the Last Judgement.) Also, in many places Paul tells us that we will receive the same physical body that Jesus has. This is the body that was raised to life, ate and drank with the disciples, walked through walls, vanished instantly, and ascended into the realm of God's Heaven.

According to Paul the first to be raised at the Great Resurrection are those who "fell asleep" in Christ; meaning all Believers throughout history who have died a physical death. 1 Corinthians 15:22–23 is quite clear: *"In the same way Adam brought about death to all mankind, so too Christ will bring about life for all mankind. But each human in their proper order – those in Christ will be raised first, then anyone who remains outside of Christ."* [364] Now let's add Pauline theology to Johannine: those raised to life in Revelation 20:12 are those who were raised in Christ, and then in 20:13 we see those not raised in Christ ascending from Sheol to stand before the Great Throne of God.

This is why full Preterism (that *all* of Scripture, including Revelation, has *already* been fulfilled) makes no sense. It is in a way a derivative of cessationism, which suggests that the gifts of the Spirit and miracles ceased after the Apostles of Jesus died. Such nonsense. If our "faith" has no margin for the supernatural, the impossible, or that which can only be accomplished by the Divine, then we have not a faith but rather a religion. Let's put this plainly: you will die. Your loved ones will die. Some already have. Remember the pain you felt? The grief? The trauma? That should trigger you to remember there will be a day (the Great Resurrection) when you and everyone else won't ever experience such pain again. Death is an *enemy* that only Yeshua the Messiah *will* defeat. That day isn't about people *dying* and going to Heaven. Heaven is simply a holding place. That day is about Believers who have already died *leaving* Heaven and returning to this realm – the renewed earth – for the greatest family reunion of all time.

"Brothers and sisters, we do not want you to be uninformed about those who sleep in death, so that you do not grieve like the rest of mankind, who

---

[364] If one does a literal comparison between the Final Judgement events written in 1 Corinthians 15 and Revelation 20, they will notice that the sound of a last trumpet (1 Cor 15:52; 1 Thes 4:16) is absent from Revelation 20. But regardless of whether Paul was being figurative or literal about said trumpet blast, the mere symbolism of a final trumpet is sufficient. As Paul sees it, the trumpet (lit. "shofar," an Old Testament image) sets off the last series of monumental events that will once and for all alter the course of human history.

have no hope. For we believe that Jesus died and rose again, **and so we believe that God will bring with Jesus those who have fallen asleep in him***... For the Lord himself will come down from heaven, with a loud command, with the voice of the archangel and with the trumpet call of God, and the dead in Christ will rise first. After that, we who are still alive and are left will be caught up together with them in the clouds to meet the Lord in the air. And so we will be with the Lord forever." 1 Thessalonians 4:13–17 (NIV, emphasis mine)*

The next time you hear this scripture read at a funeral, remember this context: we do not grieve like the rest of mankind because our hope is in the Great Resurrection, not simply dying and going to heaven. So long as physical death remains, God's story has yet to be concluded. Let's look at another Pauline Scripture that has nothing to do with dying and going to Heaven, but rather again, the Great Resurrection. Speaking of the physical and mortal body, Paul longs for the supernatural body that we will all inherit on that day:

"For we have known that if the tent of our earthly house may be thrown down, we have a building from God, a house not made with hands—perpetual—in the heavens, for also in this we groan, earnestly desiring to clothe ourselves with our dwelling that is from Heaven, if so be that, having clothed ourselves, we will not be found naked, or we also who are in the tent groan, being burdened, seeing we do not wish to unclothe ourselves, but to clothe ourselves, that the mortal may be swallowed up of life…
We are also ambitious for this reason, whether at home or away from home, to be well pleasing to Him, **for it is necessary for all of us to have appeared before the judgment seat of the Christ***, that each one may receive the things [done] through the body, in reference to the things that he did, whether good or evil…*
for the love of the Christ constrains us, having judged thus: that if one died for all, then the whole died, and He died for all, that those living may no longer live to themselves, but to Him who died for them, and was raised again. So that we, from now on, have known no one according to the flesh, and even if we have known Christ according to the flesh, yet now we know Him [thus] no longer; so that if anyone [is] in Christ—[he is] a new creature; the old things passed away, behold, all things have become new. And all things [are] of God, who reconciled us to Himself through Jesus Christ, and gave to us the ministry of the reconciliation, how that God was in Christ—reconciling the world to Himself, not reckoning to them their trespasses…"

2 Corinthians 5:1–4, 9–10, 14–19 (LSV, emphasis mine)

Again, Paul is speaking of the Great Resurrection here, not dying and going to heaven. This passage is a good connection between the Great Resurrection and the final judgement of the Saints. Standing before the tribunal (or judgment seat) of Christ has nothing to do with being sent to hell or heaven. We see the clear connection surrounding the judgment seat, the statements about receiving new bodies from God, and His ministry of reconciliation where He does not count our trespasses against us. In Aramaic, 2 Corinthians 5:10 reads a little differently than the Greek quoted above.

> *"For we are all preparing ourselves to rise before the judgment-seat of the Messiah, He who will restitute each man in his body for everything done by him, if was good and if it was bad."*

PIECING TOGETHER THE FINAL JUDGEMENT

Let me start off by stating the judgement seat of God is insulated with *mercy*. In fact, **the judgment seat is the mercy seat** (more on that later). Therefore, the act of standing before "Christ's tribunal" (Paul's words) is more likely to be part of the process that leads us unto the final step of what the Early Church Father's called *theosis*.[365] Though not implicit, if we read Paul into John's vision, then it would seem that standing before Yahweh is what leads to us receiving our glorified bodies.

> *"if we may live, we live to the LORD; if also we may die, we die to the LORD; both then if we may live, also if we may die, we are the LORD's; for because of this Christ both died and rose again, and lived again, that He may be Lord both of dead and of living.*
> *And you, why do you judge your brother? Or again, you, why do you set at nothing your brother?* **For we will all stand at the judgment seat of the Christ;** *for it has been written: 'I live! Says the LORD—Every knee will bow to Me, and every tongue will confess to God'; so, then,* **each of us will give reckoning to God concerning himself...**" *Romans 14:8–12 (LSV, emphasis mine)*

In 2 Corinthians 5, Paul is adamant that it is necessary for all humanity (Believers and unbelievers) to stand before the judgment seat of Christ so

---

[365] As much as I'd love to teach on theosis, this topic is beyond the scope of this book. But I highly recommend you research this for yourself!

that each one may receive things through the body that correspond to the things that person did, regardless if he or she was good or evil. Which body? The one to come – the supernatural body that won't die and will experience the renewed heavens and earth. In Romans 14, he calls this giving a "reckoning" (literally a statement or word) to God concerning ourselves. Yet somehow it will be for our edification and benefit.

> *"By the grace God has given me, I laid a foundation as a wise builder, and someone else is building on it. But each one should build with care. For no one can lay any foundation other than the one already laid, which is Jesus Christ. If anyone builds on this foundation using gold, silver, costly stones, wood, hay or straw, their work will be shown for what it is,* **because the Day will bring it to light***. It will be revealed with fire, and* **the fire will test the quality of each person's work***. If what has been built survives, the builder will receive a reward. If it is burned up,* **the builder will suffer loss but yet will be saved— even though only as one escaping through the flames***."*
> 1 Corinthians 3:10–15 (NIV)

Going back to Revelation 20:12, the verse at hand, again it reads:

> *And I saw the dead – great and small – who rose before the throne. And scrolls were opened, but another scroll was opened, which is of the Judgment, and the dead were judged from those things that were written in the scroll according to their deeds.*

Practically speaking, we have to walk through the steps of how things play out in order to try to make sense of what John and Paul are getting at. First, suppose you and I as Believers die. Immediately we are fully exposed to God's realm and reality (aka Heaven, Paradise. E.g. Jn 11:25). Then perhaps after what seems like both an instant and an eternity, this experience is concluded with you and me being brought back to the physical realm, back to the renewed earth (the Great Resurrection). You and I were already in God's presence and enjoying the company of the Saints (the "Great Cloud of Witnesses") and the fellowship of Yahweh God, Son, and Spirit. But now the scene shifts, and we see God is sitting on a great white throne for judgement. So tell me, does the blissful experience prior to the Great Resurrection shift into terror and dread? Does the Godhead take you from being fully enveloped in love to being gripped with fear? Impossible. We will remain in this place of love, having no fear when we see the Great White Throne.

"God is love. Whoever lives in love lives in God, and God in them. This is how love is made complete among us **so that we will have confidence on the day of judgment***: In this world we are like Jesus. There is no fear in love. But perfect love drives out fear,* **because fear has to do with punishment.** *The one who fears is not made perfect in love. We love because he first loved us."*
1 John 4:16–19 (NIV, emphasis mine)

But what will happen when we give an account before God? This is a great mystery which calls for humility and reverential awe of Father God. Perhaps that experience will entail a dialogue between us and the Godhead as we "put on Christ" once and for all. Perhaps it will be that (at that time) we will no longer *"see through a glass, darkly; but then face to face: now I know in part; but then shall I know even as also I am known"* (1 Cor 13:9–12). Perhaps we will exchange all our deeds and experiences for all of His deeds and experiences. Perhaps we will be able to talk about all the ways we walked in error, deception, or partial truths and He will illuminate it all with revelation and understanding. He isn't there to scold us, and we are not there to get punished. So if anything, it will be a moment where we are fathered by God though all the mysteries of our past life - where we failed, did our best, did our worst, and everything in between. Perhaps it brings closure to all of life's mysteries and traumas, once and for all. Again, I say perhaps.

> Such a judgment isn't aimed at distinguishing between believers and unbelievers, the elect and the non-elect, or the righteous and unrighteous, but between the victims and perpetrators of actual interpersonal, familial, social, and political injustices. God's judgments are a severe grace and a transforming fire in which perpetrators and victims must face the burdens they would rather not remember or else never want to forget in the presence of God and one another. This creative (versus retributive) judgment will save lives, heal wounds, restore dignity, and reconcile inequities, thus establishing God's just society where everything is made right.[366]

Now let me show you how I came to the conclusion that the judgment seat of Christ (aka the Great White Throne of God) is the mercy seat.

---

[366] Jersak, Bradley. *Her Gates Will Never Be Shut: Hope, Hell, and the New Jerusalem* (pp. 148-149). Wipf & Stock, an Imprint of Wipf and Stock Publishers. Kindle Edition.

THE MERCY SEAT OF JUDGEMENT

> *"My little children, these things I write to you that you may not sin: and if anyone may sin, we have an Advocate with the Father, Jesus Christ, [the] Righteous One, and He is [the]* **propitiation** *for our sins, and not only for ours, but also for the whole world."*
> 1 John 2:1–2 (LSV, emphasis mine)

Propitiation (חוֹסָיָא) in the Aramaic means "atonement, pardon, remission, the breast-plate worn by the High Priest, or the Mercy Seat in the Holy of Holies."[367] Now go back and re-read the above passage in 1 John and let that blow your mind. This same word is used in Romans 3:25, Hebrews 9:5, and again in 1 John 4:10. Christ is not just the pardon or atonement for our sins, **He is literally the mercy seat and the breast-plate of the High Priest!** So this word was my first clue in connecting the judgement seat of Christ to the mercy seat.

In Revelation 1:13, the Aramaic states that Yeshua was wearing an ephod as he walked amongst the menorahs. As I discuss in the previous book, this is a description of Jesus as High Priest. In 2:17, Jesus mentions the promise of receiving a white stone with a new name written upon it, alluding to the sacerdotal garb of the High Priest. As part of Aharon's (Aaron's) priestly ephod, a breast-plate is also mentioned extensively in Exodus 28, and is enigmatically called the Breast-Plate of Judgement.

> *"You are to summon your brother Aharon and his sons to come from among the people of Isra'el to you, so that they can serve me as cohanim [priests]…*
> *The garments they are to make are these: a breastplate, a ritual vest, a robe, a checkered tunic, a turban and a sash…*
> ***Make a breastplate for judging****. Have it crafted by a skilled artisan; make it like the work of the ritual vest…*
> *Put in it settings of stones, four rows of stones…*
> *The stones will correspond to the names of the twelve sons of Isra'el; they are to be engraved with their names as a seal would be engraved…*
> ***Aharon will carry the names of the sons of Isra'el on the breastplate for judging, over his heart****, when he enters the Holy Place, as a continual reminder before Adonai. You are to put the urim*

---

[367] See J. Payne Smith's *A Compendious Syriac Dictionary*, pp 132.

and the tumim in the breastplate for judging; they will be over Aharon's heart when he goes into the presence of Adonai. **Thus Aharon will always have the means for making decisions for the people of Isra'el over his heart when he is in the presence of Adonai…**
You are to make an ornament of pure gold and engrave on it as on a seal, 'Set apart for Adonai.' Fasten it to the turban with a blue cord, on the front of the turban, over Aharon's forehead. **Because Aharon bears the guilt for any errors committed by the people of Isra'el** *in consecrating their holy gifts, this ornament is always to be on his forehead, so that the gifts for Adonai will be accepted by him.:*
Exodus 28:1, 4, 15, 17, 21, 29–30, 36–38 (CJB, emphasis mine)

Not only is Yeshua our High Priest (read Hebrews!), He is also the embodiment of the Breast-Plate and the Mercy Seat which was situated between two cherubim on top of the Ark of the Covenant. And as discussed above, the Aramaic New Testament makes this connection for us by assigning one word חוּסָיא to mean "propitiation, Mercy Seat, Breast-Plate" in relation to Jesus.

The second clue is in Revelation 20:12 where it says, "but another scroll was opened, which is of the Judgment." It is interesting to me that the Greek writers translated this as the scroll of "Life", which is what most Bibles say today. In a sense, both "life" and "judgement" are correct because we are dealing with Jesus and He is The Life and His judgements are unto life. **The scroll of Judgement (or "life" in Greek) is the scroll of what Jesus accomplished. In contrast, the other scrolls are the scrolls of everyone's own deeds.** What is fascinating to me is that while we have these other scrolls present (containing the deeds of each person), they are not read. Instead, only the scroll of the Judgement is highlighted. Incredibly, Revelation 20:12 says that this group of people who stood before the throne were judged according to what was written in the scroll of Judgement (the Jesus scroll) as if it were their own deeds.

"And I saw the dead – great and small – who rose before the throne. And scrolls were opened, but another scroll was opened, which is of the Judgment, and the dead were judged from those things that were written in the scroll as their deeds." (Revelation 20:12)

It is my belief that the single scroll "which is of the Judgement" consists the deeds of Christ and what He accomplished. This is why people are judged according to *that* scroll, and not the many scrolls that are first mentioned. Therefore, the people in verse 12 are judged by what Jesus did and not by what they have done. However, things *may* be a bit different for the next group of people that stand before the throne, as we are about to see.

> א *(13) And the Sea yielded the dead which were in it, and Death and Sheol yielded the dead which were with them. And each of them was judged one by one according to their deeds.*

It may seem bizarre to have two groups of people at the Final Judgement, but as stated earlier, Paul provides much clarity. At the Great Resurrection, those who are in Christ rise first, so it would be a logical conclusion that these in Revelation 20:13 are those who are not in Christ. Another point that supports this notion is this group ascends from **Sheol, Death, and the Sea.**[368] As we have already discussed, those who are in Christ in this life never descend into Sheol, and in light of the previous discourse I provided regarding this locale, its *Harrowing* and Jesus' preaching circuit therein, the resurrection of those stuck in Sheol must be understood with the reality of said Harrowing in mind. Therefore, we can conclude that this group of people in Revelation 20:13 have experienced ongoing visitations from Jesus Himself.[369] Yeah, that's a bit of a theological mind trip!

> *"But God will redeem me from the realm of the dead;*
> *he will surely take me to himself." Psalm 49:15 (NASB)*

This judgment in verse 13 is very different than the one in verse 12. No scrolls are mentioned at all. It therefore seems that all are judged exclusively by what they have done. In my mind, this plays out as follows: if I were in Sheol, and Jesus came to visit and preach to me there (per 1 Pt 3:18–19, 4:4–

---

[368] "In ancient cosmology, the sea was not thought to be part of Hades [or Sheol], so those who died by drowning in the sea and were never recovered for burial, formed a separate category of the dead. But they too will now be brought to stand before the great white throne..." Wright, N. T.. Revelation for Everyone (The New Testament for Everyone) (p. 184). Presbyterian Publishing Corporation. Kindle Edition.

[369] See Psalm 139:7–8; Psalm 88:3–4, 9–14; Matthew 12:40; Revelation 1:18; Ephesians 4:8–10; 1 Peter 3:18-19; 1 Peter 4:5–6; Philippians 2:9–11; Colossians 1:16–17; Hebrews 1:3.

6), did I open my heart to receive what He accomplished for me? Did I choose to put to death the Adam in me? Or, did I hide from His light? Did I harden my heart even further and reject Him all the more?

If I said "yes" to Jesus in Sheol, then perhaps the work I'm judged by is the "yes" in my heart of hearts towards Him. I ran to the light instead of away from it. Yet if I said "no" to Jesus in Sheol, then perhaps I stand before the Thone with my hardened heart ,and that's what I'm judged by. As Paul wrote,

> *"You, therefore, have no excuse, you who pass judgment on someone else, for at whatever point you judge another, you are condemning yourself, because you who pass judgment do the same things. Now we know that God's judgment against those who do such things is based on truth. So when you, a mere human being, pass judgment on them and yet do the same things, do you think you will escape God's judgment? Or do you show contempt for the riches of his kindness, forbearance and patience, not realizing that God's kindness is intended to lead you to repentance?*
> **But because of your stubbornness and your unrepentant heart, you are storing up wrath against yourself for the day of God's wrath, when his righteous judgment will be revealed.** *God 'will repay each person according to what they have done.' To those who by persistence in doing good seek glory, honor and immortality, he will give eternal life. But for those who are self-seeking and who reject the truth and follow evil, there will be wrath and anger.* **There will be trouble and distress for every human being who does evil: first for the Jew, then for the Gentile;** *but glory, honor and peace for everyone who does good: first for the Jew, then for the Gentile. For God does not show favoritism.*
>
> *All who sin apart from the law will also perish apart from the law, and all who sin under the law will be judged by the law. For it is not those who hear the law who are righteous in God's sight, but it is those who obey the law who will be declared righteous. (Indeed, when Gentiles, who do not have the law, do by nature things required by the law, they are a law for themselves, even though they do not have the law. They show that the requirements of the law are written on their hearts, their consciences also bearing witness, and their thoughts sometimes accusing them and at other times even defending them.)* **This will take place on the day when God judges people's secrets through Jesus Christ**, *as my gospel declares." Romans 2:1-16 (NIV, emphasis mine)*

Now an argument could be made that Paul was alluding to the 70 AD judgement that came upon the Holy Land, which of course has been a major theme in this series. Regardless, his language is still fitting here in the context of the Final Judgement as well. John 12 also provides us with something to ponder:

> *"if anyone may hear My sayings, and not believe, I do not judge him, for I did not come that I might judge the world, but that I might save the world. He who is rejecting Me, and not receiving My sayings, has one who is judging him,* **the word that I spoke, that will judge him <u>in the last day</u>***, because I did not speak from Myself, but the Father who sent Me..." John 12:47–49 (LSV, emphasis mine)*

We can liken this statement of Jesus to the imagery found in Revelation 19 where we read of swords that come forth from the mouths of Christ and his angels. Those swords represent the prophetic words of Jesus, and it was those **words** that brought about the calamities that befell the Holy Land. Now, take this example from Revelation 19 and apply it to John 12, which we just read above. The **words** of Jesus will bring about judgement on the Last Day.

That said, James Matarazzo offers a fascinating perspective of the Last Day event that reconciles the love of God and the judgment of God in such a beautiful way:

> [H]uman beings will be glorified without regard to their state of grace *in hora mortis*: "Incorruptibility and glorification are given to [each human] by God in resurrection *ex opere operato*, so to speak, and enter [sic] into life as an irresistible force, as a higher reality from which man cannot hide." What human beings cannot hide from is Christ before whom they must stand. This confrontation results in each human being seeing her biography in its totality as it is reflected back to her by Christ. This results in self-judgment. However, this judgment does not happen alone. It is a relational judgment: "Both man's life and his responsibility are conditioned by and linked with the destinies of the whole human race… love's judgment (which is really the Holy Spirit) is the most terrible of any judgment. The reason for its quality as *terribilis* is because it causes a separation within the human person. All that is outside of Christ (i.e., sin) is

separated or rather excised by the fire of the Spirit... in the judgment there is wrath, but this wrath, though terrible, has no retributive function. There is no fear for perfect love casts out fear (1 John 4:18). This loving wrath is analogous to passion. Christ's passionate love results in torment in the person not due to any punishment inflicted, but due to the terrible understanding by the beloved that he did not actualize his love for Christ, the divine lover, in his past life. This encounter is "revolutionary" because the person is face to face with ontological Love, the uncreated source of love itself—love as being.[370]

For anyone stubborn enough to reject Jesus again, even after experiencing the realities of the afterlife and having a visitation from Jesus in Sheol, then indeed things won't be great for such individuals on that day. Yet, there may still be hope.

[The] act of judgment is one of absolute recognition in which human persons "see" in an unfiltered and unlimited way the reality of their own earthly lives, the reality of God, and the reality of the impact of their lives on all other persons. It is this recognition that enables not only reconciliation, but also the full constitution of human personhood. This creative act of God in the judgment is analogous to *theosis*, the incorporation of human beings into the divine life; which is an unlimited life in relationality between persons: between divine persons (using the metaphor of the Trinity) and human persons made divine...

[Divine] judgment can be understood as the event of absolute recognition of God, the self, and the other. It is the act of absolute recognition, which may be harrowing, that initiates the process of transformation and glorification. [371]

---

[370] Matarazzo Jr, James M. The Judgment of Love: An Investigation of Salvific Judgment in Christian Eschatology (Distinguished Dissertations in Christian Theology Book 15) (p. 148–151). Pickwick Publications, an Imprint of Wipf and Stock Publishers. Kindle Edition.
[371] Matarazzo Jr, James M. *The Judgment of Love: An Investigation of Salvific Judgment in Christian Eschatology (Distinguished Dissertations in Christian Theology Book 15)* (p. 286,

To summarize, the Final Judgement seems to consist of two judgements for two different groups of people (this is quite fascinating). The methods and details that describe these judgements clearly differ from each other, and this is intentional. In the absence of any immediate commentary from John or an angel (cf. Rev 17:7), we are left to speculate.[372] Thankfully there are sufficient clues spread throughout the New Testament, especially from Paul, that help us make an informed hypothesis. Still, we must tread carefully and humbly. One never "arrives" in their understanding of these deep matters, so it behooves us to continue to ask Holy Spirit to lead and guide our thoughts and studies. Humble hearts and open minds.

> א *(14) And Death and Sheol were cast down into the Sea of Fire, which this is the second death.*

Surly there could have been a great heavenly proclamation, or at least some fireworks, in commemoration of the last enemy being defeated! Since the beginning of the Messianic Age, Yeshua has had authority over Death and Sheol (Rev 1:18). Yet in Divine mystery, Jesus waits until the end of the Messianic Age to destroy the consequences that came as a result of Adam's delusion.

> *"And the Lord God commanded the man, 'You are free to eat from any tree in the garden; but you must not eat from the tree of the knowledge of good and evil,* **for when you eat from it you will certainly die.**'" *Genesis 2:16–17 (NIV, emphasis mine)*

The two-fold death that Adam died has now been destroyed – death of the image and death of the body. Adam didn't drop dead the day he and Eve ate of the tree, but the created purpose in them died. Their identity died. They cut themselves off from the Life Himself. But this symbolic death humanity has suffered is now destroyed in the Sea of Fire and Sulfur. This means that from now on, mankind is set free from inheriting the death of their identity. Humans will never again experience the death of Genesis 2:17.

Physical, bodily death is also put to an end forever. This is a most remarkable occurrence. One really needs to ponder this future event in order

---

291). Pickwick Publications, an Imprint of Wipf and Stock Publishers. Kindle Edition.

[372] Though John does receive some commentary from Yahweh Himself in Revelation 21:8, 27 and 22:15.

to fully grasp its implications. Imagine a world where no one dies a physical death – what will that be like? What does that mean for pets and animals? For creation?

> *"Never again will there be in it*
> *an infant who lives but a few days,*
> *or an old man who does not live out his years;*
> *the one who dies at a hundred*
> *will be thought a mere child;*
> *the one who fails to reach a hundred*
> *will be considered accursed."* Isaiah 65:20

The totality of death, something that God did not create yet ultimately used to His (and our) advantage, is completely defeated once and for all.

> *"On this mountain he will destroy*
> *the shroud that enfolds all peoples,*
> *the sheet that covers all nations;*
> **he will swallow up death forever.**
> *The Sovereign Lord will wipe away the tears*
> *from all faces;*
> *he will remove his people's disgrace*
> *from all the earth.*
> *The Lord has spoken."* Isaiah 25:7–8 (NIV, emphasis mine)

> *"I will deliver this people from the power of the grave;*
> *I will redeem them from death.*
> *Where, O death, are your plagues?*
> *Where, O grave, is your destruction?"* Hosea 13:14 (NASB)

> *"He shall rule from sea to sea and from the river unto the ends of the Earth! Also You, in the blood of your covenant, You have released the prisoners from the pit which has no water in it [i.e., Sheol]."* Zechariah 9:10–11 (Aramaic)

> *"For as in Adam all die, so in Christ all will be made alive… Then the end will come… For he must reign until he has put all his enemies under his feet.* **The last enemy to be destroyed is death**… *When the perishable has been clothed with the imperishable, and the mortal with immortality, then the saying that is written will come true: 'Death has*

been swallowed up in victory.'"
1 Corinthians 15:21–26, 54 (NIV, emphasis mine)

This is a prophetic anticipation that is found in both the Old and New Testaments.

> Death and Hades [Sheol] are both cast into the lake of fire along with "anyone whose name was not found written in the book of life" (Rev 20:14–15). So how should we understand such an image, given that neither Death nor Hades [Sheol] is literally a person capable of being punished? In view of Paul's prediction in 1 Corinthians 15:26 that the "last enemy to be destroyed is death," the most plausible interpretation, I would suggest, is that the lake of fire will consume and thus destroy the death in us, provided that we permit it to do so. Being cast into the lake of fire is therefore called "the second death" because it represents the death of death, that is, the place where Death itself is finally destroyed forever. But in Pauline theology, at least, death is more than a physical process; it is also a spiritual condition and includes everything that separates us from union with God. From the perspective of Pauline theology, therefore, the final destruction of death must also include a final destruction of everything that separates us from union with God…
>
> So far, so good. But more speculative, perhaps, is the idea that even in the lake of fire one may yet retain the power to continue resisting God's purifying love. For even as such resistance inevitably makes contact with the divine nature increasingly unbearable, it may also open up a theoretical possibility, at least, for this further choice: either one can submit freely to the purification that the lake of fire represents and begin to discover the bliss of union with the divine nature, or one can separate oneself altogether from God's holy presence. The latter option implies separation from every implicit experience of God, including even an experience of the material universe. The brief New Testament allusions to the outer darkness suggest further that God may indeed honor such a choice. If,

perchance, anyone in the lake of fire should retain the delusion that some good is possible apart from God, such a person would be free to act upon it and put it to the test. [373]

Well, I guess the above will be the last time I quote 1 Corinthians 15 in this series. I've certainly enjoyed the dozens of times we've read it! Now, turning our attention to Isaiah 25:7–8 (also quoted above), the prophet writes that Yahweh will "swallow up death". Compare this to the Sea of Fire and Sulfur: Death and Sheol are cast down into this Sea. Now add in 1 Corinthians 15 and the triumph of Jesus over Death. Together, these Scriptures all point to the notion that the Sea of Fire is undeniably associated with the Godhead. At minimum it is an instrument, but more than likely it is another expression of the Divine Presence.

Now, some may ask, "Isn't the Sea of Fire and Sulfur the same as Gehenna?" Emphatically not. Though I discuss Gehenna (the Hinnom Valley outside of old Jerusalem's ancient walls) at length in the first book of this series, I will in one sentence summarize my thoughts: the Gehenna fire was a judgement event unique to Israel and Judah that took place twice (586 BC and 70 AD), and only those bound by the Law of Moses experienced it. Nevertheless, the theme of Gehenna is fitting here because even to the Jewish sages Gehenna was ultimately unto purification:

> Talk of the Gehenna was part of the common religious parlance of the Jewish world before, during, and soon after the time of Jesus, but how it was interpreted by the differing schools of theology is almost impossible to reduce to a single formula or concept. Clearly it was understood sometimes as a place of final destruction, sometimes simply as a place of punishment, and sometimes as a place of purgatorial regeneration. In both of the two largest and most influential rabbinical schools of Christ's time, those of Shammai and Hillel, it was frequently described as a place of purification or punishment for a finite term; but both schools apparently also taught that there would be some state of final remorse, suffering, or ruin for souls incapable of correction. Shammai is reputed to have been the dourer of the two great rabbis, since he seems to have thought—at least, if

---

[373] Talbott, Thomas. *The Inescapable Love of God* (p. 187–188). Cascade Books, an Imprint of Wipf and Stock Publishers. Kindle Edition.

the lore has been accurately transmitted and interpreted—that a fairly substantial portion of humanity might ultimately be lost. Even so, for him the Gehenna was principally a place of purification, a refining fire for the souls of those who have been neither incorrigibly wicked nor impeccably good during their lives; and he taught that, once their penance had been completed, those imprisoned there would be released and taken up to paradise. Hillel, by contrast, is reputed to have had considerably greater trust in God's power to save the reprobate from their destruction or damnation, as far as ultimate numbers go; at least, he seemed to think that only a very few might be beyond rescue. But he apparently also thought of the Gehenna as a place of final punishment and annihilation of the bodies and souls of those too depraved to be regenerated. Needless to say, certain of the images employed by Christ to describe the final judgment would have accorded perfectly well with the teachings of either school, though perhaps perfectly with neither. As for what became the dominant view of later rabbinic tradition—that no one can suffer in the Gehenna for more than twelve months—this can be traced back at least to the teachings of Rabbi Akiva (c. 50–135), not long after the time of Christ.[374]

א *(15) And whosoever was not found engraved in The Book[375] of The Living,[376] he was cast down into the Sea of Fire.*

The pronoun at the start of verse 15, "whosoever", is significant. Many people have been inadvertently conditioned to understand this verse to mean millions of people will not be found engraved in The Book of The Living. Yet John provides no indication that there will be a multitude cast into the Sea of Fire. Elsewhere in Revelation, from the 144,000, to the myriad of myriads of Roman soldiers, to the Army of Magog that is more numerous than the sand of the seashore, the Apostle has no trouble envisioning and

---

[374] Hart, David Bentley. *That All Shall Be Saved: Heaven, Hell, and Universal Salvation* (pp. 114-115). Yale University Press. Kindle Edition.
[375] כְּתָבָא / ܟܬܒܐ *book*, which means "inscription, scripture". Like the Hebrew *ktav* (Strong's H3790).
[376] "Life" is conjugated as determined plural emphatic noun, hence "The Living".

expressing large numbers of people. Such indication is absent here in the closing sentence of chapter 20. From a purely textual sense, it would seem the use of "whosoever" instead of "all" or "every" suggests a choice. This same word is used in Mark 10:44: *"whosoever wishes to be first, must be a servant of all."*

Yahweh Himself needed to step in and be very specific with John in Revelation 21 and 22:

> *"But to the fearful, the unfaithful, the lawless, the defiled, the murderers, the sorcerers, the fornicators, the worshipers of idols, and all the false: their portion[377] is in the burning Sea of Fire and Sulfur, which is the Second Death." Revelation 21:8 (Aramaic)*

> *"And outside are the fornicators,[378] the murderers, the worshipers of idols, the defiled, the sorcerers and all the oracles and the workers of lies." Revelation 22:15 (Aramaic)*

The word "portion" here is very revealing. In the Old Testament, מָנָה "mana" was first introduced in Exodus and Leviticus as portions of sacrifices that were to be offered in ceremony. Jesus also used this word in Matthew 24 when he spoke of the Gehenna fire that the Roman soldiers would bring:

> *"[The lord of that servant] will cut him off, and will appoint his portion with the hypocrites; there will be the weeping and the gnashing of the teeth." Matthew 24:51 (LSV).*

So what are we to make of this? Those who have not been perfected in love (1 Jn 4:18) are placed in the Sea of Fire and Sulfur to be refined. In similar fashion to the ceremonies detailed in Exodus and Leviticus, the portion of these individuals, which God lists (i.e. fear, fornication, murder, etc.), is what they take into the Sea of Fire to be burned and ritually cleansed. Looking back to Revelation 20:13, we read of a second group of people who rose up from the Sheol and were judged by their deeds. It is most likely that from this group of people there may be some who still choose to be "the fearful, the unfaithful, the lawless, the defiled, the murderers, the sorcerers, the fornicators, the worshipers of idols, and all the false" (Rev 21:8), even

---

[377] This word is derived from "manna", the food of the wilderness. William Jennings, *Lexicon to the Syriac New Testament*, p. 796. It is similar to the Hebrew מָנָה (Strong's H4490).

[378] The Aramaic does not have the derogatory word "dogs". That is the Greek translation only.

after having Jesus preach to them in Sheol. **Therefore, is seems to me that those who rose up from Sheol and stood before the throne of God, if they said no to Jesus when he visited them in Sheol, then these are the ones whose portion is the Sea of Fire and Sulfur** (Cf. Rev 20:15; 21:8; 22:15).

Yet, I would place such matters under the realm of Divine mystery, leaving room in my theology for God's methodologies and foreknowledge to be beyond comprehension. What we do know is that Jesus, not Moses, is the express image of our Father. Every chance has been afforded mankind to be redeemed and renewed, to be conformed to the likeness of Jesus, and to be enjoined in union with the Holy Trinity. Both in life and in death, on earth and in Sheol, Jesus has left the ninety-nine to pursue the one. Holy Spirit has turned the house upside-down in search of lost coins. Father God has allowed countless sons and daughters to cash in their inheritance and wander off, yet He waits patiently at the foot of the driveway, arms wide open, ready to receive them back. Therefore we must trust in the Divine goodness and endgame.

THE BOOK OF THE LIVING

The Book of The Living is to be contrasted to the other various scrolls mentioned. The word כְּתָבָא "book" (like the Hebrew *ktav*) is also used elsewhere in both the Old and New Testaments, often in reference to the corpus of Jewish Scriptures, i.e. the Hebrew Bible. The distinction of the book versus the scroll is in proportion to its size. Scrolls by nature are fragmented, especially in antient times. For instance, the famous Isaiah Scroll found at Qumran doesn't contain any other prophetic works, just Isaiah's. But a book, a codex, a *biblio,* contains many volumes. The imagery is clear: The Book of The Living is massive, perhaps like a bunch of old phone books stacked on top of each other.

Moreover, names are *engraved* into The Book of The Living. The only other time you have Yahweh engraving something in a similar context is when He etched the Ten Commandments into the Tablets of Stone.

> *"When the Lord finished speaking to Moses on Mount Sinai, he gave him the two tablets of the covenant law, the tablets of stone inscribed by the finger of God." Exodus 31:18 (NIV)*

The idea of a book of life is alluded to throughout the Bible, though Revelation mentions The Book of The Living more than any other book

(Revelation 3:5; 13:8; 17:8; 20:15).

> BOOK OF LIFE, or perhaps more correctly BOOK OF THE LIVING (Heb. סֵפֶר חַיִּים, Sefer Ḥayyim), a heavenly book in which the names of the righteous are inscribed. The expression "Book of Life" appears only once in the Bible, in Psalms 69: 29 (28), "Let them be blotted out of the book of the living; let them not be enrolled among the righteous," but a close parallel is found in Isaiah 4:3, which speaks of a list of those destined (literally "written") for life in Jerusalem. The erasure of a sinner's name from such a register is equivalent to death (cf. Ps. 69: 29, and the plea of Moses, Ex. 32:32–33).
>
> The belief in the existence of heavenly ledgers is alluded to several times in the Bible (Isa. 65:6; Jer. 17:1; 22:30; Mal. 3:16; Ps. 40:8; 87:6; 139:16; Job 13:26; Dan. 7:10; 12:1; Neh. 13:14 – the exact meaning of some of these texts, along with I Samuel 25:29, however, is still in doubt), the Apocrypha and Pseudepigrapha (e.g., Jub. 30: 19–23; I En. 47:3; 81:1ff.; 97:6; 98:7ff.; 103:2; 104:7; 108:3, 7; I Bar. 24:1), and the New Testament (e.g., Luke 10:20; Phil. 4:3; Heb. 12:23).[379]

As it concerned the Jewish audience for which John primarily wrote to, being inscribed in a "book" meant you were part of a community of ones who had pledged their allegiance to Yahweh alone. To the Hebrews coming out of Egypt, being inscribed in a book had nothing to do with a final judgment or burning in hell. To be "blotted out" implied dying prematurely and outside of the covenant promises. We were first introduced to this notion in Exodus 32:

> *"But now, if you will forgive their sin—but if not,* ***please blot me out of your book that you have written.****" But the* LORD *said to Moses, "Whoever has sinned against me, I will blot out of my book." Exodus 32:32–33 (ESV, emphasis mine)*

To be inscribed in a "book" meant these Hebrew slaves, whom Yahweh had saved and delivered, were receiving a new identity. The covenant of Moses was part of that identity. Conversely, "blotting out" meant saying "no"

---

[379] Encyclopaedia Judaica. © 2008 The Gale Group. All Rights Reserved.
<https://www.jewishvirtuallibrary.org/book-of-life>

to being in covenant with Yahweh.

> *"Beware lest there be among you a man or woman or clan or tribe whose heart is turning away today from the LORD our God to go and serve the gods of those nations…*
> **the LORD will blot out his name from under heaven**. *And the LORD will single him out from all the tribes of Israel for calamity, in accordance with all the curses of the covenant written in this Book of the Law…*
> *[And when] all the nations will say, 'Why has the LORD done thus to this land? What caused the heat of this great anger?' Then people will say, 'It is because they abandoned the covenant of the LORD."*
> *Deuteronomy 29:18, 20–21, 24–25 (ESV, emphasis mine)*

Here's something to wrap your heard around: **the slaves that Moses led out of Egypt were automatically written into God's book**, having been invited by Yahweh to experience a unique and blessed life in the Promised Land. **The goal wasn't to get written in, it was to understand what it would take to be blotted out!** This life and the covenant which legally bound them to that life (like matrimony) were synonymous; to be in that God-life was to be in covenant, and to be in covenant was to be in that God-life. To say no to that God-life was to be blotted out and suffer curses from the Law and/or a premature physical death. Over time, the notion of the Book of Life and even a Book of Death was expanded upon by Biblical and extra-Biblical writers, as well as Jewish sages.

> While the prevailing tendency among apocryphal writers of the Hasidean school was to give the Book of Life an eschatological meaning—and to this inclines also Targ. Jon. to Isa. iv. 3 and Ezek. xiii. 9 (compare Targ. Yer. to Ex. xxxii. 32)—the Jewish liturgy and the tradition relating to the New-Year's and Atonement days adhered to the ancient view which took the Book of Life in its natural meaning, preferring, from a sound practical point of view, the this-worldliness of Judaism to the heavenliness of the Essenes. Instead of transferring, as is done in the Book of Enoch, the Testament of Abraham, and elsewhere, the great Judgment Day to the hereafter, the Pharisaic school taught that on the first day of each year (Rosh ha-Shanah) God sits in judgment over His creatures and has the Books of Life and Death opened, together with the books

containing the records of the righteous and the unrighteous. And out of the middle state of the future judgment (see Testament of Abraham, A, xiv.) there arose the idea of a third class of men who are held in suspense ("Benonim," the middle), and of a corresponding third book for this middle class (R. H. 15b). In Tos. Sanh. xiii. 3, however, the annual (Rosh ha-Shanah) judgment (Yom ha-Din) is not yet recognized (compare Tos. R. H. i. 13, R. Jose's opinion in opposition to that of R. Akiba and R. Meïr, which has become the universally accepted one).[380]

Therefore, in simplest terms, to be written into a Book of Life is to be a willful participant in God–life by way of relationship (covenant), while to be blotted out of a Book of Life is to willfully say "no" to the God-life and stay in a fallen state, which is death (physical and spiritual). In the Old Testament, this meant physical death, while in John's Revelation, it means the second death, which is the Sea of Fire.

Now let's grab all the mentions of the Book of The Living in Revelation and piece them together:

"He who overcomes in this way is garbed with a white garment, and I shall not blot out his name from The Book of The Living, but I shall confess his name before my Father and before his Angels." (Revelation 3:5)

And all the inhabitants of The Land will bow in submission to it – those who are not written in The Book of Living of the Lamb slain before the foundations of the Age. (Revelation 13:8)

"'The savage animal which you saw – which was, and is not – prepares to come up from the Sea and it moves forth for destruction. But they that inhabit the Land will marvel – whose names are not written in The Book of The Living from the foundations of the Age – when they see the savage animal which was, and is not, and is approaching." (Revelation 17:8)

"And whosoever was not found engraved in The Book of The Living, he

---

[380] Jewish Encyclopedia Vol 3, *Book of Life,* Kaufmann Kohler, Max L. Margolis, p 313 < https://www.jewishencyclopedia.com/articles/3554-book-of-life>

was cast down into the Sea of Fire." (Revelation 20:15)

In Revelation 3:5, speaking to the church at Sardis, Jesus is admonishing those who were living a life of mixture between Law and Grace. Sardis in those days had the largest synagogue of all,[381] and there was a strong Jewish community in that city. Having their names blotted out meant putting themselves back under the Law of Moses (cf. Gal 5:1–4). Both 13:8 and 17:8 speak of those in the Holy Land who would fall prey to the calamities of the Roman invasion. They specify that anyone under the curse of the Law will be forced to bow in submission to the Romans and will marvel in astonishment at the savage animal (even John did momentarily in 17:7!). Lastly, Revelation 20:15 can be understood as anyone who chooses to remain apart from a God-life through covenant is actually choosing to remain in the death that Adam died. They are therefore cast down into the Sea of Fire to have that death die.

For the first three mentions of the Book of The Living (Rev 3:5; 13:8; 17:8), it is probable to assume that those who suffered under the curses of the Law died prematurely, as we just discussed. It does not mean their eternal fate was determined or that they are eternally damned. Absurd! Yeshua met them all in Sheol. Remember the Divine mystery found in Romans 11:26: all Israel will live ("be saved"). The final mention of the Book of The Living (Rev 20:15), which is broad and eschatological, deals with two groups - people in a future time who will be living on earth but hostile to God when the Great Resurrection comes about, and whosoever happens to come out of the Sheol experience with hardened hearts.

Again, the group of people that Revelation 20:15 most likely applies to are those are alive at the Great Resurrection and Final Judgement and are hostile to God, as well as anyone who still has a hardened heart after the Sheol experience. Because both Death and Sheol are destroyed at that time, there is no traditional afterlife experience for these people. Perhaps then it is in the Sea of Fire and Sulfur where they are given an opportunity (or ultimatum?) to allow the death of Adam in them to be purged by fire and salt (cf. Mk 9:49). If the Sea of Fire and Sulfur is somehow a manifestation of the Divine Presence, where God is the refining fire and Yeshua is the fuller's sulfur (cf. Mal 3:2–3), then the Sea of Fire suddenly becomes a baptismal tank to baptize the newly arrived inhabitants with Holy Spirit and Fire (cf. Mat 3:11).

---

[381] Seager, Andrew R. (1972-10-01). "The Building History of the Sardis Synagogue". American Journal of Archaeology. 76 (4): 425–435.

Perhaps.

Or you can stick with the traditional hypothesis rooted in Dante Alighieri's *Inferno* instead. To each their own!

To conclude, it seems to me that in a climactic crescendo of eschatological hopes and prophecies, the start and end of Revelation 20 stretches our hearts and faith to believe that God will indeed make all things new. Every wrong will be made right, and creation will be purged of evil. But as is the case with God's Kingdom, there are humble beginnings, and all promises are initiated in seed form. Nevertheless, our Father is faithful, and His words will not return void. In order to save a few pages in an already long book, I will list Scriptures below that I highly encourage you to read. Let them remind you of what God not only intends to do, but in fact is actively doing even as you read these words.

- Genesis 1:28
- Isaiah 2:2-4
- Isaiah 9:7
- Isaiah 11:9–11
- Isaiah 42:1–4
- Isaiah 65:17–25
- Zechariah 9:9–12
- Ezekiel 16:53–55, 60–63 (cf. Gen 13:10–11)
- Ezekiel 47:1–12
- Luke 1:31–33
- Matthew 28:18
- John 17:20-23
- 1 Corinthians 15:24-26

A few more concluding thoughts to close this chapter. When Paul visited Athens, Greece, he had the opportunity to share the Gospel to dozens, if not hundreds, of Greek bystanders. Here was his big chance to get all the most important points across to a group of people who have likely never heard of Yahweh God, never heard of Jesus, never heard of salvation, never heard of going to church, and never heard of praying a prayer that keeps you from going to hell. Certainly, whatever was *most* important to Paul as it pertains to the Gospel is what he chose to share in his street-evangelism message. So, let's take a look at the words of Paul, as transcribed by Saint Luke, in the Book of Acts:

"Now from one bloodline He made the entire age of all humanity to be dwelling upon the face of all the Earth. And He organized the times in His decrees, and placed limits of the habitation of humans,

So that they would be searching after God, investigating and finding Him in His creation. Also because He doesn't exist far removed from any one of us.

In Him we indeed have life, and are moved, and exist; just as some of the wise men among you have said, 'Our lineage is from Him.'

Men, therefore, our lineage is from God. You should not be obligated to think that gold or silver or stone carved by the skill and knowledge of a man resembles the Godhead.

For God has made the times of deception to cross over. And now in this time, His decree for all humanity – each person in every place – is to come back.

Because He has established the Day in which He is prepared to try the whole earth in righteousness, through the agency of the Man He has ordained. And He will cause every person to turn back to his truth, since He has raised Him from the house of the dead."
Acts 17:26–31 (Aramaic)

Paul clearly failed evangelism school. No one was invited to the front to pray the sinner's prayer. No one was warned about burning in hell forever. No one was told about the wrath of God and how Jesus was the only way to be saved from that wrath. Basically, everyone who was there that day must have ended up in hell, burning forever. Paul has a lot of blood on his hands.

Of course, I write all this not merely for jest! Rather, by forcing a stark contrast between the modern Protestant-Evangelical doctrine of salvation to all that we have studied in Revelation thus far, the differences are so very apparent. Everything the Protestant West has been taught to focus on when it comes to soteriology (study of salvation) is absent from the Book of Revelation, the Gospels, the Epistles, and even here in this simple example from Acts 17. Many look to the Scriptures for fire insurance, when they should instead be looking for the Author's story. God is not out for blood, He is out for sons and daughters.

> *"The Lord is not slow in keeping his promise, as some understand slowness. Instead he is patient with you, not wanting anyone to perish, but everyone to come to repentance."* 2 Peter 3:9 (NIV)

Consider also the prophetic irony of the Jewish mob's fateful words at the trail of Jesus before Pilate:

> *"Now when Pilate saw that he was accomplishing nothing, but rather that a riot was starting, he took water and washed his hands in front of the crowd, saying, 'I am innocent of this Man's blood; you yourselves shall see.' And all the people replied,* **'His blood shall be on us and on our children!'"** *Matthew 27:24–25 (NASB, emphasis mine)*

Though the thought never crossed their minds, consider the implication of their words – may the blood of Jesus be upon us and our children.[382] Every single event and every single word surrounding the Passion of Christ is prophetic and eschatological. These words are no exception. The blood of Jesus covered them in the height of their delusion of deception. Hence, on the cross, Jesus makes this statement:

> *"Father, forgive them, for they do not know what they are doing."* Luke 23:34 (NIV)

God means to restore *all things,* to be *all in all.* And He will succeed. Indeed, every knee will bow and every tongue will confess that Jesus is Lord. But not by force, as the Romans did to those they subdued. Knees will bow and hearts will cry out because of the measure of encounter everyone will have with the fiery eyes of Yeshua. With unveiled faces and our very essence fully exposed and laid bare before Him, we will know Him fully in the same way we are fully known (1 Cor 13:12). Jesus not only undoes all the effects of Adam, He recapitulates mankind beyond Adam's original state and makes us *like Him* instead (1 Jn 3:2, 4:17; 2 Pet 1:4; 1 Cor 15:49).

> Reconciliation is the goal.
> I have yet to see God fail.

> *"But if [Israel's] transgression means riches for* **the world,** *and their loss means riches for the Gentiles, how much greater riches will* **[Israel's] full inclusion** *bring!*
> *…For if [Israel's] rejection brought* **reconciliation to the world,** *what will their acceptance be but* **life from the dead?**

---

[382] Credit to my friend Caleb W. Brown for sharing this revelation with me.

> *... After all, if [Gentiles] were cut out of an olive tree that is wild by nature, and contrary to nature* **were grafted into** *a cultivated olive tree, how much more readily will these, the natural branches, be* **grafted into their own olive tree!**
>
> *...I do not want you [Gentiles] to be ignorant of this mystery, brothers and sisters, so that you may not be conceited: Israel has experienced a hardening in part until* **the full number of the Gentiles has come in**, *and in this way* **all Israel will be saved...**
>
> *For God has bound everyone over to disobedience so that he may have* **mercy on them all.**"
> *(Romans 11:12, 15, 24–26, 32, NASB, emphasis mine)*

God chose to characterize Himself as fire (Deut 4:24; Heb 12:29) in the same way He chose to characterize Himself as love (1 Jn 4:8). He is as much fire as He is love, and the two attributes are not at odds with one another. When wood is burned, we think of the ash left over. But the divine imagery therein is the fire and wood become one. That which the fire desired became one with it, and that which it did not desire was left. This is also another way of seeing the refining of gold through fire.

Fire is also a symbol of life. That the "I AM THAT I AM" statement came from a burning bush (Ex 3:14) speaks to this. Indeed, all living things can be burned, and all living things have a burning that is within them: metabolism. Metabolism is a defining feature of life. We are called the light of the world by Jesus, and we are called to walk in the light as He is in the light (Mt 5:14; 1 Jn 1:7). The interesting thing is all natural light requires something to be burned. **That which burns is that which produces light.** We are His burning ones.

> "He makes the winds His messengers,
> Flaming fire His ministers." Psalm 104:4 (NIV)

Revelation 20 can therefore be understood as the whole of creation being exposed to the consuming fire of God, even in the Sea of Fire. Fire is the gateway back into the Garden of Eden. In Genesis 3, cherubim where placed at the entrance to Paradise to guard the Tree of Life. With these cherubim was a flaming sword which turned every which way (Gen 3:24), meaning nothing could escape the reach of this sword. More profoundly, all that Mankind was never created to be has to be cut off and burned away in order to enter back into the Garden of Eden. This is what is taking place in Revelation 20. The fire is the gateway into the New Eden, the New Jerusalem, the New Creation. God's grand narrative has always been one in which He is taking us from garden to garden. Revelation 21 and 22 is a glimpse of this story's end.

15 ALL THINGS NEW: CH. 21

"Hope is being able to see that there is light despite all of the darkness."
— Desmond Tutu

Revelation 21 must be seen as a succession of events that begins in chapter 20 verse 9: fire fills the earth for the refining and purifying of all things. On the other side of that purification and refinement is a renewed cosmos and Spirit-Waters that heal and restore (Rev 21:6; 22:1–2). The focus of John's vision here is not a cloud-floored abode in a faraway place called "Heaven", but rather a merging of the realms of heaven and earth, culminating in a proximal and intimate experience.

> *"For I reckon the sufferings of the present time to be of no worth before the coming glory that will be revealed to us. For the earnest expectation of creation anxiously awaits the revelation of the sons of God. For creation was made subordinate to pointlessness, not willingly but because of the one who subordinated it, in the hope. That creation itself will also be liberated from decay into the freedom of the glory of God's children. For we know that all creation groans together and labors together in birth pangs, up to this moment; Not only this, but even we ourselves, having the firstfruits of the spirit, groan within ourselves as well, anxiously awaiting adoption,*

emancipation of our body." Romans 8:18–23 (Hart Translation)[383]

Though the First Adam subjected creation to futility, the Last Adam (Jesus) delivered it from that subjection. The one who lead humanity out of the Garden of Eden (Adam) now follows the One who leads humanity back into a New Eden. Garden to Garden. The failed endeavor to bring order into the earth (Gen 1:28) is recapitulated by the Last Adam who rules and reigns as King of all kings and Lord of all lords.

Our minds must shift away from the notion that Revelation 21 and 22 is all about heaven, and realize that the text is emphatically speaking of a new reality here on earth. What you are about to read pertains to the future of the dirt you and I tread upon. Moses removed his sandals because the ground near the bush that was consumed by the ethereal fires of Yahweh was holy. Yet a day is coming where we will all remove our sandals because the whole earth will be holy ground.

Surprisingly absent from chapters 21 and 22 is the mention of fire. Revelation 20 especially was filled will fire as Yahweh's purifying presence consumed all creation. Now, on this side of restoration and renewal, fire is not required. Still, Yahweh God is ever present as He establishes His abode right in the midst of humanity. What does this mean? It means that on the other side of a Sinai theophany, on the other side of a consuming fire, on the other side of a Gehenna judgement, on the other side of a burning Sea of Fire and Sulfur, we experience Yahweh God as Abba Father. "I shall be his God and he shall be My son" (Rev 21:7). We can't escape the fire, so embrace it in this life. "[Jesus] will baptize you with the Holy Spirit and fire" (Mat 3:11). Let Him. Better His baptism here and now than the baptism in the Sea of Fire and Sulfur. Better a gradual lifetime of sanctification than intense purification in an instant. Astonishingly, chapter 22 of Revelation then becomes an expression of the Godhead as life-giving and *healing* water.

Yes, this line of thought rattles theological paradigms of soteriology. Such is the nature of an unfettered exploration of the Bible and why the verse "Thus you nullify the word of God by your tradition that you have handed down" (Mark 7:13) is necessary. We cannot be reckless in our exploration, yet more importantly, we cannot shrink back from our conclusions. Let us boldly take hold of all that Christ accomplished for us through His Incarnation, Passion, and Resurrection. Amen!

---

[383] Hart, David Bentley. The New Testament: A Translation (pp. 302-303). Yale University Press. Kindle Edition.

> א *(1) And I saw the new heavens and the new earth, for the first heavens and the first earth had gone, and the sea didn't exist anymore.*

Revelation 21 and 22 are reminiscent of Genesis 1 and 2: creation and Eden. But in this future *genesis* event, we do not have the Spirit hovering over the depths. The "sea" described here in 21:1 is not a topographical illustration, but rather a qualitative statement – there will be no more chaos. In the Old Testament, the Sea was a picture of both chaos and the realm of Leviathan.[384] Hence Jesus speaking over the winds and waves (cf. Mt 14:22-27) is significant in an eschatological sense. The point here is that chaos and the depths (תְהוֹם "tehom") will be no more.

> א *(2) And the Holy City, the New Jerusalem, I saw descending from Heaven, from God's side, prepared as the Bride adorned for her Husband.*

Betrothal is a key theme in God's grand love story. This verse right here is why I gave my first book the subtitle *The Victorious Bridegroom King*. A day will come when the marriage between Jesus and His Bride is consummated. Perhaps this is a graphic depiction for you, but this truth must be viewed from a redemptive lens: what happens in intercourse is a prophetic picture of what will take place between God and humanity – He will come into us, and the two will become one.

Also, you will notice that twice in Revelation 21 (21:2 and 21:10) we read that the New Jerusalem, which is you and me, the Body and Bride of Christ, **descends** from Heaven to earth. So for anyone who still thinks that God's ultimate plan is for us to all escape this earth and spend eternity in the clouds, you will be hard-pressed to find evidence of that plan in Revelation. All the good things you are about to read in chapters 21 and 22 of John's vision take place right here, on the ground where you and I stand.

An important thing to note in the upcoming verses (and also chapter 22) is the narrative flow will shift back and forth from vision to commentary.

---

[384] Gen 1:2, 7:11; Ps 18:15–16, 29:3–10, 69:14–15, 74:10–17, 77:16, 93:3–4, 104:6–9, 144:7; Isa 17:12-14; Job 38:8–11. See also Isa 27:1, 51:9–10, and Job 7:12, 26:13.

The commentary sections MUST NOT be read as part of the chronological sequence of the visions. This is where much confusion is created.[385] **Often, either God or an angel will interject commentary that will speak to John's present age, even though the comments that are being made in the vision is for those in an age to come.** The following verses are the first instance of this.

> א *(3) Then I heard a great voice from Heaven saying, "Behold! The house of God[386] is with the children of men, and He dwells with them and they shall be His people. And God Himself will be with them, and shall be their God. (4) And He shall blot out[387] every tear from their eyes, and henceforth there shall be no death, nor grieving, nor contention, nor disease again, for His sake."*

> א *(5) As I turned, He who sat upon the throne said to me,*
>
> *"Behold! I am making all things new!"* [388]
>
> *And He said to me,*
>
> *"Write these words, they are trustworthy and true."*

> א *(6) Then He said to me,*
>
> *"It's done.*
> *I am Aleph and I am Tav,[389]*
> *Genesis[390] and Consummation.*

---

[385] For instance, advocates of Full Preterism, or what I will loosely call Hyper Universalism, tend to misread these two chapters as a linear chronological sequence of events.

[386] A euphemism for the Holy Temple. But John is intentional in his nuance, for he does not wish to re-introduce any hint of the previous Levitical system (cf. Rev 21:22).

[387] The same verb is used in Revelation 3:5 ("I will not blot their name…").

[388] It is fascinating that the verb "making" is conjugated as a participle! He is *making*, He is *renewing*, something ongoing. Perhaps this explains why nations and kings are seen walking into the new Jerusalem after the Great Judgement.

[389] This is the Hebrew equivalent. In Aramaic it is "I am Alaf and I am Taw".

[390] "Genesis" here is רֵישִׁיתָא , which is equivalent to the Hebrew רֵאשִׁית found in Genesis 1:1, "In the *beginning*". In Jewish literature, the Book of Genesis is named

> *To he who is thirsty I give freely from the spring of the Waters of Life. (7) And to he who is victorious, he shall inherit these things, and I shall be his God and he shall be My son. (8) But to the fearful, the unfaithful, the lawless, the defiled, the murderers, the sorcerers, the fornicators, the worshipers of idols, and all the false: their portion[391] is in the burning Sea of Fire and Sulfur, which is the Second Death.*

In verses 5 to 8, Yahweh Himself pauses the vision and begins offering John commentary. This is extraordinary! God's like, "Angel, you're doing a great job hosting John on this journey, but let me take the microphone for a second." **God then starts speaking to John directly and offers him pastoral insights for John's here and now.** The message is simple: come *now* to the Waters of Life, come *in this life* to the baptism of fire. For in *that* life to come, only that which has been purified will be able to participate. It's like an operating room in a hospital – you can't have dirty shoes or unwashed hands and walk in to that O.R., otherwise you bring in the risk of disease and infection with you. And central to God's commentary is the invitation to be *fathered* by Him. In the Gospels, Jesus introduces God exclusively as Father, and save for when quoting a Scripture on the cross, Jesus only referred to God as such. You and I are invited right now by Yahweh God Himself to approach Him and know Him as Father!

Now, let's talk about the "portion" some may have in the Sea of Fire. I mentioned in the previous chapter the word "portion" (מְנָה "mana") is first introduced in Exodus and Leviticus in the context of sacrifices. These sacrifices were ultimately unto purification. Therefore, those not yet perfected in love (1 Jn 4:18) are baptized in the Sea of Fire and Sulfur. The portion these individuals place in the fire are things like fear, fornication, murder, etc., to be burned. The mystery we touched on in previous chapters surrounding the notion of one's choice and free will in the Sea of Fire remains, and I will not try to step beyond the grace of God allotted me to comprehend it. It is a divine mystery, and we are wise to honor it. But what we do know from Jesus is that everyone will be salted with fire, and that He

---

Bereshit, which literally means "in the beginning". The names of the first five books of the Old Testament are named in this manner. Therefore, I have highlighted the obvious wordplay here.

[391] This word is derived from "manna", the food of the wilderness. William Jennings, *Lexicon to the Syriac New Testament*, p. 796. It is similar to the Hebrew מָנָה (Strong's H4490).

said this salt is good (Mk 9:49–50).

> ✡ *(9) And there came one of the seven Angels who had with them the seven vessels full of the seven last bowls, and he spoke with me saying, "Come! I will show you the Bride, the Wife of the Lamb!"*

Hold on. Why is the angel who dealt such heavy calamity and judgement upon the Holy Land and Jerusalem the one to now show John the New Jerusalem ("the Wife of the Lamb")? Because all of God's judgements are restorative, not retributive. On the other side of the calamity, on the other side of Sheol, there is always restoration. Remember Ezekiel 16? Remember Romans 11? I have cited those passages enough times now that we should all have them memorized! God said it Himself: He will restore Sodom, He will restore Jerusalem, and *all* Israel shall be saved! This isn't conjecture, this is exactly what Ezekiel 16 and Romans 11 say.

> ✡ *(10) And he carried me in the Spirit to a great and high mountain, and he showed me the Holy City Jerusalem coming down from Heaven from God's side,*

> ✡ *(11) And it had the glory of God,[392] and its light was as the likeness of precious stones, like jasper, as the appearance of crystal.*

> ✡ *(12) And it had a wall, great and high. And it had twelve gates, and over the gates, twelve angels, and names written which are the names of the Twelve Tribes of Israel.*

> ✡ *(13) From the east, three gates, from the north, three gates, and from the south, three gates, and from the west, three gates.*

If God is done with Israel, then why bother naming new gates with the same names of the former Twelve Tribes? Why even call this new city a New Jerusalem? I mean, by the time Jesus came on the scene in the flesh, ten of the twelve ancient tribes of Israel had already been displaced! Because God means to restore humanity – every race, every tribe, every tongue, and this

---

[392] Jesus' prayer is fully realized here: "I have given them the glory that you gave me" (John 17:22).

includes Israel. The future is not a picture of religious segregation, tiered systems, or divided citizen groups (Gal 3:28).

> "Now the body of Christ, as I often have said, is the whole of humanity." — St. Gregory of Nyssa (d. 394 AD)

The Jerusalem to come is a picture of how God takes even the worst offenders, elevates them, and makes them beautiful. It's the prodigal son being taken out of the pig pen and clothed in royalty. This is what God does. Jerusalem is symbolically depicted here (remember it's a bride made up of billions of people, not physical real estate) as a banner that states to all humanity:

> "I restore all things! I am making all things new! Even YOU!"[393]

Further, as Dr. Jordan Peterson has helped me understand, "Paradise" literally means "walled garden", just as Eden was to be understood as a walled garden. Otherwise, what would the point have been of placing cherubim to guard the entrance back into Eden if Adam and Eve could have just walked around it? Gates need walls to be sustained. Therefore, the walls of Jerusalem represent a walled off garden. This walled space where humanity is placed at the center is a symbol of social agreement. Because the New Jerusalem is literally people, its figurative walls are ever expanding as more and more walk in through her gates (cf. Rev 21:24–26, more on this below). This walled garden also represents a balance between culture and nature, structure and possibility, perfect harmony in all creation. Order has been restored.

> א *(14) And the wall of the city has twelve foundations, and on them, the twelve names of the Apostles of the Son.*
>
> א *(15) But the one who was speaking with me had with him a measuring reed of gold to measure the city and its wall.*[394]
>
> א *(16) And the city was laid out foursquare, and its length was as its width. And he measured The City with the reed: twelve thousand stadia was its length, its width, and its height. They were equal.*[395]

---

[393] Go read all of Ezekiel 16 and Romans 11 again if you disagree!
[394] John measured the Temple in Jerusalem for destruction in Revelation 11. Now an angel of Yahweh measures the New Jerusalem for restoration.
[395] "[Initially] the city is described as a square, 12,000 stadia in each direction. The beast has the triangular number 666, but the people of God have the square

> *(17) And he measured its wall one hundred and forty four cubits in the measurement of a man, that is, of the angel.*
>
> *(18) So the building of the wall was jasper, and the city was of purified gold, in the likeness of clear glass.*

There are two qualitative statements in verse 18 that I must mention – the purified gold and the clear glass. The City, representing you, me, and billions of other Saints, is described as being made up of pure gold and pure glass (the words "purified" and "clear" are the same one).

> In this most pure gold, which is purified by the heat of fire and so is proven, we perceive the chorus of the saints who have been tested in the furnace of suffering and by the heat of temptation and so have been made pure through the power of the Lord. They are compared with pure glass to indicate the transparent and pure brightness of the holiness that is in them. (Apringius of Beja [c. 6th C. AD], Tractate On The Apocalypse 21.18)[396]

In other words, those who have been baptized in fire and have stood in the sea of glass mingled with fire are those who make up the essence of Yeshua's Bride.

---

number 144 (12 x 12) (7:4–8; 14:1; 21:17). Then the city is shown not only to have a square ground plan, but to be a perfect cube, like no city ever imagined, but like the holy of holies in the temple (1 Kings 6:20). We learn later that it needs no temple (v. 22): the whole city is the holiest place of God's presence. Verse 17, as well as echoing Ezek 40:5, this verse ('144 cubits by the measure of a human being, that is, of an angel', my tr.) resembles 13:18 ('the number of the beast, for it is the number of a human being: its number is 666', my tr.). Just as Nero Caesar, written in Hebrew characters, has the numerical value 666, a triangular number, so the Greek word 'angel' (aggelos), written in Hebrew characters, has the numerical value 144, a square number." Richard Bauckham, *Revelation*, eds. John Barton and John Muddiman, Oxford Commentary. Accordance electronic ed. (Oxford: Oxford University Press, 2001), 1304.

[396] William C. Weinrich, eds. *Revelation*. vol. 12 of Ancient Christian Commentary on Scripture. ICCS/Accordance electronic ed. (Downers Grove: InterVarsity Press, 2005), 372.

> *(19) And the foundation of the wall of the city was adorned with precious stones. Now the first foundation, jasper, and the second, sapphire, and the third, chalcedony, and the fourth, emerald, (20) and the fifth, sardonyx, and the sixth, sardius, and the seventh, goldstone, and the eighth, beryl, and the ninth, topaz, and the tenth, chrysoprasus, the eleventh, jacinth, the twelfth, amethyst.*

It can be painful at times to read through lost lists like this, especially if you don't even know what half (or more?) of the items listed even look like! Simply put, the precious stones are symbols of Eden.

> [New Jerusalem] is built out of the jewels and metals of Paradise: cf. Gen 2:11–12; Ezek 28:13. The twelve precious stones (vv. 19–20) are those of the high priest's breastplate (Ex 28:17–20); and the same twelve occur in Ezek 28:13 (LXX Gk. version; in the MT the first nine) described as 'every precious stone', and in Eden. Thus the list of twelve in Revelation represents all precious stones, all to be found in Paradise. Jewish traditions claimed that the jewels of the high priest's breastplate in Solomon's temple came from Paradise, along with other precious materials used in the temple, and were also the precious stones of which, according to Isa 54:11–12, the new Jerusalem is to be built (cf. 4QpIsa[a] 1:4–9; LAB 26:13–15). Thus the jewels and the gold characterize the new Jerusalem as a temple-city adorned with all the fabulously radiant precious materials of Paradise. The glory of God is reflected in the jewels and the translucent gold of the city. These are not to be understood merely as allegories for attributes of redeemed people, but as the beauty of the new creation, Paradise restored, and a home for glorified humanity. The city's relation to Paradise here and in 22:1–2 points to the harmony of nature and human culture in the new creation.[397]

It was also common for the Early Church Fathers to ascribe stones to the

---

[397] Richard Bauckham, *Revelation*, eds. John Barton and John Muddiman, Oxford Commentary. Accordance electronic ed. (Oxford: Oxford University Press, 2001), 1304.

Start here checking Bible verses: Apostles. For example: jasper was Peter, sapphire was Paul, chalcedony was Andrew, etc.[398]

> ℵ *(21) And twelve gates of twelve pearls,[399] one to each, and every one of the gates was of one pearl, but the street of the City of purified gold, as if there was glass in it.[400]*

> ℵ *(22) But I did not see the Temple in her; for Yahweh God, Keeper of All, He is her Temple.[401]*

> ℵ *(23) Now the Lamb and the City are not needing the Sun or the Moon to illuminate them, for the glory of God illuminates her, and the Lamb is her lamp.[402] (24) And the nations[403] are walking in her light, and the kings of the earth are bringing forth praise to her. (25) And her gates will never be shut by day, for there will never be night there. (26) And they will be bringing forth to her the praise and honor of the nations. (27) But there will never be anything defiled there, nor one who performing abomination or falsehood. Rather, only those who are written in The Book of the Lamb.*

---

[398] You can read all about it in Andrew of Caesarea's *Commentary On The Apocalypse*, written in the 6th century AD.

[399] Pearls are a reference to Matthew 13:44–46 and the Parable of the Merchant and the Pearl. Jesus sold everything to buy a field because *we* were the treasure hidden in that field. *We* are the beautiful pearls that mesmerized the Merchant (Jesus). He gave everything up so that He would reconcile us back to Himself.

[400] Refinement and transparency, naked and unashamed. This is the repeated image John is shown of the polis made up of God's people.

[401] The city's symbolic dimensions are that of a perfect cube, symbolizing the Holy of Holies (as mentioned above). Verse 22 takes things further: God is the Holy Temple. This notion is echoed in John 2:19 when Jesus referred to Himself as the Temple. Therefore, we have a depiction of the Trinity in perfect union with humanity in shared sacred union. God and man are one in sacred intimacy.

[402] The Lamb and the City are personified as husband and wife – Jesus and us. The affectionate glory and light radiating from God and Jesus respectively is directed towards us ("her") as Wife.

[403] Your Bible likely reads "the nations <u>of the saved</u>". This addition is not found in the Syriac (Aramaic) text, highlighting the grace-centric theology of the early Semitic Orthodox churches, in contrast to the Greek/Latin West which limits the grace to only the "saved" in the sense the western churches currently teach.

Jersak offers thoughtful insights into the symbolic meaning of the "kings" and "nations" mentioned here:

> History of the Kings and the Nations in Revelation
>
> 1. Deception, Immorality, and Dominance: The kings and all the nations are deceived by Babylon's sorcery. She gives them authority to rule, yet she rules over their kings. The kings and all the nations are in league with Babylon against God and his kingdom. They persecute God's people, city, temple, and witnesses (Rev 11:2, 9, 18; 14:8; 17:2, 10–12, 15, 18; 18:3, 9, 23).
>
> 2. Rebellion and Defeat: The kings and nations gather for war against God. They assemble for battle, but fire comes down to devour them, and birds devour their flesh. For a while, the nations are freed from the dragon's deception (Rev 20:3), after which they rebel against the Lamb a second time, only to be defeated utterly (Rev 6:15; 16:12–14; 17:14,19; 19:18–19; 20:8; Isa 34:1–2; 60:12, 20).
>
> 3. Surrender and Submission: Christ becomes King of Kings and rules all nations with a rod of iron (Rev 12:5; 15:3; 17:14; 19:15–16; Ps 2:8).
>
> 4. Homage and Restoration: The kings and all the nations come to worship the Lamb (Rev 15:4), to walk in God's light (Isa 60:3), and to bring their glory and riches (Isa 60:5–9, 11) into the city (Rev 21:24, 26). As they enter, the leaves of the tree of life are given to heal the nations (Rev 22:2).
>
> 5. Honor and Servitude: The kings and nations rebuild the city walls, serve God's people, and adorn her sanctuary (Isa 60:10, 13). God's people are given authority over kings, and the nations bow to honor them (Rev 1:5; 2:26; Isa 60:14, 16). This represents the hope of our eternal calling (Eph 1:18; 4:4).[404]

The last five verses of chapter 21 must be read and understood as one

---

[404] Jersak, Bradley. *Her Gates Will Never Be Shut: Hope, Hell, and the New Jerusalem* (pp. 172-173). Wipf & Stock, an Imprint of Wipf and Stock Publishers. Kindle Edition.

continuous thought. The soteriological implications of this last block are astounding. Some of the glaring questions we should all be asking are:

- How is it possible to have billions of people being personified as Jerusalem, the Wife of Christ, walking hand-in-hand with Jesus in the New Eden; yet at the same time have *other* groups of people making their way to the garden setting?
- Why do we need gates at all, and why are they open?
- How it is possible for there to still be people who are not part of the New Jerusalem, the Wife of Christ, to be making their way into that union?
- Where are these nations and kings coming from?
- What on earth is going on here?

We have to admit that this picture right here – in plain sight, in the Bible – does not fit the "turn or burn" and "heaven and hell" paradigm we have inherited in the Church at large. Yet it fits the narrative flow of Revelation perfectly. And God knew that people would be asking such questions. Which is why **the answer to the enigmatic verses that conclude Revelation 21 is immediately found in the very verse first verse of Revelation 22.** See you there.[405]

---

[405] I highly recommend you read *Her Gates Will Never Be Shut: Hope, Hell, and the New Jerusalem* by Bradley Jersak. He unpacks many thoughts and themes as they relate to these nations that gradually make their way into the fold.

16 FINAL EXORTATIONS: CH. 22

"Water does not resist. Water flows. When you plunge your hand into it, all you feel is a caress. Water is not a solid wall, it will not stop you. But water always goes where it wants to go, and nothing in the end can stand against it. Water is patient. Dripping water wears away a stone. Remember that, my child."

— Margaret Atwood, The Penelopiad

Ezekiel's prophetic book crescendos with a powerful prophetic vison of the Spirit Waters of Yahweh God. In Ezekiel 47, the prophet sees the River of Life flowing from the *Renewed Temple in a Renewed Jerusalem,* and this torrential river floods Gehenna, the wilderness of temptation (Arabah), before it descends to the lowest sea in the world. Out of this New Jerusalem in Ezekiel's vision, Yahweh God brings healing and restoration to the cities of Sodom and Gomorrah, traditionally believed to have been at the bottom of the Dead Sea.

"When [the River] empties into the [Dead Sea], the salty water there becomes fresh. Swarms of living creatures will live wherever the river flows. There will be large numbers of fish, because this water flows there and makes the salt water fresh; so where the river flows everything will live…

Fruit trees of all kinds will grow on both banks of the river. Their leaves will not wither, nor will their fruit fail. Every month they will bear fruit, because the water from the sanctuary flows to them. Their fruit will serve for food and their leaves for healing." Ezekiel 47:8–9, 12 (NIV)

The concept of a Holy Spirit River, echoed in Revelation 22:2, is the key that unlocks the mysteries of the last five verses of Revelation 21. Like Ezekiel, John too sees a future Jerusalem which has Yahweh Himself as her Temple. **Both prophets see a lifeline flowing out from God's polis to those in the Dead Sea – the Sea of Fire and Sulfur**, and over time, Ezekiel's Dead Sea is healed and restored. Taking a clue from Ezekiel 16, we conclude the implication is the restoration of even the worst offenders – Sodom and Gomorrah. It is my belief that this understanding of Ezekiel is to be applied to Revelation 20 to 22. The Spirit River flows out of the New Jerusalem, situated in a New Eden, to those in the Sea of Fire and Sulfur, which is the Dead Sea.

As these nations and kings are refined by fire and healed (cf. Ezek 47:12; Rev 22:2), they start "walking in [Jerusalem's] light, and the kings of the earth are bringing forth praise to her" (21:24). For this reason "her gates will never be shut" (21:25). And the Spirit River gives life to trees who's "leaves [are] for the healing of the nations" (22:2). The concept of the Spirit River in Ezekiel 47 and Revelation 22 shatters all legalistic religious paradigms. It should leave us in awe and wonder as we ponder this reality to come.

For Jerusalem's gates to **NEVER BE SHUT** suggests the
**DOOR TO GOD IS ALWAYS OPEN,
FOR ALL ETERNITY,
EVEN AFTER THE FINAL JUDGEMENT.**
It seems that the Father of the prodigal son
WILL ALWAYS WAIT AT THE FOOT OF THE DRIVEWAY
for the lost ones to come home.[406]

---

[406] Perhaps in this sense there is a notion of perpetuity when it comes to the duration of the Sea of Fire and Sulfur: *"Now the Accuser, their Deceiver, was cast down into the Sea of Fire and Sulfur, where the savage animal and the false prophet are. And they shall be severely chastised day and night unto the Age of Ages"* (Rev 20:10). This is the only time the Sea of Fire is mentioned **and a quantitative statement about duration** is given. This may suggest the Sea of Fire crosses over into the Age of Ages, which is the final age where God makes all things new (per Revelation 21 and 22). But there is no mention here of *people*, only spiritual beings. Remember that the "false prophet" and "savage animal" are

Now, you may be wondering if I'm in any way suggesting that we can live our lives today in debauchery and waywardness because in the end we can still make it in to the New Jerusalem. If so, please stop and go back and re-read the last 3 chapters of this book! Such a thought is lunacy. The harrowing in Sheol is no laughing matter. The Sea of Fire is the last thing anyone wants to experience. Why play with fire – literally! This is serious.

> "...the cities of Sodom and Gomorrah having turned to ashes, with an overthrow did [God] condemn, an example to those about to be impious...
> 2 Peter 2:6 (YLT)

> "...Sodom and Gomorrah, and the cities around them, in like manner to these, having given themselves to whoredom, and gone after other flesh, have been set before – an example, of fire age-during, justice suffering."
> Jude 1:7 (YLT)

Yet the more important question I have in return is this: is your relationship with Jesus based on what you will escape or receive? If it is based on what you will escape, then you are operating in a rules-based salvation paradigm. But if your relationship with Jesus is genuinely rooted in love and intimacy with Him, then a typical response to the above issue is: why would I want to live in debauchery and waywardness if I know how much it would grieve His heart? Why would I let anything come between our intimate union? I am my Beloved's and He is mine.

Revelation 22 brings us all back to Genesis 1. Why did Abba Father, Son, and Spirit decide to create mankind in the image of love, knowing all They knew? Including:

- the deception of Adam of Eve
- this impact on humanity
- the introduction of death and sin
- the need for the incarnation and Passion of Yeshua

Knowing all these things before creation ever took place, They decided it was worth the endeavor. We need to take inventory of the implications of this once more. Knowing **every single thing that would take place in advance**, which meant that that the Cross of Calvary was not plan B but

---

not people! Compare with Revelation 19:20, 20:15, 21:8.

rather plan A from the beginning (Rev 13:8), ask yourself this: Did God plan **in advance** to torture people for their failures in hell for all eternity? If God is love, wouldn't the most loving thing to do be to not create people at all?

How about this: if you knew that having a son or daughter meant they would immediately be sold into human trafficking for the rest of their lives, and there would be nothing at all that you could do to stop that from happening, would you still go ahead and conceive? Of course not. So, are you more loving that God? Of course not. See how absurd our modern framework for understanding God's grand love story is? The paradigm itself is fundamentally flawed. God is not powerless, and He eventually wins with any hand that He is dealt. He would only proceed to create mankind if He knew in advance how He would bring about His desired outcome. *"[God] wants all people to be saved and to come to a knowledge of the truth"* (1 Tim 2:4). You can't say that God is all knowing, all powerful, and all present, but then say He didn't devise a plan before creation began that somehow ends with Him not accomplishing what He desires.

Alas, I digress.

In Revelation 20 we saw a multifaceted manifestation of Yahweh God as fire. Now, in Revelation 22, we have Holy Spirit expressed as living waters. **Fire is a symbol of refining and purification, and water is a symbol of healing and life.** Both are equally powerful and equally representative of the Triune God. The Bible gives us several nouns that describe the Godhead: Yahweh is fire and love; Holy Spirit is wind and water; Yeshua is a lion and a lamb. They are all of these things in equal measure. This is significant in our interpretation of Revelation 20, 21, and 22. **Those exposed to the fires of chapters 20, and the "outsiders" of chapter 21, are all exposed to the waters of chapter 22.**

Lastly, similar to Revelation 21, chapter 22 is a mix of vision and commentary. However, unique to this chapter is a final pastoral exhortation to John's immediate audience. First century Jews and Yahwists were told repeatedly that Yeshua's coming to bring about the end of the Mosaic Age was "soon". These timestamps are crucial for us today in the 21st century as they help us contextualize the urgency for that time and setting.

Now, it's time to land this plane! How remarkable to think that after 7 years of writing, I have the privilege of coming to the final chapter of John's Apocalypse. What a humbling and thought-provoking journey this has been for me. Thank you for joining me for this wild ride! I am happy to report that I am forever changed – for the better.

(Note: for this chapter, because there are several different voices speaking in succession, I will make note of who is speaking before each verse begins.)

[John]
א *(1) Then he showed me the River of the Waters of Life; pure, even bright like crystal. And it was flowing from the throne of God and of the Lamb.*[407]

א *(2) And in the middle of the street – from one end to another – upon the river was the Tree of Life, which was producing twelve fruits, and in every month it is yielding its fruits and its leaves for the healing of the nations.*[408]

א *(3) But every cursed thing will never be there. And the throne of God and of the Lamb shall be in her, and His Servants will minister to Him.*[409]

א *(4) And they will see His face and His Name will be upon their foreheads.*[410]

א *(5) And there will be no night there. But they will not need light, lamp, or sunlight, because Yahweh God is illuminating them. And He is their King for the Age of Ages.*

This is where the prophetic vision, encounter, experience, visitation, apocalypse – whatever you want to call it – ends. We are not given any

---

[407] Cf. Ezekiel 47:1. Ezekiel 47 as a whole is alluded to in Revelation 22.
[408] Why would there need to be healing for nations (aka peoples) in the New Heavens and New Earth? How is there anything sick or ill in that final Age? Because the "outsiders" are still coming in from the Sea of Fire and Sulfur. If you disagree then ask yourself where else would they be coming from?
[409] There are still many cursed things in the earth today. Again, this makes a Full Preterist view of Revelation impossible to reconcile with reality, especially for those who live in impoverished and/or totalitarian nations and labor and/or sexual slavery (or both).
[410] Face to face, in intimacy and union. The picture here is one of a Father holding his child. The name on the forehead is a symbol of identity as a legitimate child, as discussed in Revelation 14. Cf. also 1 Corinthians 13:12.

indication as to how the scene changes from future to present from John's perspective. Perhaps the scenery began to dissipate, or perhaps he became aware of his immediate surroundings again. God only knows. What we do know is from this point on the focus shifts from prophecy to pastorate. In the same way in which John's Apocalypse begins, it now ends with a pastoral exhortation to John's immediate ecclesiastical audience.

[Angel]

א *(6) Then he said to me, "These words are trustworthy and true. And Yahweh, God of the Spirit of the Holy Prophets, sent his angel to show His servants what has been permitted to happen soon."*

[Yeshua]

א *(7) "So behold! I am coming soon! Blessed is he who keeps the words of the prophecy of this book."*

[John]

א *(8) I, Yohannan, saw and heard these things. And when I saw and heard, I knelt down in obeisance before the feet of the angel who was showing me these things.*

[Angel]

א *(9) And he said to me, "Seer,[411] no! I am your fellow-servant, and of your brothers the prophets, and of those who observe these words of this book. Give homage to God!" (10) Then he said to me, "Do not seal the words of the prophecy of this book, for the time is near. (11) And he who does evil will again do evil. He who is filthy will again be filthy. But the righteous will again practice righteousness, and the holy will again be consecrated."[412]*

[Yeshua]

א *(12) "Behold! I'm coming immediately! And my wages are with*

---

[411] חזי "seer" is also used in Revelation 22:15.
[412] Though one could project this statement across the timeline of humanity, we cannot forget it is first addressing the apostates within the Holy Land. Cf. also Daniel 12:10, which was also a prophecy about the end of the Mosaic Age.

Me, and I shall give to every person according to his work."[413]

א *(13)*

"I am Aleph and I am Tav,[414]

The First and The Last,

Commencement[415] *and Consummation."*

א *(14) "Blessed are those who are doing what He commands. Their authority shall be over the Tree of Life, and through the gates shall they enter the City. (15) But outside are the fornicators,*[416] *the murderers, the worshipers of idols, the defiled, the sorcerers and all the oracles,*[417] *and the workers of lies."*

א *(16) "I, Yeshua, have sent my angel to be testifying of these things amongst you before the messianic communities."*[418]

"I am the Root and the Offspring of David,

and his companion,[419]

and the Bright Morning Star."

[John]
א *(17) And the Spirit and the Bride were saying,*

---

[413] A statement for those still bound under the Law of Moses.
[414] This is the Hebrew equivalent. In Aramaic it is "I am Alaf and I am Taw".
[415] A different word is used here than in Revelation 21:6.
[416] The Aramaic does not have the derogatory word "dogs". That is the Greek translation only.
[417] חזי or "seer". Same word is used in Revelation 22:9.
[418] As I did with Revelation chapters 1 to 3, I am translating "churches" as "messianic communities" under no affiliation or reference to modern-day Messianic movements. I rather want to emphasize that the first century church was primarily comprised of Jewish followers of Yeshua.
[419] The Aramaic uniquely has וְעָמָה "and his companion". It can also be translated "and beside him" or "and with him". But "companion" is a legitimate translation.

"Come!"

And,

"Let him who hears say, 'Come!'

And,

"Let him who thirsts come and freely receive the Waters of Life."

There is a missional summons to the "lost" here clearly meant for the Church at large: our disposition, our prayers, our declarations – these are to be in harmony with what Holy Spirit is saying, which is, "Come to the Waters of Life!" This must be our heart's cry for those who do not know Yeshua. It must never be, "Get saved or burn in hell!" Holy Spirit is constantly inviting all humanity to come to the living waters. Indeed, as personified in Luke 15:8–10, Holy Spirit is constantly searching for the precious coins that have become lost yet always belong. When the Bride reflects this heart-cry, then we may hope to see prodigals return.

[Yeshua]
(18) "I am testifying to everyone who hears the word of the prophecy of this book. Whosoever sets aside these things, God shall set upon him the blows that are written in this book. (19) And whosoever subtracts from the words of the book of this prophecy, God shall subtract his part from the Tree of Life and from the Holy City, which has been written in this book."

This is a pretty intense statement from Yeshua Himself. We must pay attention. These two verses have been used by many for centuries to instill fear or even threats against any perceived tampering with the Book of Revelation. **Yet the heart behind the words is much more practical than that: the lives of over a million Jews was on the line. These words were their lifeline. Don't mess with the instructions laid out in this prophecy, otherwise their blood will be on your hands.** It was a big deal to Yeshua because His heart went out to those first-century Jews and Yahwists still bound under the heavy burden of the Mosaic Covenant.

[John]

א *20. When He testified these things He said,*

"Yes! I am coming soon!" [420]

Come, Yahweh Yeshua! [421]

א *21. The loving-kindness[422] of our Lord Yeshua the Messiah be with each of you, His Saints.*

Amen!

---

[420] Five times (v 6, 7, 10, 12, 20) warnings are given concerning the immediacy of the calamities about to befall the Holy Land. Rome would soon be upon it.
[421] "Yahweh Yeshua". What a beautiful name John gives to Jesus. Thank you Lord that we have the beauty of the Aramaic (Syriac) Bible still available to us today!
[422] Your Bible reads "grace" here. But the word טיבותא is the equivalent to the Hebrew חֶסֶד "hesed" (Strong's H2617), meaning "mercy, kindness, goodness, favor," and many other good things!

17 CONCLUDING THOUGHTS

"The end of all our exploring will be to arrive where we started."
— T. S. Eliot

I weep as I write this last section. Chapters 21 and 22 are so filled with the presence, the glory, the loving-kindness of God that they seem so tangible as I worked through the text. I wish there was more! I also weep because this project has taken seven years to complete. Never would I have imagined that it would have spanned three books (it was supposed to be one!) or taken this long. Much like good wine, you cannot rush the process. Yet alas, here we are at the end. It's hard to believe.

I'm left in awe.

God is so much greater, kinder, and sovereign that I ever thought possible. His economy of salvation and restoration – His Garden to Garden plan – has blown my mind. Several times throughout this body of work I would come across a section of Scripture that I was almost afraid to approach. "Surely", I thought, "I'm now going to see the wrath-filled side of God." Yet that was never the case. In fact, it was the passages I was most afraid of that often left me in the greatest state of adoration and wonder.

Now, this series on Revelation is merely a primer – a baseline. There is so much more to the Book. For instance, I didn't touch on the significance of the numbers, the colors, the precious stones, the recurring patterns, etc. And like so many other prophetic books of the Hebrew Scriptures, Revelation continues to speak to us even today. Its themes and messages transcend time and culture. But it was necessary to build a proper framework first in order to have a healthy foundation to build upon.

Where was the anti-christ?
Where was the rapture?
Where was the rebuilding of the third Temple?

These were nowhere to be found in John's Apocalypse. Fascinating, isn't it? When we come into the Book of Revelation with these themes in mind, there is no limit to how far off track we can go. But by rightly dividing the Word, we restore dignity to the intended audience and their story (the Jewish people).

So where does one go from here? There are many other great commentaries on Revelation, and I encourage you to read them. We all see in part, and each of us has a puzzle piece from God. It's only when we bring our pieces together that we begin to get a wholistic picture of who God is.

I would also encourage you to study Orthodox Christianity. If you didn't read my Preface, please go and do so now.

"This is what the LORD says: "Stand at the crossroads and look; ask for the ancient paths, ask where the good way is, and walk in it, and you will find rest for your souls." Jeremiah 6:16 (NIV)

The further back you go, and the further away from Rome and Carthage you get, the more grace-centric the doctrines and beliefs are. The earliest Semitic Church Fathers (with some exceptions) mostly believed that God's economy of salvation was to bring about the restoration of all humanity.

I'm not advocating for becoming Oriental or Eastern Orthodox. I'm not saying they have a better liturgy, or that they have it all figured out. In fact, forget the labels. I'm saying take a look at what the church from AD 100 to AD 400 believed. Since that time, our doctrines haven't evolved; they've regressed. Let's not peddle new iterations of the same Reformation-Era beliefs that were hand-me-downs of Augustine, Dante, Calvin, Darby, and the like. Let's get back to our Semitic Patristic roots.

I know that my views and conclusions are outside the norm. If you have fundamentally disagreed with most of the things I have written, please pray for me. I ask this in all sincerity. Pray that God may give me the Spirit of wisdom and revelation so that I may know Him better, and that the eyes of my heart may be enlightened in order that I may know the hope to which he has called me (Eph 1:17–19). Pray that Holy Spirit will guide me into all truth (Jn 16:13). And pray that God will fill me with the knowledge of His will through all the wisdom and understanding that the Spirit gives, so that I may live a life worthy of the Lord and please Him in every way (Col 1:9–10).

Thank you for participating on this journey of discovery with me. I sincerely hope it launches you on your own path of learning and adventure. But more importantly, hopefully this body of work encourages you to find deeper intimacy with Abba Father, Yeshua, and Holy Spirit. Ultimately – what matters most – is union with our Divine Family. You are unconditionally loved and unconditionally accepted. You are safe to get it wrong, to make mistakes. There is grace to help you get up and try again. You cannot fall from grace, you can only fall into it. Therefore, always run into His arms, especially on your worst day and in your darkest hour. That's where you find the most profound grace.

"It is the goodness of God that leads you to repentance." Romans 2:4

John is known as the Apostle of Love, so isn't it fitting that the one who laid his head against Jesus' chest was the one entrusted with this prophetic message to his Jewish kin? The Book of Revelation can only be understood through the eyes of love. John had eyes of love, and we can too.

To the glory and honor of our Lord Yeshua the Messiah, our Heavenly Father the Creator of all things, and Holy Spirit which continually leads and nurtures us into union with Them.

Amen! Amen!

ABOUT THE AUTHOR

Leo De Siqueira has a passion to dig deeper into the Scriptures in order to better understand the heart of God towards mankind. While attending Tyndale University College in Toronto, Leo focused his studies on translating Biblical Hebrew and early church history. He and his family live in Calgary, Canada.

www.ingramcontent.com/pod-product-compliance
Lightning Source LLC
Chambersburg PA
CBHW070526090426
42735CB00013B/2871